THE COLUMBIA SOURCEBOOK
OF MORMONS IN THE UNITED STATES

the

COLUMBIA
SOURCEBOOK
of
MORMONS
in the
UNITED STATES

Edited by Terryl L. Givens and Reid L. Neilson

COLUMBIA UNIVERSITY PRESS | NEW YORK

Columbia University Press
Publishers Since 1893
New York   Chichester, West Sussex
Copyright © 2014 Columbia University Press
All rights reserved

Library of Congress Cataloging-in-Publication Data
The Columbia sourcebook of Mormons in the United States / edited by
Terryl L. Givens and Reid L. Neilson.
pages cm
Includes bibliographical references and index.
ISBN 978-0-231-14942-6 (cloth : alk. paper) — ISBN 978-0-231-52060-7 (ebook)
1. Church of Jesus Christ of Latter-Day Saints—History—Sources.
2. Mormon Church—History—Sources. 3. Mormons—Correspondence.
4. American prose literature—Mormon authors. I. Givens, Terryl, editor of compilation.
BX8611.C63 2014
289.3′73—dc23
2014000714

Columbia University Press books are printed on permanent
and durable acid-free paper.
This book is printed on paper with recycled content.
Printed in the United States of America
c 10 9 8 7 6 5 4 3 2 1

Jacket Design: Michelle Taormina
Jacket Image: © iStockphoto/© jhack

References to Internet Web sites (URLs) were accurate at the time of writing.
Neither the author nor Columbia University Press is responsible for URLs
that may have expired or changed since the manuscript was prepared.

To Marlin K. Jensen

CONTENTS

PREFACE

A MONOGRAPH HAS THE ADVANTAGE of not pretending to be more than a particular scholar's interpretation of his or her subject. A documentary sourcebook, in contrast, is intended as a resource and aims to satisfy the interests and pedagogical needs of an array of researchers and teachers across a span of contexts. We present the current offering as an effort to provide access to core documents that illuminate Mormon history and culture in America, from its nineteenth century beginning to the twenty-first century present. It is our hope that the array of primary sources here reproduced (many excerpted due to space restrictions, although original spelling and grammar have been retained) will serve as a nucleus for courses or class segments that deal with The Church of Jesus Christ of Latter-day Saints, popularly known as the Mormon or LDS Church. The featured texts and introductions are intended to capture pivotal moments in LDS history, to demonstrate textual foundations for its theology, and to illuminate the practices, issues, and challenges that define the Mormon community in the present.

While preparing this sourcebook for publication, we deferred to the church's official style guide, posted on its "Newsroom" Web site (http://newsroom.lds.org), which states: "The official name of the Church is The Church of Jesus Christ of Latter-day Saints. This full name was given by revelation from God to Joseph Smith in 1838. While the term 'Mormon Church' has long been publicly applied to the Church as a nickname, it is not an authorized title, and the Church discourages its use." Accordingly, we use the full name of the church as the first reference in each chapter and use *the church* as a shortened reference thereafter. When referring to church members, we use *Latter-day Saints* and *Mormons* interchangeably. We also use the term *Mormon* in proper names (like Book of Mormon, Mormon Tabernacle Choir, or Mormon Trail) or as an adjective (like Mormon pioneers) per the LDS Newsroom style guide.[1] To avoid confusion, we did not apply the term *Mormon* to the hundreds of schismatic groups that followed the 1844 martyrdom of Joseph Smith, including the Reorganized Church of Jesus Christ of Latter Day Saints (renamed the Community of Christ in 2001), as instructed by the *Associated Press Stylebook*.[2]

The Utah-headquartered church already appears as a topic in many religious survey courses in American classrooms. A number of universities are also offering specific courses in Mormon studies. At present, a few useful surveys of Mormonism (the combination of doctrine, culture, and lifestyle unique to the church) exist, and a number of outstanding monographs on LDS history, scripture, and culture are produced annually. Nothing on the market, however, affords college students or serious researchers access to Mormon primary sources in any systematic or comprehensive way. A wonderful collection by William Mulder and A. Russell Mortensen, *Among the Mormons* (1958), continued in print for many years; but it consisted almost entirely of historical and sociological observations by contemporary outsiders. In contrast, our current collection consists wholly of documents produced by Latter-day Saints themselves and expands considerably the historical scope, the subject matter, and the genres represented. It therefore breaks new ground in the range and type of texts made available in one place. Still, our volume focuses on the Mormon experience in America, following the template of Edward Curtis's *Columbia Sourcebook of Muslims in the United States* (2008), which centers on Islam in America, not abroad. Like Islam, the church is a worldwide religious movement with members in nearly every nation. At present, more than half of its members reside outside the United States. But neither we nor any other editorial team could hope to do justice to both the North American and international Mormon past and present in a single volume.

Considering the difficulty of capturing the essence of the American church experience in one collection through the limited perspective of only ourselves, we solicited input from dozens of Mormon and non-Mormon scholars in the fields of American religion, sociology, theology, and history, as noted in our acknowledgments. While their suggestions have considerably altered and improved our original plan, we are confident no one will be fully satisfied with the final list of what is included and what has of necessity fallen by the way. Misrepresentation is, we fear, an inevitable casualty of the genre. To include a dissident voice in a section of three texts, for example, is to overrepresent a minority perspective. To omit it is to silence it altogether. To provide an official version of history, to give another example, is to privilege a dominant, institutional voice. To provide an alternative account is to obscure the canonical text that endowed an entire people with the sense of identity they now possess. With these limitations in mind, we have sought to balance the mainstream and the peripheries, the institutional and the personal, the theoretical and the practical.

We have included a variety of orthodox and heterodox Latter-day Saint voices in this volume. But we have made no attempt to incorporate nonmember sources or anti-Mormon rhetoric as both would widen the scope of the text unmanageably and would constitute separate subjects. About half of the authors of the primary sources are male and half female. As the church is led by a male priesthood, women's voices are principally found in the social and cultural, rather than theological, sections. About half of the selections are of an institutional nature, while the balance of the texts come from the church laity. We have included a sample of voices that critique or question mainline LDS teachings on sexuality, gender, and other issues. However, it is a sociological fact that the church is authoritarian and that there is a strikingly (and statistically demonstrable) high level of correspondence between official doctrine and rank and file adherence. The church and its members, in other words, are by and large notably traditionalists. That very conservatism is one of Mormonism's hallmark features and as such is reflected in the selection.

We deliberately privileged The Church of Jesus Christ of Latter-day Saints over other "Mormon" groups. Our focus is, quite explicitly, on the religious organization that follows in the wake of Brigham Young's succession to Joseph Smith and which constitutes, numerically, probably 98 percent of restorationist adherents. That said, we are aware of the variety of "Mormon" movements that need to be recognized, including polygamy-practicing, self-described "Mormon fundamentalists," which derived from Joseph Smith. Approximately two hundred splinter groups have emerged in the aftermath of Smith's assassination in 1844. The Community of Christ (formerly the Reorganized Church of Jesus Christ of Latter Day Saints, or RLDS Church) is one group often accorded some emphasis in Mormon studies circles. However, numerically their 250,000 members represent a tiny fraction (1.8 percent) compared to the church's 14 million members.[3] And doctrinally, the leadership of the Community of Christ has been moving further and further away from their roots in Joseph Smith and the Book of Mormon, conspicuously de-emphasizing both. In an edited collection of limited size and scope, it would clearly be impossible to cover the range of topics presented as they pertain to two or more groups rather than one. Nevertheless, in chapter two we describe what led to the "scattering of the Saints" after the assassination of Joseph Smith and include some of the pivotal documents of those groups. This arrangement allowed us to focus the body of the sourcebook on the LDS tradition while also helping readers understand both the similarities and differences between the various "Mormon" groups.

Our organization is thematic, with a largely chronological arrangement within those categories. We were thus able to cover the widest variety of subjects while giving some sense of historical and doctrinal development. We have also sought to balance foundational and traditional with those topics and issues that are the subjects of current debate and in a process of evolving definition, such as gender roles, sexual orientation, and race.

The church and its members are too often caricatured and exoticized by observers, including well-meaning scholars, who want to reconstruct Latter-day Saints in their own images and according to their own interests. While there will likely be debate over what we have included and omitted, we are confident that the vast majority of past and present American Mormons would recognize themselves and their church in this volume's pages. Sir Richard F. Burton was perhaps the most successful European ever to blend into the Arab cultures he studied and was the first outsider to explore such forbidden cities as Harar in Somaliland, as well as Mecca and Medina. But even he sensed that "there is in Mormondom . . . an inner life into which I cannot flatter myself or deceive the reader with the idea of my having penetrated."[4] It is our hope that these texts will provide multiple windows into a religion and a people that Burton—and many others—have found so baffling.

ACKNOWLEDGMENTS

ATTEMPTING TO TELL THE STORY of the Mormon experience in America through less than one hundred documents was a daunting task. Thankfully, we were aided by a number of friends and colleagues who found value in such an undertaking. Historian Edward E. Curtis IV generously provided the template and initial encouragement for this volume with his *Columbia Sourcebook of Muslims in the United States.*

The following scholars and members of the American religious and Mormon history communities have our appreciation for their content suggestions and editorial guidance throughout the project: Grant Anderson, Mark Ashurst-McGee, Ron Barney, Mel Bashore, Alex Baugh, Richard Bennett, Susan Black, Gideon Burton, Claudia Bushman, Richard Bushman, Richard Cowan, Jo Lyn Curtis, Karen Davidson, Jill Derr, John Charles Duffly, Ron Esplin, Scott Esplin, Lawrence Flake, Spencer Fluhman, Arnold Garr, Alonzo Gaskill, Michael Goodman, John Hamer, Steve Harper, Bill Hartley, Richard Holzapfel, Mike Hunter, Elder Marlin K. Jensen, Robin Jensen, Christopher Jones, Roger Keller, Hyrum Lewis, Carol Madsen, Laurie Maffly-Kipp, Craig Manscill, Patrick Mason, Robert Millet, Steven Olsen, Michael Paulos, Glenn Rowe, Heather Seferovich, Bill Slaughter, Stan Thayne, Richard Turley, Tom Tweed, Grant Wacker, Jack Welch, Mary Jane Woodger, Fred Woods, and Dan Wotherspoon.

The librarians and professional staffs of the L. Tom Perry Special Collections, the Utah Valley Regional Family History Center, and the Harold B. Lee Library at Brigham Young University; the Church History Library and the Family History Library at The Church of Jesus Christ of Latter-day Saints; the Special Collections and the J. Willard Marriott Library at the University of Utah; the Special Collections and Archives at Utah State University; and the Research Library and Collections at the Utah State Historical Society all provided access to needed primary source documents to tell the story of the Latter-day Saints.

In addition, the management teams of the Arthur H. Clark Company, Associated Press, Bonneville Books, Brigham Young University, *BYU Studies*, Cedar Fort, The Church of Jesus Christ of Latter-day Saints, Community of Christ, Deseret Book Company, *Deseret News*, *Dialogue*, *Journal of American History*, Organization of American Historians, *Segullah*, Signature Books, *Sunstone*, University of Arizona Press, University of Chicago Divinity School, University of Oklahoma Press, University of Utah, and Utah State University Press, along with a number of individual contributors and copyright holders generously allowed us to reprint the material found herein. Senior Executive Editor Wendy Lochner, Publisher, and the editorial and production staff of Columbia University Press were a delight to work with from concept to printed page. Lastly, we wish to thank our families for encouraging us to produce this volume that tells the story of the Mormon experience in America.

We have made every effort to trace copyright holders and give proper credit for all copyrighted material used in this book. We regret any oversights. The publisher will be pleased to hear from any copyright holders not acknowledged in this edition so that a correction might be made at the next opportunity.

THE COLUMBIA SOURCEBOOK
OF MORMONS IN THE UNITED STATES

ONE

THEOLOGY AND DOCTRINE

THE CHURCH OF JESUS CHRIST OF LATTER-DAY SAINTS (hereafter referred to as *the church*) took shape amidst a flood of other-worldly phenomena. Visitations of God and Christ, miraculously preserved golden plates and seerstones, along with Old Testament prophets, New Testament apostles, ancient American kings and warrior-priests, all appearing now as holy angels, converged on a young seeker named Joseph Smith. Even by the standards of an age prone to supernaturalism and folk magic, the restorationist movement popularly known today as *Mormonism* unfolded as a spectacular effusion of the miraculous. To the church's early faithful, this manifold merging of heaven and earth was a sign of the end times, a fulfillment of millennial expectations, and the harbinger of a final gathering preparatory to Christ's return and the building of a New Jerusalem, as described in the Bible and the Book of Mormon.

A number of historians have observed that the church's theology is its history. This is essentially true in the same sense it could be said of Christianity, especially primitive Christianity. The earliest creed, the Apostles', was primarily an attestation of events, not dogmas: Christ was conceived by the Holy Ghost, born of a virgin, suffered under Pilate, was crucified, died, and was buried. And, most importantly, faith rested on assent to the historical claim that on "the third day He rose again from the dead." Before scriptural canons or Trinitarian formulas took shape, the brute fact of a literal resurrection of the man Jesus on the first Easter Sunday was the heart and soul of Christian belief.

Latter-day Saints continue in affirming these traditional Christian fundamentals, but they have extended the historical bases of such faith into the present age. This historical focus operates to at least two purposes. First, to more contemporary Mormons, this history is a hedge against the mythologizing common in liberal Protestantism. The relatively recent accounts of Joseph Smith's visions attest to the continuing interaction of God with humans in the modern age. And this is a God who is fully realized in Smith's descriptions as embodied and capable of human speech and of weeping real tears. The history of the church, in other words, points to a particular kind of divine nature and divine activity.

Second, the litany of miraculous events and heavenly visitations confirms in the LDS mind the special status of the church. Latter-day Saints frequently refer to their belief in "the only true and living church" (Doctrine and Covenants 30:1), language outsiders interpret as exclusivist and jingoistic. What the Mormons mean is perhaps what the Roman Catholic Church has traditionally meant, insofar as both traditions emphasize the divinely appointed role the church has as the earthly vehicle for human salvation. Mormon history is therefore inextricably connected to claims for a specific kind of authority that is central to their people's religious understanding. And Latter-day Saints in the twenty-first century still look for and appreciate the continuation of charismatic spiritual gifts and otherworldly blessings in their lives, despite the church's more institutional nature.

Authority functions in the LDS tradition in several related, important ways. First is the Mormon claim of authority for the restoration of the church itself, which they believe to have been instituted by Christ but fatally maimed through the historical loss of apostolic authority and the corruption of the original "apostasy." Latter-day Saints usually date Joseph Smith's calling as a prophet to the event known as the "First Vision," wherein God the Father and his son Jesus Christ appeared to the fourteen-year-old boy and informed him that no true church then existed on the earth. Mormons sing and testify of this event as the cardinal symbol of Smith's status as God's latter-day prophet. He viewed the significance of the event as an affirmation of the Lord's scriptural promise to answer the humble seeker of wisdom and as a supernal moment of forgiveness and spiritual cleansing.

Joseph Smith's mandate to organize a church came just years later. He only prepared for public dissemination an account of this First Vision more than two decades after the event. Figuring much more prominently in early LDS mentality was Smith's role in translating the Book of Mormon. Remarkably, the book that garnered such notoriety—and so many converts—for the faith was relatively unremarkable for conspicuously new theology. But its material reality was the paramount sign of Joseph Smith's prophetic status, confirming his claims to be acting under divine authority in restoring the church. It was no coincidence that the formal organization occurred mere weeks after the book's publication. Smith subsequently used this seership, or ability to reveal ancient texts, to produce writings from more familiar biblical figures, like Moses, Abraham, and, reproduced later in this chapter, Enoch. He also dictated dozens of revelations in the voice of God, the most celebrated of which was his vision of the three degrees of glory, describing a multitiered heaven.

Latter-day Saints also see authority as necessary to the performance of saving ordinances (sacraments). This power, which they term *priesthood*, must be traceable to Jesus Christ through a line of unbroken transmission. In the aftermath of the apostasy, such divine provenance could only be reestablished by the appearance of resurrected apostles. No contemporary account exists of the visit of Peter, James, and John to Joseph Smith to bestow the "Melchizedek Priesthood," but Smith and Oliver Cowdery both attested to the appearance of John the Baptist to confer the lesser, "Aaronic Priesthood" (see the selection later in this chapter). Old Testament figures like Moses and Elijah conferred on Joseph Smith more specific "keys"; that is, rights and authority pertaining to more specific powers or dispensational functions, like the gathering of Israel (Moses) or the perpetuation of the family united beyond the grave (Elijah).

Finally, a particular kind of authority inheres in the position of prophet. For Latter-day Saints, the generic use of the word *prophet* refers to a general category of the Lord's anointed mouthpieces, or any who enjoy the spiritual gift described by the New Testament Apostle Paul. But more particularly, *the prophet* is Joseph Smith or any successor to his office, who is the one individual in whom all priesthood authority and keys reside and who alone is authorized to speak the Lord's will to the church and to the world.

The Mormon prophet has the further prerogative of pronouncing new doctrine for the church. Protestantism developed largely as a consequence of theological reflection, with revisionist readings of biblical passages generating new understandings of grace, Christology, or the role of and necessity for the sacraments, for example. LDS doctrine developed largely as a consequence of production of scripture via revelations dictated to Joseph Smith in a process initiated by an intellectual response to some theological quandary or scriptural enigma, but which Latter-day Saints believe eventuated in a visionary experience or oracular pronouncement vouchsafed to the prophet. However, when Smith stood outside his charismatic role to preach spontaneously, he could produce doctrinal sermons whose status as scripture is therefore fairly ambiguous in the LDS faith. The most famous such example is his King Follett sermon, which represents the acme of his theology, incorporating such themes as the eternal existence of spirit, *creatio ex materia*, the potential for deification of humans, and the anthropomorphic nature and origins of God. Some of these, but not all, were elaborated or reaffirmed through revelations canonized in the church's Doctrine and Covenants volume of scripture.

Although the office of prophet survived Joseph Smith's death (after a three-year hiatus when Brigham Young led the church as president of the Quorum of the Twelve Apostles), the pentecostal era of visions, visitations, and production of scripture largely abated. The last prophetic vision recorded and canonized was that of President Joseph F. Smith (Joseph Smith's nephew) received in 1918, which elaborated the Mormon doctrine of the evangelizing of the dead in the spirit world (and explains the Latter-day Saints' massive, worldwide genealogical program). Subsequent prophets would speak with authority comparable to that of Joseph Smith, and the principle of ongoing revelation to living prophets continues to the present, but such pronouncements are in general carefully crafted affirmations or clarifications of standing doctrine. This is the case with declarations on such subjects as the principle of evolution and the status of gender, marriage, and the family in this world and beyond. However, for a contemporary Latter-day Saint, the most essential calling of a prophet is as a testator of the divinity of Jesus Christ. It is in that sense that all living apostles (a quorum of twelve and all members of the First Presidency) are sustained by church members as prophets, seers, and revelators.

1. Joseph Smith, "Latter Day Saints"

Writing in 1835, Joseph Smith dated his prophetic career to 1827, when he began work on the Book of Mormon. At that time, few of his contemporaries knew the details of his First Vision, which occurred when he was a youth of fourteen in 1820. Apostle Orson Pratt published a second-hand account in an 1839 Edinburgh publication, An Account of Several Remarkable Visions. *Only in 1842 did Smith prepare for publication a sketch of the rise, progress, persecution, and faith of the Latter-day Saints that included the first autobiographical account of his visions and angelic visitations, as well as a summary of Mormon beliefs. This version was published in the March 1 edition of the Church's newspaper,* Times and Seasons. *The next year, historian Israel Daniel Rupp submitted a request to Joseph Smith to prepare a statement for his encyclopedia of American religions. Smith complied with a slightly edited and updated version of his 1842 narrative. This version, which saw print in 1844, was thus the only first-person account of the foundational events of the church published to a non-Mormon readership during Joseph Smith's lifetime. The thirteen "Articles of Faith" with which he concluded his narrative is a curious blend of the familiar and the iconoclastic. While it affirms some Latter-day Saint distinctives (the Book of Mormon; no original sin), it was silent on others (an embodied God, pre-mortal existence, and human theosis).*

The Church of Jesus Christ of Latter Day Saints, was founded upon direct revelation, as the true church of God has ever been, according to the scriptures (Amos, iii. 7, and Acts, i. 2). And through the will and blessings of God, I have been an instrument in his hands, thus far, to move forward the cause of Zion. Therefore, in order to fulfil the solicitation of your letter of July last, I shall commence with my life.

I was born in the town of Sharon, Windsor county, Vermont, on the 23d of December, A.D. 1805. When ten years old, my parents removed to Palmyra, New York, where we resided about four years, and from thence we removed to the town of Manchester, a distance of six miles.

My father was a farmer, and taught me the art of husbandry. When about fourteen years of age, I began to reflect upon the importance of being prepared for a future state; and upon inquiring the place of salvation, I found that there was a great clash in religious sentiment; if I went to one society they referred me to one place, and another to another; each one pointing to his own particular creed as the summum bonum of perfection. Considering that all could not be right, and that God could not be the author of so much confusion, I determined to investigate the subject more fully, believing that if God had a church, it would not be split up into factions, and that if he taught one society to worship one way, and administer in one set of ordinances, he would not teach another principles which were diametrically opposed. Believing the word of God, I had confidence in the declaration of James, If any man lack wisdom let him ask of God, who giveth to all men liberally and upbraideth not, and it shall be given him.

I retired to a secret place in a grove, and began to call upon the Lord. While fervently engaged in supplication, my mind was taken away from the objects with which I was surrounded, and I was enrapt in a heavenly vision, and saw two glorious personages, who exactly resembled each other in features and likeness, surrounded with a brilliant light, which eclipsed the sun at noonday. They told me that all the religious denominations were believing in incorrect doctrines, and that none of them was acknowledged of God as his church and kingdom. And I was expressly commanded to go not after them, at the same time receiving a promise that the fulness of the gospel should at some future time be made known unto me.

On the evening of the 21st September, A.D. 1823, while I was praying unto God and endeavouring to exercise faith in the precious promises of scripture, on a sudden a light like that of day, only of a far purer and more glorious appearance and brightness, burst into the room; indeed the first sight was as though the house was filled with consuming fire. The appearance produced a shock that affected the whole body. In a moment a personage stood before me surrounded with a glory yet greater than that with which I was already surrounded. This messenger proclaimed himself to be an angel of God, sent to bring the joyful tidings, that the covenant which God made with ancient Israel was at hand to be fulfilled; that the preparatory work for the second coming of the Messiah was speedily to commence; that the time was at hand for the gospel in all its fulness to be preached in power, unto all nations, that a people might be prepared for the millennial reign.

I was informed that I was chosen to be an instrument in the hands of God to bring about some of his purposes in this glorious dispensation.

I was informed also concerning the aboriginal inhabitants of this country, and shown who they were, and from whence they came;—a brief sketch of their origin, progress, civilization, laws, governments, of their righteousness and iniquity, and the blessings of God being finally withdrawn from them as a people, was made known unto me. I was also told where there was deposited some plates, on which was engraven an abridgment of the records of the ancient prophets that had existed on this continent. The angel appeared to me three times the same night and unfolded the same things. After having received many visits from the angels of God, unfolding the majesty and glory of the events that should transpire in the last days, on the morning of the 22d of September, A.D. 1827, the angel of the Lord delivered the records into my hands.

These records were engraven on plates which had the appearance of gold; each plate was six inches wide and eight inches long, and not quite so thick as common tin. They were filled with engravings in Egyptian characters, and bound together in a volume, as the leaves of a book, with three rings running through the whole. The volume was something near six inches in thickness, a part of which was sealed. The characters on the unsealed part were small and beautifully engraved. The whole book exhibited many marks of antiquity in its construction, and much skill in the art of engraving. With the records was found a curious instrument which the ancients called Urim and Thummim, which consisted of two transparent stones set in the rim on a bow fastened to a breastplate.

Through the medium of the Urim and Thummim I translated the record, by the gift and power of God.

In this important and interesting book the history of ancient America is unfolded, from its first settlement by a colony that came from the tower of Babel, at the confusion of languages, to the beginning of the fifth century of the Christian era.

We are informed by these records, that America, in ancient times, has been inhabited by two distinct races of people. The first were called Jaredites, and came directly from the tower of Babel. The second race came directly from the city of Jerusalem, about six hundred years before Christ. They were principally Israelites, of the descendants of Joseph. The Jaredites were destroyed, about the time that the Israelites came from Jerusalem, who succeeded them in the inheritance of the country. The principal nation of the second race fell in battle towards the close of the fourth century. The remnant are the Indians who now inhabit this country. This book also tells us that our Saviour made his appearance upon this continent after his resurrection; that he planted the gospel here in all its fulness, and richness, and power, and blessing; that they had apostles, prophets, pastors, teachers, and evangelists; the same order, the same priesthood, the same ordinances, gifts, powers, and blessing, as was enjoyed on the eastern continent; that the people were cut off in consequence of their transgressions; that the last of their prophets who existed among them was commanded to write an abridgment of their prophecies, history, &c., and to hide it up in the earth, and that it should come forth and be united with the Bible, for the accomplishment of the purposes of God, in the last days. For a more particular account, I would refer to the Book of Mormon, which can be purchased at Nauvoo, or from any of our travelling elders.

As soon as the news of this discovery was made known, false reports, mis-representation and slander flew, as on the wings of the wind, in every direction; my house was frequently beset by mobs, and evil designing persons; several times I was shot at, and very narrowly escaped, and every device was made use of to get the plates away from me; but the power and blessing of God attended me, and several began to believe my testimony. . . .

Believing the Bible to say what it means and mean what it says; and guided by revelation according to the ancient order of the fathers to whom came what little light we enjoy; and circumscribed only by the eternal limits of truth: this church must continue the even tenor of her way, and spread undivided, and operate unspent.

We believe in God the Eternal Father, and in his son Jesus Christ, and in the Holy Ghost.

We believe that men will be punished for their own sins and not for Adam's transgression.

We believe that through the atonement of Christ all men may be saved by obedience to the laws and ordinances of the gospel.

We believe that these ordinances are: 1st, Faith in the Lord Jesus Christ; 2d, Repentance; 3d, Baptism by immersion for the remission of sins; 4th, Laying on of hands for the gift of the Holy Ghost.

We believe that a man must be called of God by prophecy, and by laying on of hands, by those who are in authority to preach the gospel and administer in the ordinances thereof.

We believe in the same organization that existed in the primitive church, viz. apostles, prophets, pastors, teachers, evangelists, &c.

We believe in the gift of tongues, prophecy, revelation, visions, healing, interpretation of tongues, &c.

We believe the Bible to be the word of God as far as it is translated correctly; we also believe the Book of Mormon to be the word of God.

We believe all that God has revealed, all that he does now reveal, and we believe that he will yet reveal many great and important things pertaining to the kingdom of God.

We believe in the literal gathering of Israel, and in the restoration of the Ten Tribes. That Zion will be built upon this continent. That Christ will reign personally upon the earth, and that the earth will be renewed and receive its paradisal glory.

We claim the privilege of worshipping Almighty God according to the dictates of our conscience, and allow all men the same privilege, let them worship how, where, or what they may.

We believe in being subject to kings, presidents, rulers, and magistrates in obeying, honouring, and sustaining the law.

We believe in being honest, true, chaste, benevolent, virtuous, and in doing good to all men; indeed we may say that we follow the admonition of Paul; we believe all things: we hope all things: we have endured many things, and hope to be able to endure all things. If there is any thing virtuous, lovely, or of good report, or praiseworthy, we seek thereafter.

From *He Pasa Ekklesia: An Original History of the Religious Denominations at Present Existing in the United States* (1844)

2. Joseph Smith, Selection from The Book of Mormon

The earliest and most conspicuous emblem of the Mormon faith, which gave the movement its popular appellation, was the book published a few weeks before the church's formal 1830 organization. Joseph Smith used "the gift and power of God" to translate a set of ancient plates he retrieved, under the angel Moroni's supervision, from a hillside near his home in upstate New York in 1827. The record chronicled various peoples who migrated to ancient America. The principal group, whose prophets created the plates and maintained a thousand years of history, traveled from Jerusalem to the Western hemisphere in the sixth century BCE. The text Smith produced is a mixture of political and military history, with copious quotations from Isaiah, midrashic readings adapted to the narrators' ancient American audience, and a history of a pre-Christian church established in the second century BCE. The worshipful anticipation of Jesus Christ by New World inhabitants and religious tenets that parallel New Testament teachings comprise the thematic core of the Book of Mormon. The dramatic high point of the narrative occurs when, subsequent to tempests and destructions that occur in Book of Mormon territory at the time of Christ's Old World crucifixion, the resurrected Jesus makes an appearance among his New World disciples (called Nephites). The scene is described in the excerpt that follows.

And now it came to pass that there were a great multitude gathered together, of the people of Nephi, round about the temple which was in the land Bountiful; and they were marvelling and wondering one with another, and were shewing one to another the great and marvellous change which had taken place; and they were also conversing about this Jesus Christ, of which the sign had been given, concerning his death.

And it came to pass that while they were thus conversing one with another, they heard a voice, as if it came out of Heaven; and they cast their eyes round about, for they understood not the voice which they heard; and it was not a harsh voice, neither was it a loud voice; nevertheless, and notwithstanding it being a small voice, it did pierce them that did hear, to the centre, insomuch that there were no part of their frame that it did not cause to quake; yea, it did pierce them to the very soul, and did cause their hearts to burn.—And it came to pass that again they heard the voice, and they understood it not; and again the third time they did hear the voice, and did open their ears to hear it; and their eyes were towards the sound thereof; and they did look steadfastly towards Heaven, from whence the sound came; and behold, the third time they did understand the voice which they heard; and it saith unto them, Behold, my beloved Son, in whom I am well pleased, in whom I have glorified my name, hear ye him.

And it came to pass as they understood, they cast their eyes up again towards Heaven, and behold, they saw a man descending out of Heaven: and he was clothed in a white robe, and he came down and stood in the midst of them, and the eyes of the whole multitude was turned upon him, and they durst not open their mouths, even one to another, and wist not what it meant: for they thought it was an angel that had appeared unto them.

And it came to pass that he stretched forth his hand, and spake unto the people, saying: Behold I am Jesus Christ, of which the prophets testified that should come into the world; and behold I am the light and the life of the world, and I have drank out of that bitter cup which the Father hath given me, and have glorified the Father in taking upon me the sins of the world, in the which I have suffered the will of the Father in all things, from the beginning.

And it came to pass that when Jesus had spake these words, the whole multitude fell to the earth, for they remembered that it had been prophesied among them that Christ should shew himself unto them after his ascension into Heaven.

And it came to pass that the Lord spake unto them saying: Arise and come forth unto me, that ye may thrust your hands into my side, and also that ye may feel the prints of the nails in my hands, and in my feet, that ye may know that I am the God of Israel, and the God of the whole earth, and have been slain for the sins of the world.

And it came to pass that the multitude went forth, and thrust their hands into his side, and did feel the prints of the nails in his hands and in his feet; and this they did do, going forth one by one, until they had all gone forth, and did see with their eyes, and did feel with their hands, and did know of a surety, and did bear record, that it was he, of whom it was written by the prophets that should come.

And it came to pass that when they had all gone forth, and had witnessed for themselves, they did cry out with one accord, saying: Hosanna! Blessed be the name of the Most High God! And they did fall down at the feet of Jesus, and did worship him.

And it came to pass that he spake unto Nephi, (for Nephi was among the multitude,) and he commanded him that he should come forth. And Nephi arose and went forth, and bowed himself before the Lord, and he did kiss his feet.—And the Lord commanded him that he should arise. And he arose and stood before him. And the Lord said unto him, I give unto you power that ye shall baptize this people, when I am again ascended into heaven. And again the Lord called others, and said unto them likewise; and he gave unto them power to baptize. And he saith unto them, On this wise shall ye baptize; and there shall be no disputations among you. Verily I say unto you, that whoso repenteth of his sins through your words, and desireth to be baptized in my name, on this wise shall ye baptize them: Behold, ye shall go down and stand in the water, and in my name shall ye baptize them. And now behold, these are the words which ye shall say, calling them by name, saying: Having authority given me of Jesus Christ, I baptize you in the name of the Father, and of the Son, and of the Holy Ghost. Amen. And then shall ye immerse them in the water, and come forth again out of the water. And after this manner shall ye baptize in my name, for behold, verily I say unto you, that the Father, and the Son, and the Holy Ghost are one; and I am in the Father, and the Father in me, and the Father and I are one. And according as I have commanded you, thus shall ye baptize. And there shall be no disputations among you, as there hath hitherto been; neither shall there be disputations among you concerning the points of my doctrine, as there hath hitherto been; for verily, verily I say unto you, he that hath the spirit of contention, is not of me, but is of the Devil, which is the father of contention, and he stirreth up the hearts of men to contend with anger, one with another.

Behold, this is not my doctrine, to stir up the hearts of men with anger, one against another; but this is my doctrine, that such things should be done away. Behold, verily, verily I say unto you, I will declare unto you my doctrine. And this is my doctrine, and it is the doctrine which the Father hath given unto me; and I bear record of the Father, and the Father beareth record of me, and the Holy Ghost beareth record of the Father and me, and I bear record that the father commandeth all men, every where, to repent and believe in me; and whoso believeth in me, and is baptized, the same shall be saved; and they are they which shall inherit the kingdom of God. And whoso believeth not in me, and is not baptized, shall be damned.—Verily, verily I say unto you, that this is my doctrine; and I bear record of it from the Father; and whoso believeth in me, believeth in the Father also; and unto him will the Father bear record of me; for he will visit him with fire, and with the Holy Ghost; and thus will the Father bear record of me; and the Holy Ghost will bear record unto him of the Father and me: for the Father, and I, and the Holy Ghost, are one. And again I say unto you, ye must repent, and become as a little child, and be baptized in my name, or ye can in nowise receive these things. And again I say unto you, Ye must repent, and be baptized in my name, and become as a little child, or ye can in nowise inherit the kingdom of God. Verily, verily I say unto you, that this is my doctrine; and whoso buildeth upon this, buildeth upon my rock; and the gates of hell shall not prevail against them. And whoso shall declare more or less than this, and establish it for my doctrine, the same cometh of evil, and is not built upon my rock, but he buildeth upon a sandy foundation, and the gates of hell standeth open to receive such, when the floods come, and the winds beat upon them. Therefore go forth unto this people, and declare the words which I have spoken, unto the ends of the earth.

The Book of Mormon [3 Nephi 9–11] (1830)

3. Oliver Cowdery, "Letter to W. W. Phelps on Priesthood Restoration"

One of the distinguishing features of the church was Joseph Smith's claim that he received authority for his actions through the ministry of angels. His translation of the Book of Mormon was an act delegated by a heavenly messenger—Moroni— who appeared to him in 1823, as well as a sign of his divine calling and implicit authority. While working together on the translation, Oliver Cowdery and Smith were impressed by the Book of Mormon precedent of immersive baptism, done by men "having authority" (Mosiah 18:17; 3 Nephi 11:25). Prayerfully seeking authorization to perform this ordinance, Joseph Smith, accompanied by Cowdery this time, again heard the voice of God, followed by the receipt of authority from a ministering angel in May 1829. The important development in this case was the formal bestowing of authority through the laying on of hands, rather than through a simple verbal commission. Smith and Cowdery subsequently identified the angel as the resurrected John the Baptist. Evidence is incomplete, but indicates that a short time later, Joseph Smith and Cowdery declared the similar bestowal of additional authority from resurrected apostles Peter, James, and John. Gradually, Smith would refer to this authority as priesthood and associate it with the several offices that emerged in subsequent years. With a revelation in 1835, Joseph Smith first explicitly differentiated the two forms, the lesser or Aaronic Priesthood coming from the Baptist, and the higher or Melchizedek Priesthood derived from the New Testament apostles. Latter-day Saints thus trace their priesthood authority back through an unbroken chain of succession to Jesus Christ himself.

Dear Brother,

Before leaving home, I promised, if I tarried long, to write; and while a few moments are now allowed me for reflection, aside from the cares and common conversation of my friends in this place, I have thought that were I to communicate them to you, might, perhaps, if they should not prove especially beneficial to yourself, by confirming you in the faith of the gospel, at least be interesting, since it has pleased our heavenly Father to call us both to rejoice in the same hope of eternal life. . . .

On Friday, the 5th, in company with our brother Joseph Smith Jr. I left Kirtland for this place (New Portage,) to attend the conference previously appointed. To be permitted, once more, to travel with this brother, occasions reflections of no ordinary kind. Many have been the fatigues and privations which have fallen to my lot to endure, for the gospel's sake, since 1828, with this brother. Our road has frequently been spread with the fowler's snare, and our persons sought with the eagerness, of the Savage's ferocity, for innocent blood, by men, either heated to desperation by the insinuations of those who professed to be guides and way marks to the kingdom of glory, or the individuals themselves!—This,

I confess, is a dark picture to spread before our patrons, but they will pardon my plainness when I assure them of the truth. In fact, God has so ordered, that the reflections which I am permitted to cast upon my past life, relative to a knowledge of the way of salvation, are rendered doubly endearing. Not only have I been graciously preserved from wicked and unreasonable men, with this our brother, but I have seen the fruit of perseverance in proclaiming the everlasting gospel, immediately after it was declared to the world in these last days, in a manner not to be forgotten while heaven gives my common intellect. And what serves to render the reflection past expression on this point is, that from his hand I received baptism, by the direction of the angel of God—the first received into this church, in this day.

Near the time of the setting of the Sun, Sabbath evening, April 5th, 1829, my natural eyes, for the first time beheld this brother. He then resided in Harmony, Susquehanna County Penn. On Monday the 6th, I assisted him in arranging some business of a temporal nature, and on Tuesday the 7th, commenced to write the Book of Mormon. These were days never to be forgotten—to sit under the sound of a voice dictated by the inspiration of heaven, awakened the utmost gratitude of this bosom! Day after day I continued, uninterrupted, to write from his mouth, as he translated, with the Urim and Thummim, or, as the Nephites would have said, Interpreters, the history, or record, called The book of Mormon.

To notice, in even few words, the interesting account given by Mormon, and his faithful son Moroni, of a people once beloved and favored of heaven, would supersede my present design: I shall therefore defer this to a future period, and as I said in the introduction, pass more directly to some few incidents immediately connected with the rise of this church, which may be entertaining to some thousands who have stepped forward, amid the frowns of bigots and the calumny of hypocrites, and embraced the gospel of Christ.

No men in their sober senses, could translate and write the directions given to the Nephites, from the mouth of the Savior, of the precise manner in which men should build up his church, and especially, when corruption had spread an uncertainty over all forms and systems practiced among men, without desiring a privilege of showing the willingness of the heart by being buried in the liquid grave, to answer a good conscience by the resurrection of Jesus Christ.

After writing the account given of the Savior's ministry to the remnant of the seed of Jacob, upon this continent, it was easily to be seen, as the prophet said would be, that darkness covered the earth and gross darkness the minds of the people. On reflecting further, it was as easily to be seen, that amid the great strife and noise concerning religion, none had authority from God to administer the ordinances of the gospel. For, the question might be asked, have men authority to administer in the name of Christ, who deny revelations? when his testimony is no less than the spirit of prophecy? and his religion based, built, and sustained by immediate revelations in all ages of the world, when he has had a people on earth? If these facts were buried, and carefully concealed by men whose craft would have been in danger, if once permitted to shine in the faces of men, they were no longer to us; and we only waited for the commandment to be given, Arise and be baptized.

This was not long desired before it was realized. The Lord, who is rich in mercy, and ever willing to answer the consistent prayer of the humble, after we had called upon him in a fervent manner, aside from the abodes of men, condescended to manifest to us his will. On a sudden, as from the midst of eternity, the voice of the Redeemer spake peace to us, while the veil was parted and the angel of God came down clothed with glory, and delivered the anxiously looked for message, and the keys of the gospel of repentance!—What joy! what wonder! what amazement! While the world were racked and distracted—while millions were groping as the blind for the wall, and while all men were resting upon uncertainty, as a general mass, our eyes beheld—our ears heard. As in the blaze of day; yes, more—above the glitter of the May Sun beam, which then shed its brilliancy over the face of nature! Then his voice, though mild, pierced to the center, and his words, I am thy fellow servant, dispelled every fear. We listened—we gazed—we admired! 'Twas the voice of the angel from glory—'twas a message from the Most High! and as we heard we rejoiced, while his love enkindled upon our souls, and we were rapt in the vision of the Almighty! Where was room for doubt? No where: uncertainty had fled, doubt had sunk, no more to rise, while fiction and deception had fled forever!

But, dear brother think, further think for a moment, what joy filled our hearts and with what surprise we must have bowed, (for who would not have bowed the knee for such a blessing?) when we received under his hand the holy priesthood, as he said, upon you my fellow servants, in the name of Messiah I confer this priesthood and this authority, which shall remain upon earth, that the sons of Levi may yet offer an offering unto the Lord in righteousness!

I shall not attempt to paint to you the feelings of this heart, nor the majestic beauty and glory which surrounded us on this occasion; but you will believe me when I say, that earth, nor men, with the eloquence of time, cannot begin to clothe language in as interesting and sublime a manner as this holy personage. No; nor has this earth power to give the joy, to bestow the peace, or comprehend the wisdom which was contained in each sentence as they were delivered by the power of the Holy Spirit! Man may deceive his fellow man; deception may follow deception, and the children of the wicked one may have power to seduce the foolish and untaught, till nought but fiction feeds the many, and the fruit of falsehood carries in its current the giddy to the grave; but one touch with the finger of his love, yes, one ray of glory from the upper world, or one word from the mouth of the Savior, from the bosom of eternity, strikes it all into insignificance, and blots it forever from the mind! The assurance that we were in the presence of an angel; the certainty that we heard the voice of Jesus, and the truth unsullied as it flowed from a pure personage, dictated by the will of God, is to me, past description, and I shall ever look upon this expression of the Savior's goodness with wonder and thanksgiving while I am permitted to tarry, and in those mansions where perfection dwells and sin never comes, I hope to adore in that day which shall never cease!

From *Messenger and Advocate* (1834)

4. Joseph Smith, "Extract from the Prophecy of Enoch [Moses 7]"

Joseph Smith's production of the Book of Mormon burst open the traditional Christian belief in a closed canon. Within months of publishing that new scripture, he began work on a revision ("translation" he called it) of the Bible. Almost immediately, Smith began incorporating new material into Genesis, which he considered inspired restoration through his gift of revelation. The most remarkable of these interpolations was "the Prophecy of Enoch," an extended narrative based on the Old Testament figure of that name. The narrative adds to an already considerable number of variants of the Enoch tradition, which include Ethiopic, Old Slavonic, and Kabalistic accounts. Joseph Smith's version is noteworthy, among other details, for its depiction of the Weeping God, a motif appearing in many ancient noncanonical sources. In Smith's earliest version of the text, it is the heavens that actually weep. The redaction to a God himself who weeps (in current Mormon scripture) is a deliberate step away from poetic personification of the heavens, toward the literal assignment of emotions to God. Later, Joseph Smith would add physical embodiment to his divine anthropology, to arrive at a Mormon God—in contradistinction to the Christian creedal God—who emphatically is possessed of body and parts, as well as passions. The Weeping God of Enoch was an early, crucial step in the elaboration of a godhead that consists of three separate and distinct beings. This LDS divergence from classical Trinitarianism may be the single most consequential aspect of the Mormon gospel, one that puts the church in direct tension with creedal Christianity.

And it came to pass that Enoch continued his speech saying, Behold our father Adam taught these things, and many have believed and become the sons of God, and many have believed not and have perished in their sins, and are looking forth with fear, in torment, for the fiery indignation of the wrath of God to be poured out upon them. And from that time forth Enoch began to prophesy, saying unto the people, That, as I was journeying and stood upon the place Mahujth, and I cried unto the Lord, there came a voice out of heaven, saying, Turn ye and get ye upon the mount Simeon. And it came to pass that I turned and went upon the mount, and as I stood upon the mount, I beheld the heavens open, and I was clothed upon with glory, and I saw the Lord; he stood before my face, and he talked with me, even as a man talketh one with another face to face; and he saith unto me, Look, and I will shew unto thee the world for the space of many generations. . . .

And it came to pass that Enoch continued to call upon all the people, save it were the people of Canaan, to repent: And so great was the faith of Enoch that he led the people of God, and their enemies came to battle against them, and he spake the word of the Lord, and the earth trembled; and the mountains fled, even according to his command; and the rivers of water were turned out of their course; and the roar of the lions was heard out of the wilderness; and all nations feared greatly, so powerful was the word of Enoch, and so great was the power of the language, which God had given him. There also came up a land out of the depth of the sea; and so great was the fear of the enemies of the people of God, that they fled and stood afar off, and went upon the land which came up out of the depths of the sea. And the giants of the land, also, stood afar off; and there went forth a curse upon all the people which fought against God; and from that time forth there was wars and bloodsheds among them, but the Lord came and dwelt with his people, and they dwelt in righteousness. The fear of the Lord was upon all nations, so great was the glory of the Lord, which was upon his people: And the Lord blessed the land, and they were blessed upon the mountains, and upon the high places, and did flourish. And the Lord called his people Zion, because they were of one heart and of one mind, and dwelt in righteousness; and there was no poor among them: and Enoch continued his preaching in righteousness unto the people of God. And it came to pass in his days, that he built a city that was called The City of Holiness, even ZION. And it came to pass that Enoch talked with the Lord, and he said unto the Lord, Surely Zion shall dwell in safety forever:—But the Lord said unto Enoch, Zion hath I blessed, but the residue of the people have I cursed. And it came to pass that the Lord showed unto Enoch all the inhabitants of the earth; and he beheld, and lo, Zion, in process of time, was taken up into heaven! And the Lord said unto Enoch, Behold mine abode forever: and Enoch also beheld the residue of the people which were the sons of Adam, and they were a mixture of all the seed of Adam, save it were the seed of Cain, for the seed of Cain were black, and had not place among them. And after that Zion was taken up into heaven, Enoch beheld and lo, all the nations of the earth were before him! and there came generation upon generation, and Enoch was high and lifted up, even in the bosom of the Father, and the Son of man; and behold the power of Satan was upon all the face of the earth! And he saw angels descending out of heaven; and he heard a loud voice, saying, Wo, wo, be unto the inhabitants of the Earth! And he beheld Satan, and he had a great chain in his hand, and it veiled he whole face of the earth with darkness, and he looked up and laughed, and his angels rejoiced. And Enoch beheld angels descending out of heaven bearing testimony of the Father and Son, and the Holy Ghost fell on many, and they were caught up by the powers of heaven into Zion: And it came to pass that the God of heaven looked upon the residue of the people, and he wept, and Enoch bore record of it, saying, How is it the heavens weep and shed forth her tears as the rain upon the mountains? And Enoch said unto the Lord, How is it that thou canst weep seeing thou art holy and from all eternity from all eternity? and were it possible that man could number the particles of the earth, yea, and millions of earths like this, it would not be a beginning to the number of thy creations; and thy curtains are stretched out still; and yet thou art there, and thy bosom is there; and so, thou art just; thou art merciful and kind forever; thou hast taken Zion to thine own bosom from all thy creations, from all thy creations, from all eternity to all eternity, and nought at peace, justice and truth is the habitation of thy throne; and mercy shall go before thy face and have no end: how is it that thou canst weep? The Lord said unto Enoch,

Behold these thy brethren; they are the workmanship of mine own hands, and I gave unto them their knowledge, in the day I created them; and in the garden of Eden gave I unto man his agency; and unto thy brethren have I said, and also, gave commandment, That they should love one another; and that they should choose me their father, but behold they are without affection; and they hate their own blood; and the fire of mine indignation is kindled against them; and in my hot displeasure will I send in the floods upon them, for my fierce anger is kindled against them: Behold I am God; Man of Holiness is my name; Man of council is my name, and Endless and Eternal is my name, also. Wherefore, I can stretch forth mine hands and hold all the creations which I have made; and mine eye can pierce them, also; and among all the workmanship of mine hand, there has not been so great wickedness, as among thy brethren, but behold their sins shall be upon the heads of their fathers: Satan shall be their father, and misery shall be their doom; and the whole heavens shall weep over them, even all the workmanship of mine hands: Wherefore, should not the heavens weep, seeing these shall suffer? But behold, these, which thine eyes are upon, shall perish in the floods; and behold I will shut them up: a prison have I prepared for them:—And that which I have chosen hath plead before my face: Wherefore he sufferth for their sins, inasmuch as they will repent in the day that my chosen shall return unto me; and until that day, they shall be in torment: Wherefore, for this shall the heavens weep; yea, and all the workmanship of mine hands.

And it came to pass, that the Lord spake unto Enoch and told Enoch all the doings of the children of men: wherefore Enoch knew, and looked upon their wickedness, and their misery, and wept, and stretched forth his arms, and his heart swelled wide as eternity; and his bowels yearned, and all eternity shook.

From *The Evening and the Morning Star* (1832)

5. Joseph Smith, "A Vision [Doctrine and Covenants 76]"

Contemporary Latter-day Saints, if queried on Joseph Smith's "vision," would assume his 1820 theophany was the subject. But that "First Vision," as it is now called, came into greater prominence many decades after his 1844 assassination. Of Smith's myriad visitations, revelations, prophecies, and pronouncements, only one so transcended all others in its scope, detail, and theological ramifications, to later be labeled "The Vision" in the nineteenth century. Adding to its considerable authority is Joseph Smith's claim that the revelation was actually "a transcript from the records of the eternal world." Virtually all Christians believe in a dualistic afterlife: salvation and heaven for the righteous, damnation and hell for the rest. This revelation ironically moves in two seeming contradictory directions— both iconoclastic. First, it explicates that the "many mansions" to which Jesus Christ referred to mean a multitiered heaven, differentiated into distinct realms. At the same time, however, in considering all three kingdoms to be kingdoms of glory, the vision makes salvation quasi-universal. Only a few, the intractably rebellious sons of perdition, will suffer everlasting punishment. As for hell, it is revealed in this revelation as a temporary abode of suffering prior to judgment. Even the unbelievers, eventually, "shall be heirs of salvation." It thus comes close to Universalism in its generous conception of heaven. A final significance of this revelation was its allusion to humans as "gods, even the sons of god." A potentially metaphorical reference, it became a contested passage around which the LDS doctrine of theosis (human deification) would first emerge in a public forum as writers like Apostle Parley P. Pratt rushed to defend it. All of these unorthodoxies startled even the Mormon faithful. Brigham Young himself initially struggled with the doctrine here revealed, and some membership defections resulted. Today, it is one of the most loved and invoked revelations of Joseph Smith.

We, Joseph and Sidney, being in the Spirit on the sixteenth of February, in the year of our Lord, one thousand eight hundred and thirty two, and through the power of the Spirit, our eyes were opened, and our understandings were enlightened, so as to see and understand the things of God; even things which were from the beginning before the world was, which was ordained of the Father, through his only begotten Son, who was in the bosom of the Father, even from the beginning, of whom we bear record, and the record which we bear is the fulness of the Gospel of Jesus Christ, which is in the Son whom we saw and with whom we conversed in the Heavenly Vision; for as we sat doing the work of translation, which the Lord had appointed unto us, we came to the twenty ninth verse of the fifth chapter of John, which was given unto us thus: speaking of the resurrection of the dead who should hear the voice of the Son of man, and shall come forth; they who have done good in the resurrection of the just, and they who have done evil in the resurrection of the unjust. Now this caused us to marvel, for it was given us of the Spirit; and while we meditated upon these things, the Lord touched the eyes of our understandings, and they were opened, and the glory of the Lord shone round about; and we beheld the glory of the Son, on the right hand of the Father, and received of his fulness; and saw the holy angels, and they who are sanctified before his throne, worshiping God and the Lamb forever and ever. And now after the many testimonies which have been given of him, this is the testimony, last of all, which we give of him, that he lives; for we saw him, even on the right hand of God; and we heard the voice bearing record that he is the only begotten of the Father; that by him, and through him, and of him, the worlds are made, and were created; and the inhabitants thereof are begotten sons and daughters unto God. This we saw also and bear record, that an angel of God, who was in authority in the presence of God, who rebelled against the only begotten Son, (whom the Father loved, and who was in the bosom of the Father,) and was thrust down from the presence of God and the Son, and was called Perdition; for the Heavens wept over him; for he was Lucifer, even the son of the morning; and we behold and lo, he is fallen! is fallen! even the son of the morning. And while we were yet in the Spirit, the Lord commanded us that we should write the Vision; for behold satan, that old serpant, even the devil, who rebelled against God, and sought to take kingdoms of our God, and of his Christ; wherefore he maketh war with the saints of God, and encompasses them about: And we saw a vision of the eternal sufferings of those with whom he maketh war and overcometh, for thus came the voice of the Lord unto us.

Thus saith the Lord, concerning all those who know my power, and who have been made partakers thereof, and suffered themselves, through the power of the devil, to be overcome unto the denying of the truth, and the defying of my power: they are they who are the sons of perdition, of whom I say it had been better for them never to have been born; for they are vessels of wrath doomed to suffer the wrath of God, with the devil and his angels, throughout eternity: concerning whom I have said there is no forgiveness for them in this world nor in the world to come; having denied the Holy Ghost after having received it, and having denied the only begotten Son of the Father, crucifying him unto themselves, and putting him to an open shame: these are they who shall go away into the lake of fire and brimstone, with the devil and his angels, and the only ones on whom the second death shall have any power; yea, verily the only ones who shall not be redeemed in the due time of the Lord, after the sufferings of his wrath, who shall be brought forth by the resurrection of the dead, through the triumph & the glory of the Lamb; who was slain, who was in the bosom of the Father before the worlds were made. And this is the Gospel, the glad tidings which the voice out of the heavens bore record unto us, that he came into the world, even Jesus to be crucified for the world, and to bear the sins of the world, and to sanctify the world, and to cleanse it from all unrighteousness; that through him all might be saved, whom the Father had put into his power; and made by him who glorifieth the Father; and saveth all the work of his hands, except those sons of perdition, who denieth the Son after the Father hath revealed him: wherefore he saveth all save them, and these shall go away into everlasting punishment, which is endless punishment, which is eternal punishment, to reign with the devil and his angels throughout eternity, where their worm dieth not and the fire is not quenched, which is their torment, but the end thereof, neither the place thereof, and their torment, no man knoweth, neither was revealed, neither is, neither will be revealed unto man, save to them who are made partakers thereof: nevertheless I the Lord showeth it by vision unto many, but straightway shutteth it up again: wherefore the end, the width, the height, the depth, and the misery thereof, he understandeth not, neither any man save them who are ordained unto this condemnation. And we heard the voice saying, Write the Vision for lo, this is the end of the vision of the eternal sufferings of the ungodly!

And again, we bear record for we saw and heard, and this is the testimony of the Gospel of Christ, concerning them who come forth in the resurrection of the just: they are they who received the testimony of Jesus, and believed on his name, and were baptized after the manner of his burial, being buried in the water in his name, and this according to the commandment which he hath given, that, by keeping the commandment, they might be washed and cleansed from all their sins, and receive the Holy Ghost by the laying on of the hands of him who is ordained and sealed unto this power; and who overcome by faith, and are sealed by that Holy Spirit of promise, which the Father shedeth forth upon all those who are just and true: they are they who are the church of the first-born: they are they into whose hands the Father hath given all things: they are they who are priests and kings, who having received of his fulness, and of his glory, are priests of the most High after the order of Melchisedek, which was after the order of Enoch, which was after the order of the only begotten Son: wherefore, as it is written, they are gods, even the sons of God: wherefore all things are theirs, whether life or death, or things present, or things to come, all are theirs, and they are Christ's, and Christ is God's; and they shall overcome all things: wherefore let no man glory in man, but rather let him glory in God, who shall subdue all enemies under his feet: these shall dwell in the presence of God and his Christ forever and ever: these are they whom he shall bring with him, when he shall come in the clouds of heaven, to reign on the earth over his people: these are they who shall have part in the first resurrection: these are they who shall come forth in the resurrection of the just: these are they who are come unto mount Zion, and unto the city of the living God, the heavenly place, the holiest of all: these are they who have come to an innumerrable company of angels; to the general assembly and church of Enoch, and of the first born: these are they whose names are written in Heaven, where God and Christ is the judge of all: these are they who are just men made perfect through Jesus the Mediator of the new covenant, who wrought out this perfect atonement through the shedding of his own blood: these are they whose bodies are celestial, whose glory is that of the Son, even of God the highest of all; which glory the Sun of the firmament is written of as being typical.

And again, we saw the Terrestrial world, and behold and lo! these are they who are of the terrestrial, whose glory differeth from that of the church of the first born, who have received of the fulness of the Father, even as that of the Moon differeth from the Sun of the firmament. Behold, these are they who died without law; and also they who are the spirits of men kept in prison, whom the Son visited and preached the Gospel unto them, that they might be judged according to men in the flesh, who received not the testimony of Jesus in the flesh, but afterwards received it: these are they who are honorable men of the earth, who were blinded by the craftiness of men: these are they who receive of his glory, but not of his fulness: these are they who receive of the presence of the Son, but not of the fulness of the Father: wherefore they are bodies terrestrial, and not bodies celestial, and differeth in glory as the Moon differeth from the Sun: these are they who are not valiant in the testimony of Jesus: wherefore they obtained not the crown over the kingdoms of our God. And now this is the end of the vision which we saw of the terrestrial, that the Lord commanded us to write while we were yet in the Spirit.

And again, we saw the glory of the Telestial, which glory is that of the lesser, even as the glory of the stars differeth from that of the glory of the Moon in the firmament: these are they who receive not the Gospel of Christ, neither the testimony of Jesus: these are they who deny not the Holy Ghost: these are they who are thrust down to hell: these are they who shall not be redeemed from the devil, until the last resurrection, until the Lord, even Christ the Lamb, shall have finished his work: these are they who receive not of his fulness in the eternal world, but of the Holy Ghost through the administration of the terrestrial; and the terrestrial through the administration of the celestial; and also the telestial receive it of the administering of angels, who are appointed to minister for them, or who are appointed to be ministering spirits for them, for they shall be heirs of salvation. . . . But behold and lo, we saw the inhabitants of the telestial world, that they were in number as innumerable as the stars in the firmament of Heaven, or as the sand upon the sea shore, and heard the voice of the Lord saying: These all shall bow the knee, and every tongue shall confess to him who sitteth upon the throne forever and ever: for they shall be judged according to their works; and every man shall receive according to his own works, and his own dominion, in the mansions which are prepared; and they shall be servants of the most High, but where God and Christ dwells they cannot come, worlds without end. This is the end of the vision which we saw, which we were commanded to write while we were yet in the Spirit.

From *The Evening and the Morning Star* (1832)

6. Joseph Smith, Journal Account of Kirtland Temple Visitations

With meager resources and at tremendous sacrifice, the modest Ohio Mormon community of a few hundred (most had "gathered" to Missouri) had just completed their first temple, resulting in the following pentecostal outpouring and heavenly visitations. Though the Kirtland Temple was also used for church meetings, Joseph Smith conceived of temples along Old Testament lines, as sacred structures where ordinances like washings and anointings (Exodus 40:12–13) would be performed. (Over time, more ordinances were added, and common worship services would be relegated entirely to churches, tabernacles, and other structures.) The language of the revelation reflects the great and growing significance Smith attached to keys, or priesthood authority to administer particular duties or phases of the restored gospel. As a resurrected John the Baptist had earlier given Joseph Smith authority to baptize, Moses now committed the keys of gathering. Almost immediately, Smith would organize the first overseas mission as a result. The gospel of Abraham, which Elias committed, received unique interpretation in Mormon theology. His promise of an innumerable posterity later became interpreted in Mormon thought as the promise of eternal posterity sired in the world to come. Looming larger in Joseph Smith's thinking, however, would be the figure of Elijah, whose return was prophesied by Malachi. The keys he conveyed led Smith to develop a theology of the sealing power of the priesthood, by which couples, families, and generations would be bound together with cords stronger than death. "The spirit of Elijah" is today commonly invoked by Latter-day Saints to account for the worldwide interest in genealogy or family history work, which of itself forges intergenerational connections consistent with the words of Malachi, but also enables church members to perform vicarious sealings, to weld families together in their temples.

Sabbath April 3d [1836] He [Joseph Smith] attended meeting in the Lords House, assisted the other Presidents of the Church in seating the congregation and then became an attentive listener to the preaching from the Stand. T. B. Marsh & D. W. Patten spoke in the A.M. to an attentive audience of about 1000 persons. In the P.M. he assisted the other Presidents in distributing the elements of the Lords Supper to the church, receiving them from the Twelve whose privilige it was to officiate in the sacred desk this day. After having performed this service to his brethren, he retired to the pulpit, the vails being dropped, and bowed himself with O. Cowdery, in solemn, but silent prayer to the Most High.

After rising from prayer the following vision was opened to both of them.

The vail was taken from their minds and the eyes of their understandings were opened. They saw the Lord standing upon the breast work of the pulpit before them, and under his feet was a paved work of pure gold, in color like amber: his eyes were as a flame of fire; the hair of his head was like the pure snow, his countenance shone above the brightness of the sun, and his voice was as the sound of the rushing of great waters, even the Voice of Jehovah, saying, I am the first and the last, I am he who liveth, I am he who was slain. I am your Advocate with the Father. Behold your sins are forgiven you. You are clean before me, therefore, lift up your heads and rejoice, let the hearts of your brethren rejoice and let the hearts of all my people rejoice, who have with their might, built this house to my name. For behold I have accepted this house and my name shall be here; and I will manifest myself to my people, in mercy, in this House, yea I will appear unto my servants and speak unto them with mine own voice, if my people will keep my commandments and do not pollute this Holy House. Yea the hearts of thousands and tens of thousands shall greatly rejoice in consequence of the blessings which shall be poured out, and the endowment with which my servants have already been endowed and shall hereafter be endowed in this House. And the fame of this House shall spread to foreign lands, and this is the beginning of the blessing, which shall be poured out upon the heads of my people. even so Amen. After this vision closed, the Heavens were again opened unto them and Moses appeared before them and committed unto them the keys of the gathering of Israel from the four parts of the Earth and the leading of the ten tribes from the Land of the North. After this Elias appeared and committed the dispensation of the gospel of Abraham, saying, that in them and their seed all generations after them should be blessed. After this vision had closed, another great and glorious vision burst upon them, for Elijah, the Prophet, who was taken to Heaven without tasting death, also stood before them, and said, behold the time has fully come which was spoken of by the Mouth of Malachi, testifying, that he should be sent before the great and dreadful day of the Lord come, to turn the hearts of the Fathers to the children, and the children to the fathers, lest the whole earth be smitten with a curse. Therefore, the keys of this dispensation are committed into your hands, and by this ye may know that the great and the dreadful day of the Lord is near, even at the doors.

Doctrine and Covenants 110 (1836)

7. Joseph Smith, "Letter from Joseph Smith [on Baptisms for the Dead]"

Joseph Smith was several years in working out the full implications of the priest-hood keys he had received in 1836 from the resurrected Elijah, with the reference to the turning of the hearts of children and the fathers to each other. Two related beliefs took gradual shape more or less concurrently. First was the emphasis on eternal familial relationships, which would eventually morph into the daunting objective of binding together the entire human family, living and dead, through the priesthood's sealing power. But the biblical words of Malachi also came to represent for Smith not an aspiration as much as obligation—to perform on behalf of those generations now deceased those ordinances essential to salvation. Primary among these was baptism. The fate of the earth's billions who have died without hearing the gospel or receiving its ordinances has been a perennial problem in Christian theology. Limbo, the harrowing of hell, or regrettable but inevitable damnation have all been suggested as the consequence of innocent non-baptism.

Another possibility raised intermittently has been vicarious baptism, practiced occasionally by early Christians and alluded to by the New Testament Apostle Paul (1 Cor. 15:29). Joseph Smith may also have heard of the practice as engaged in by the seventeenth-century Ephrata community in Pennsylvania or from apocryphal New Testament sources, but it was in the course of developing his temple theology, and a few years after the Kirtland Temple visitations, that he began to teach the doctrine. He first preached on the Pauline passage in 1840. At the church's October conference, he lectured on the subject again and allowed several church members to do vicarious baptisms for the dead in the Mississippi River. A year later, Smith ordered an end to the practice, until a temple could be built for that purpose (the Kirtland Temple had been abandoned by his followers to a dissident group in 1838). The cornerstone for the Nauvoo, Illinois, temple would be laid in April 1841, and baptisms for the dead commenced in the completed basement font that November. In the following revelation, Joseph Smith ordered and added definition to the practice, while providing a fully detailed account of the doctrine of salvation for the dead.

As I stated to you in my letter before I left my place, that I would write to you from time to time, and give you information in relation to many subjects, I now resume the subject of the baptism for the dead; as that subject seems to occupy my mind, and press itself upon my feelings the strongest, since I have been pursued by my enemies.

I wrote a few words of Revelation to you concerning a Recorder. I have had a few additional views in relation to this matter, which I now certify. That is, it was declared in my former letter that there should be a Recorder, who should be eye witness, and also to hear with his ears, that he might make a record of a truth before the Lord. Now, in relation to this matter, it would be very difficult for one recorder to be present at all times, and to do all the business. To obviate this difficulty, there can be a recorder appointed in each ward of the city, who is well qualified for taking accurate minutes: and let him be very particular and precise in making his record, in taking the whole proceedings; certifying in his record that he saw with his eyes, and heard with his ears; giving the date, and names, &c., and the history of the whole transaction; naming also, some three individuals that are present, if there be any present, who can at any time when called upon, certify to the same, that in the mouth of two or three witnesses every word may be established. Then let there be a general Recorder, to whom these other records can be handed, being attended with certificates over their own signatures; certifying that the record which they have made is true. Then the general church recorder can enter the record on the general church book, with the certificates and all the attending witnesses, with his own statement that he verily believes the above statement and records to be true, from his knowledge of the general character and appointment of those men by the church. And when this is done on the general church book, the record shall be just as holy, and shall answer the ordinance just the same as if he had seen with his eyes, and heard with his ears, and made a record of the same on the general church book.

You may think this order of things to be very particular, but let me tell you that they are only to answer the will of God, by conforming to the ordinance and preparation that the Lord ordained and prepared before the foundation of the world, for the salvation of the dead, who should die without a knowledge of the gospel.

And further, I want you to remember that John the Revelator was contemplating this very subject in relation to the dead, when he declared as you will find recorded in Revelations, xx: 12. "And I saw the dead, small and great, stand before God: and the books were opened: and another book was opened, which is the book of life; and the dead were judged out of those things which were written in the books, according to their works." You will discover in this quotation that the books were opened; and another book was opened, which was the book of life. But the dead were judged out of those things which were written in the books, according to their works; consequently the books spoken of must be the books which contained the record of their works; and refers to the records which are kept on the earth. And the book which was the book of life, is the record which is kept in heaven; the principle agreeing precisely with the doctrine which is commanded you in the revelation contained in the letter which I wrote you previous to my leaving my place, "that in all your recordings it may be recorded in heaven." Now the nature of power of the priesthood, by the revelation of Jesus Christ; wherein it is granted that whatsoever you bind on earth shall be bound in heaven, and whatsoever you loose on earth shall be loosed in heaven. Or in other words, taking a different view of the translation, whatsoever you record on earth shall be recorded in heaven; and whatsoever you do not record on earth shall not be recorded in heaven; for out of the books shall your dead be judged, according to their works, whether they themselves have attended to the ordinances in their own propria persona, or by the means of their own agents, according to the ordinance which God has prepared for their salvation from before the foundation of the world; according to the records which they have kept concerning their dead.

It may seem to some to be a very bold doctrine that we talk of: a power which records or binds on earth, and binds in heaven: nevertheless, in all ages of the world, whenever the Lord has given a dispensation of the Priesthood to any man by actual revelation, or any set of men, this power has always been given. Hence whatsoever those men did in authority, in the name of the Lord, and did it truly and faithfully, and kept a proper and faithful record of the same, it became a law on earth and in heaven, and could not be annulled, according to the decrees of the great Jehovah. This is a faithful saying! Who can hear it? And again for a precedent, Matthew, xvi: 18,19. "And I say also unto thee, that thou art Peter: and upon this rock I will build my church; and the gates of hell shall not prevail against it: and I will give unto thee the keys of the kingdom of heaven, and whatsoever thou shalt bind on earth shall be bound in heaven: and whatsoever thou shalt loose on earth shall be loosed in heaven." Now the great and grand secret of the whole matter, and the sum and bonum of the whole subject that is lying before us, consists in obtaining the powers of the Holy Priesthood. For him to whom these keys are given there is no difficulty in obtaining a knowledge of facts in relation to the salvation of the children of men, both as well for the dead as for the living. Herein is glory and honor and immortality and eternal life. The ordinance of baptism by water, to be immersed therein in order to answer to the likeness of the dead, that one principle might accord with the other. To be immersed in the water and come forth out of the water is in the likeness of the resurrection of the dead in coming forth out of the graves; hence, this ordinance was instituted to form a relationship with the ordinance of baptism for the dead, being in likeness of the dead. Consequently the Baptismal Font was instituted as a simile of the grave, and was commanded to be in a place underneath where the living are wont to assemble, to shew forth the living and the dead: and that all things may have their likeness, and that they may accord one with another; that which is earthly, conforming to that which is heavenly, as Paul hath declared, 1 Corinthians, xv: 46, 47, and 48. "Howbeit that was not first which is spiritual, but that which is natural, and afterwards that which is spiritual. The first man is of the earth, earthy; the second man is the Lord, from heaven. As is the earthy such are they also that are earthy; and as is the heavenly, such are they also that are heavenly."

And as are the records on the earth in relation to your dead, which are truly made out, so also are the records in heaven. This therefore is the sealing and binding power, and in one sense of the word the keys of the kingdom, which consists in the key of knowledge. And now my dearly and beloved brethren and sisters, let me assure you that these are principles, in relation to the dead and the living, that cannot be lightly passed over, as pertaining to our salvation. For their salvation is necessary and essential to our salvation, as Paul says concerning the fathers, "that they without us can not be made perfect"; neither can we without our dead, be made perfect. And now in relation to the dead, I will give you another quotation of Paul, 1 Corinthians, xv: 29. Else what shall they do which are baptized for the dead if the dead rise not at all; why are they then baptized for the dead. And again, in connection with this quotation, I will give you a quotation from one of the prophets, who had his eye fixed on the restoration of the priesthood, the glories to be revealed in the last days, and in an especial manner this most glorious of all subjects belonging to the everlasting gospel, viz: the baptism for the dead; for Malachi says, last chapter, verses 5th and 6th, Behold I will send you Elijah the prophet, before the coming of the great and dreadful day of the Lord: and he shall turn the heart of the fathers to the children, and the heart of the children to their fathers, lest I come and smite the earth with a curse. I might have rendered a plainer translation to this, but it is sufficiently plain to suit my purpose as it stands. It is sufficient to know in this case, that the earth will be smitten with a curse, unless there is a welding link of some kind or other, between the fathers and the children, upon some subject or other, and behold, what is that subject. It is the baptism for the dead. For we without them cannot be made perfect; neither can they without us be made perfect. Neither can they or us, be made perfect without those who have died in the gospel also; for it is necessary in the ushering in of the dispensation of the fulness of times; which dispensation is now beginning to usher in, that a whole, and complete, and perfect union, and welding together of dispensations, and keys, and powers, and glories should take place, and be revealed, from the days of Adam even to the present time; and not only this, but those things which never have been revealed from the foundation of the world, but have been kept hid from the wise and prudent, shall be revealed unto babes and sucklings in this the dispensation of the fulness of times.—Now what do we hear in the gospel which we have received? A voice of gladness! A voice of mercy from Heaven; and a voice of truth out of the earth, glad tidings for the dead: a voice of gladness for the living and the dead; glad tidings of great joy.

How beautiful upon the mountains are the feet of those that bring glad tidings of good things; and that say unto Zion, behold! thy God reigneth. As the dews of Carmel, so shall the knowledge of God descend upon them. And again, what do we hear? Glad tidings from Cumorah! Moroni, an Angel from heaven, declaring the fulfilment of the prophets—the book to be revealed. A voice of the Lord in the wilderness of Fayette, Seneca county, declaring the three witnesses to bear record of the book. The voice of Michael on the banks of the Susquehanna, detecting the devil when he appeared as an angel of light. The voice of Peter, James and John, in the wilderness between Harmony, Susquehanna county, and Colesville, Broom county, on the Susquehanna River, declaring themselves as possessing the keys of the kingdom, and of the dispensation of the fulness of times. And again, the voice of God in the chamber of old father Whitmer, in Fayette, Seneca county, and at sundry times, and in divers places, through all the travels and tribulations of this Church of Jesus Christ of Latter Day Saints. And the voice of Michael, the archangel; the voice of Gabriel, and of Raphael, and of divers angels, from Michael or Adam, down to the present time, all declaring each one their dispensation, their rights, their keys, their honors, their majesty and glory, and the power of their priesthood; giving line upon line, precept upon precept; here a little and there a little—giving us consolation by holding forth that which is to come, confirming our hope.

Brethren shall we not go on in so great a cause? Go forward and not backward. Courage, brethren; and on, on to the victory! Let your hearts rejoice, and be exceeding glad.—Let the earth break forth into singing. Let the dead speak forth anthems of eternal praise to the King Immanuel, who hath ordained before the world was, that which would enable us to redeem them out of their prisons; for the prisoners shall go free.

Let the mountains shout for joy, and all ye valleys cry aloud and all ye seas and dry lands tell the wonders of your eternal King. And ye rivers, and brooks, and rills, flow down with gladness. Let the woods, and all the trees of the field praise the Lord: and ye solid rocks weep for joy. And let the sun, moon, and the morning stars sing together, and let all the sons of god shout for joy. And let the eternal creations declare his name for ever and ever. And again I say, how glorious is the voice we hear from heaven proclaiming in our ears, glory, and salvation, and honor, and immortality, and eternal life: kingdoms, principalities, and powers. Behold the great day of the Lord is at hand, and who can abide the day of his coming, and who can stand when he appeareth, for he is like a refiners fire and like fullers soap; and he shall sit as a refiner and purifier of silver, and he shall purify the sons of Levi, and purge them as gold and silver, that they may offer unto the Lord an offering in righteousness. Let us therefore, as a church and a people, and as Latter Day Saints, offer unto the Lord an offering in righteousness, and let us present in his holy Temple when it is finished, a book containing the records of our dead, which shall be worthy of all acceptation.

Brethren, I have many things to say to you on the subject; but shall now close for the present, and continue the subject another time.

I am, as ever, your humble servant and never deviating friend.

From *Times and Seasons* (1842)

8. Joseph Smith, "The King Follett Discourse"

No full contemporary transcript exists of any discourse by Joseph Smith. Fortunately, the most complete account we do have is of his theologically richest and most significant oration. Given to an outdoor Nauvoo congregation of perhaps ten thousand on April 7, 1844, the sermon is named after a church member whose funeral had been held days earlier. Smith's own funeral would occur less than three months later; the sermon therefore reflects the culmination of his religion-making thought. Most of Mormonism's radical cosmology, with its heterodox human and divine anthropology, is here: the eternity of matter, and creation as divine organization; the eternity of the human spirit; God as anthropomorphic and the head of a council of Gods; the human potential to become gods. Some of these ideas had appeared earlier in LDS scripture and Apostle Parley P. Pratt's writings but were never so forcefully, explicitly, and officially presented to the public. Most controversial, even within the church, were Joseph Smith's remarks about a God who evolved from human origins, "working out his kingdom with fear and trembling."

No canonized version of this teaching exists in the church, and the sermon as a whole has had a fluctuating status in Mormon history. The sermon was published in the church newspaper a few months after Smith's death. It was left out of the first official version of the church's history, but added in 1950, and printed in the church's magazine, The Ensign, in 1971. In an official church manual of Joseph Smith's teachings published in 2007, portions pertaining to human pre-existence and exaltation (the Mormon term for becoming gods) are included, but not the sermon in its entirely. The following version of the King Follett Discourse

is an amalgamated text, incorporating notes taken by four contemporary audi-
tors: Thomas Bullock (basic running text), William Clayton (superimposed ver-
sion and refinements), Apostle Willard Richards (confirming text), and Apostle
Wilford Woodruff (additional material added). Weaving these contemporary pri-
mary sources together offers the fullest text available, as no one scribe captured
Joseph Smith's entire sermon.

I now call the attention of this congregation while I address you on the subject
which was contemplated in the fore-part of the conference. As the wind blows
very hard it will be hardly possible for me to make you all hear unless there is
profound attention. It is a subject of the greatest importance and the most solemn of any that could occupy our attention, and that is the subject of the dead.
I have been requested to speak on the subject on the decease of our beloved
brother, Elder King Follett, who was crushed to death in a well, by the falling of
a tub of rock on him. I have been requested to speak by his friends and relatives
but inasmuch as there are a great many others here in this congregation, who
live in this city as well as elsewhere, who have lost friends, their case will be had
in mind this afternoon, and I feel disposed to speak on the subject in general
and offer you my ideas as far as I have ability and as far as I will be inspired by
the Holy Spirit to treat and dwell upon this subject. . . .

I do not calculate to please your ears with superfluity of words, with oratory,
or with much learning, but I calculate to edify you with the simple truths of
heaven.

In the first place I wish to go back to the beginning of creation. There is
the starting point in order to know and be fully acquainted with the mind,
purposes, decrees, and ordinations of the great Elohim that sits in the heavens.
For us to take up beginning at the creation it is necessary for us to understand
something of God Himself in the beginning. If we start right, it is very easy for
us to go right all the time; but if we start wrong, we may go wrong, and it is a
hard matter to get right.

There are but very few beings in the world who understand rightly the character of God. If men do not comprehend the character of God, they do not
comprehend their own character. They cannot comprehend anything that is
past or that which is to come; they do not know—they do not understand their
own relationship to God. The world knows and comprehends but little more

than the brute beast. If a man knows nothing more than to eat, drink, sleep, arise, and not any more, and does not comprehend what any of the designs of Jehovah are, what better is he than the beast, for it comprehends the same things—it eats, drinks, sleeps, comprehends the present and knows nothing more about God or His existence. This is as much as we know, unless we are able to comprehend by the inspiration of Almighty God. And how are we to do it by any other way?

I want to go back, then, to the beginning that you may understand and so get you to lift your minds into a more lofty sphere and exalted standing than what the human mind generally understands. I want to ask this congregation— every man, woman, and child—to answer this question in their own heart: What kind of a being is God? Ask yourselves! I again repeat the question: What kind of a being is God? Does any man or woman know? Turn your thoughts in your hearts, and say, Have any of you seen Him? Or heard Him? Or communed with Him? Here is a question that will, peradventure, from this time henceforth occupy your attention while you live.

The Apostle says that this is eternal life to know the only wise God and Jesus Christ whom He has sent—that is eternal life. If any man inquire, What kind of a being is God?—if he will cast his mind to know and search diligently his own heart—if the declaration of the Apostle be true, he will realize that unless he knows God he has not eternal life for there can be eternal life on no other principle.

My first object is to go back and find out the character of the only wise and true God and what kind of a being He is. . . .

I am going to inquire after God because I want you all to know God and to be familiar with Him. If I can get you to know Him, I can bring you to Him. And if so, all persecution against me will cease. This will let you know that I am His servant, for I speak as one having authority and not as a scribe.

What kind of a being was God in the beginning, before the world was? I will go back to the beginning to show you. I will tell you, so open your ears and eyes, all ye ends of the earth, and hear, for I am going to prove it to you with the Bible. I am going to tell you the designs of God for the human race, the relation the human family sustains with God, and why He interferes with the affairs of man. First, God Himself who sits enthroned in yonder heavens is a Man like unto one of yourselves—that is the great secret! If the veil were rent today and the great God that holds this world in its sphere and the planets in their orbit and who upholds all things by His power—if you were to see Him today, you would see Him in all the person, image, fashion, and very form of a man, like yourselves. For Adam was a man formed in His likeness and created in the very fashion and image of God. Adam received instruction, walked, talked, and conversed with Him as one man talks and communicates with another.

In order to understand the subject of the dead and to speak for the consolation of those who mourn for the loss of their friends, it is necessary to understand the character and being of God. For I am going to tell you how God came to be God and what sort of a being He is. For we have imagined that God was God from the beginning of all eternity. I will refute that idea and take away the veil so you may see. Truth is the touchstone. These things are incomprehensible to some, but they are simple. The first principle of truth and of the Gospel is to know for a certainty the character of God, and that we may converse with Him the same as one man with another, and that He once was a man like one of us and that God Himself, the Father of us all, once dwelled on an earth the same as Jesus Christ himself did in the flesh and like us.

I will show it from the Bible. I wish I were in a suitable place to tell it. I wish I had the trump of an archangel. If I had the privilege, I could tell the story in such a manner that persecution would cease forever. The scriptures inform us (Mark it, Brother Rigdon) that Jesus Christ said:—What did Jesus say?—As the Father has power in Himself, even so has the Son power in himself. To do what? Why, what the Father did. That answer is obvious; even in a manner to lay down His body and take it up again. Jesus, what are you going to do? To lay down my life as my Father laid down His body that I might take it up again. Do you believe it? If you don't believe it, you don't believe the Bible. The Scriptures say it and I defy all hell—all the learned wisdom and records and all the combined powers of earth and hell together to refute it!

Here then is eternal life—to know the only wise and true God. You have got to learn how to make yourselves Gods in order to save yourselves and be kings and priests to God, the same as all Gods have done—by going from a small capacity to a great capacity, from a small degree to another, from grace to grace, until the resurrection of the dead, from exaltation to exaltation—till you are able to sit in everlasting burnings and everlasting power and glory as those who have gone before, sit enthroned. I want you to know that God in the last days, while certain individuals are proclaiming His name, is not trifling with you nor me.

I want you to know the first principles of consolation. How consoling to the mourners when they are called to part with a husband, father, wife, mother, child, dear relative, or friend, to know, though they lay down this body and all earthly tabernacles shall be dissolved, that their very being shall rise in immortal glory to dwell in everlasting burnings and to sorrow, die, and suffer no more. And not only that, but to contemplate the saying that they will be heirs of God and joint-heirs with Jesus Christ. What is it? To inherit and enjoy the same glory, powers, and exaltation until you ascend a throne of eternal power and arrive at the station of a God, the same as those who have gone before. What did Jesus Christ do? Why I do the same things that I saw my Father do when worlds came rolling into existence. Saw the Father do what? I saw the Father work out His kingdom with fear and trembling and I am doing the same, too. When I get my kingdom, I will give it to the Father and it will add to and exalt His glory. He will take a higher exaltation and I will take His place and I am also exalted, so that He obtains kingdom rolling upon kingdom. So that Jesus treads in His tracks as He had gone before and then inherits what God did before. God is glorified in the salvation and exaltation of His creatures.

It is plain beyond comprehension and you thus learn that these are some of the first principles of the Gospel, about which so much has been said. When you climb a ladder, you must begin at the bottom rung. You have got to find the beginning of the history and go on until you have learned the last principle of the Gospel. It will be a great while after the grave before you learn to understand the last, for it is a great thing to learn salvation beyond the grave and it is not all to be comprehended in this world.

I suppose I am not allowed to go into an investigation of anything that is not contained in the Bible. If I should, you would cry treason, and I think there are so many learned and wise men here who would put me to death for treason. I will, then, go to the old Bible and turn commentator today. I will go to the very first Hebrew word—BERESHITH—in the Bible and make a comment on the first sentence of the history of creation: In the beginning. . . . I want to analyze the word BERESHITH. BE—in, by, through, and everything else; next, ROSH—the head, ITH. Where did it come from? When the inspired man wrote it, he did not put the first part—the BE—there; but a man—an old Jew without any authority—put it there. He thought it too bad to begin to talk about the head of any man. It read in the first: The Head One of the Gods brought forth the Gods. This is the true meaning of the words. ROSHITH [BARA ELOHIM] signifies [the Head] to bring forth the Elohim. If you do not believe it, you do not believe the learned man of God. No learned man can tell you any more than what I have told you. Thus, the Head God brought forth the Head Gods in the grand, head council. I want to simplify it in the English language.

O, ye lawyers, ye learned doctors, who have persecuted me, I want to let you know and learn that the Holy Ghost knows something as well as you do. The Head One of the Gods called together the Gods and the grand councillors sat in grand council at the head in yonder heavens to bring forth the world and contemplated the creation of the worlds that were created at that time. When I say doctors and lawyers, I mean the doctors and lawyers of the Scriptures. I have done so hitherto, to let the lawyers flutter and let everybody laugh at them. Some learned doctor might take a notion to say that the Scriptures say thus and so, and we must believe the Scriptures, for they are not to be altered. . . .

Come here, ye learned men, and read, if you can. I should not have introduced this testimony, only to show that I am right and to back up the word ROSH—the Head Father of the Gods. In the beginning the Head of the Gods called a council of the Gods. The Gods came together and concocted a scheme to create this world and the inhabitants. When we begin to learn in this way, we begin to learn the only true God. We find out God and what kind of a being we have got to worship. Having a knowledge of God, we know how to approach Him and ask so that He will answer. When we begin to know how to come to Him, He begins to come to us. When we are ready to come to Him, He is ready to receive us. As soon as we begin to understand the character of God, He begins to unfold the heavens to us and tell us all about it before our prayers get to His ears.

Now, I ask all the learned men who hear me, why the learned doctors who are preaching salvation say that God created the heavens and the earth out of nothing. They account it blasphemy to contradict the idea. If you tell them that God made the world out of something, they will call you a fool. The reason is that they are unlearned but I am learned and know more than all the world put together—the Holy Ghost does, anyhow. If the Holy Ghost in me comprehends more than all the world, I will associate myself with it.

You ask them why, and they say, Doesn't the Bible say He created the world? And they infer that it must be out of nothing. The word create came from the word BARA, but it doesn't mean so. What does BARA mean? It means to organize; the same as a man would organize and use things to build a ship. Hence, we infer that God Himself had materials to organize the world out of chaos—chaotic matter—which is element and in which dwells all the glory. Element had an existence from the time He had. The pure principles of element are principles that never can be destroyed. They may be organized and reorganized, but not destroyed. Nothing can be destroyed. They never can have a beginning or an ending; they exist eternally. It is associated with the subject in question, the resurrection of the dead.

I have another subject to dwell on which is calculated to exalt man, but it isn't possible for me to say much but to touch upon it. Time will not permit me to say all. So I must come to what I wish to speak of—the resurrection of the dead—the soul—the immortal spirit—the mind of man. Where did it come from? All doctors of divinity say that God created it in the beginning, but it is not so. The very idea lessens the character of man, in my estimation. I don't believe the doctrine. Hear it, all ye ends of the earth: I know better for God has told me so. I will make a man appear a fool before he gets through. If he doesn't believe it, it won't make the truth without effect. I am going to tell of things more noble.

We say that God Himself is a self-existent God. Who told you so? It's correct enough, but how did it get into your heads? Who told you that man did not exist in like manner upon the same principle? [He refers to the Bible.] How does it read in the Hebrew? It doesn't say so in the old Hebrew. God made the tabernacle of man out of the earth and put into him Adam's spirit (which was created before), and then it became a living body or human soul. Man existed in spirit; the mind of man—the intelligent part—is as immortal as, and is coequal with, God Himself. I know that my testimony is true.

Hence, when I talk to these mourners, what have they lost? You who mourn the loss of friends are only separated for a small moment from their spirits, and their spirits are only separated from their bodies for a short season. But their spirits existed coequal with God and they now exist in a place where they hold converse together one with another the same as we do on the earth. Does not this give you satisfaction?

I want to reason more on the spirit of man for I am dwelling on the immutability of the spirit and on the body of man—on the subject of the dead. Is it logical to say that a spirit is immortal and yet have a beginning? Because if a spirit of man had a beginning, it will have an end, but it does not have a beginning or end. This is good logic and is illustrated by my ring. I take my ring from my finger and liken it unto the mind of man—the immortal spirit—because it has no beginning or end. Suppose you cut it in two—as the Lord lives there would be a beginning and an end. So it is with man. All the fools and learned and wise men from the beginning of creation, who come and say that man had a beginning, prove that he must have an end. If that doctrine be true, then the doctrine of annihilation would be true. But if I am right, then I might with boldness proclaim from the housetop that God never had the power to create the spirit of man at all. God Himself could not create Himself.

Intelligence is eternal and exists upon a self-existent principle. It is a spirit from age to age and there is no creation about it. The first principles of man are self-existent with God. All the minds and spirits that God ever sent into the world are susceptible of enlargement and improvement. The relationship we have with God places us in a situation to advance in knowledge. God Himself found Himself in the midst of spirits and glory. Because He was greater He saw proper to institute laws whereby the rest, who were less in intelligence, could have a privilege to advance like Himself and be exalted with Him, so that they might have one glory upon another in all that knowledge, power, and glory. So He took in hand to save the world of spirits.

This is good doctrine. It tastes good. You say honey is sweet and so do I. I can also taste the spirit and principles of eternal life, and so can you. I know it is good and that when I tell you of these words of eternal life that are given to me by the inspiration of the Holy Spirit and the revelations of Jesus Christ, you are bound to receive them as sweet. You taste them and I know you believe them. I rejoice more and more. . . .

A question about parents receiving their children. Will mothers have their children in eternity? Yes! Yes! Mothers, you will have your children. For they will have it without price; for their debt of redemption is paid. There is no damnation awaiting them for they are in the spirit. But as the child dies, so will it rise from the dead and be living in the burning of God and possessing all the intelligence of a God. It will never grow, it will be the child in its precise form as it was before it died out of your arms. Children dwell and exercise power, throne upon throne, dominion upon dominion, in the same form just as you laid them down. Eternity is full of thrones upon which dwell thousands of children, reigning on thrones of glory, with not one cubit added to their stature. . . .

I have intended my remarks to all—to all the rich and poor, bond and free, great and small. I have no enmity against any man. I love all men—I love you all, but hate your deeds. I am their best friend, and if persons miss their mark it is their own fault. If I reprove a man, and he hate me, he is a fool; for I love all men, especially these my brethren and sisters. I rejoice in hearing the testimony of my aged friend.

You don't know me—you never will. You never knew my heart. No man knows my history. I cannot do it. I shall never undertake it. I don't blame you for not believing my history. If I had not experienced what I have, I could not have believed it myself. I never did harm any man since I have been born in the world. My voice is always for peace. I cannot lie down until my work is finished. I never think evil nor think anything to the harm of my fellowman. When I am called at the trump and weighed in the balance, you will know me then. I add no more. God bless you. Amen.

From *BYU Studies* (1844)

9. Joseph F. Smith, "Vision of the Redemption of the Dead [Doctrine and Covenants 138]"

Although Latter-day Saints believe in an open canon, and added three volumes of scripture to the Holy Bible to constitute their "Standard Works," most of these additions were produced by Joseph Smith. He dictated the Book of Mormon, the writings of Moses and Abraham along with other texts comprising the Pearl of Great Price, and more than 130 revelations that formed the bulk of the modern Doctrine and Covenants. After his death, Apostle John Taylor penned a eulogy, and Apostle Brigham Young issued a directive pertaining to the westward exodus. Both texts were added to the Mormon canon in 1844 and 1876, respectively. Except for an official "Manifesto" by President Wilford Woodruff announcing the end of new plural marriages (first included in the Doctrine and Covenants in 1908), no other Mormon prophet added to the body of scripture until 1981. In that year, a 1978 declaration by President Spencer W. Kimball extending the priesthood to men of every race and a 1918 vision received by President Joseph F. Smith were presented to church membership for inclusion in the canon. In October 1918, the deadliest month in American history, 195,000 people perished in the flu pandemic, while the slaughter on World War I battlegrounds continued unabated. Added to a personal legacy of enormous loss (orphaned as a boy, Joseph F. Smith buried one wife and thirteen children as an adult), this immersion in the trauma of death doubtless led him to ponder deeply the matter of the afterlife. His ensuing vision added considerable detail to Mormon belief in an extensive missionary work taking place among the souls in the spirit world. The vast enterprise among Latter-day Saints of family history work and temple ordinances for the deceased is predicated on the belief that, as intimated in 1 Peter 3:19–20, the gospel is taught to the deceased wicked (in "spirit prison") and righteous (in "paradise"), affording them the opportunity for salvation they did not have in this life.

On the third of October, in the year nineteen hundred and eighteen, I sat in my room pondering over the Scriptures and reflecting upon the great atoning sacrifice that was made by the Son of God for the redemption of the world, and the great and wonderful love made manifest by the Father and the Son in the coming of the Redeemer into the world, that through his Atonement and by obedience to the principles of the gospel, mankind might be saved.

While I was thus engaged, my mind reverted to the writings of the Apostle Peter to the primitive saints scattered abroad throughout Pontus, Galatia, Cappadocia, and other parts of Asia where the gospel had been preached after the crucifixion of the Lord. I opened the Bible and read the third and fourth chapters of the first epistle of Peter, and as I read I was greatly impressed, more than I had ever been before, with the following passages:

> For Christ also hath once suffered for sins, the just for the unjust, that he might bring us to God, being put to death in the flesh, but quickened by the Spirit:
>
> By which also he went and preached unto the spirits in prison;
>
> Which sometime were disobedient, when once the longsuffering of God waited in the days of Noah, while the ark was a preparing, wherein few, that is, eight souls were saved by water. (1 Peter 3:18–20.)
>
> For this cause was the gospel preached also to them that are dead, that they might be judged according to men in the flesh, but live according to God in the spirit. (1 Peter 4:6.)

As I pondered over these things which are written, the eyes of my understanding were opened, and the Spirit of the Lord rested upon me, and I saw the hosts of the dead, both small and great. And there were gathered together in one place an innumerable company of the spirits of the just, who had been faithful in the testimony of Jesus while they lived in mortality, and who had offered sacrifice in the similitude of the great sacrifice of the Son of God, and had suffered tribulation in their Redeemer's name. All these had departed the mortal life, firm in the hope of a glorious resurrection, through the grace of God the Father and his Only Begotten Son, Jesus Christ.

I beheld that they were filled with joy and gladness, and were rejoicing together because the day of their deliverance was at hand. They were assembled awaiting the advent of the Son of God into the spirit world, to declare their redemption from the bands of death. Their sleeping dust was to be restored unto its perfect frame, bone to his bone, and the sinews and the flesh upon them, the spirit and the body to be united never again to be divided, that they might receive a fulness of joy.

While this vast multitude waited and conversed, rejoicing in the hour of their deliverance from the chains of death, the Son of God appeared, declaring liberty to the captives who had been faithful, and there he preached to them the everlasting gospel, the doctrine of the resurrection and the redemption of mankind from the fall, and from individual sins on conditions of repentance. But unto the wicked he did not go, and among the ungodly and the unrepentant who had defiled themselves while in the flesh, his voice was not raised, neither did the rebellious who rejected the testimonies and the warnings of the ancient prophets behold his presence, nor look upon his face. Where these were, darkness reigned, but among the righteous there was peace, and the saints rejoiced in their redemption, and bowed the knee and acknowledged the Son of God as their Redeemer and Deliverer from death and the chains of hell. Their countenances shone and the radiance from the presence of the Lord rested upon them and they sang praises unto his holy Name.

I marveled, for I understood that the Savior spent about three years in his ministry among the Jews and those of the house of Israel, endeavoring to teach them the everlasting gospel and call them unto repentance; and yet, notwithstanding his mighty works and miracles and proclamation of the truth in great power and authority, there were but few who hearkened to his voice and rejoiced in his presence and received salvation at his hands. But his ministry among those who were dead was limited to the brief time intervening between the crucifixion and his resurrection; and I wondered at the words of Peter wherein he said that the Son of God preached unto the spirits in prison who sometime were disobedient, when once the longsuffering of God waited in the days of Noah, and how it was possible for him to preach to those spirits and perform the necessary labor among them in so short a time.

And as I wondered, my eyes were opened, and my understanding quickened, and I perceived that the Lord went not in person among the wicked and the disobedient who had rejected the truth, to teach them; but behold, from among the righteous he organized his forces and appointed messengers, clothed with power and authority, and commissioned them to go forth and carry the light of the gospel to them that were in darkness, even to all the spirits of men. And thus was the gospel preached to the dead. And the chosen messengers went forth to declare the acceptable day of the Lord, and proclaim liberty to the captives who were bound; even unto all who would repent of their sins and receive the gospel. Thus was the gospel preached to those who had died in their sins, without a knowledge of the truth, or in transgression, having rejected the prophets. These were taught faith in God, repentance from sin, vicarious baptism for the remission of sins, the gift of the Holy Ghost by the laying on of hands, and all other principles of the gospel that were necessary for them to know in order to qualify themselves that they might be judged according to men in the flesh, but live according to God in the spirit.

And so it was made known among the dead, both small and great, the unrighteous as well as the faithful, that redemption had been wrought through the sacrifice of the Son of God upon the cross. Thus was it made known that our Redeemer spent his time during his sojourn in the world of spirits, instructing and preparing the faithful spirits of the prophets who had testified of him in the flesh, that they might carry the message of redemption unto all the dead unto whom he could not go personally because of their rebellion and transgression, that they through the ministration of his servants might also hear his words.

Among the great and mighty ones who were assembled in this vast congregation of the righteous, were Father Adam, the Ancient of Days and father of all, and our glorious Mother Eve, with many of her faithful daughters who had lived through the ages and worshiped the true and living God. Abel, the first martyr, was there, and his brother Seth, one of the mighty ones, who was in the express image of his father Adam. Noah, who gave warning of the flood; Shem, the great High Priest; Abraham, the father of the faithful; Isaac, Jacob, and Moses, the great law-giver of Israel; Isaiah, who declared by prophecy that the Redeemer was anointed to bind up the broken hearted, to proclaim liberty to the captives, and the opening of the prison to them that were bound, were also there.

Moreover, Ezekiel, who was shown in vision the great valley of dry bones which were to be clothed upon with flesh to come forth again in the resurrection of the dead, living souls; Daniel, who foresaw and foretold the establishment of the kingdom of God in the latter days, never again to be destroyed nor given to other people; Elias, who was with Moses on the Mount of Transfiguration, and Malachi, the prophet who testified of the coming of Elijah—of whom also Moroni spake to the Prophet Joseph Smith—declaring that he should come before the ushering in of the great and dreadful day of the Lord, were also there. The prophet Elijah was to plant in the hearts of the children the promises made to their fathers, foreshadowing the great work to be done in the temples of the Lord in the Dispensation of the Fulness of Times, for the redemption of the dead and the sealing of the children to their parents, lest the whole earth be smitten with a curse and utterly wasted at his coming.

All these and many more, even the prophets who dwelt among the Nephites and testified of the coming of the Son of God, mingled in the vast assembly and waited for their deliverance, for the dead had looked upon the long absence of their spirits from their bodies as a bondage. These the Lord taught, and gave them power to come forth, after his resurrection from the dead, to enter into his Father's kingdom, there to be crowned with immortality and eternal life, and continue thenceforth their labors as had been promised by the Lord, and be partakers of all blessings which were held in reserve for them that love him.

The Prophet Joseph Smith, and my father, Hyrum Smith, Brigham Young, John Taylor, Wilford Woodruff, and other choice spirits, who were reserved to come forth in the fulness of times to take part in laying the foundations of the great Latter-day work, including the building of temples and the performance of ordinances therein for the redemption of the dead, were also in the spirit world. I observed that they were also among the noble and great ones who were chosen in the beginning to be rulers in the Church of God. Even before they were born, they, with many others, received their first lessons in the world of spirits, and were prepared to come forth in the due time of the Lord to labor in his vineyard for the salvation of the souls of men.

I beheld that the faithful elders of this dispensation, when they depart from mortal life, continue their labors in the preaching of the gospel of repentance and redemption, through the sacrifice of the Only Begotten Son of God, among those who are in darkness and under the bondage of sin in the great world of the spirits of the dead. The dead who repent will be redeemed, through obedience to the ordinances of the house of God, and after they have paid the penalty of their transgressions, and are washed clean, shall receive a reward according to their works, for they are heirs of salvation.

Thus was the vision of the redemption of the dead revealed to me, and I bear record, and I know that this record is true, through the blessing of our Lord and Savior, Jesus Christ, even so. Amen.

From *Improvement Era* (1918)

10. First Presidency (Heber J. Grant, Anthony W. Ivins, and Charles W. Nibley), "'Mormon' View of Evolution"

Like many Christian institutions, the church suffered the spasms of Charles Darwin's disruption of the classical creationist paradigm, but a tendency toward scriptural literalism was counterbalanced by a crucial scriptural emendation and Joseph Smith's progressivism. Smith recast the creation narrative, in his Abraham texts, as involving creational "times" rather than days; in addition, he said that this "system" was billions of years old. President Brigham Young criticized other religious leaders for believing in that which was contrary to demonstrated science, and reserved judgment on Darwinism, though most LDS apostles were skeptical or dismissive. In 1909, the First Presidency first issued a public statement on "The Origin of Man," which referred to Darwin's writings on evolution as the "theories of men," without explicitly rejecting them. In 1925, in the midst of the "Scopes Monkey Trial" and extensive controversy, church leaders issued a revised statement, this time titled "The Mormon View of Evolution." It was, once again, a model of studied ambiguity. Emphatically affirming the role of God as Creator, and belief in Adam as human progenitor, the document nowhere uses the term "evolution," nor does it mention Darwin. The silence at the most crucial point allowed the church's most influential theologians of the era, Apostles Joseph Fielding Smith and James Talmage, subsequently to embrace opposite sides of the evolution debate. Brigham Young University, the church's flagship institution of higher learning located in Provo, Utah, has itself played a role as both opponent and proponent. Four evolutionists from the BYU faculty were dismissed in 1911. Today, by contrast, there is a small dinosaur museum and a top evolutionary biology program at the university.

"God created man in his own image, in the image of God created he him; male and female created he them."

In these plain and pointed words the inspired author of the book of Genesis made known to the world the truth concerning the origin of the human family. Moses, the prophet-historian, who was "learned" we are told, "in all the wisdom of the Egyptians," when making this important announcement, was not voicing a mere opinion. He was speaking as the mouthpiece of God, and his solemn declaration was for all time and for all people. No subsequent revelator of the truth has contradicted the great leader and law-giver of Israel. All who have since spoken by divine authority upon this theme have confirmed his simple and sublime proclamation. Nor could it be otherwise. Truth has but one source, and all revelations from heaven are harmonious one with the other.

Jesus Christ, the Son of God, is "the express image" of his Father's person (Hebrews 1:3). He walked the earth as a human being, as a perfect man, and said, in answer to a question put to him: "He that hath seen me hath seen the Father" (John 14:9). This alone ought to solve the problem to the satisfaction of every thoughtful, reverent mind. It was in this form that the Father and the Son, as two distinct personages, appeared to Joseph Smith, when, as a boy of fourteen years, he received his first vision.

The Father of Jesus Christ is our Father also. Jesus himself taught this truth, when he instructed his disciples how to pray: "Our Father which art in heaven," etc. Jesus, however, is the first born among all the sons of God—the first begotten in the spirit, and the only begotten in the flesh. He is our elder brother, and we, like him, are in the image of God. All men and women are in the similitude of the universal Father and Mother, and are literally sons and daughters of Deity.

Adam, our great progenitor, "the first man," was, like Christ, a pre-existent spirit, and, like Christ, he took upon him an appropriate body, the body of a man, and so became a "living soul." The doctrine of pre-existence pours wonderful flood of light upon the otherwise mysterious problem of man's origin. It shows that man, as a spirit, was begotten and born of heavenly parents, and reared to maturity in the eternal mansions of the Father, prior to coming upon the earth in a temporal body to undergo an experience in mortality.

The Church of Jesus Christ of Latter-day Saints, basing its belief on divine revelation, ancient and modern, proclaims man to be the direct and lineal offspring of Deity. By his Almighty power God organized the earth, and all that it contains, from spirit and element, which exist co-eternally with himself.

Man is the child of God, formed in the divine image and endowed with divine attributes, and even as the infant son of an earthly father and mother is capable in due time of becoming a man, so that undeveloped offspring of celestial parentage is capable, by experience through ages and aeons, of evolving into a God.

From *Improvement Era* (1925)

11. First Presidency and Quorum of the Twelve Apostles (Gordon B. Hinckley, Thomas S. Monson, James E. Faust, et al.), "The Family: A Proclamation to the World"

Ever since the sexual revolution of the 1960s, religious leaders and populist politicians have invoked the specter of a disintegrating American family. By 1989, concern was widespread enough that the United Nations General Assembly designated 1994 the International Year of the Family, declaring that "the widest possible protection and assistance should be accorded to the family." In 1995, church leaders issued a proclamation to the world, in which the leadership mixed theology, admonition, and warning. The church and its membership occupy an ironic position, insofar as they combine a historic legacy of unconventional marriage practice (polygamy), a novel theology of the family (eternal marriage and eternal family relationships), and a modern reputation as exemplifying the most conservative and traditional of family values in America. Latter-day Saints who intermarry have the lowest divorce rate in America, Mormons have the lowest abortion and teen pregnancy rates in the nation, and their youth are the most religiously observant of all faith groups measured.[1] Nevertheless, exceptions to these ideals are significant enough to disturb church leaders, as does the unsettling incidence of pornography and sexual and spousal abuse. There is nothing new by way of doctrine in this proclamation, being mostly a reaffirmation of long-standing moral standards. Its clear statement of parental roles and responsibilities, on the eternity of gender and the role of procreation in marriage, laid a foundation—if not a self-imposed imperative—for church involvement in controversial legislative battles such as the gay-marriage initiatives of 2008 and later. (Only five proclamations have been issued by the church, which are binding official utterances, though not canonized as scripture.)

We, the First Presidency and the Council of the Twelve Apostles of The Church of Jesus Christ of Latter-day Saints, solemnly proclaim that marriage between a man and a woman is ordained of God and that the family is central to the Creator's plan for the eternal destiny of His children.

All human beings—male and female—are created in the image of God. Each is a beloved spirit son or daughter of heavenly parents, and, as such, each has a divine nature and destiny. Gender is an essential characteristic of individual premortal, mortal, and eternal identity and purpose.

In the premortal realm, spirit sons and daughters knew and worshiped God as their Eternal Father and accepted His plan by which His children could obtain a physical body and gain earthly experience to progress toward perfection and ultimately realize his or her divine destiny as an heir of eternal life. The divine plan of happiness enables family relationships to be perpetuated beyond the grave. Sacred ordinances and covenants available in holy temples make it possible for individuals to return to the presence of God and for families to be united eternally.

The first commandment that God gave to Adam and Eve pertained to their potential for parenthood as husband and wife. We declare that God's commandment for His children to multiply and replenish the earth remains in force. We further declare that God has commanded that the sacred powers of procreation are to be employed only between man and woman, lawfully wedded as husband and wife.

We declare the means by which mortal life is created to be divinely appointed. We affirm the sanctity of life and of its importance in God's eternal plan.

Husband and wife have a solemn responsibility to love and care for each other and for their children. "Children are an heritage of the Lord" (Psalms 127:3). Parents have a sacred duty to rear their children in love and righteousness, to provide for their physical and spiritual needs, to teach them to love and serve one another, to observe the commandments of God and to be law-abiding citizens wherever they live. Husbands and wives—mothers and fathers—will be held accountable before God for the discharge of these obligations.

The family is ordained of God. Marriage between man and woman is essential to His eternal plan. Children are entitled to birth within the bonds of matrimony, and to be reared by a father and a mother who honor marital vows with complete fidelity. Happiness in family life is most likely to be achieved when founded upon the teachings of the Lord Jesus Christ. Successful marriages and families are established and maintained on principles of faith, prayer, repentance, forgiveness, respect, love, compassion, work, and wholesome recreational activities. By divine design, fathers are to preside over their families in love and righteousness and are responsible to provide the necessities of life and protection for their families. Mothers are primarily responsible for the nurture of their children. In these sacred responsibilities, fathers and mothers are obligated to help one another as equal partners. Disability, death, or other circumstances may necessitate individual adaptation. Extended families should lend support when needed.

We warn that individuals who violate covenants of chastity, who abuse spouse or offspring, or who fail to fulfill family responsibilities will one day stand accountable before God. Further, we warn that the disintegration of the family will bring upon individuals, communities, and nations the calamities foretold by ancient and modern prophets.

We call upon responsible citizens and officers of government everywhere to promote those measures designed to maintain and strengthen the family as the fundamental unit of society.

From *Ensign* (1995)

12. First Presidency and Quorum of the Twelve Apostles (Gordon B. Hinckley, Thomas S. Monson, James E. Faust, et al.), "The Living Christ: The Testimony of the Apostles"

It is ironic that a religious denomination named "The Church of Jesus Christ of Latter-day Saints" should frequently find its right to the designation of Christian challenged. Prominent in these debates is the Mormon doctrine of deity, which is not Trinitarian, like that of Catholic and Protestant Christianity. Jesus Christ is, however, central to LDS faith and worship. On the first day of the new millennium, the Council of the First Presidency and Quorum of the Twelve Apostles jointly produced a statement that both affirmed their faith in and defined the role and status of Jesus Christ. Other than the identification of Jesus with the Jehovah of the Old Testament, the Christology of the document is generally the same as orthodox Christian belief. Christ is divine, the literal Son of God and his firstborn in the flesh, savior of mankind, physically resurrected from the tomb, and he who will come again. The repeated emphasis on a Christ "who lives" is not accidental. For Latter-day Saints, that Christ is a living Christ is most abundantly manifest in his current direction of the church, through literal revelation to modern day prophets and apostles. The members of the First Presidency, as well as members of the Quorum of the Twelve, are ordained apostles. The essence of their calling, as defined in LDS scripture, is to be "special witnesses of the name of Christ in all the world" (Doctrine and Covenants 107:23). This testimony represents an emphatic, collective fulfillment of that commission.

As we commemorate the birth of Jesus Christ two millennia ago, we offer our testimony of the reality of His matchless life and the infinite virtue of His great atoning sacrifice. None other has had so profound an influence upon all who have lived and will yet live upon the earth.

He was the Great Jehovah of the Old Testament, the Messiah of the New. Under the direction of His Father, He was the creator of the earth. "All things were made by him; and without him was not any thing made that was made" (John 1:3). Though sinless, He was baptized to fulfill all righteousness. He "went about doing good" (Acts 10:38), yet was despised for it. His gospel was a message of peace and goodwill. He entreated all to follow His example. He walked the roads of Palestine, healing the sick, causing the blind to see, and raising the dead. He taught the truths of eternity, the reality of our premortal existence, the purpose of our life on earth, and the potential for the sons and daughters of God in the life to come.

He instituted the sacrament as a reminder of His great atoning sacrifice. He was arrested and condemned on spurious charges, convicted to satisfy a mob, and sentenced to die on Calvary's cross. He gave His life to atone for the sins of all mankind. His was a great vicarious gift in behalf of all who would ever live upon the earth.

We solemnly testify that His life, which is central to all human history, neither began in Bethlehem nor concluded on Calvary. He was the Firstborn of the Father, the Only Begotten Son in the flesh, the Redeemer of the world.

He rose from the grave to "become the first fruits of them that slept" (1 Corinthians 15:20). As Risen Lord, He visited among those He had loved in life. He also ministered among His "other sheep" (John 10:16) in ancient America. In the modern world, He and His Father appeared to the boy Joseph Smith, ushering in the long-promised "dispensation of the fulness of times" (Ephesians 1:10).

Of the Living Christ, the Prophet Joseph wrote: "His eyes were as a flame of fire; the hair of his head was white like the pure snow; his countenance shone above the brightness of the sun; and his voice was as the sound of the rushing of great waters, even the voice of Jehovah, saying:

"I am the first and the last; I am he who liveth, I am he who was slain; I am your advocate with the Father" (D&C 110:3–4).

Of Him the Prophet also declared: "And now, after the many testimonies which have been given of him, this is the testimony, last of all, which we give of him: That he lives!"

"For we saw him, even on the right hand of God; and we heard the voice bearing record that he is the Only Begotten of the Father—

"That by him, and through him, and of him, the worlds are and were created, and the inhabitants thereof are begotten sons and daughters unto God" (D&C 76:22–24).

We declare in words of solemnity that His priesthood and His Church have been restored upon the earth—"built upon the foundation of . . . apostles and prophets, Jesus Christ himself being the chief corner stone" (Ephesians 2:20).

We testify that He will someday return to earth. "And the glory of the Lord shall be revealed, and all flesh shall see it together" (Isaiah 40:5). He will rule as King of Kings and reign as Lord of Lords, and every knee shall bend and every tongue shall speak in worship before Him. Each of us will stand to be judged of Him according to our works and the desires of our hearts.

We bear testimony, as His duly ordained Apostles—that Jesus is the Living Christ, the immortal Son of God. He is the great King Immanuel, who stands today on the right hand of His Father. He is the light, the life, and the hope of the world. His way is the path that leads to happiness in this life and eternal life in the world to come. God be thanked for the matchless gift of His divine Son.

From *Ensign* (2000)

TWO

SCATTERING OF THE SAINTS

EARLY OPPOSITION TO THE CHURCH of Jesus Christ of Latter-day Saints arose in a variety of contexts and for an array of reasons. Joseph Smith claimed that while yet a young man, his story of being visited by divine beings and angelic messengers brought intense and prolonged persecution upon his head. As leader of the fledgling church, he asserted not just prophetic gifts, but also the authority to direct followers in temporal as well as spiritual matters. When thousands of Latter-day Saints settled in Missouri, their rhetoric of being chosen by God and their intimations that they would inherit lands in Missouri (which they called Zion) infuriated old non-Mormon settlers. Swelling LDS numbers upset the political balance of power, further alarming locals. Latter-day Saints responded to harassment with increasingly militant and threatening speeches and expressed sympathy for abolition in a state full of slaveholders. Forcibly relocated to Illinois, they founded a virtual city-state in Nauvoo, where they established their own judicial system and a thousands-strong militia. To many outsiders, Smith seemed a fanatical tyrant with theocratic intentions, repugnant to democratic institutions and principles. These allegations were compounded by rumors of sexual misconduct and plural marriage being practiced in the Mormon capital. When Joseph Smith launched a campaign for the U.S. presidency in 1844, he seemed to confirm the public's worst fears. Delusions of grandeur now seemed to be fueling dangerous ambition, and the number of his followers had reached well over ten thousand.

The last straw was the decision of the Nauvoo City Council, over which Joseph Smith presided, to destroy as a public nuisance the printing press of the *Nauvoo Expositor*, a newspaper run by dissidents who vowed to alert the public to the worst of Smith's purported crimes, especially his practice—then spreading among his associates—of polygamy. A furious public outcry resulted, and at the urging of Illinois Governor Thomas Ford, Joseph Smith surrendered himself to authorities in the non-Mormon community of Carthage. Charged with treason, he was committed to the local jail. In the late afternoon of June 27, 1844, before a trial was held, the jail was stormed by a mob of some two hundred people with blackened faces. Smith, with his brother Hyrum and two associates, Apostles Willard Richards and John Taylor, tried to fend off their attackers with walking sticks and a pepperbox pistol. Hyrum was hit by several musket balls and died immediately; Taylor received a similar number but survived. Richards, behind the forced door, was unscathed. Joseph Smith attempted to jump from the second story window and was shot several times in the process. He pitched forward and fell through the window and to the ground where he died. The next day, Latter-day Saints retrieved the bodies of Joseph and Hyrum and took them home to Nauvoo for burial. Given his frequently expressed intimations of an imminent death, it is surprising that Smith did not make clearer provisions for an heir to his position of leadership. Throughout his ministry, he had given hints and occasionally clear signals to a number of possible successors. As a consequence, in the aftermath of Joseph Smith's death, the church went through a time of both splintering and reconsolidation known as the succession crisis.

Hyrum Smith, Joseph's older brother and close confidant, had been designated Presiding Patriarch and Assistant President of the church. In all likelihood he would have succeeded Joseph Smith if they had not died together; Apostle Brigham Young said as much weeks later. Now, in the absence of an unambiguous claimant to the position, several individuals were plausible contenders. Apostles like John Taylor and Willard Richards were originally considered "traveling councilors" with jurisdictional authority only outside organized "stakes." As a quorum, they were at this time coming to function as a presiding body second to, and supervised by, the First Presidency. Sidney Rigdon, Smith's counselor in the First Presidency, was in Pittsburgh. With Joseph Smith dead, the status of remaining First Presidency members and the Quorum itself was unclear. William Marks, as president of the Nauvoo Stake, was the presiding church authority on the scene. Word of the Carthage killings took days and weeks to reach most of the widely dispersed church leadership. Young and all other quorum members besides Taylor and Richards were scattered throughout the Midwest and Eastern states on missions. Apostle Parley P. Pratt reached Nauvoo on July 8, and his colleagues filtered in over the next four weeks.

A public meeting was convened on the morning of August 8 to decide the succession question. No one presumed to fill Joseph Smith's shoes or inherit his title as prophet. Sidney Rigdon, the church's most powerful orator, stood and claimed the right to serve the church as "guardian." In the afternoon, Brigham Young arose and asked the throng of thousands if they wished to choose a prophet or guardian. When no support was expressed, he then declared that "the quorum of the twelve have the keys of the kingdom of God in all the world" and promised to build upon the foundation Smith had laid. In later narratives of the occasion, many in the audience claimed that Young had been transfigured as he spoke, in voice and person, into the likeness of Joseph Smith. Supporters of Young spoke to support his claim; Rigdon declined an opportunity to speak further, and the assembly voted overwhelmingly to support Young and the twelve of the Twelve Apostles.

Brigham Young had several advantages going into the Nauvoo public meeting, but principal among them was his combination of on-scene presence and steadfast prominence in church service. Sidney Rigdon had once shared comparable stature but had been publicly disavowed by Joseph Smith almost a year earlier, whereupon his involvement in church leadership declined. For years, Smith had questioned Rigdon's loyalty to him and his commitment to the growing church. Church members were aware of the strained relationship between the two men. In the aftermath of the August 1844 meeting, however, a number of claimants began to emerge who either had missed the opportunity to address the core membership assembled at Nauvoo or were slower to formulate their own desires and justification for succession. Young's strained relations with Joseph Smith's wife, Emma, and his support for the unpopular and guarded practice of polygamy were two strikes against him. The Smith name, claims to angelic calling, public opposition to plural marriage, and purported letters and blessings given personally by Joseph Smith worked to the advantage of competing claimants.

The most successful challenge to Brigham Young initially came from James Strang, a recent convert who had a formidable array of support for his position. He had a letter of appointment he said was in Joseph Smith's hand, his own testimony of angelic visitation and confirmation of his calling, a scriptural record that (like Smith's Book of Mormon) Strang claimed to have translated, and within a short time, a printing press to promulgate his message. He would go on to form his own church, move his followers to Michigan, practice plural marriage, and eventually be murdered by some estranged disciples. By the end of the twentieth century, there were less than three hundred Strangites. But the most numerically successful challenge that survives to this day was the Reorganized Church of Jesus Christ of Latter Day Saints (RLDS Church, which became the Community of Christ in 2001). It coalesced in 1860 around Joseph Smith's son, Joseph Smith III, out of several scattered groups that had earlier rejected Young's leadership.

The documents selected for this chapter sample a very small portion of the myriad restorationist groups that claim descent from Joseph Smith's teachings and authority. Most were of short duration, and not many had more than a few hundred members, except for a number of modern polygamous groups. (Not surprisingly, Smith's prophetic authority and claims to be the *only* one called to lead by revelation were challenged during his lifetime as well.) Given the fluidity, brevity, and obscurity of some of these descendent churches, it is impossible to give an exact number; some scholars claim there have been more than four hundred. The seeds for their vitality—as well as their fragmentation—were established early on, with Joseph Smith's celebration of continuing "direct revelation" from God as the hallmark of the restoration.[1]

1. Isaac Russell, "Letter to the Saints in England"

In 1844, Mormon Apostle Parley P. Pratt published a "Dialogue Between Joseph Smith and the Devil," in which the latter fumed most fiercely against the "abominable doctrine ... of direct communication with God, by new revelation."[2] Latter-day Saints represented this power of personal revelation as the destroyer of Satan's dominion, the mainspring of their movement, key to the restoration, and proof of the church's divine origins. But the idea of personal revelation was far too potent an idea to contain easily once it had been unleashed. Within six months of the church's founding, some members like Hiram Page were claiming to receive their own revelations for the guidance of the church. An 1830 revelation declared that "no one shall be appointed to receive . . . revelations in this church excepting my servant Joseph" (Doctrine and Covenants 28:2), but competitors would emerge from time to time. One example of how the restorationist movement could fracture even before Smith's martyrdom is the case of Isaac Russell, a Canadian converted by Pratt in 1836. In late 1838, leading Latter-day Saints were arrested and imprisoned, and the bulk of the Mormons were forcefully expelled from their gathering places in Missouri. Russell appealed to those reluctant to pull up stakes and depart, claiming he had a revelation authorizing him to head up a new gathering further west. His revelation incorporated several familiar themes: the retreat of a righteous remnant to the wilderness, building Zion, preparation for an imminent millennium, and the ministering of angels (in this case, by the "Three Nephites" mentioned in the Book of Mormon). After attracting initial followers, Russell's effort fizzled. Nevertheless, it stands as an early illustration of the religious volatility created among restorationists by the principle of ongoing, heavenly revelation and the potential for widespread fracturing upon Joseph Smith's death.

Far West, January 30, 1839

To the Faithful Brethren and Sisters of the Church
of Latter-day Saints in Alston:

Dear Brethren:—Inasmuch as wisdom is only to be spoken amongst those who are wise, I charge you to read this letter to none but those who enter into a covenant with you to keep those things that are revealed in this letter from all the world, and from all the churches, except the churches to whom I myself have ministered, viz.—the church in Alston and the branches round about, to whom I ministered, and to none else; and to none but the faithful amongst you; and wo be to the man or woman that breaketh this covenant.

Now the Indians, who are the children of the Nephites and the Lamanites, who are spoken of in the Book of Mormon, have all been driven to the western boundaries of the States of America, by the Gentiles, as I told you; they have now to be visited by the gospel, for the day of their redemption is come, and the Gentiles have now well nigh filled up the measure of their wickedness, and will soon be cut off, for they have slain many of the people of the Lord, and scattered the rest; and for the sins of God's people, the Gentiles will now be suffered to scourge them from city to city, and from place to place, and few of all the thousands of the Church of Latter-day Saints will stand to receive an inheritance in the land of promise, which is now in the hands of our enemies. But a few will remain and be purified as gold seven times refined; and they will return to Zion with songs of everlasting joy, to build up the old waste places that are now left desolate.

Now the thing that I have to reveal to you is sacred, and must be kept with care; for I am not suffered to reveal it at all to the churches in this land, because of their wickedness and unbelief—for they have almost cast me out from amongst them, because I have testified of their sins to them, and warned them of the judgments that have yet to come upon them; and this thing that I now tell you, will not come to the knowledge of the churches until they are purified.

Now the thing is as follows—The Lord has directed me, with a few others, whose hearts the Lord has touched, to go into the wilderness, where we shall be fed and directed by the hand of the Lord until we are purified and prepared to minister to the Lamanites, and with us the Lord will send those three who are spoken of in the Book of Mormon, who were with Jesus after His resurrection, and have tarried on the earth to minister to their brethren in the last days.

Thus God is sending us before to prepare a place for you and for the remnant who will survive the judgments which are now coming on the Church of Latter-day Saints, to purify them, for we are sent to prepare a Zion, (as Joseph was before sent into Egypt), a city of Peace, a place of Refuge, that you may hide yourselves with us and all the Saints in the due time of the Lord, before His indignation shall sweep away the nations.

These things are marvelous in our eyes, for great is the work of the Lord that He is going to accomplish. All this land will be redeemed by the hands of the Lamanites, and room made for you, when you hear again from me. Abide where you are, and be subject to the powers that be amongst you in the church. Keep diligently the things I taught you, and when you read this, be comforted concerning me, for though you may not see me for some few years, yet as many of you as continue faithful, will see me again, and it will be in the day of your deliverance. Pray for me always, and be assured that I will not forget you. To the grace of God I commend you in Christ. Amen.

Isaac Russell

P. S.—We have not yet gone in the wilderness, but we shall go when the Lord appoints the time. If you should hear that I have apostatized, believe it not, for I am doing the work of the Lord.

From *History of the Church* (1839)

2. Brigham Young, "An Epistle of the Twelve"

So unclear were the provisions that Joseph Smith had made for succession that upon learning of the martyrdom, even senior Apostle Brigham Young was momentarily uncertain where presiding authority now lay. Young later said that the first fear he had was "whether Joseph had taken the keys of the kingdom with him." After a moment's reflection, he slapped his knee with the epiphany that "The keys of the kingdom are right here with the Church."³ After Brigham Young's passing in 1877, President Wilford Woodruff clarified the determinative occasion that Young apparently had in mind:

John Taylor and Wilford Woodruff are the only two men now living in the flesh who listened to the words and charge of Joseph Smith the Prophet to the Twelve Apostles before his death when he said, "Brethren, I have had sorrow of heart for fear I might be taken away with the keys of the Kingdom of God upon me before I sealed them upon the heads of other men. But I thank God I have lived to see the day when I have had power to give the Twelve Apostles their endowments. And I have now sealed upon your heads all the keys of the kingdom of God and the powers of the Holy Priesthood, which God has sealed upon me. And now I roll off the labor and work of the Church and Kingdom of God upon the shoulders of the Twelve Apostles. And I now command you in the name of Jesus Christ to round up your shoulders and bear off this church and Kingdom of God on the earth before heaven and earth, and before God, angels, and men, and if you do not do it you will be damned."⁴

A week after the 1844 Nauvoo public meeting where Brigham Young was sustained as the church's new leader, the group of apostles over which he presided published a letter laying forth their understanding of Young's claims to preside over the church as president of that quorum. Herein Brigham Young insists that no man can take Joseph Smith's place; nevertheless, three years later Young would assume the title of prophet, as has every successor since in the church.

Beloved Brethren: Forasmuch as the Saints have been called to suffer deep affliction and persecution, and also to mourn the loss of our beloved Prophet and also our Patriarch, who have suffered a cruel martyrdom for the testimony of Jesus, having voluntarily yielded themselves to cruel murderers who had sworn to take their lives, and thus like good shepherds have laid down their lives for the sheep, therefore it becomes necessary for us to address you at this time on several important subjects.

You are now without a prophet present with you in the flesh to guide you; but you are not without apostles, who hold the keys of power to seal on earth that which shall be sealed in heaven, and to preside over all the affairs of the church in all the world; being still under the direction of the same God, and being dictated by the same spirit, having the same manifestations of the Holy Ghost to dictate all the affairs of the church in all the world, to build up the kingdom upon the foundation that the prophet Joseph has laid, who still holds the keys of this last dispensation, and will hold them to all eternity, as a king and priest unto the most high God, ministering in heaven, on earth, or among the spirits of the departed dead, as seemeth good to him who sent him.

Let no man presume for a moment that his place will be filled by another; for, remember he stands in his own place, and always will; and the Twelve Apostles of this dispensation stand in their own place and always will, both in time and in eternity, to minister, preside and regulate the affairs of the whole church.

How vain are the imaginations of the children of men, to presume for a moment that the slaughter of one, two or a hundred of the leaders of this church could destroy an organization, so perfect in itself and so harmoniously arranged that it will stand while one member of it is left alive upon the earth. Brethren be not alarmed, for if the Twelve should be taken away still there are powers and offices in existence which will bear the kingdom of God triumphantly victorious in all the world. This church may have prophets many, and apostles many, but they are all to stand in due time in their proper organization, under the direction of those who hold the keys.

On the subject of the gathering, let it be distinctly understood that the City of Nauvoo and the Temple of our Lord are to continue to be built up according to the pattern which has been commenced, and which has progressed with such rapidity thus far.

The city must be built up and supported by the gathering of those who have capital, and are willing to lay it out for the erection of every branch of industry and manufacture, which is necessary for the employment and support of the poor, or of those who depend wholly on their labor; while farmers who have capital must come on and purchase farms in the adjoining country, and improve and cultivate the same. In this way all may enjoy plenty, and our infant city may grow and flourish, and be strengthened an hundred fold; and unless this is done, it is impossible for the gathering to progress, because those who have no other dependence cannot live together without industry and employment.

Therefore, let capitalists hasten here; and they may be assured we have nerves, sinews, fingers, skill and ingenuity sufficient in our midst to carry on all the necessary branches of industry.

The Temple must be completed by a regular system of tithing, according to the commandments of the Lord, which he has given as a law unto this church, by the mouth of his servant Joseph.

Therefore, as soon as the Twelve have proceeded to a full and complete organization of the branches abroad, let every member proceed immediately to tithe himself or herself, a tenth of all their property and money, and pay it into the hands of the Twelve; or into the hands of such Bishops as have been, or shall be appointed by them to receive the same, for the building of the Temple or the support of the priesthood, according to the scriptures, and the revelations of God; and then let them continue to pay in a tenth of their income from that time forth, for this is a law unto this church as much binding on their conscience as any other law or ordinance. And let this law or ordinance be henceforth taught to this church, that they may know the sacrifice and tithing which the Lord requires, and perform it; or else not curse the church with a mock membership as many have done heretofore. This will furnish a steady public fund for all sacred purposes, and save the leaders from constant debt and embarrassment, and the members can then employ the remainder of their capital in every branch of enterprise, industry, and charity, as seemeth them good; only holding themselves in readiness to be advised in such manner as shall be for the good of themselves and the whole society; and thus all things can move in harmony, and for the general benefit and satisfaction of all concerned.

The United States and adjoining provinces will be immediately organized by the Twelve into proper districts, in a similar manner as they have already done in England and Scotland, and high priests will be appointed over each district, to preside over the same, and to call quarterly conferences for the regulation and representation of the branches included in the same, and for the furtherance of the gospel; and also to take measures for a yearly representation in a general conference. This will save the trouble and confusion of the running to and fro of elders; detect false doctrine and false teachers, and make every elder abroad accountable to the conference in which he may happen to labor. Bishops will also be appointed in the larger branches, to attend to the management of the temporal funds, such as tythings, and funds for the poor, according to the revelations of God, and to be judges in Israel.

The gospel in its fulness and purity, must now roll forth through every neighborhood of this wide-spread country, and to all the world; and millions will awake to its truths and obey its precepts; and the kingdoms of this world will become the kingdoms of our Lord and of his Christ.

As rulers and people have taken counsel together against the Lord; and against his anointed, and have murdered him who would have reformed and saved the nation, it is not wisdom for the Saints to have any thing to do with politics, voting, or president making, at present.—None of the candidates who are now before the public for that high office, have manifested any disposition or intention to redress wrong or restore right, liberty or law; and therefore, wo unto him who gives countenance to corruption, or partakes of murder, robbery or other cruel deeds. Let us then stand aloof from all their corrupt men and measures, and wait, at least, till a man is found, who, if elected, will carry out the enlarged principles, universal freedom, and equal rights and protection, expressed in the views of our beloved prophet and martyr, General Joseph Smith.

We do not, however, offer this political advise as binding on the consciences of others; we are perfectly willing that every member of this church should use their own freedom in all political matters; but we give it as our own rule of action, and for the benefit of those who may choose to profit by it.

Now, dear brethren, to conclude our present communication, we would exhort you in the name of the Lord Jesus Christ, to be humble and faithful before God, and before all the people, and give no occasion for any man to speak evil of you; but preach the gospel in its simplicity and purity, and practice righteousness, and seek to establish the influence of truth, peace and love among mankind, and in so doing the Lord will bless you, and make you a blessing to all people.

You may expect to hear from us again.

From *Times and Seasons* (1844)

3. Lyman Wight and George Miller, "Lyman Wight to the First Presidency—Preaching the Gospel to the Indians and Proposing to Migrate to Texas"

Lyman Wight was part of the first harvest of Mormon converts from the Kirtland, Ohio, area. He suffered with the Latter-day Saints in Missouri, was imprisoned in Liberty Jail with Joseph Smith, and became an apostle in 1841. Soon thereafter, along with George Miller, who succeeded Edward Partridge as a bishop of the church, he ran a church sawmill in Wisconsin, providing lumber for major construction projects in the city of Nauvoo, Illinois. By 1843, the golden age of church tranquility in Illinois was coming to an end, as conflicts with neighbors created a dreadful sense of déjà vu. Smith began to consider, yet again, new places to reestablish Zion. While supervising the lumber mill in Wisconsin, Wight and Miller explored opportunities for church expansion in that area and grew convinced that the Southwest was far better suited as a field for church settlement and growth, as the accompanying letter reveals. Miller later testified that in spring 1844, Joseph Smith convened a council to discuss the future of the church. There, he confirmed his intention to run for president in the coming national election. In addition, Smith reportedly confirmed on that occasion plans to move the church to the Republic of Texas, after negotiating with its cabinet for official recognition of the Mormons "as a nation." Joseph Smith was killed that June, and Wight broke with the Quorum of the Twelve Apostles over the question of succession. Using funds from the logging and mill operations, he led a band of almost two hundred followers southward down the Missouri River to Texas in four boats, in accordance with what he believed to be Smith's intention. By summer 1846, they had established themselves southeast of Austin, Texas. For the next decade, Wight and his followers persisted in efforts to establish a thriving colony. By then, Wight came to believe Joseph Smith should be succeeded by a lineal descendant, but Joseph Smith III (the late prophet's son) was still too young to assume the mantle. Wight died in 1858, en route to unite with other Saints who were likewise still seeking an alternative to Brigham Young's leadership.

Black River Falls, Feb. 15, 1844.

To the First Presidency and the Quorum of the Twelve of the Church of Christ of Latter-day Saints.

Dear Brethren,—Through the goodness and mercy of God, the Eternal Father, and grace of our Lord and Savior Jesus Christ, we are permitted to write and send by a special messenger a concise account of our lumbering operations, together with the apparent prospects of the introduction and spread of the Gospel among the Chippewa and Menomanee Indians, and also the projects of our hearts in regard to future operations in spreading the Gospel south in all the extent of America, and the consequences growing out of the same, all of which we beg leave to submit to your consideration that we may have your concurrence, or such views as shall be in accordance with the mind and will of the Lord, and govern ourselves in accordance therewith.

Since we have been here lumbering, we have had many difficulties to encounter; but the main hindrance to our successful operations was the feeding, clothing, and transporting a great many lazy, idle men, who have not produced anything by their pretended labor, and thus eating up all that the diligent and honest could produce by their unceasing application to labor; and we have not yet got entirely clear of such persons.

But under all these mighty clogs and hindrances, we have been able to accomplish and have in progress, so that we can deliver in Nauvoo about one million feet of lumber by the last of July next, which will be a great deal more than what is necessary to build the Temple and the Nauvoo House. Besides all this, we have made valuable improvements here,—all the result of much labor done under trying circumstances.

We have recently ascertained that the lands from the falls of Black River to its sources are the property of the Menomanee Indians, and the general government having urged them to move off the lands in the vicinity of Green Bay to their own lands. The Indians say they will, provided the Government will remove all strange Indians and trespassing white men off their lands; consequently, the agent and superintendent of Indian Affairs are taking such steps as will stop all further trespassing on the Indian lands, on the Wisconsin, Black and Chippewa rivers, under the penalties of the laws relative to the cases.

We sent Brothers Miller and Daniels, in company with the principal chief of the Menomanee Indians, overland to the Wisconsin river, to ascertain more about the matter. They saw the agent; found him a gruff, austere man, determined to stop all trespassing on Indian lands.

The Indians are willing to sell privileges to individuals for lumbering and cutting timber, as they have hitherto done; but the agent is opposed to it. Thus a difficulty arises between themselves.

Now, as regards the introduction of the Gospel of Christ among the Indians here, it will require more exertion, to all appearances, to check the enthusiastic ardor of these our red brethren, until the full principles of faith in our Lord and Savior Jesus Christ shall be reasoned into their minds, than to urge them on to receive it. They have great confidence in us.

The country belonging to these northern Indians is a dreary, cold region, and to a great extent, cranberry marshes, pine barrens, and swamps, with a small amount of good lands, scarce of game, and only valuable in mill privileges and facilities for lumbering purposes.

As to mineral resources, they have not been fully developed. There is no doubt as to the abundance of iron ore, but uncertain as to quality.

Now, under all these circumstances, a few of us here have arrived at this conclusion in our minds (such as can undergo all things,)—that as the Gospel has not been fully opened in all the South and Southwestern States, as also Texas, Mexico, Brazil. &c., together with the West Indian Islands, having produced lumber enough to build the Temple and Nauvoo House,—also having an influence over the Indians, so as to induce them to sell their lands to the United States, and go to a climate southwest (all according to the policy of the U.S. Government),—and having also become convinced that the Church at Nauvoo or in the Eastern States will not build the Nauvoo House according to the commandment, neither the Temple in a reasonable time, and that we have, so far as we have made trials, got means in the south,—we have in our minds to go to the table-lands of Texas, to a point we may find to be the most eligible, there locate, and let it be a place of gathering for all the South (they being incumbered with that unfortunate race of beings, the negroes); and for us to employ our time and talents in gathering together means to build according to the commandments of our God, and spread the Gospel to the nations according to the will of our Heavenly Father. We, therefore, our beloved brethren, send our worthy Brother Young, with a few of our thoughts, on paper, that you may take the subject-matter under consideration, and return us such instructions as may be according to the mind and will of the Lord our God.

We have thought it best to sell the mills here, if you think it expedient. We feel greatly encouraged to spend and be spent in the cause of Christ, according to the will of our Heavenly Father.

You will, therefore, after due deliberation, send us, by the hands of Brother Young, such instructions as may be the result of your deliberations.

Holding ourselves ready under all circumstances in life to try to do all things whatsoever commanded or instructed to do by those ordained to direct the officers of the Church of Jesus Christ; subscribing ourselves yours truly, while life shall endure.

From *History of the Church* (1844)

4. James J. Strang, "Pastoral Letter" (1845)

Among contenders for succession to leadership of the Latter-day Saints, James Strang had the briefest history of involvement in the movement. Joseph Smith baptized him in late February 1844, only a few months before his own martyrdom. Strang was at that time visiting Nauvoo, Illinois, and after his baptism he was sent by Smith to help establish the church in Wisconsin. Upon Joseph Smith's death, Strang invoked two proofs of his right of succession. First was his alleged "letter of appointment," dated June 18, 1844, authorizing him to preside over "a stake of Zion in Wisconsin and the gathering of the saints there."⁵ Strang and his followers interpreted the jurisdiction referred to as being church-wide. Second was his claim to have been appointed by an angel at the moment of Joseph Smith's assassination. Strang's claims were persuasive with several prominent Latter-day Saints (including three apostles and four Book of Mormon witnesses), as well as a thousand or more of the rank and file, who gathered to Wisconsin under their new leader. Membership would peak a few years later with several thousand, but decline to few more than a thousand a decade later.⁶ Strang buttressed his prophetic claims by finding and translating a set of three tiny brass leaves, known as the Voree Plates, in 1845. Subsequently he moved his group to Beaver Island in Lake Michigan and there translated another discovery, a smallish set of plates he claimed were the Plates of Laban mentioned in the Book of Mormon. Together with sundry revelations, he published them as "The Book of the Law of the Lord." Strang's appeal as a religious leader waned when he incorporated plural marriage into his colony, a practice that he had originally rejected, and as his role and function as a political leader aroused opposition and hostility. After he was murdered by disgruntled followers in 1856, Strang's membership largely migrated into the Reorganized Church of Jesus Christ of Latter Day Saints. Today, "Strangites," or members of the Church of Jesus Christ of Latter Day Saints as they call themselves, number between a few dozen and a few hundred. Strang's ability to publish and disseminate the following letter that endorsed his claims (in the Voree Herald *and as a tract) contributed greatly to his influence.*

Pastoral Letter, December 25, 1845

James J. Strang, a Prophet of the Most High God, and an Apostle of the Lord Jesus Christ, unto the Elders of the Church of Jesus Christ of Latter Day Saints:

1. I am in continual remembrance of your past work in the upbuilding of the Kingdom of God and of the evils done at the hands of ungodly men, and I would that ye remain no longer ignorant of the refuge that God has appointed you, and follow not after any who usurp the authority of God in the Holy City.

2. Be not unmindful of the flock who know not the true Shepherd, but are following hirelings, among whom are grievous wolves, and they bleat like sheep by day and devour by night. God be praised that some of you have escaped them. I would that none of you go astray but that you all unitedly might follow after the true Shepherd: lest coming short after escaping the first perils you enter not into your rest.

3. I beseech you, brethren, that you be not unmindful of the words of the Lord by the mouth of the prophet Joseph; that you be not deceived; that you receive not the teachings of any that come before you as revelations and commandments, except they come in at the gate and be ordained according to the command of God. (1835 D.C. 14:2; Utah D.C. 43:5–7; Reor. D.C. 43:2b)

4. I wist ye are not ignorant of the office and place of the prophet Joseph, that he was an Elder and an Apostle, (1835 D.C. 46:1; Utah D.C. 21:1; Reor. D.C. 19:1a.) a Prophet, Seer, Revelator and Translator, called to go before the church as Moses went before Israel. (1835 D.C. 3:42; Utah D.C. 107:91–92; Reor. D.C. 104:42a–b)

5. Suffer me in all patience to remind you of the law of the Lord which he revealed unto us aforetime that the place of the prophet Joseph should be filled by another; (1835 D.C. 14:1–2; 11:4 last clause; 51:2 last clause; 84:2; Utah D.C. 43:4; 35:18; 28:7; 90:4; Reor. D.C. 43:2a; 34:41; 27:ld; 87:2a); that the appointment of his successor is by revelation from God; (1835 D.C. 5:6; 11:4; Utah D.C. 102:9; 35:18; Reor. D.C. 99:6a; 34:4f); and that through Joseph only could that

appointment be made. (1835 D.C. 14:2; 84:2; Utah D.C. 43:4; 90:4; Reor. D.C. 43:2a; 87:2a)

6. For it is said in one place that if his gift be taken from him he shall not have power except to appoint another in his stead; and in another place it is said, if he abide not in me another will I plant in his stead. And at the organization of the High Council of the church it was written that the President of the church, who is also President of the council, is appointed by revelation. Finally it is said, I have given unto him the keys of mysteries and revelations which are sealed until I appoint unto them (the church) another in his stead.

7. By these testimonies and by many more it doth clearly appear that it was the duty of the prophet Joseph before his martyrdom to appoint another to fill his place when he should be removed. If he has not done so then we have no evidence that he was a prophet for what he hath spoken hath not come to pass.

8. The only rational conclusion which any man can arrive at in view of these testimonies is that in the order of this church the Presidency, with its several gifts, offices, and duties, is perpetual. God having thus organized the church, and the power of the devil having accomplished the martyrdom of two of the chief officers, will any saint teach that satan has changed the order of the church and abolished those offices which God instituted, and by the martyrdom of prophets established a new and better order? I trust not.

9. I am well aware that Sidney Rigdon claimed his place above the Twelve, and that he sought to do some acts by virtue of his office as one of the First Presidency which were generally very much disapproved of, but though he had a perfect right to officiate in his place he had no right to place himself at the head of the church.

10. His office as an associate or member of the First Presidency does not constitute him a regular successor to Joseph Smith, the claim in his favor to succeed as the highest surviving officer of the church, not being a claim of an appointment of God by revelation through Joseph Smith to fill his place, which is the only form of appointment known to the law of God.

11. I am aware, also, that the Twelve claim in their first Apostolic letter after the death of Joseph (Letter of Brigham Young, Aug. 15, 1844, in the Times and Seasons of that date) to preside over and dictate all the affairs of the church in all the world. And they emphatically charge us, Let no man presume for a moment that his place (Joseph's) will be filled by another. Thus they assumed to abolish the First Presidency of the church and usurp its duties to themselves.

12. This claim, however, is not only utterly unsupported by any one testimony, but is in many points directly contrary to the word of God. The Twelve are a traveling and not a local or general, high council, and though they are required to build up the church, and regulate all the affairs thereof in all nations, they are to do so expressly *under the direction of the Presidency of the church,* agreeable to the institution of Heaven. (1835 D.C. 3:12; Utah D.C. 107:33; Reor. D.C. 104:12) They hold the keys of the opening of the gospel to the nations, (1835 D.C. 3:13; Utah D.C. 107:34; Reor. D.C. 104:13a), but the keys of mysteries and revelations belong to Joseph as First President, Prophet, Seer, and so forth, and to his successors regularly appointed by revelation through him. (1835 D.C. 5:6; 11:4; 14:1–2; Utah D.C. 102:9–11: 35:17–18; 43:1–7; Reor. D.C. 99:6a–c: 34:4e–f; 14:1a–2c). The keys of the kingdom belong to Joseph, for time and eternity, but still with a regular succession as to the oracles or gift of receiving revelation for the church. (1835 D.C. 84:2; Utah D.C. 90:3–5; Reor. D.C. 87:2a–b) The Melchizedek priesthood, by its presidency, holds the keys of ordinances and spiritual blessings. (1835 D.C. 3:9 & 31; Utah D.C. 107:18–19 & 60–67; Reor. D.C. 104:9a–b & 31b–f) And in all these things the Twelve are without power, their duties being to open the preaching of the gospel.

13. Moreover, it cannot be that the Twelve should dictate all the affairs of the church in all the world, because they not only are under the direction of the First Presidency, but the high council is above them, and they are amenable to it. "The most important business of the church, and the most difficult cases of the church, in as much as there is not satisfaction upon the decision of the Bishop or Judges, it shall be handed over and carried up to the council of the church before the Presidency of the high priesthood; and the Presidency of the council of the high priesthood shall have power to call other high priests, even twelve, to assist as counselors; and thus the Presidency of the high priesthood and its counselors shall have power to decide upon testimony according to the laws of the church. And after this decision it shall be had in remembrance no more before the Lord, for this is the highest council of the church of God, and a final decision upon controversies, in spiritual matters. (1835 D.C. 3:35; Utah D.C. 107:78–80; Reor. D.C. 104:35a–c) There is not any person belonging to the church, who is exempt from this council of the church. (1835 D.C. 3:36; 5:13; Utah D.C. 107:81; 102:30–32; Reor. D.C. 104:36; 99:13a–b)

14. Upon what pretense is this claim of the Twelve founded? Upon the trial of Sidney Rigdon, they took pains to state it as strongly as possible, and they make out no more than this, that when Joseph Smith was candidate for President of

the United States, and knew by the Spirit that some great thing was to happen, *but did not know what it was,* he gave them an endowment of ordinances (not the oracles), and told them that on their shoulders would rest the responsibility. (See trial of S. Rigdon, Times and Seasons, Sept. 15, 1844, page 647, remarks of Orson Hyde). These ordinances are intended for the whole church—men, women and children. Will they all have power to dictate all the affairs of the church in all the world then? If not, how do these ordinances give the Apostles that power now? If these ordinances gave certain power to some men, why not to others?

15. All the Twelve were not present and did not receive these ordinances. Whence their claim of power? Several persons, not of the Twelve, were present and received all these ordinances with such of the Twelve as were there. Why are not they included in the favored number? Joseph survived this meeting some months. Why did not they find out that he had resigned his office and devolved its duties on them, till after he was dead? If his giving an endowment of ordinances, and rolling the responsibility of giving counsel, etc., upon some twenty-five men *with their wives,* as he commenced a political career *vacated his office* and those of his *counselors,* and *superseded the First Presidency and an entire quorum of the church,* it is certainly most extraordinary. A very moderate share of common sense, or any acquaintance whatever with the laws of the church, accompanied with integrity of heart, will reject so preposterous a claim at first blush. The responsibility of leading the church by good counsel in proper order would devolve on a few of its most influential members, necessarily, whenever Joseph's attention was turned from them, by any means whatever, not in virtue of any offices they might hold, but as leading men. Since the death of Joseph, they have used that responsibility to lead the church *from* the rock of revelation, out of the true order, and from the place of refuge God has appointed unto them. Thus have a few led, sanctioned by the votes of Conferences instead of the voice of God, till the destruction which not only lurks in midnight darkness, but stalks boldly at noonday, is upon them.

16. The Twelve have never, in any known publication, claimed, either for themselves or any one of their number, to be First President of the church, or President of the high priesthood. Their claim is to supersede the First Presidency, put the high council which God has made the highest council of the church, (1835 D.C. 3:35; Utah D.C. 107:78–80; Reor. D.C. 104:35a–c), below themselves, and put a bishop over it, where God placed a President, (1835 D.C. 3:9; Utah D.C. 107:18–19; Reor. D.C. 104:9a–b), and finally, that ex officio, as

Apostles and not as Presidents of the high priesthood, they are to hold the keys and powers which devolved on the First Presidency and its counselors, and to discontinue the offices of Seer, Revelator and Translator in the church.

17. Nothing is more certain than that no law was made at the death of Joseph, or for some years previous, changing the order of the church, or abolishing any of its offices or quorums. Down to the time of his death, it was properly understood by the whole of the church that he alone received revelations from God to be taught by way of commandment in the church; that he and his two associates in the Presidency had the chief administration of the affairs of the church, and that they, with the twelve high counselors, were a court or judicatory of final resort in all important cases, and that the Twelve Apostles were the chief traveling elders and under the direction of the Presidency. And the man who, during the life-time of Joseph, had said that the Twelve were at the head of the church, would have been looked upon either as a reckless and hair-brained liar, or utterly insane. To have held this then was unblushing apostasy. To hold now that they are not so is equally apostasy with the leaders in Nauvoo. Whence is the change? In God or man? Does truth thus belie itself?

18. Why should not the place of Joseph be filled by another? Says Brigham Young, "Because he stands in his own place and always will." (Apostolic Letter, Aug. 15, 1844). But in the same paragraph he also says the Twelve Apostles of this dispensation stand in their own places and always will. Brother Young, will not their places be filled by others when they fill the measure of their days? Then why was Brother Patten's place filled? Again: Who will be at the head of the church when the Twelve are all fallen asleep? Will not the High Priests and the Seventies all hold their own places? If so, shall anyone succeed them? Then where will the priesthood be when the present generation is dead?

19. But, says someone, God promised Joseph that the keys of the kingdom should never be taken from him in this world, neither in the world to come. Very well. They were never taken from Christ, but his holding them did not prevent Joseph, and in the eternal worlds all who are joint heirs with Jesus Christ will hold them at one and the same time.

20. Brethren, I exhort you as you look for the coming of the Lord Jesus, follow not after these blinding fables. Set up no more the work of men's hand against the voice of God. Trust not in your own wisdom to improve or alter the law of God. You that have gone astray return to the order of God's house. Let all the quorums take their proper order as God has established them. Let the President who has wandered in darkness return to his proper place which God gave,

nor covet that which men may offer. Let the Twelve take their place as a traveling high council with the keys of the opening of the gospel to the nations. Let the high counselors give counsel and assistance to the Presidency, which has been called to the high and responsible calling of leading the church to peace and happiness and preparing a people for the coming of the Son of God. Let the high priests teach the law of God unto the people. Let all the elders learn not to put their faith in some great man and say all is well, but let them buckle on the whole armor of God and stand up, bold defenders of truth, rather than men.

21. Now in my weakness and in the infancy of my ministry I call upon you to assist me. It hath pleased God to put it into the heart of Joseph to appoint me to receive mysteries and revelations unto this church. And he has been faithful unto the vision and voice of God by sending me his epistle containing the revelation which God gave him, the Lord God confirming the same by sending his angels unto me to charge me with this ministry in the same hour that Joseph was taken away, and by witnessing the same to the brethren in those wonderful works which the brethren here are ready to testify unto you.

22. Let not my call to you be in vain. The destroyer has gone forth among you and has prevailed. You are preparing to resign country and houses and lands to him. Many of you are about to leave the haunts of civilization and of men to go into an unexplored wilderness among savages, and in trackless deserts, to seek a home in the wilds where the foot-print of the white man is not found. The voice of God has not called you to this. His promise has not gone before to prepare a habitation for you. The hearts of the Lamanites are not turned unto you, and they will not regard you. When the herd comes the savages shall pursue. The cloud which surrounds by day shall bewilder, and the pillar of fire by night shall consume and reveal you to the destroyer; and the men in whom you trusted when you rejected the promises of God shall leave you early and not be found of you in your greatest need.

23. Let the oppressed flee for safety unto Voree, and let the gathering of the people be there. Let the evil who have gone to the holy city be rejected and given to the law. Let the Twelve go out and preach the gospel to the nations according to the command of God, instead of staying at home as a prominent mark to bring cruel enemies on their brethren. Let the filth of Zion be cleansed and her garments of peace put on. Let neither gun nor sword be lifted in defiance, nor rest be taken upon the arm of flesh, and the city of our God shall be saved and the Temple of his holiness be unpolluted by the hand of the Gentile.

24. Causeless the curse has not come, and causeless it shall not fall. They that ask justice let them do it. They that cry out against mobs let them abstain from violence. Those who hate persecution let them regard the rights of others.

They that preach God and the gospel let them remember the Law and forget not the order which he has revealed and their own mouths have proclaimed. Let them not buffet others for changing the ordinances and breaking the everlasting covenant unless they themselves will abide the word of God.

5. Jason W. Briggs, "Revelation"

The largest non-LDS restorationist movement descending from Joseph Smith was also one of the latest to develop. Smith was believed to have given a blessing to his eldest surviving son, Joseph Smith III, which indicated his future leadership of the church. Proponents of his succession believed the promise was binding, while others believed it was, like most pronounced blessings, contingent on many factors. In any case, no transcription of the blessing exists. Joseph Smith III had been an eleven-year old boy at his father's death in 1844, but by the 1850s, many were beginning to urge the young man to assume the leadership in a reconstituted church. One pivotal event in this regard was a revelation received by Jason Briggs, who migrated from James Strang's movement to that of William Smith, younger brother of the prophet, before leaving each in disillusionment. In 1851, Briggs asked for divine guidance, and received the promise that a descendant of Joseph Smith would soon arise to preside over the Lord's church. When Joseph Smith III was persuaded to accept that role in 1860, it was in part because of the foundation Briggs's revelation had laid. Members of the new movement traced it to the 1830 beginnings of Mormonism, but considered the period from 1844 to 1860 a period of disorganization. Hence, they named their organization the Reorganized Church of Jesus Christ of Latter Day Saints (RLDS Church). Once the Strangites embraced polygamy, the RLDS Church became virtually the only viable refuge for those who repudiated the unorthodox marital practice or who, like Emma Smith and Joseph Smith III, maintained that Joseph Smith had never himself taken plural wives. Because Strang had not announced a successor, his death made the transition of many of his followers to a movement led by a descendant of Joseph Smith even easier. Beginning with a membership of a few hundred, Community of Christ (the RLDS Church's name since 2001) has some 250,000 members in some fifty nations.

While pondering in my heart the situation of the church, on the 18th day of November, 1851, on the prairie, about three miles northwest of Beloit, Wisconsin, the Spirit of the Lord came upon me, and the visions of truth opened to my mind, and the Spirit of the Lord said unto me,

"Verily, verily, saith the Lord, even Jesus Christ, unto his servant, Jason W. Briggs, concerning the church: Behold, I have not cast off my people; neither have I changed in regard to Zion. Yea, verily, my people shall be redeemed, and my law shall be kept which I revealed unto my servant, Joseph Smith, Jr., for I am God and not man, and who is he that shall turn me from my purpose, or destroy whom I would preserve? Wolves have entered into the flock, and who shall deliver them? Where is he that giveth his life for the flock? Behold, I will judge those who call themselves shepherds, and have preyed upon the flock of my pastures.

"And because you have asked me in faith concerning William Smith, this is the answer of the Lord thy God concerning him: I, the Lord, have permitted him to represent the rightful heir to the presidency of the high priesthood of my church by reason of the faith and prayers of his father, and his brothers, Joseph and Hyrum Smith, which came up before me in his behalf; and to respect the law of lineage, by which the holy priesthood is transmitted, in all generations, when organized into quorums. And the keys which were taught him by my servant Joseph were of me, that I might prove him therewith. And for this reason have I poured out my Spirit through his ministrations, according to the integrity of those who received them.

"But as Esau despised his birthright, so has William Smith despised my law, and forfeited that which pertained to him as an apostle and high priest in my church. And his spokesman, Joseph Wood, shall fall with him, for they are rejected of me. They shall be degraded in their lives, and shall die without regard; for they have wholly forsaken my law, and given themselves to all manner of uncleanness, and prostituted my law and the keys of power intrusted to them, to the lusts of the flesh, and have run greedily in the way of adultery.

"Therefore, let the elders whom I have ordained by the hand of my servant Joseph, or by the hand of those ordained by him, resist not this authority, nor faint in the discharge of duty, which is to preach my gospel as revealed in the record of the Jews, and the Book of Mormon, and the Book of Doctrine and Covenants; and cry repentance and remission of sins through obedience to the gospel, and I will sustain them, and give them my Spirit; and in mine own due time will I call upon the seed of Joseph Smith, and will bring one forth, and he shall be mighty and strong, and he shall preside over the high priesthood of my church; and then shall the quorums assemble, and the pure in heart shall gather, and Zion shall be reinhabited, as I said unto my servant Joseph Smith; after many days shall all these things be accomplished, saith the Spirit. Behold, that which ye received as my celestial law is not of me, but is the doctrine of Baalam. And I command you to denounce it and proclaim against it; and I will give you power, that none shall be able to withstand your words, if you rely upon me; for my Spirit shall attend you." And the Spirit said unto me, "Write, write, write; write the revelation and send it unto the saints at Palestine, and at Voree, and at Waukesha, and to all places where this doctrine is taught as my law; and whomsoever will humble themselves before me, and ask of me, shall receive of my Spirit a testimony that these words are of me. Even so. Amen."

From *The Messenger* (1851)

6. William Smith, *Epistle of the Twelve* (1851)

William was a volatile Smith, clashing with his younger brother Joseph physically as well as verbally. Called as one of the original twelve apostles in 1835 at Joseph's insistence, he served erratically. After Joseph's death in 1844, William lineally inherited the office of presiding patriarch from his deceased brother Hyrum. He soon quarreled with Apostle Brigham Young over the purview of his office as patriarch and was disfellowshipped and then excommunicated by church leaders in late 1845. Joseph Smith Sr. and Lucy Mack had had seven sons, but by then all had been lost to illness or violent death save only William. The largest group to break with Young would be the RLDS Church under Joseph Smith III. But at the time of William's excommunication, Joseph Smith III was not yet a teenager, leaving William as the only Smith heir apparent of adult age. Joseph Smith III thus had a powerful claim to the succession, for those attracted to a principle of hereditary—or in this case filial—right to the office. Even so, William initially threw his lot in with James Strang, as did his sisters. Two years later, he broke with Strang and declared himself "First President, Prophet, Seer, Revelator, Translator, and Patriarch over the whole Church of Jesus Christ of Latter Day Saints."[7] In a lengthy epistle that William's supporter Joseph Wood published, several points buttressed his claim. William invoked a blessing received at the hands of his father Joseph Smith Sr., prophesying that "thou shalt be made equal with thy brethren (Joseph and Hyrum) and thy seed with their seed," as well as a blessing at the hands of Joseph Jr., promising him a time of sorrow following which he would be "endowed with power from on high." One final appeal he made was the claim that it was James, the brother of Jesus, who succeeded the Christ.[8] The revelation William alludes to in the following letter—a summation of his succession claims—was the moment when "he called on the name of the Lord and found forgiveness, and the Lord commanded him to arise and put on his whole armor, &c., and endowed him with power from on high according to the predictions." Nevertheless, William Smith's movement failed to gain much traction and disintegrated two years later.

Palestine Stake of Zion, Dec. 25th, 1851.

Brother Powell.— I have concluded to spend my Christmas in writing you a few lines. As to question in regard to my right of standing as Joseph's successor, I reply. In my first step in acting as the representative of Joseph's son, the matter was not made plain to me then as it now is. The increase in light began small at first, and so increased by degrees until the full right of my authority was made known by revelation. Something over two years ago, or thereabout, it may not be so long; by references to the record I can ascertain the time exact. By reference to the enclosed drawing, you will get the idea perfectly. No. 1 is old Father Smith holding the Patriarchy ordaining his seven sons, Alvin, Hyrum, Joseph, Samuel, Ephraim, William and D. Carlos. On the second line, No. 2, you will see the places for six of the sons are blank, all being dead but William, who now stands as the only head of the Church, holding the patriarchy, and also the only person now representing the old patriarch, Father Smith. This of course makes William Smith the successor of Joseph Smith. Also on the third line, No. 3, is William's son, ordaining Joseph's and Hyrum's posterity. And as none of these are ordained as yet, who shall preside over the Church of God but William Smith, who was ordained before Joseph's death, Prophet, Seer, Revelator and Translator; thus keeping up a regular chain of priesthood, as you can see in the drawing. On line No. 2, you will see William ordaining his son as his successor in office. It is in this manner my inheritance is preserved unto my children, and thus answering to the revelation I have received of late on the subject. Should William have no son, he would have the power to ordain one of Joseph's sons, provided one of them came forward and claimed rights. But should William have a son, or sons, the right of Patriarchy, not by expediency, but by law, rests in his family,—a stream can never rise higher than its fountain, consequently Joseph's children, (nor Hyrum's, nor any of the brothers), can not preside over William, nor over his sons. The question is again, Is the building greater than the builder? Neither Joseph nor Hyrum ordained their sons, and no one can ordain them now but William, or his (William's) successor in office. To this you will add, the position takes away rights from Joseph's children, and also from Hyrum's children. To this I reply it does not. For the have no right of office in the Church, no more than Tom, Dick or Harry; not until they have been ordained. It is the priesthood after the order of Melchisedec, which is after the order of the Son of God, that is handed down from Father to Son; not the offices of Prophet, Patriarch, Apostle, High Priest, Elder, Priest, Teacher and Deacon. This is the error of Jason (J. W. Briggs), as well as many others that have fallen. They do not make the proper distinction between the orders of priesthood, (there being two orders, the Aaronic and the Melchisedec; see sec. 3, on Priesthood), and the different offices of these two priesthoods. The ORDER of priesthood, (not *offices*), is handed down from father to son. The offices are ordained by those holding authority, as the Holy Ghost shall direct; see sec. 2, par. 12, page 96. But the two orders of priesthood, meaning the Aaronic and the Melchisedec, is handed down from father to son, according to the flesh, &c., &c. A great ado is made over the blessing put upon Joseph's posterity. Now read the promised blessing, revelation of 1841, and you will see two things only mentioned; first, an inheritance for Joseph's children, in the Nauvoo house; second, the blessing upon Joseph's head that his children shall be blessed as Abraham's seed was. And to all this I have not the least objection. The Nauvoo House is not finished yet, and no prospects that it ever will be, at least not for many years to come. And then you will discover by the drawing, that should the time ever come that Joseph's children, or children's children, desired a place in the church of God, the authority to ordain them to the various offices in the Church is preserved unto William Smith and his posterity *forever*. It is in this way you will discover that the promise made to Joseph is fulfilled upon the head of his posterity; being ordained one an Elder, one an High Priest, and so on; holding a right of priesthood, (not of office), according to the flesh. If the right of office, as Jason affirms, is handed down from father to son, then Joseph would have four prophets in his family, and Hyrum three patriarchs and Samuel two High Priests, and D. Carlos none, his children all being girls. But Paul says, 'Not all apostles, not all prophets;' consequently it is the order of priesthood that is the inheritance, and not the grades of office, as I have previously stated. Jason makes an utter great *blunder* on the *spokesmanship*. No priesthood is taken from Hyrum's children; it is the office of spokesman conferred on Br. Wood. Jason makes another brush at the order, by placing the spokesman on the right hand of the Father. *Will Jason tell us where Brother Wood* (Joseph Wood) will be seated after his work is done? And as to certain parts of that celestial law, it was referred to future generations. If Brother Wood has done wrong, Jason should have given him the extent of the rule, if he repents.—Read revelation of February, 1831, sec. 13, par. 7; consequently, Jason's revelation to cut off, is premature. Without applying the rule I however deny all such charges. God is on our side.

7. Sidney Rigdon, Joseph H. Newton, William Richards, and William Stanley, *An Appeal to the Latter-day Saints* (1863)

Sidney Rigdon was a member of immense influence among the church's first generation. A hugely effective preacher in the Campbellite movement, he joined the fledgling church in 1830 through the preaching of the man he had previously mentored, Parley P. Pratt. Over a hundred members of his congregation joined along with him. When Joseph Smith moved the church to Rigdon's home territory of Kirtland, Ohio, Rigdon quickly became his right-hand man. He was ordained as Smith's counselor, traveled with him, worked on the Bible revisions with him, experienced visions with him, was tarred and feathered with him, and served as unofficial spokesman for the church. In the Nauvoo era, however, Rigdon resided in Pennsylvania and grew gradually estranged from the prophet. Even so, he was sustained as Joseph Smith's counselor again in 1843 against Smith's wishes. Rigdon was by one measure the highest ranking leader at the time of Joseph Smith's assassination in 1844, given his tenure in the First Presidency. He was supported in his claim to the succession by William Marks, president of the Nauvoo Stake and himself a credible contender to succeed Smith. In the public meeting to determine the succession, Rigdon and Apostle Brigham Young were the principal claimants. When Young prevailed by general acclamation of the audience, Rigdon withdrew with some of his supporters to Pittsburgh, Pennsylvania. There he reorganized as "The Church of Christ," but his movement did not thrive. In 1863, some of his supporters organized Rigdon's arguments supporting his claims to the succession and published them in a lengthy pamphlet, "An Appeal to the Latter-day Saints." His succession claims rested on his past positions of obvious prestige and influence, and what he inferred was a clear destiny to finish the prophetic mission of Joseph

Smith, aborted by his martyrdom. But by that time, the majority of Sidney Rigdon's followers had reformed under the leadership of William Bickerton as the Church of Jesus Christ. Today that church numbers more than ten thousand worldwide.[9]

Having brought with us the prophecies and promises written and published by Joseph Smith, we have come to a knowledge of his mission by virtue of his own writings, without any conjectures or opinions of ourselves or others. He was sent of the Lord as prophet and revelator to inform the Gentiles the Lord was preparing to do a great and marvellous work, that would either prove to their salvation or condemnation; and, prophetically, to make known the great events connected with it, and to let us all understand that unless we gave diligent heed to the requirements of heaven, we should perish in the general ruin; as also to bring to light the priesthood, through and by whose administration the great and marvellous work would be brought to pass, and give instructions and directions in relation to giving such notice of the great and coming work to the Gentiles, as the Lord deemed necessary; organizing a church, ordaining priesthoods, and things pertaining to the notification of the Gentiles generally, and to fill up the volume of revelation and prophecy, sufficiently so as to enable all honest seekers after truth to obtain the knowledge necessary for their salvation. But he was not called to do the work; the Lord prepared another man for that purpose, and gave power to Joseph Smith and Oliver Cowdery to bring that priesthood to light; and this they did in a manner beyond the possibility of a successful contradiction, that all might see and understand; and if they did not, it was their sin and not their excuse. It was said to the church through Joseph Smith, that if he were taken, he should have power only to appoint another in his stead. (Section 14th, paragraph 2d, Book of Doctrine and Covenants.) Now to say that if a man should be equal to himself in holding the keys of the kingdom, and also the keys of the school of the prophets, was not making that appointment, we should like to know what would do or could do it. Put in connection with this his carrying to the Lamanites the gospel of their salvation, and their receiving it at his hand; and that he should turn to the Jews, and then the arm of the Lord should be revealed in power; and then all should hear the gospel in their own tongue; that through him the Lord's people should be pure as Christ was; and that the blind should see, the lame should walk, the deaf should hear, and devils should be cast out, and the heavens should shake for his good. All this said concerning one man, to the exclusion of all others. From all these facts, let any and all judge whether Joseph Smith did or did not appoint a man to lead Zion. . . .

The entire effort of the Devil since the beginning, has been to falsify the word of the Lord, and to get men to act in opposition to it; he always knows, if he can succeed in that, he has them in his power. It matters nothing to him how religious they are, if their religion is not in obedience to the revealed will of heaven. Those who, among us, obey the voice of the Lord, and turn to the Book of Mormon and the former commandments, see that Satan, true to his instincts, has attacked us as he has done all others before us. What is or was ever said about Brigham Young's ever ruling the church of God? nothing; or what was about Strang's doing it? nothing; or about Beneemy's doing it? nothing; or about young Joseph Smith's doing it? nothing; but about another man's doing it? half the prophecies and promises in the books are devoted to the purpose of making all know it: that he was the chosen of God to the exclusion of all others. What are these men then doing? *falsifying the word of God,* and nothing else: the very work that the Devil wants them to do, in order that he may get possession of both them and the world.

It is almost universally the case, that those who place themselves in such a relation to the Deity, mark some man as a victim, against whom they lavish their vituperation with unmitigated viciousness: too ignorant to see that it is the Almighty himself against whom they are levelling their shafts. It is his word that they are falsifying, and not man's. Take Brigham Young, for example. He professes to be acting under the power of a priesthood obtained from and through Joseph Smith, while he uses it for the purpose of falsifying the burden of all the prophecies and promises written by Joseph Smith; in fact, his whole course and all those who are with him, is to falsify what Smith caused to be written, and has left behind him. Could inconsistency reach a higher degree of perfection than this? Be sure they have tried to make a scapegoat of Sidney Rigdon, and corruption itself could not have gone to greater lengths in vilification than they have; but all such attempts are only worthy of their authors. Sidney Rigdon did not write the revelations in the Book of Mormon and the Book of Doctrine and Covenants, but the Spirit of the Lord through Joseph Smith; and after all their vilification and slander, to-day they read as they always did. It was the Lord, through Joseph Smith, who chose him, called, ordained and qualified him for his great calling, and all their railings are against the Lord himself; and this they will find out, in that day, when the olive-trees are broken down, the people affrighted and fled, and their works destroyed.

There are two organizations now in existence, both of which are operating to thwart the purposes of Heaven, to make his prophecies and promises which he has caused to be written false, and by doing so, undeify him in the world, and give Satan power in the world, and full sway over the whole empire of man: one led by Brigham Young, and the other by Joseph Smith the younger. The one led by Smith is the most forbidding of the two, because it was his own father that was revelator, and it is the prophecies and promises which came through him, that the son is trying to falsify. If it were possible for him to do so, he would sink his father's memory into everlasting shame and would undeify the Lord in the world, and give Satan full dominion on the earth; but the decree of Jehovah has already gone forth that he will fail, be cut off and cast into the fire. But here we will leave them to their fate. . . . When the Lord rejected the house of Eli, he cut it off; when he rejected that of Saul, he cut that off also; and when John the Baptist stepped aside from the duty assigned to him, and took it upon himself to meddle with the affairs of the political rulers, Christ let him be cut off; and when we come nearer to our own times, when the Smith family was rejected of God, he cut them off. Strang has also been cut off for setting his feet in places where the Lord had not authorized him to do it; and we have the Lord's word for it that Brigham Young and those with him will be cut off. From all these examples, surely the people whom the Lord has notified that through them he is going to proceed to begin the work of *preparing* to fulfill the covenant made to the house of Israel, will find it important to study well the word of the Lord, and walk as he has directed.

Now, for the sum of the whole matter. If Sidney Rigdon does not convert the Lamanites, restore the tribes of Jacob, bring salvation to Zion, and purify the saints, so they can see the face of the Lord; and if, under his administration, the blind do not see, the lame walk, the dumb speak, the heavens shake, and the arm of the Lord be revealed in power, in convincing the nations; then, indeed, the books of revelation we have are a tissue of falsehoods, and all our religion vain; Joseph Smith, a base falsifier, an imp of Satan, instead of a prophet of the living God.

8. John Taylor, Revelation (1886)

In the 1880s, the U.S. federal campaign against Mormon plural marriage was in overdrive. Increasingly, the continued viability of the church's temporal existence was in doubt, given the arrest of leaders, disenfranchisement of members, and federal expropriation of assets. In this climate, President John Taylor (Brigham Young's successor) purportedly sought heavenly guidance and recorded an 1886 revelation insisting that the "law of Abraham" would never be revoked. The next year Taylor died, without having made the revelation public, and in 1890, the "Manifesto" of his prophetic successor, Wilford Woodruff, officially led to the end of the practice of plural marriage. Self-described Mormon fundamentalists, who continue to practice polygamy, believe John Taylor transferred the keys of the practice to several associates to keep it alive in the face of such an eventuality. The Salt Lake City, Utah-based church has long refused to consider the Taylor revelation authentic.[10] In any case, Latter-day Saints observe that the phrase "works of Abraham" is ambiguous. Found in the revelation known as Doctrine and Covenants 132, this terminology is confusing; interconnected but not clearly differentiated principles related to the subject include eternity of the marriage covenant, plurality of wives, authority of the priesthood officiators, and the affirming seal of the Holy Spirit. To this day, no official LDS position is held on the question of what role, if any, plural marriage will have in the eternities. Regardless, the Mormon prophet as presiding authority has the keys to administer plural marriage, and he has refused to employ or authorize their use since the early twentieth century. Polygamy is today grounds for automatic excommunication from the church. The many groups who today practice plural marriage and claim affinity with Joseph Smith's restorationist tradition generally invoke the contested Taylor revelation as the basis of their authority.

September 27, 1886

My son John: You have asked me concerning the New and Everlasting Covenant and how far it is binding upon my people.

Thus saith the Lord All commandments that I give must be obeyed by those calling themselves by my name unless they are revoked by me or by my authority and how can I revoke an everlasting covenant; For I the Lord am everlasting and my covenants cannot be abrogated nor done away with; but they stand forever. Have I not given my word in great plainness on this subject? Yet have not great numbers of my people been negligent in the observance of my law and the keeping of my commandment, and yet have I borne with them these many years and this because of their weakness because of the perilous times. And furthermore it is more pleasing to me that men should use their free agency in regard to these matters. Nevertheless I the Lord do not change and my word and my covenants and my law do not. And as I have heretofore said by my servant Joseph all those who would enter into my glory must and shall obey my law. And have I not commanded men that if they were Abraham's seed and would enter into my glory they must do the works of Abraham. I have not revoked this law nor will I for it is everlasting and those who will enter into my glory must obey the conditions thereof, even so Amen.

9. David Whitmer, *An Address to All Believers in Christ: By a Witness to the Divine Authenticity of The Book of Mormon* (1887)

David Whitmer befriended Joseph Smith in 1828, was one of three witnesses to see the gold plates and an accompanying angel, and with Oliver Cowdery and Martin Harris selected the first twelve apostles to serve with Smith. After the center of Mormon gathering shifted from Ohio to Missouri, Whitmer, with his brother John and William W. Phelps, was appointed to preside over the church there. He grew disaffected by 1838, largely as a result of what he saw as Joseph Smith's mingling of civil with ecclesiastical authority. Along with other dissenters, he fled Far West as the church—under increasing threat from Missourians—became intolerant of internal opposition. He remained in Richmond, Missouri, aloof from Mormon affairs until after Joseph Smith's death in 1844. Whitmer half-heartedly acquiesced in a short-lived "Church of Christ" led by former Apostle William McLellin in 1847, based on his public 1834 ordination to be Joseph Smith's successor. He launched a second, more concerted effort to re-inaugurate a restorationist church in 1876. John Whitmer published the next year his "Address to All Believers in Christ," which largely targeted other branches of the Mormon faith. Whitmer died in 1888, but his movement attracted enough adherents to survive until most "Whitmerites" merged with the Church of Christ (Temple Lot) a generation later. John Whitmer's pamphlet is perhaps most significant for what he revealed about the ways in which restorationists could compartmentalize the different segments of Joseph Smith's life and ministry. For Whitmer, Smith's principal error was in not confining his role to the translation of the Book of Mormon and a restored church built up on its (and the Bible's) teachings. Like members of the RLDS Church, Whitmer believed that many doctrinal developments subsequent to the Kirtland era were not inspired. But Whitmer insisted the RLDS Church needed to acknowledge, rather than evade, the historical evidence for what he considered Joseph Smith's uninspired teachings. Polygamy, especially, Whitmer renounced, making the striking claim that Smith had ultimately renounced that practice as well.

In June 1829, the translation of the Book of Mormon was finished. God gave it to us as his Holy Word, and left us as men to work out our own salvation and set in order the Church of Christ according to the written word. He left us as men to receive of His Spirit as we walked worthy to receive it; and His Spirit guides men into all truth; but the spirit of man guides man into error. When God had given us the Book of Mormon, and a few revelations in 1829 by the same means that the Book was translated, commanding us to rely upon the written word in establishing the church, He did His part; and it left us to do our part and to be guided by the Holy Ghost as we walked worthy to receive. God works with men according to their faith and obedience. He has unchangeable spiritual laws which He cannot break; and He could not be so merciful as to give more of His Spirit to any man, than that man was worthy to receive by his faith and obedience.

In the beginning we walked humble and worthy to receive a great portion of the Spirit of God, and we were guided rightly at first in establishing the Church, but we soon began to drift into errors, because we heeded our own desires too much, instead of relying solely upon God and being led entirely by His Spirit. . . . I will state a few facts concerning some of Brother Joseph's errors in the beginning, also the errors of us all, in order to show you these most important truths, viz: How humble and contrite in heart a man must be to receive revelations from God: and how very weak man is, and how liable to be led into error, thinking at the time that he is doing God's will. . . .

Brother Hyrum said it had been suggested to him that some of the brethren might go to Toronto, Canada, and sell the copyright of the Book of Mormon for considerable money: and he persuaded Joseph to inquire of the Lord about it. Joseph concluded to do so. He had not yet given up the stone. Joseph looked into the hat in which he placed the stone, and received a revelation that some of the brethren should go to Toronto, Canada, and that they would sell the copyright of the Book of Mormon. Hiram Page and Oliver Cowdery went to Toronto on this mission, but they failed entirely to sell the copyright, returning without any money. Joseph was at my father's house when they returned. I was there also, and am an eye witness to these facts. Jacob Whitmer and John Whitmer were also present when Hiram Page and Oliver Cowdery returned from Canada. Well, we were all in great trouble; and we asked Joseph how it was that he had received a revelation from the Lord for some brethren to go to Toronto and sell the copyright, and the brethren had utterly failed in their undertaking. Joseph did not know how it was, so he enquired of the Lord about it, and behold the following revelation came through the stone: "Some revelations are of God: some revelations are of men: and some revelations are of the devil." So we see that the revelation to go to Toronto and sell the copyright was not of God, but was of the devil or of the heart of man. When a man enquires of the Lord concerning a matter, if he is deceived by his own carnal desires, and is in error, he will receive an answer according to his erring heart, but it will not be a revelation from the Lord. This was a lesson for our benefit and we should have profited by it in future more than we did. . . .

I will say here, that I could tell you other false revelations that came through Brother Joseph as mouthpiece, (not through the stone) but this will suffice. Many of Brother Joseph's revelations were never printed. The revelation to go to Canada was written down on paper, but was never printed. When Brother Joseph was humble he had the Spirit of God with him; but when he was not humble he did not have the Spirit. Brother Joseph gave many true prophesies when he was humble before God: but this is no more than many of the other brethren did. Brother Joseph's true prophesies were almost all published, but those of the other brethren were not. I could give you the names of many who gave great prophesies which came to pass. I will name a few: Brothers Ziba Peterson, Hiram Page, Oliver Cowdery, Parley P. Pratt, Orson Pratt, Peter Whitmer, Christian Whitmer, John Whitmer, myself and others had the gift of prophesy. Hiram Page prophesied a few days before the stars fell in November, 1833, that the stars would fall from heaven and frighten many people. This prophesy was given in my presence. I could give you many instances of true prophesies which came through the above named brethren, but I desire to be brief. I could also tell you of some false prophesies which some of them gave, when they were not living humble.

After the translation of the Book of Mormon was finished, early in the spring of 1830, before April 6th, Joseph gave the stone to Oliver Cowdery and told me as well as the rest that he was through with it, and he did not use the stone any more. He said he was through the work that God had given him the gift to perform, except to preach the gospel. He told us that we would all have to depend on the Holy Ghost hereafter to be guided into truth and obtain the will of the Lord. The revelations after this came through Joseph as "mouth piece"; that is, he would enquire of the Lord, pray and ask concerning a matter, and speak out the revelation, which he thought to be a revelation from the Lord; but sometimes he was mistaken about it being the word of the Lord. As we have seen, some revelations are of God and some are not. In this manner, through Brother Joseph as "mouth piece" came every revelation to establish new doctrines and offices which disagree with the New Covenant in the Book of Mormon and New Testament! I would have you to remember this fact.

In June, 1829, the Lord called Oliver Cowdery, Martin Harris, and myself as the three witnesses, to behold the vision of the Angel, as recorded in the fore part of the Book of Mormon, and to bear testimony to the world that the Book of Mormon is true. I was not called to bear testimony to the mission of Brother Joseph Smith any farther than his work of translating the Book of Mormon, as you can see by reading the testimony of us three witnesses. . . .

Now, when April 6, 1830, had come, we had then established three branches of the "Church of Christ," in which three branches were about seventy members: One branch was at Fayette, N.Y.; one at Manchester, N.Y., and one at Colesville, Pa. It is all a mistake about the church being organized on April 6, 1830, as I will show. We were as fully organized—spiritually—before April 6th as we were on that day. The reason why we met on that day was this; the world had been telling us that we were not a regularly organized church, and we had no right to officiate in the ordinance of marriage, hold church property, etc., and that we should organize according to the laws of the land. On this account we met at my father's house in Fayette, N.Y., on April 6, 1830, to attend to this matter of organizing according to the laws of the land. . . . I do not consider that the church was any more organized or established in the eyes of God on that day than it was previous to that day. I consider that on that day the first error was introduced into the Church of Christ, and that error was Brother Joseph being ordained as "Prophet Seer and Revelator" to the church.

The Holy Ghost was with us in more power during the eight months previous to April 6, 1830, than ever at any time thereafter. Almost everyone who was baptized received the Holy Ghost in power, some prophesying, some speaking in tongues, the heavens were opened to some, and all the signs which Christ promised should follow the believers were with us abundantly. We were a humble happy people, and loved each other as brethren should love.

Just before April 6, 1830, some of the brethren began to think that the church should have a leader, just like the children of Israel wanting a king. Brother Joseph finally inquired of the Lord about it. He must have had a desire himself to be their leader, which desire in any form is not of God, for Christ said "If any man desire to be first, the same shall be last of all, and servant of all." "He that would be great, let him be your servant." "For he that is least among you all, the same shall be great." A true and humble follower of Christ will never have any desire to lead or be first, or to seek the praise of men or brethren. Desiring any prominence whatever is not humility, but it is pride; it is seeking praise of mortals instead of the praise of God. Joseph received a revelation that he should be the leader; that he should be ordained by Oliver Cowdery as "Prophet Seer and Revelator" to the church, and that the church should receive his words as if from God's own mouth. Satan surely rejoiced on that day, for he then saw that in time he could overthrow them. Remember, "Some revelations are of God, some revelations are of man, and some revelations are of the devil." God allowed them to be answered according to their erring desires. They were like the children of Israel wanting a king, and God gave them a king, but it was to their final destruction. He gave the church a leader, but it proved their destruction and final landing of the majority of them in the Salt Lake valley in polygamy, believing that their leader had received a revelation from God to practice this abomination. This was the first error that crept into the church. . . .

The next grievous error which crept into the church was in ordaining high priests in June, 1831. This error was introduced at the instigation of Sydney Rigdon. The office of high priests was never spoken of, and never thought of being established in the church until Rigdon came in. . . . Sydney Rigdon was the cause of almost all the errors which were introduced while he was in the church. . . . In this manner the revelations came through Brother Joseph as mouthpiece from time to time. Brother Joseph would listen to the persuasions of men, and inquire of the Lord concerning the different things, and the revelations would come just as they desired and thought in their hearts. . . .

Now you have thought that because Brother Joseph was given a gift to translate the Book, that he could not fall into error; and you worship and give credit to the man, when all the credit is due to God. You should think of this matter. Brother Joseph did not write a word of the Book of Mormon; it was already written by holy men of God who dwelt upon this land. . . . Now when we look at it aright, the fact of Brother Joseph having the gift to translate the Book, is that any reason why you should put any more trust in him than any other man? Not at all. Is that any reason why he should be a man who could not fall? Not at all. . . .

I will now pass over a recital of the errors which came into the church by revelation from time to time, and speak of them hereafter. I desire to speak here on the subject of polygamy. A few years ago I had doubts in regard to Brother Joseph's connection with the Spiritual Wife doctrine, but I have recently seen Vol. I, No. 1, of the old Latter Day Saints Herald, which has settled this matter in my mind. . . . I see that when the Reorganized Church was established, the fact that Joseph received this revelation was then known and acknowledged in editorials in the Herald. The reason why these articles were written in the Herald, was to explain why the Reorganized Church rejected the revelation received by Brother Joseph on polygamy, and to explain that he repented of his connection with polygamy just previous to this death. . . . The inspired writers did not try to hide the polygamy of David and Solomon. Their transgressions do not make the Psalms and Proverbs untrue. . . . You should have acknowledged belief in the errors of Joseph Smith, and not tried to hide them when there is so much evidence by the scriptures to make his question very clear to any one. . . . Today nearly all of the Reorganization do not believe that Brother Joseph received that revelation on polygamy, ever had any connection whatever with the doctrine of polygamy, openly and firmly denying this fact; some through ignorance, and some who should not be so ignorant about this matter. They charge it all to Brigham Young. Now, all honest men will understand, after they have read this pamphlet through, that I am doing God's will in bringing the truth to light concerning the errors of Brother Joseph. They will see that it is necessary, as he is the man who introduced many doctrines of error into the Church of Christ; and his errors must be made manifest and the truth brought to light, in order that all Latter Day Saints shall cease to put their trust in this man, believing his doctrines as if they were from the mouth of God.

I quote from Volume 1, Number 1, of The True Latter Day Saints Herald, page 24, from an article written by Isaac Sheen, who was a leader in establishing the Reorganization. . . . Here we have Isaac Sheen's testimony as follows: That Joseph Smith did not have connection with this spiritual wife doctrine; that he repented of it just before his death, having come to the conclusion that the revelation was not of God, but was of the devil; and he caused the revelation to be burned. Brother Sheen does not state how long Brother Joseph had connection with this doctrine, but of course we suppose from the time the revelation was given, July 12, 1843, until the time of his repentance just before his death, in June, 1844; at which time he concluded that the revelation was not of God, but was of the devil, and caused it to be burned, voluntarily giving himself up to his enemies, saying he was going to Carthage to die. . . .

On page 22, in the same number of the Herald, is an article of like testimony, by Wm. Marks, who, as he states in his article, was Presiding Elder at Nauvoo in 1844, when Brother Joseph was killed, and was with Brother Joseph up to his death. His testimony is the same as that given in the two foregoing articles.

He states that Brother Joseph said to him just before his death, concerning polygamy as follows: He (Joseph) said it eventually would prove the overthrow of the church, and we should soon be obliged to leave the United States unless it could be speedily put down. He was satisfied that it was a cursed doctrine, and that there must be every exertion made to put it down, etc. . . .

The foregoing evidence is sufficient to convince any one that Brother Joseph received the revelation on polygamy; that he gave the doctrine to the church; that he had connection with this spiritual wife doctrine himself; and afterwards became convinced that this revelation was of the devil, and repented of this iniquity just before his death. . . .

If Christ did not mean for Brother Joseph to be ordained a Seer to the church, it is a most serious error. If Christ did not mean for three first presidents to be ordained in his church, it is a most serious error to have ordained them. If Christ did not mean for high priests to be ordained in his church, it is a most serious error to have ordained them. If Christ did not mean for the doctrine of baptism for the dead to be an ordinance in his church, it is a serious error. If you are in error concerning the gathering and building the city New Jerusalem, it is a serious error. If Christ did not mean for them to change the name which he gave the church in 1829, it is a serious error; and likewise other errors taught in the book of Doctrine and Covenants; as the doctrine of revenge—cursing one's enemies in the name of the Lord; etc. For the Salt Lake church, I will also add, the doctrine of polygamy and other doctrines which are not to be found in the teachings of Christ. So you see that if you are in error in taking the book of Doctrine and Covenants as the law of God to the church, you are in many grave and serious errors. The object of this epistle is to show you that you are in serious error in taking that book as a law of God to the church; and that God's law is all contained in the written word—the Bible and the Book of Mormon.

10. Joseph Musser, "Announcement"

Joseph Musser is a key figure in those self-described Mormon fundamentalist movements that have continued to adhere to the practice of plural marriage. The church's commitment to abandoning polygamy, even after the President Wilford Woodruff Manifesto of 1890, was not clear even to many Latter-day Saints. Musser claimed that in this period of uncertainty, a "messenger" from Woodruff's successor President Lorenzo Snow (or President Joseph F. Smith he said elsewhere) directed him to enter plural marriage and "help keep the principle alive."[11] He took a second wife in 1902 and another in 1907 (after the second Manifesto of 1904, which effectively ended Mormon polygamy). After Joseph Musser prepared to marry a fourth in 1921, he was severed from the church. Musser subsequently associated with others of like mind, including Lorin Woolley, who believed that church leaders had gone astray in forsaking plural marriage. Woolley claimed to have been outside the door when a post-mortal Joseph Smith appeared to John Taylor in 1886 and revealed that polygamy would never be divinely rescinded as a practice. He also described a meeting and series of ordinations that are the source of the authority for plural marriage claimed by most Mormon fundamentalists. In that meeting, Lorin Woolley said Taylor shared the revelation he had received guaranteeing polygamy's continuation and ordained five men, including Woolley, with the authority to perform plural marriages. In 1929, Woolley ordained Joseph Musser an apostle in the "Council of Seven Friends," a group over which Woolley presided and which he claimed as the repository of real priesthood authority on the earth. By 1933, Musser had begun editing the journal Truth, *wherein he "brought together virtually all the arguments and doctrines that have become the basis for fundamentalist theology today," making him in the opinion of many the "father of the fundamentalist movement."[12]*

With this issue TRUTH begins its life journey. There is need for the message its columns will bear. The world is sick. It gropes in darkness. Complete dissolution threatens the established governments. The situation can be saved only by quick and heroic action. God is the great Physician. Man must turn unto him. It will be our aim to help blaze the way leading through the maze of perplexity, prejudice, hatred and ignorance, up toward the "great white throne."

We approach this delicate but all-important task with a deep sense of dependence on the Lord. We shall work hard to discharge our duty.

As we view it, the fundamentals governing man's existence on earth and his efforts to achieve salvation in the life to come, may be grouped under four general headings: POLITICAL, SOCIAL, ECONOMIC, and SPIRITUAL. These four must be fully coordinated in the lives and actions of mankind before a complete success is possible. To the extent that this co-ordination is perfect, just to that extent may man hope to achieve. Growing out of these four governing principles are, of course, countless shoots and branches, all designed to strengthen and beautify the parent tree. But it is to the four principles mentioned that special attention is now directed.

The POLITICAL part of the world mechanism is sadly out of order. All governments are feverishly restless, continuously engaged in talking peace while preparing for war, and the whole earth is in commotion, and men's hearts are failing them. This situation can be corrected only when Jesus Christ shall set up his reign under the form of government known as the Kingdom of God, which is destined to subvert all other kingdoms and governments and sweep them from the earth.

TRUTH will endeavor to teach "this gospel of the Kingdom" as Christ has outlined it, to the end that mankind may receive full protection in civil and religious rights, finally arriving at a state of righteousness and universal peace.

The SOCIAL structure of modern Christendom is toppling to ruin. A complete breakdown threatens. The monogamic order of marriage, the boast of modern civilization, has failed. Gnawing at its very vitals, to which the glorious principle of marriage is slowly but surely succumbing, are the death-dealing agencies of infidelity, birth control and divorce. The remedy is comprehended in God's order of marriage known today as Celestial or Patriarchal marriage. It was revealed to Abraham by the Lord, and in the present dispensation was restored through the "Mormon" Prophet, Joseph Smith.

TRUTH will champion the cause of this great social law and will endeavor to lead men to a clearer light.

The world has fallen into an ECONOMIC maelstrom, which threatens commercial destruction. It struggles seemingly to no purpose, each effort taking it deeper into the quagmire of failure. God, through his Prophet, has said: "The wisdom of their wise men shall perish and the understanding of their prudent men shall be hid." This prophetic edict is fulfilled in the present state of world economic bankruptcy. God alone can correct the evil. His cure involves acceptance of what is known as the "Order of Enoch" or the "United Order," as instituted during the Apostolic age:

> And the multitude of them that believed were of one heart and of one soul: neither said any of them that aught of the things which he possessed was his own; but they had all things common (Acts 4:32)

TRUTH adopts this plan as God's method of bringing men to a common level, and will advocate its practical adoption in accordance with latter-day revelation on the subject.

SPIRITUAL life is palsied. The death rattle in the throat is heard. "Lo, here is Christ; or, lo, He is there," is being thundered from the house-tops by those who have no rational conception of either Christ or his mission. The modern Pharisee has out-done his ancient brother in hypocrisy and ignorance. God's remedy for this bedlam of conflicting creeds and philosophies is that men shall accept the principle of present and continuous revelation. A constant communion between heaven and earth is the cure. Without this communion man cannot succeed; for "where there is no vision, the people perish."

TRUTH accepts this hypothesis as a self-evident fact. Its columns will seek to clarify those of God's revelations which are meant for the guidance of his children in this day, whether these revelations come through the ancient Jewish scriptures or through modern sources; whether they are voiced by the mouth of a Moses, a Confucius, a Swedenborg, a Luther, an Ingersol, or through our modern Prophets, of which Joseph Smith was the leader.

The four great pillars of light and progress classified as POLITICAL, SOCIAL, ECONOMIC, and SPIRITUAL, with all their devious branches and ramifications will be elucidated on and championed by TRUTH in accordance with the wisdom and understanding of its contributors. We know the task to be a difficult one. We approach it in meekness. In the defense of truth or in battling error, we will neither court fear nor favor. In the words of the late Theodore Roosevelt, "Our spear knows no brother." Our guide shall be light and truth. We shall always welcome constructive criticism and wholesome comments. The columns of TRUTH will teem with the best thoughts of the great minds of the past as well as those of the present, upon the subjects treated.

It will be noted that TRUTH begins its career on a very important date— June 1st—the one hundred and thirty-fourth anniversary of the birth of Brigham Young. It is fitting that this enterprise should be thus launched.

Brigham Young, though a greatly abused character, and much misunderstood, yet is known the world over as one of the America's greatest colonizers. He was clean, wise and courageous—a true Christian. Perhaps no other man in this dispensation contributed more towards establishing the truth as revealed through the "Mormon" Prophet, Joseph Smith, than this great leader.

TRUTH will endeavor to maintain the high standard of faith and essential works reflected by the life of this great leader, whose birth is celebrated by our first issue.

———————

From *Truth* (1935)

11. Wallace B. Smith, Revelation on Priesthood [RLDS D&C 156] (1984)

Like those of kindred restorationist movements, the Reorganized Church of Jesus Christ of Latter Day Saints (RLDS Church; renamed Community of Christ since 2001) faithful believe revelation to their prophet is continuing. RLDS members go even further than their LDS counterparts in continually expanding their canon of scripture by frequent addition of new revelations. While the Latter-day Saints have added only one section and two official declarations to their canon since 1846, the Reorganites have added more than forty. Most of the RLDS revelations are administrative in nature, addressing changes to the leadership. Some, however, deal with substantive doctrinal changes, such as RLDS Doctrine and Covenants section 156, which addresses the two topics of priesthood and temples. Whereas Latter-day Saints have granted the priesthood as a matter of routine to all "worthy" male members over the age of twelve (with the exception of blacks before 1978), RLDS practice was more selective. The RLDS were cautioned by revelation to "be not hasty in ordaining men of the Negro race" (RLDS Doctrine and Covenants 116:4a), but even white males were ordained only upon evidence of divine calling. In the following 1984 revelation, RLDS President Wallace B. Smith shattered the male monopoly on priesthood ordination, delighting many members, but alienating thousands of others (as many as 25 percent are thought to have defected as a consequence). Temple building was one of the principal motivations behind the early Mormon practice of gathering, and the exclusivity of temple participation has been a long-standing irritant and source of suspicion to outsiders. RLDS members rejected most LDS temple theology, including vicarious ordinances done on behalf of the dead. This variance in views on Joseph Smith's temple-building initiatives and ritual emphasis is one of the largest defining features separating the two largest denominations with a shared theological heritage. Nevertheless, in 1968, RLDS leaders announced a revelation directing them to build a temple whose "functions" would be revealed at a later time (RLDS Doctrine and Covenants 149). That promise was fulfilled also in this 1984 revelation. Today members of the LDS and RLDS churches worship in temples very differently; the former experience a closed ritualistic learning environment while the latter enjoy a more public place of prayer and meditation.

My servants have been diligent in the work of planning for the building of my temple in the Center Place. Let this work continue at an accelerated rate, according to the instructions already given, for there is great need of the spiritual awakening that will be engendered by the ministries experienced within its walls.

Indeed, these ministries shall be the means of great blessing for you, my people, if you will heed the counsel of my servants of the First Presidency who are rightly charged with the responsibility of developing the specific details of these ministries.

The priesthood offices already provided for in my church have always had the potential of supplying these blessings. Some of their functions, however, will be expanded and given additional meaning as the purposes of temple ministries are revealed more fully.

The temple shall be dedicated to the pursuit of peace. It shall be for reconciliation and for healing of the spirit.

It shall also be for a strengthening of faith and preparation for witness.

By its ministries an attitude of wholeness of body, mind, and spirit as a desirable end toward which to strive will be fostered.

It shall be the means for providing leadership education for priesthood and member.

And it shall be a place in which the essential meaning of the Restoration as healing and redeeming agent is given new life and understanding, inspired by the life and witness of the Redeemer of the world.

Therefore, let the work of planning go forward, and let the resources be gathered in, that the building of my temple may be an ensign to the world of the breadth and depth of the devotion of the Saints.

The following is also presented as the voice of the Spirit:

Hear, O my people, regarding my holy priesthood. The power of this priesthood was placed in your midst from the earliest days of the rise of this work for the blessing and salvation of humanity.

There have been priesthood members over the years, however, who have misunderstood the purpose of their calling. Succumbing to pride, some have used it for personal aggrandizement.

Others, through disinterest or lack of diligence, have failed to magnify their calling or have become inactive.

When this has happened, the church has experienced a loss of spiritual power, and the entire priesthood structure has been diminished.

It is my will that my priesthood be made up of those who have an abiding faith and desire to serve me with all their hearts, in humility and with great devotion.

Therefore, where there are those who are not now functioning in their priesthood, let inquiry be made by the proper administrative officers, according to the provisions of the law, to determine the continuing nature of their commitment.

I have heard the prayers of many, including my servant the prophet, as they have sought to know my will in regard to the question of who shall be called to share the burdens and responsibilities of priesthood in my church.

I say to you now, as I have said in the past, that all are called according to the gifts which have been given them. This applies to priesthood as well as to any other aspects of the work.

Therefore, do not wonder that some women of the church are being called to priesthood responsibilities. This is in harmony with my will and where these calls are made known to my servants, they may be processed according to administrative procedures and provisions of the law.

Nevertheless, in the ordaining of women to priesthood, let this be done with all deliberateness. Before the actual laying on of hands takes place, let specific guidelines and instructions be provided by the spiritual authorities, that all may be done in order.

Remember, in many places there is still much uncertainty and misunderstanding regarding the principles of calling and giftedness. There are persons whose burden in this regard will require that considerable labor and ministerial support be provided. This should be extended with prayer and tenderness of feeling, that all may be blessed with the full power of my reconciling Spirit.

Dear Saints, have courage for the task which is yours in bringing to pass the cause of Zion. Prepare yourselves through much study and earnest prayer.

Then, as you go forth to witness of my love and my concern for all persons, you will know the joy which comes from devoting yourselves completely to the work of the kingdom. To this end will my Spirit be with you. Amen.

RLDS Doctrine & Covenants 156 (1984)

12. Stephen M. Veazey, "A Defining Moment"

In the early twenty-first century, the RLDS Church was renamed Community of Christ and moved to emphasize Christian fundamentals over restoration-ist distinctives. Joseph Smith III had de-emphasized the more radical, later teachings of his murdered father Joseph Smith, including polygamy, human theosis, vicarious temple work, and the Abrahamic texts. Eventually, mention of Joseph Smith's theophanies and his production of scripture (including the Book of Mormon) all but disappeared. Among the distinctive aspects of the Mormon faith tradition, three that stand out are a history that is providential, steeped in conspicuous moments of divine participation; a scriptural canon that is open, expanding, and more immediate than the Judeo-Christian texts; and a prophet who is considered God's mouthpiece and source of continuing revelation. In this progressive document, a kind of Vatican II moment for Community of Christ, President Stephen M. Veazey gave substantial redefini-tion—or refocus—to each of the three, marking a significant departure from Mormon readings of these key elements of the faith. For Latter-day Saints, it is oft said, history is theology. Their faith is grounded in affirmation of piv-otal historical events, like the First Vision, or the visit of priesthood-bearing Peter, James, and John to Joseph Smith. God is seen as personally inaugurat-ing the restoration through his visit to Smith and superintending its unfolding through divine guidance and heavenly emissaries. As for scripture, Joseph Smith dictated much of it under the immediate influence of the Spirit, and he pronounced the Book of Mormon "the most correct of any book on earth." Even morally troubling scriptural elements like plural marriage and curs-ing with blackness become inspired words to fit into a large, restorationist mosaic. The prophet's keys are considered radically distinct, empowering him to receive revelation as God's word to the church and to the world, unlike personal revelation vouchsafed the rank and file members. Veazey challenges each of these views in turn. Considering also Community of Christ's decision to ordain women to the priesthood and its affirmation of a triune God, the church now has less in common with the current LDS faith than with more liberal varieties of contemporary Christianity.

This is a defining moment in the life of the church! Defining moments occur at the juncture of fear and hope, challenge and opportunity, hesitancy and faithful response.

The church has faced defining moments before. Times when deliberate choices had to be made to clarify priorities in the face of difficult circumstances. Such defining moments brought the best out of us and prepared us for the next phase of our journey with God.

What is this defining moment? In general, it can be framed by two questions: Will we allow certain circumstances and issues to divert us from our mission? Or will we clarify our mission priorities and focus on what matters most? . . .

To become the Community of Christ that God is calling us to become we must address some important issues. The first has to do with how we relate to our history.

Our early church history is the story of faithful, inspired people who heard the call to embrace and share the gospel of Christ more fully. They did so with great enthusiasm. They responded with unusual commitment and creative energy, giving tangible expression of the gospel in community life together.

Over the generations, though, we have tailored their story to put the church in the best possible light. We have raised early church leaders to the status of spiritual heroes of mythical proportions, while downplaying their humanity and struggles.

In recent decades many books and articles have been written about the earliest years of the Restoration movement. While some previous works approached this period of history mainly by describing events, the more recent works explore the interrelated religious, social, and political factors that influenced the early church and its leaders. Many historians, with access to additional historical information, are writing with increased frankness and openness.

The Presidency recently released a set of "Church History Principles." The "History Principles" were created to bring perspective to the relationship between history and matters of faith. While affirming the essential role of historical study, the principles state that history does not have the final word on matters of faith and unfolding direction in the church today. The history principles provide the guidelines needed to treasure our history, but not be totally defined by it.

Let me give you an example. Despite how our story often is told, we no longer can claim that we were just the innocent victims of violence during the church's early years. While our forbearers were certainly the targets of persecution on various occasions, more than once they provoked and initiated violence because of judgmental attitudes toward others. In the pressure-filled years of the early church, violence and militancy overtook Christ's message of reconciliation, forgiveness, and peace.

To move ahead with integrity in our emphasis on sharing the peace of Jesus Christ, we must repent of and learn from the violent episodes in church history. Only through honest examination, including identifying any remaining signs of these tendencies, can we continue on the restoring path of peace, reconciliation, and healing of the spirit to which God calls us.

We can take these steps because we know that our history does not have to be without blemish to reveal the hand of God working in the movement. Ironically, one of the primary principles of scripture is that God's grace is revealed most clearly by its working in and through humanity, especially human weakness and sin. Viewing our history through this lens allows us to be affirming, honest, and sympathetic. . . .

Besides putting our history in perspective, we need to deepen our understanding of the nature of scripture.

For this part of our journey we need a light and a compass. Our light is the witness of the Holy Spirit that illuminates divine truth. Our compass is the church's "Statement on Scripture" that provides reliable direction. Basic to the "Statement on Scripture" is the understanding that scripture is an amazing collection of inspired writings that is indispensable to encountering the Living God revealed in the Living Word, Jesus Christ. Scripture speaks with many voices, including testimonies, stories, poetry, metaphors, commentary, and parables. All of these ways of communicating point us to divine truths beyond the ability of any language to express fully. Scripture is authoritative,

SCATTERING OF THE SAINTS | 98 |

not because it is perfect or inerrant in every literal detail, but because it reliably keeps us grounded in God's revelation.

Here is the heart of our challenge. Over the last several centuries a doctrine of scripture emerged in Christianity that insists that all scripture—every single word—was dictated directly by God and is inerrant in every detail. This belief emerged as a response to the questioning of religious authority from those who held that human reason alone was the most reliable pathway to truth. So, a doctrine of scripture emerged that enshrined the literal words of scripture as inerrant and as the sole authority on all matters.

This view still dominates much of global Christianity. It also strongly influences more than a few members of Community of Christ who have adopted it from the larger culture.

However, that doctrine is not how scripture was understood in Christianity for many centuries after its birth. It is not how Jesus used scripture. And, it is not how Community of Christ officially views scripture today.

The church affirms that scripture is inspired and essential to our knowledge of God and the gospel. In addition, we believe that scripture should be interpreted responsibly through informed study, guided by the Spirit working in the church. Scripture was formed by the community to shape the community. Therefore, interpreting scripture is the constant work of the community. In other words, understanding and applying scripture is not just a matter of reading a passage and deciding on our own what it means.

Community of Christ also stresses that all scripture must be interpreted through the lens of God's most-decisive revelation in Jesus Christ. So if portions of scripture don't agree with our fullest understanding of the meaning of the revelation of God in Christ, as illuminated by the Holy Spirit and discerned by the faith community, the teachings and vision of Christ take precedence. This principle applies to all of our books of scripture, especially any passage used by some to assign God's disfavor, negative characteristics, or secondary roles to others.

This is why our belief in "continuing revelation" is so important. This belief keeps us open to "yet more light and truth" so we can grow in understanding of God's supreme will as revealed in Christ.

[RLDS] Doctrine and Covenants 163:7d states that "Scripture, prophetic guidance, knowledge, and discernment in the faith community must walk hand in hand to reveal the true will of God. Follow this pathway, which is the way of the Living Christ, and you will discover more than sufficient light for the journey ahead." . . .

The 2007 World Conference passed a resolution asking the Presidency to bring guidance to the church about our practice of rebaptism as a condition for church membership. After a time of study and reflection, the Presidency is inviting the whole church to engage with us in prayerful discernment about this issue. We believe this approach is in harmony with [RLDS] Doctrine and Covenants 162:2c, which states: "As a prophetic people you are called, under the direction of the spiritual authorities and with the common consent of the people, to discern the divine will for your own time and in the places where you serve."

The obvious opportunity before us is to sharpen our skills as a prophetic and discerning people. The importance of the process is much greater than how we will resolve the issue. Its ultimate importance lies in enriching our capacity to engage in fair, Spirit-led dialogue about important issues. . . .

It is telling that much of what I have addressed so far is about internal church issues. This is the greatest challenge we face. Will we be able to put internal church issues in proper perspective so we can focus first on our mission to Proclaim Jesus Christ and Promote Communities of Joy, Hope, Love and Peace? Everything else which may be of concern is secondary to pursuing this mission.

For example, I began by addressing economic challenges facing the church and by assuring you that our long-term financial viability is not in question. Is that the most important question we should be asking? The most important question for a missional church is not about long-term survival. It is about how we passionately pursue Christ's mission in a suffering world that groans for the liberating truths of the gospel ([RLDS] Doctrine and Covenants 155:7).

Are we mobilizing to provide pastoral care and tangible help to individuals and families that are barely surviving because of economic pressures? Are we responding to the increasing hatred and violence toward immigrants and ethnic minorities because others want to make them scapegoats for our common difficulties? What about the children in your community? How are they doing? What does it mean to be a prophetic people who speak and act in the name of God and Christ in times like these?

Many of our members live in countries with developing or nonfunctional economic and political systems. Their situation is much worse than anything many of us in more affluent areas are experiencing. What matters most to them is how to free themselves and their neighbors from the devastating effects of poverty, disease, and human conflict. The missional question for the church is, "How does the hope of God's peaceful kingdom become more than a faint dream for them?" What will we do as a church whose mission is grounded in restoring people to wholeness in community?

I am pleased to announce the Presidency, in concert with the Community of Christ Peace Support Network, is convening a summit this September to address this question. We are inviting leaders of church-related ministries and all our affiliates—such as Outreach International, World Accord, Graceland University, and the Seminary, just to name a few—to meet with us.

Our goal is to create a vision and cooperative action plan for promoting communities of economic justice and peace throughout the world. Coordinating and integrating our compassionate relief, educational, advocacy, and community-development ministries will allow us to make an even greater impact.

In many parts of the western world a primary concern is sustaining, reviving, and growing congregations to carry out the church's mission. The Co-Missioned Pastors Initiative is a pilot project designed to discover the most effective pastoral training, resources, and support for leading healthy congregations that engage all ages in focusing on Christ's mission.

We have learned a lot from the pilot project. Despite the financial challenges we face, it is essential that we expand access to this support and training for more pastors, congregational leaders, and priesthood. Instead of one hundred pastors who now are completing the pilot, I see five hundred, eight hundred, or one thousand pastors and congregational leaders who will respond to the call to become effective, visionary congregational leaders. Leaders who know how to incorporate all generations in congregational life. Leaders who have the insights and skills to guide congregations in discovering the ministries God is calling them to pursue in the communities they serve.

I am aware of the frustrations of some youth and young adults with the seemingly slow pace of congregational life in response to mission. I also am aware of your disappointment with not having opportunities to serve and lead as you feel called. In response, let me say the church needs the insights and gifts of all ages to be healthy. Congregations that ignore this principle do so at their own peril.

I also know words are not enough. We need to do something now. I and other church leaders personally commit to meet with young adults in various locations to listen to concerns, perspectives, and hopes. We want to envision the future of the church with you. We want to explore models of ministry, mission, and leadership to open more doors for your participation. We are making plans for such gatherings right now. The first will be here in the Temple Lecture Hall immediately following this address. I invite all young adults present to meet with us tonight. Yes, there will be food. (And, if your children are young adults or older youth, you are no longer a young adult. I have had to accept this fact, and so can you.)

Young adults, the church needs you. We need you now. We need you to help us become who we are all yearning to become.

If you are ready to cause change right now, go to www.we-cause.org. At this site you will find a special video message from me and additional information about our plans for meeting with young adults. You also will find information and links for specific opportunities for involvement, and tangible ways to support the church's mission right now.

So, after all that is said, what matters most? I hope it has become clear. The vision and mission of Jesus Christ matters most! What matters most is for us to become who God is calling us to become so the restoring ministry of Christ can be shared in every possible way in every possible place.

As I was preparing this address, I prayerfully asked God many times, "What more does the church need to hear?" On several occasions, I sensed the impress of the Spirit. In response, I want to give voice to what I sensed through the following words to the church:

Fear not! Do not be afraid to become who God is calling you to become. God, the Eternal One, has been with you in your past, continues with you in the present, and already is waiting patiently for you in the future. Through your lives the sacred story of the Restoration still is being written.

Engage the current challenges and opportunities before you with commitment and hope worthy of the dedication and sacrifices of those who went before you. Creatively build on the faith foundations they laid. Open windows and doors to the future.

Beloved community, God has chosen you to assist in accomplishing divine purposes if you will choose to live out of your better natures and potential. Deepen your faith. Refine your sensitivity to the guidance of the Spirit so that you are not distracted by other influences. Explore your scriptures with openness to new insights that will come. Increase your compassion and generosity. Strengthen your relationships so the peace of Christ may be magnified through you.

Have courage and hope. Gather in the gifts of all ages and cultures so the ministries of the body can become whole and fully alive. Others are being prepared around the world to join their efforts with yours, if you will move ahead according to the direction offered to you by the Spirit. Amen.

Brothers and sisters, there is a way into the future that holds the promise that our best days are yet before us.

May we choose it is my fervent hope and prayer.

From *Community of Christ Herald* (2009)

THREE

GATHERING TO ZION

"IT WAS THE DESIGN OF THE COUNCILS of heaven before the world was," Joseph Smith taught, "that the principles and laws of the priesthood should be predicated upon the gathering of the people in every age of the world." At least two purposes were accomplished by the physical congregating of members of The Church of Jesus Christ of Latter-day Saints in one area. First was the mustering of resources necessary to engage in the daunting undertaking of temple building. Smith explained a second reason as well: "Intelligence is the great object of our holy religion," he declared. And intelligence, he continued, "is the result of education, and education can only be obtained by living in compact society; One of the principal objects, then, of our coming together, is to obtain the advantages of education; and in order to do this, compact society is absolutely necessary."[1]

But in Mormon history, that gathering proved to be provisional and portable. New York, Ohio, Missouri, Illinois, and Utah all served in turn as sites where the Latter-day Saints assembled, seeking spiritual and physical refuge. The Mormons sacralized the American frontier settlements of Kirtland, Independence, Far West, Adam-Ondi-Ahman, Nauvoo, and Salt Lake City in their quest to build temples to anchor their sacred cities, following the pattern found in ancient scripture. For it was in the Missouri heartland of America, they believed, that Adam and Eve dwelt in the Garden of Eden before being cast out into the mortal world, and where God's people would gather in the last days to build the New Jerusalem, where Jesus Christ would rule and reign throughout the millennium.

Although Brigham Young is lionized in the American imagination as the consummate mover of persecuted peoples and planner of pioneer cities, it was his mentor Joseph Smith who shepherded the fledgling church from New England to Ohio's Western Reserve and then to the borders of the Missouri River. In 1833, Smith produced a detailed plat map for the city of Zion, here included (figure 3.1), with temples at its center and farms at its periphery. The account of the convert Sarah Studevant Leavitt is a reminder that the church was born in an age when, as in the Great Awakening, thousands of Americans were stirred to a quest for personal salvation. In this newer age, the quest for personal renewal often accompanied an expectation of institutional renewal or restoration as well. Like all religious innovators, Joseph Smith encountered external opposition and internal dissension. However, conflicts became increasingly violent as Latter-day Saints gathered in threatening numbers at a time of precarious political tensions. Church members were sometimes their own worst enemies by using rhetoric that could at times be triumphalistic and bellicose. Artemisia Sidnie Meyers recorded her experience of the worst pogrom to ensue in the "Mormon Wars" of Missouri. Only men and boys were massacred at Haun's Mill in 1838, but women bore a more constant burden in an era when Mormon men were frequently called to serve long missions, leaving wives and children to fend for themselves amidst destitution and persecution. Vilate Kimball's brief but poignant letter to her husband captures the largely unnoted sacrifices of myriad Mormon women.

By 1839, the center of Mormon gathering had shifted to the swampland of Commerce, Illinois. Joseph Smith and his counselors issued a clarion call in 1841 for the European Latter-day Saints to gather to the renamed Nauvoo, where they could consecrate their labors for the building of a temple and thereafter receive sacred ordinances available in no other place. To their litany of challenges, Mormon women were here for the first time called upon to sacrifice public respectability and popular conceptions of morality to obey "the principle," the practice of plural marriage. Elizabeth Ann Smith Whitney records the mixed trauma and blessing of yielding both herself and daughter as plural wives. For the first years of their residence in "the city of Joseph," Mormons experienced a temporary age of peace and harmony, captured in Joseph Smith's epistle to church members scattered abroad. Mormon women at this time achieved some relative autonomy, through the establishment of their own organization, the Relief Society, as chronicled later in this chapter.

After the martyrdom of Joseph Smith, the Latter-day Saints reorganized and resolutely sought new refuge in the distant American West, where Brigham Young would echo Smith's gathering call from the mountain valleys of Utah. The poem-turned-hymn "All Is Well" captures the gratitude and determination of William Clayton, a Mormon pioneer who, while struggling for survival on the tundra of Iowa, learned that his wife had given birth to a healthy baby. His stirring words, put to an English folk melody, became the anthem of gathering for subsequent Latter-day Saints on the trail west. In 1846, from their staging station in Winter Quarters, Young received a revelation that mirrored Jehovah's instructions to Moses and the ancient children of Israel as they embarked on their journey to a promised land. Like downtrodden African Americans who appropriated the Exodus motif to the struggles of their people, the Latter-day Saints followed their own American Moses through the wilderness in search of a land they could call their own. Of the many images of sturdy, suffering Mormon exiles, the "handcart pioneer" stands out, in spite of the relatively small numbers who engaged in the ever pragmatic Brigham Young's economy-minded experiment. Meanwhile, converts continued to pour in from England and Europe. The autobiographical account of young Danish girl Valborg Rasmussen offers a glimpse of why tens of thousands of European church members were willing to abandon family and friends in the old country to gather to Zion. Although the physical gathering to Utah had tapered off by the end of the nineteenth century, the First Presidency formally reversed the decades-old emigration policy in 1907, urging those Latter-day Saints still in Europe to remain in their homelands. From that time to the present, church members around the globe have been counseled to build up spiritual Zion in their native lands.

1. Joseph Smith, "Plat for the City of Zion" (1833)

The first hint that the Latter-day Saints' gathering was to be more than metaphor came only months after the church was organized. "No man knoweth where the city [Zion] shall be built, but it shall be given hereafter" said a September 1830 revelation to Joseph Smith (Doctrine and Covenants 28:9). A month later, the Mormons were told that they were "called to bring to pass the gathering of mine elect," in biblical language understood by generations of preachers and missionaries to refer to the process of conversion to the body of believers in Christ. But the revelation in this case clarified "that they shall be gathered in unto one place upon the face of this land . . . to be prepared in all things" (Doctrine and Covenants 29:7–8). Subsequently directed by revelation to Missouri, Smith arrived in Jackson County, Missouri, and there, he recounted, "God . . . manifested himself unto us, and designated, to me and others, the very spot upon which he designed to commence the work of the gathering, and the upbuilding of an 'holy city,' which should be called Zion."[2] Joseph Smith first produced a city plan in 1833 (figure 3.1), two years after the first Latter-day Saints began arriving in Jackson County. The

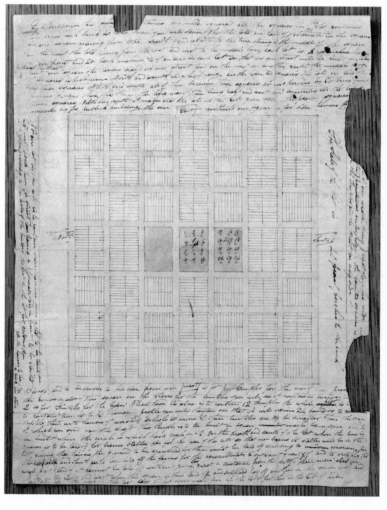

FIGURE 3.1. Plat for the City of Zion (1833).

plat encompasses one mile square, a common practice with city planning of the era. But additional features included the reservation of central blocks for church buildings, of other special blocks for public buildings, and the inclusion of farmer and rancher domiciles within the city boundaries. Barns, corrals, and agricultural zones were relegated to the outskirts or beyond.

Plat for the City of Zion, Church History Library (1833)

2. Sarah Studevant Leavitt, "Autobiography"

Born in New Hampshire, Sarah Studevant married Jeremiah Leavitt in 1817 and moved afterwards to Canada. The spiritual pilgrimage she recounts parallels thousands of contemporary accounts: raised in a mainline Protestant tradition, she determined at a young age that the churches she knew were far removed from the Christianity of the New Testament and "was looking forward" to a restoration of the primitive religion. Her fervent expectations found fulfillment in personal signs, ecstatic trances, and, eventually, the revelations of Joseph Smith printed in the church newspaper and the writings of Apostle Parley P. Pratt in the Voice of Warning. *By this time, most Latter-day Saints were gathering to Missouri. Leavitt and her husband, together with their nine children and an extended family, set out for Zion. The narrative reprinted below recounts her life until their arrival in Kirtland, Ohio, where Joseph Smith still maintained church headquarters and the site of the Mormon Temple. Shortly after reaching Kirtland, the family's funds were exhausted and they settled temporarily in Mayfield, ten miles away. Before they could fulfill their goal of reaching Zion, the Latter-day Saints had been expelled from Missouri; when Mormon gathering shifted to Nauvoo, Illinois, the Leavitts joined the main body of church members. In 1846, the Saints were outcasts once more. Sarah and her family left with Brigham Young for the West, but Jeremiah died before they could reach Winter Quarters in Iowa. She eventually completed the journey to Salt Lake with the rest of her family. She died in 1878.*

I was born in the town of Lime, County of Grafton, New Hampshire, and am now seventy-six years, seven months, and fifteen days old. My father was Lemuel Studevant and my mother was Priscilla Tompson. My parents were very strict with their children, being descendants of the old Pilgrims. They taught them every principle of truth and honor as they understood it themselves. They taught them to pray and read the Bible for themselves. My father had many books that treated on the principle of man's salvation and many stories that were very interesting and I took great pleasure in reading them. He was Dean of the Presbyterian Church. For years his house was open to all denominations, so his children had the privilege of hearing the interesting religious conversations, but as I had the privilege of reading the Bible for myself, I found that none of them understood the Bible as I did. I knew of no other way to understand it only as it read. The Apostle said, "Though we, or angels from heaven, preach any other gospel than that which we preach, let him be accursed," and it was very evident to my understanding that they all came short of preaching the doctrine that Paul preached, but I was confident we should have the faith.

From childhood I was seriously impressed and desired very much to be saved from that awful hell I heard so much about. I believed in the words of the Savior, that said, "Ask, and you shall receive." I prayed much and my prayers were sometimes answered immediately; this was before I made any pretentions to having any religion. When I was eighteen years old the Lord sent me a good husband. We were married at my father's house, March 6, 1817, in the town of Barton, County of Orleans, State of Vermont. The next June we moved to Canada, fifteen miles from the Vermont line, into a very wicked place. They would swear and drink and play cards on Sunday and steal and do any wicked act their master, the devil, would lead them to. This was very different from what I was brought up to [do]. My father would never suffer any profane language in his house. The next February I had a daughter born. She lived only twelve days. There was some things very strange connected with the birth of this child, which I do not think best to write, but I shall never forget, which I never shall know the meaning of until the first resurrection, when I shall clasp it again in my arms.

The next January I had another daughter born. When she was about six months old I had a vision of the damned spirits in hell, so that I was filled with horror more than I was able to bear, but I cried to the Lord day and night until I got an answer of peace and a promise that I should be saved in the kingdom of God that satisfied me. That promise has been with me through all the changing scenes of life ever since. . . .

There was a minister come from the states and formed a church, called the Baptist, which I joined because I wanted to be baptized by immersion. I had been sprinkled when an infant, but as I said before, I did not believe in any church on earth, but was looking forward to a time when the knowledge of

God would cover the earth, and that glorious time is rolling, all glory to the Lord. I lived very watchful and prayerful, never neglecting my prayers, for I felt that I was entitled to no blessing unless I asked for them, and I think so yet.

We took a free-will Baptist paper that I thought always told the truth, but there was a number of columns in this paper concerning a new sect. It had a prophet that pretended he talked with God. They had built a thing they called a meetinghouse, a huge mass of rock and wood, on the shores of Lake Cryenth (I am not sure as to the spelling of this word) to make the blue waters of the lake blush for shame. In this Joe would go talk, he said, with the Lord and come out and tell them what the Lord said. But if I should go on and tell all the lies in that paper, how they healed the sick and managed their affairs, it would be too much for me. If you ever read the Arabian Night tales, you might guess of what importance they were, for I could compare them to nothing else. No person of common sense would believe a word of it, and yet they wrote it for truth, thinking that would hinder Mormonism from spreading. But in this the devil overshot himself, for they were too big lies for anyone to believe.

But I will go on with my experience. I had a place that I went every day for secret prayers. My mind would be carried away in prayer so that I knew nothing of what was going on around me. It seemed like a cloud was resting down over my head. If that cloud would break, there was an angel that had a message for me or some new light. If the cloud would break, there would be something new and strange revealed. I did not know that it concerned anyone but myself. Soon after this there was one of my husband's sisters came in, and after spending a short time in the house she asked me to take a walk with her. She had heard the gospel preached by a Mormon and believed it and been baptized. She commenced and related the whole of Joseph's vision and what the Angel Moroni had said the mission he had called him to.

It came to my mind in a moment that this was the message that was behind that cloud, for me and not for me only, but for the whole world, and I considered it of more importance than anything I had ever heard before, for it brought back the ancient order of things and laid a foundation that could be built upon that was permanent; a foundation made by Him that laid the foundation of the earth, even the Almighty God; and he commanded his people to build up the kingdom of God upon the foundation he had laid, and notwithstanding the heathen raged and Satan mustered all his forces against the work, it has gone onward and upward for more than forty years, and will continue until the work is finished.

I read the Book of Mormon, the Doctrine and Covenants, and all the writings I could get from the Latter-day Saints. It was the book of Doctrine and Covenants that confirmed my faith in the work. I knew that no man, nor set of men, that could make such a book or would dare try from any wisdom that man possessed. I knew it was the word of God and a revelation from heaven and received it as such. I sought with my whole heart a knowledge of the truth and obtained a knowledge that never has nor never will leave me.

The next thing was to gather with the Saints. I was pondering over in my heart how it was possible for such a journey with what means we could muster. We had a good farm, but could not get much for it, but the voice of the Spirit said, "Come out of Babylon, O my people, that you be not partakers of her plagues." From the time the voice spoke so loud, clear and plain to my understanding, I knew the way would be open for us to gather with the Saints. For the Lord never gives a commandment to man but what he gives them a chance to obey. From this time we set out in earnest and was ready to start with the rest of the company July 20, 1835. The company was made up of the Leavitt family, Mother Sarah Shannon Leavitt, and her children, consisting of twenty-three souls. Franklin Chamberlain, her oldest son-in-law, took the lead. He did not belong to the Church, but his wife did.

We had a prosperous journey of eight hundred miles to Kirtland, Ohio. I had no chance to be baptized and join the Church until I got there. My daughter, Louisa, and myself and some others were baptized at this place and were confirmed. Louisa had been sick for a year, under the doctor's care, and had taken very much medicine, but all to no purpose. She was very feeble, could sit up but little. She had been in the states with my friends for more than a year. Her father and myself went after her with a light carriage. As she was eighteen years old, I gave her her choice to go home with us or stay with my sister. My sister told her if she would stay with her she should never want for anything, but she said she would go with her father and mother. My sister said, "Louisa, if you ever get well, don't say that Mormonism cured you." So much for her judgment on Mormonism. She was rich, high spirited, and proud, and belonged to a church that was more popular than the Latter-day Saints.

Now I will go back to my story. We stayed at Kirtland about a week and had the privilege of hearing Joseph preach in that thing the Baptists said they called a meetinghouse, which proved to be a very good house. We went into the upper rooms, saw the Egyptian mummies, the writing that was said to be written in Abraham's day, Jacob's ladder being pictured on it, and lots more wonders that I cannot write here, and that were explained to us.

From *Women's Voices* (1875)

3. Artemisia Sidnie Meyers, "Haun's Mill Massacre Account"

The Mormon gathering to Missouri, undertaken in summer 1831 with such soaring hopes, was in disarray two years later, when Latter-day Saints agreed to abandon their stakes in Jackson County under intense pressure from citizens and mob attacks. In November 1833, Latter-day Saints fled north to welcoming Clay County, but the refuge proved a temporary respite; the old tensions emerged in their new setting, and summer 1836 found them fleeing further north, principally into newly created Caldwell but also adjoining counties. By August 1838, political tensions, intemperate Mormon language, and mutual hostility finally erupted in election-day violence at polls in Gallatin, Daviess County. Violence on both sides immediately escalated out of control, and on October 28 Missouri Governor Lilburn Boggs ordered the state militia to drive the Latter-day Saints from the state. In the vicinity of Haun's Mill settlement in northeastern Caldwell County, two hundred militiamen, acting without knowledge of Boggs's order, were at that moment planning a violent attack. Artemisia Sidnie Meyers was at this time a nine-year-old girl living in the Mormon settlement. Her recollection was recorded years later but agrees in detail with other contemporary accounts. No legal consequences followed in the wake of this pogrom, which remains enshrined in Mormon memory as the greatest atrocity perpetuated against the Latter-day Saints in America as a consequence of their religious beliefs.

I was born in Richland County Ohio on the 24th day of January 1829. My father, Jacob Myers and my Mother Sarah Coleman Myers embraced the gospel about the year 1834 and moved to Missouri in 1836. They settled in the eastern part of Caldwell County near Shoal Creek, about 16 miles from Far West. He built a grist mill for Mr. Haun which afterwards was the scene of the massacre. I was baptized in the summer of 1837 when in my ninth year. In 1838 when the war broke out against the Saints, my brother Jacob Myers, Jr., was living near the mill and had been assisting in running it. My brother-in-law, James

Houston, who was a blacksmith, built and owned the shop in which the massacre occurred. On the 30th of October 1838 most of the brethren living in the
vicinity of Haun's Mill assembled there, among whom were my father and my
brother George. My father with my brother-in-law accompanying him started
for home before the mob came upon them at the mill. My brother-in-law's
wife was at father's home. About dark word came to us that the mobbers were
coming and that men, women and children had better hide in the woods as
they intended to kill all they could find. The men were told to hide by themselves. There were three families at father's house. After the men were gone the
women took the children, and went about a mile and one-half to the woods.
After the children were asleep and lights put out my mother put on a man's
coat and stood guard until one or two o'clock, when word came to us they had
had a battle at the mill and two of my brothers were wounded. We all then
went home and found father there. Mother told him he had better stay with
the children and she would go to the mill to see my wounded brothers. I clung
to my mother and wanted to go with her to which she consented. My brother
George's wife also went with us. We lived three miles from the mill. My brother
George lived one and a quarter miles from the mill. When we came to his
house we found him lying on the bed. When Mother saw him she exclaimed:
"Oh! Lord have mercy on my boy." He replied: "Don't fret Mother, I shall not
die." He was very weak from the loss of blood. I will here relate the manner of
his escape in his own words as he told us after he was better.

Our guns were in the blacksmith shop when the Mob came unexpectedly upon
us. Orders were given to run to the shop. The mob formed a half circle on the
north side of, the shop, extending partly across the east and west ends so as to
cover all retreat from the shop. They commenced firing before we could escape
with our arms. I looked for a chance to run out but as soon as I arose to run one
fellow behind a tree leveled, his gun at me and I had to stop down again. One of
the brethren by my side had just loaded his gun when he fell, mortally wounded.
I seized his gun and raised my hat so that the mobber could see it immediately
when he came around the tree so I could see him level his gun again at me, but I
was too quick for him when I fired he clasped his arms around the tree and slid
to the ground. I now thought it was my time to escape. I made two or three jumps
from the door when a bullet struck me a little below the right shoulder blade and
lodged against the skin near the pit of my stomach. I fell to the ground, Mother,
if ever a boy prayed I did at this time. I thought it would do me no good to lie

there so I arose and ran up the hill, the bullets whistling by me all the time. When I came to the fence and was climbing over it, a ball passed through my shirt collar. I walked as far as I could but soon became so weak from loss of blood that I had to get on my hands and knees and crawl the rest of the way home. I was very thirsty, and finding no one at home, crawled to the spring and drank freely. When I got back to the house I became very sick and vomited a large quantity of blood. Then I felt more easy. I suffered terribly before this.

After Mother dressed George's wounds we went on to the mill where we arrived just at the break of day. I shall never forget the awful scene that met our eyes. When we first arrived at Haun's Mill the first scene that presented itself, in his dooryard, was the remains of father York and McBride and others covered with sheets. We went down the hill to cross the mill dam and there stood a boy over a pool of blood. He said: "Mother Myers this is the blood of my poor father." This, with the groans of the wounded, which we could distinctly hear, affected Mother so that she was unable to make any reply to the boy. We made our way to brother Jacob's house and found him with his left leg broken by a bullet about half way between his knee and ankle and a flesh wound in his thigh. After he fell to the ground the mobber saw him sitting there holding his left and one of them ran up to him with a corn cutter to kill him. As he raised his arm to strike, another one of the mob called out to him and told him if he touched my brother he would shoot him. Running up to them he said my brother was a damned fine man for he had ground many a grist for him. After the mob had ceased firing my brother's wife and her sister saw him sitting where he had fallen. They went out and asked two of the mobbers to carry him into his house. The mobbers asked them if there were any Mormons in the house. They said there were not. They told the women that they would throw them into the millpond if they lied to them. They then took him up and carried him into his house and threw him on the bed, and hurried out of doors as though they expected to be shot the next moment. From my brother's house we went to the blacksmith shop where we beheld a most shocking sight. There layed dead, the dying and the wounded, weltering in their blood where they fell. A young man, whose name was Simon Cox who lived with my father, lay there with four bullets, having passed through his body the kidneys. He was still alive. He said to Mother. "All I want is a bowl of sweet milk and a feather bed to lie on." He had just got a pair of new boots a few days before and he told Mother how they dragged him about the shop to get them off. He told us to be faithful and said to me: "Be a good girl and obey your parents." He died in the afternoon about twenty-four hours after he was shot.

After we came back to my brother's house my father, David Evans and Joseph Young, with one of two more came and gathered up the dead and carried them to my brother's place, put the bodies on a wide board, and slid them off feet foremost into a well which he had been digging but had not yet come to water. Every time they brought one and slid him in I screamed and cried. It was such an awful sight to see them piled in the bottom in all shapes. After the dead were buried (which was done in a great hurry), father and the brethren went away and secreted themselves for fear the mobbers would return. The mobbers returned, I do not remember how soon, camping there about 20 days during which time they killed cattle and hogs to live on. They also took six or eight stands of bees belonging to Father which were at the mill. During the time they camped there they were very civil to the women folks. They chopped wood and brought water for my brother's folks. They wanted to come in the house and sit around the fire but Mother would not allow them to do so. In the following spring my brothers had so far recovered as to be able to go on board a steamer on the Missouri River and return to Ohio where Jacob had to have his leg amputated above the knee. George never became a sound man again. Father moved his family in the spring of 1839 and settled near Payson, Adams County, and continued to live in that region till the exodus from Nauvoo.

From *Bones in the Well* (ca. 1850)

4. Vilate Kimball, Letter to Her Husband Heber C. Kimball

At the time of the 1838 Mormon expulsions from Missouri, Joseph Smith (along with several other high-ranking leaders) was arrested and imprisoned for several months. From his cell in Liberty Jail, Clay County, he directed the church's acquisition of holdings in Commerce, Illinois, beautifully situated on a bend of the Mississippi River, but full of swampland. When Smith arrived in the city in May 1839, workmen had not yet drained the miasmic swamps, which harbored malarial mosquitoes that were infecting and sickening large numbers of Latter-day Saints, many of whom had yet to recuperate fully from the rigors of the past autumn's expulsions. Cholera and typhoid were also rampant. In July, Joseph Smith and other church leaders ministered to many prostrate members, in what Latter-day

Saints later called "Day of God's Power." But as summer wore on, illness and destitution continued to take their toll. As usual, Smith chose a time of crisis to launch another initiative—a second mission to overseas soil. Brigham Young, president of the Quorum of the Twelve Apostles, and Heber C. Kimball, next in apostolic seniority, were among the first to depart for England. Young left behind a wife and several sick children, the youngest ten days old. He made it as far as Kimball's home and collapsed for several days. On July 18, still sick and weak, Brigham Young and Heber Kimball heaved themselves into a wagon and headed for New York and their port of departure. The mission of the apostles would be phenomenally successful, yielding thousands of converts. But three days after her husband left, Vilate Kimball penned a simple letter that documented the price paid by the women and children left behind.

My very Dear Husband

With a weak and trembleing hand I attempt to write a few lines, agreable to your request to let you know how we do; which is very poorly I can assure you. As to my feelings I dont know but I am perfectly reconciled to your going. But I must say I have got a trial of my faith as I never had before.

The day you left home, was as sick a one as I ever experianced, the pain in my back and head was almost intolerable. No doubt the pain in my head was worse on the account of my much weeping. But I did not weep any after you left, for my distress was so great I could think of not much els. William moaned and cried about all day, and had a chill in the evening. Sister Bently staid with me through the day. She was sick, but she did all she could for me. Fanny Dort came over and stayed all night with me. I was a lone a little while before she came. I then cralled out of bed, and bowed before the Lord and pled with him to give us a good nights rest and he did so, and be assured I did not forget to pray for you.

The next morning I felt free from pain; [*but I was so light*] headed that I could not walk without staggering. William and Helen was not able to do any thing so I was obliged to crall round and do my chores, and wash a little for the babe; no one to help me but little Heber P. I soon got over done and brought on my chill and fever, so that I had a very sick afternoon, and did not rest but little last night.

To day I have not ben able to do any thing. I was taken early this morning with a shake, and shook about an hour and a half as hard as I ever saw any body in my life, and then weltered under a fever and extream pain until almost night. William has just had the hardest chill that he has had in a number of days. Br Rogors has ben here and left more pills for him, and he has taken them up, but they dont seem to do him any good. He offered to leave some for me, but I told him I would try what virtue there was in bone set first. But it has not done me any good. And what to [do I] dont k[n]ow. I have no one to get any thing for me, or to do any thing for my comfort. Br Bently has moved in here, but sister Ann is very feble hardly able to do her own work. She is very kind and would be glad to doctor us if she was able. Helen is complaining all the time, but is able to do some chores to day.

Now I have given you a statement of our situation, not to make you feel bad, but because you requested it of me. Thus you see I have got a trial of my weak faith as I said before. But all that I can ask of you is to pray that I may have patience to endure to the end whether it be long or short. I feel as though if you ever see your famaly all alive again it will be through your faith.

Saterday morning, dear Heber we are all alive and tolerable comfortable this morning. Would to God we could remain so through the day. We will hope for the best. Mother Bemon stayed with me last night. She said I [must] tell you she had slept with your little Prophet. I must draw to a close for Br George is waiting. Unless my health should improve I shall not be able to write next week as you requested, for im groing weak every day. You had better enquire for a letter at New York, perhaps I shall direct there. So fare you well my dear Heber. I pray that it may be well with you.

> Sister Ann send love to you.
> The children all send love to you.

From *Men with a Mission* (1839)

5. Elizabeth Ann Smith Whitney, "Reminiscence"

Elizabeth Whitney joined the church with the first great waves of converts, members of Sidney Rigdon's Campbellite congregations living in the Kirtland, Ohio, area when Apostle Parley P. Pratt and three missionary companions passed through in 1830. A woman of intellectual gifts and spiritual sensitivities, she later became a prominent leader in the church's organization for women, the Relief Society. Elizabeth Whitney's recollections of being "ordained" by Joseph Smith "to administer to the sick and comfort the sorrowful" recalls a time when women had a greater role in priesthood functions than subsequently became the case. Her record strikingly reveals her husband and herself to be part of Smith's inner circle, privy to teachings like the one on plural marriage well before they were generally promulgated. The privilege of hearing the doctrine soon became the responsibility of living it, and Whitney noted that her husband was one of the first Mormons, after Joseph Smith, to take a plural wife. While most practitioners of "the principle" found the practice difficult and emotionally burdensome, Whitney powerfully defended plural marriage as a potent refiner's fire, and one that revealed the sublimity of woman's "true nature." After the deaths of Joseph and his brother Hyrum Smith, Whitney emigrated to Utah with the majority of the Latter-day Saints, dying there in 1882.

In the Fall of 1838 we left Kirtland, and with what we considered necessary for our immediate wants we commenced our journey to Far West. Our family then consisted of six children, the two youngest being very delicate in health. My eldest son was then fifteen years of age. While we were on our way, a report reached us that the Saints in Missouri were being driven, mobbed and persecuted in a most shocking and terrible manner; we were careful to investigate the matter, in order to ascertain its truth. We went on to St. Louis and waited there until we could obtain the facts in relation to the matter, which we soon learned were most startlingly true. We considered it safest to go over into Illinois to spend the winter, and decided upon Carrollton, Greene Co., Illinois. Here I remained with my children alone, while my husband returned to Kirtland to settle some business and wait further orders from the Prophet Joseph. We were informed the goods we had sent up to Missouri were thrown into the street, and the store burnt to the ground. My eldest son taught school while we remained there, and as the persecution was at that time most extreme, we kept quiet in regard to religion. We were kindly treated, but more particularly by two families who were our near neighbors. In the Spring my husband returned, and shortly after, accompanied by my eldest son, went up to Commerce, since called Nauvoo. At that place they found that the Prophet Joseph and many others of the Saints had settled and commenced to re-organize and sustain each other and the doctrines in which they believed. Joseph then told my husband to return to his family and as quickly as practicable join the Saints there. Meantime a man named Bellows, who had formerly known my husband in Kirtland, recognized us as the Mormon Bishop's family, and determined to have us mobbed and driven from the town; but those two families who had all the time befriended us, offered to render us assistance in getting away, by crossing the river in the night. So in a neighborhood where we had been looked upon with the greatest respect, we were treated like outlaws, and compelled to flee for safety. My husband and son returned in time to cross the river with us; when we reached the opposite bank and felt comparatively safe from our immediate enemies, I shall never forget my husband's taking off his hat, wiping the perspiration from his brow, and thanking God for our deliverance. Strange how trifling incidents like these, sometimes leave indelible impressions upon the memory which can never be effaced. From there we went up the river to Quincy, Illinois, where several families of the Saints who had been driven from Missouri were living; among these was the family of Titus Billings, one of our nearest neighbors in Kirtland; his wife was the first woman baptized in Kirtland, and is still living. We found many other friends and their families. We remained in Quincy during the winter, and passed the time rather pleasantly; my eldest son was fond of music, and so were the Billings' boys, and they used to go out together to play for parties, and thus rendered some assistance in obtaining a living, for we had left our means in Kirtland.

Early in the Spring of 1840 we went up to Commerce, as the upper portion of the City of Nauvoo continued to be called. We rented a house belonging to Hiram Kimball, whose widow and children are residents of this city. Here we were all sick with ague, chills and fever, and were only just barely able to crawl around and wait upon each other. Under these trying circumstances my ninth child was born. Joseph, upon visiting us and seeing our change of circumstances, urged us at once to come and share his accommodations. We felt the climate, the water, and the privations we were enduring could not much longer be borne; therefore we availed ourselves of this proposal and went to live in the Prophet Joseph's yard, in a small cottage; we soon recruited in health, and the children became more like themselves. My husband was employed in a store Joseph had built and fitted up with such goods as the people were in actual need of.

One day while coming out of the house into the yard the remembrance of a prophecy Joseph Smith had made to me, while living in our house in

Kirtland, flashed through my mind like an electric shock; it was this: that even as we had done by him, in opening our doors to him and his family when he was without a home; even so should we in the future be received by him into his house. We afterwards moved up stairs over the brick store, as it was designated. It was during our residence in the brick store that the Relief Society was organized, March 17, 1842, and I was chosen Counselor to the President of the Society, Mrs. Emma Smith. In this work I took the greatest interest, for I realized in some degree its importance, and the need of such an organization. I was also ordained and set apart under the hand of Joseph Smith the Prophet to administer to the sick and comfort the sorrowful. Several other sisters were also ordained and set apart to administer in these holy ordinances. The Relief Society then was small compared to its numbers now, but the Prophet foretold great things concerning the future of this organization, many of which I have lived to see fulfilled; but there are many things which yet remain to be fulfilled in the future of which he prophesied, that are great and glorious; and I rejoice in the contemplation of these things daily, feeling that the promises are sure to be verified in the future as they have been in the past. I trust the sisters who are now laboring in the interest of Relief Societies in Zion realize the importance attached to the work, and comprehend that upon them a great responsibility rests as mothers in Israel. President Joseph Smith had great faith in the sisters' labors, and ever sought to encourage them in the performance of the duties which pertained to these Societies, which he said were not only for benevolent purposes and spiritual improvement, but were actually to save souls. And my testimony to my sisters is that I have seen many demonstrations of the power and blessing of God through the administration of the sisters, but they should be ever humble, for through great humility comes the blessing. The Lord remembers His daughters and owns and acknowledges, in a perceptible manner, those who are striving to be faithful. I could say much to my sisters on this subject, for it is one in which I am deeply interested. I have been a living witness to the trials, sacrifices, patience and endurance of thousands of them, and my heart goes out to all those who are seeking to walk the narrow way and keep fast hold of the iron rod. The Father has great blessings in store for His daughters; fear not, my sisters, but trust in God, live your religion and teach it to your children.

It was during the time we lived at the Brick Store that Joseph received the revelation pertaining to Celestial Marriage; also concerning the ordinances of the House of the Lord. He had been strictly charged by the angel who committed these precious things into his keeping that he should only reveal them to such persons as were pure, full of integrity to the truth, and worthy to be entrusted with divine messages; that to spread them abroad would only be like casting pearls before swine, and that the most profound secrecy must be maintained, until the Lord saw fit to make it known publicly through His servants. Joseph had the most implicit confidence in my husband's uprightness and integrity of character; he knew him capable of keeping a secret, and was not afraid to confide in him, as he had been a Free Mason for many years. He therefore confided to him, and a few others, the principles set forth in that revelation, and also gave him the privilege to read it and to make a copy of it, knowing it would be perfectly safe with him. It was this veritable copy, which was preserved, in the providence of God, that has since been published to the world; for Emma (Joseph's wife) afterwards becoming indignant, burned the original, thinking she had destroyed the only written document upon the subject in existence. My husband revealed these things to me; we had always been united, and had the utmost faith and confidence in each other. We pondered upon them continually, and our prayers were unceasing that the Lord would grant us some special manifestation concerning this new and strange doctrine. The Lord was very merciful to us; He revealed unto us His power and glory. We were seemingly wrapt in a heavenly vision, a halo of light encircled us, and we were convinced in our own minds that God heard and approved our prayers and intercedings before Him. Our hearts were comforted, and our faith made so perfect that we were willing to give our eldest daughter, then only seventeen years of age, to Joseph, in the holy order of plural marriage. She had been raised in the strictest manner as regarded propriety, virtue and chastity; she was as pure in thought, in feeling and in impulse as it was possible for a young girl to be. Yet, laying aside all our traditions and former notions in regard to marriage, we gave her with our mutual consent. She was the first woman ever given in plural marriage by or with the consent of both parents. Of course these things had to be kept an inviolate secret; and as some were false to their vows and pledges, persecution arose, and caused grievous sorrow to those who had obeyed, in all purity and sincerity, the requirements of the celestial order of marriage.

The Lord commanded his servants; they themselves did not comprehend what the ultimate course of action would be, but were waiting further developments from heaven. Meantime the ordinances of the house of the Lord were given, to bless and strengthen us in our future endeavors to promulgate the

principles of divine light and intelligence; but coming in contact with all pre-
conceived notions and principles heretofore taught as the articles of religious
faith, it was not strange that many could not receive it; others doubted, and
only a few remained firm and immovable. Among that number were my husband and myself; yet although my husband believed and was firm in teaching
this Celestial order of Marriage, he was slow in practice. Joseph repeatedly told
him to take a wife, or wives, but he wished to be so extremely cautious not to
do what would probably have to be undone, that in Joseph's day he never took
a wife. When he did so, he did it to fulfill a duty due to the principles of divine
revelation as he understood his duty, and believing sincerely that every man
should prove his faith by his works; but he afterwards took several wives, and
with one or two exceptions, they came into the same house with me, and my
children; therefore, I believe I am safe in saying that I am intimately acquainted
with the practical part of polygamy.

We learn to understand human nature by being brought into close connection with each other, and more especially when under trying and difficult
circumstances; and we seldom think more unkindly of persons from gaining
an insight into their real hearts and character. Instead of my opinion of women
being unfavorable or my feelings unkindly in consequence of being intimately
associated in family relationship with them, I am more favorably disposed to
women as a class, learning more of the true nature of woman-kind than I ever
could without this peculiar experience; and I am willing and ready to defend
enthusiastically those of my sisters who have been genuine enough and who
possessed sufficient sublimity of character, to practically live the principles of
divine faith, which have been revealed in these the last days, in the establishing
of the kingdom of God upon the earth. It has required sterling qualities indeed
to battle with the opposition on every hand, and not be overcome.

That this is God's work and not man's should be apparent to all those who
are acquainted with the history of the saints, their persecutions, their trials,
their difficulties, and the marvelous means of their deliverance,—when dangerous and various untoward circumstances environed them.

My husband built a comfortable dwelling house on Parley Street in Nauvoo,
but still we endured many privations, which in our own home in Ohio would
probably never have fallen to our lot; but we always felt we must be thus tried
to prepare us for future exaltation, and that we might be able to participate
with those whom God had approved and owned, who "came up out of great
tribulation."

Every one acquainted with the history of our people know the terrible results of the apostacy of "Bennett, Foster and the Laws." Joseph Smith had no peace, his life was sought continually by his enemies, and this was the occasion of constant anxiety and trouble to the saints.

The persecutions brought upon our people in Nauvoo and other places adjacent, by the wicked misrepresentations of such men as Dr. Bennett, William and Wilson Law, and others who had been members of our church, increased rapidly. Every now and then Joseph Smith was arraigned before the magistrates on some pretext or other, and the Saints were threatened with mobs, and they felt there was no security for them because of their betrayal by designing and treacherous men.

In January, 1844, my youngest daughter was born. She was the first child born heir to the Holy Priesthood and in the New and Everlasting Covenant in this dispensation. I felt she was doubly a child of promise, not only through the priesthood, but through Joseph's promise to me when I gave him my eldest daughter to wife. He prophesied to me that I should have another daughter, who would be a strength and support to me to soothe my declining years; and in this daughter have these words been verified. My health was very poor, but I remained strong in the faith of the Gospel, and full of courage to persevere in the latter-day work. My two youngest children were frail little tender blossoms and required the most constant care.

During the ensuing summer a fearful and continuous storm of persecution raged, until it led to the massacre of Joseph and Hyrum Smith; and John Taylor, who, although pierced with bullets until his life scarce hung by a single thread, afterwards recovered. After this horrible tragedy, the people sorrowed and mourned for their Patriarch and Prophet. Indeed, the terrible grief and consternation which were the result of the untimely death of these noble men was beyond description.

The Gentiles, our opposers, thought they had destroyed our religion, overthrown our cause, and destroyed the influence of our people, and actually had accomplished all that was necessary to do away with Mormonism.

But God's work cannot be thus ignored; another prophet, Brigham Young, was raised up to succeed Joseph, and the work rolled on. We were not allowed, however, to rest in peace; those who had apostatized from us and were filled with a spirit of rebellion against the work sought by all their power and influence to stir up the authorities of government in the State of Illinois, and to drive us from the bounds of civilization. At this time the people were energetically at work upon the Temple, and President Brigham Young and his brethren of the Quorum of the Twelve, with the Bishops and all the leading men, were pushing everything forward towards completing the Temple, in order to obtain certain blessings and confirmations that had been promised to the Saints when the Temple should be so far finished as to enable them to work in it. The people were most of them poor, and they denied themselves every comfort they possibly could to assist in finishing the Lord's house. In the latter part of the fall of 1845 we commenced work in the Temple, and then I gave myself, my time and attention to that mission. I worked in the Temple every day without cessation until it was closed.

We were making preparations to leave Nauvoo and go into the wilderness. I had a large family, and my household cares and my many other duties were indeed arduous; I worked constantly day and night, scarcely sleeping at all, so great was my anxiety to accomplish all that was necessary and go with the first company who left in February, 1846, crossing the Mississippi River on the ice.

From *In Their Own Words: Women and the Story of Nauvoo* (1878)

6. First Presidency (Joseph Smith, Sidney Rigdon, and Hyrum Smith), "A Proclamation, to the Saints Scattered Abroad"

With the swamps drained and an orderly and growing community of several thousand Latter-day Saints established, Commerce became Nauvoo—"the Beautiful." The redemption of "Zion" in Jackson County, Missouri, would "wait for a little season," the Lord had revealed to Joseph Smith (Doctrine and Covenants 105:9). Meanwhile, the Mormon principle of the gathering was undiminished— merely transferred to the banks of the Mississippi. From the three thousand stated in this 1841 proclamation, the population, aided largely by the immigration of British converts, soared over the next few years to more than ten thousand, rivaling Chicago to the north. The jewel of the city would be the new temple, an imposing stone structure more than a hundred feet tall that dominated the horizon for miles. In Nauvoo, the Latter-day Saints would enjoy their longest golden age to date, in large part because of the privileges granted in their city charter. As Joseph Smith indicates, the Illinois legislature gave Nauvoo the right to its own militia, the "Nauvoo Legion," its own university, and most significant if ambiguous, a high degree of judicial autonomy. In the space of less than a decade, Nauvoo would become the largest city ever founded as a place of religious refuge from other Americans, and then the largest city to be forcibly depopulated at the hands of fellow citizens. The same charter-vested autonomy and powers that facilitated their peace and independence also sowed fatal seeds of suspicion and resentment. Control over the local courts and a showy military legion thousands strong exacerbated fears that Smith was creating a dangerous theocracy that countenanced both illegality and immorality.

The name of our city (Nauvoo) is of Hebrew origin, and signifies a beautiful situation, or place, carrying with it, also, the idea of rest; and is truly descriptive of the most delightful location. It is situated on the east bank of the Mississippi river, at the head of the Des Moines Rapids, in Hancock county, bounded on the east by an extensive prairie of surpassing beauty, and on the north, west, and south, by the Mississippi. This place has been objected to by some on account of the sickness which has prevailed in the summer months, but it is the opinion of Doctor Bennett, that Hancock county, and all the eastern and southern portions of the City of Nauvoo, are as healthful as any other portions of the western country, to acclimatized citizens; whilst the northwestern portion of the city has experienced much affliction from fever and ague, which, however, Doctor Bennett thinks can be easily remedied by draining the sloughs on the adjacent islands in the Mississippi.

The population of our city is increasing with unparalleled rapidity, numbering more than 3,000 inhabitants. Every facility is afforded, in the city and adjacent country, in Hancock county, for the successful prosecution of the mechanical arts and the pleasing pursuits of agriculture. The waters of the Mississippi can be successfully used for manufacturing purposes to almost an unlimited extent.

Having been instrumental, in the hands of our heavenly Father, in laying a foundation for the gathering of Zion, we would say, let all those who appreciate the blessings of the Gospel, and realize the importance of obeying the commandments of heaven, who have been blessed of heaven with the possession of this world's goods, first prepare for the general gathering; let them dispose of their effects as fast as circumstances will possibly admit, without making too great sacrifices, and remove to our city and county; establish and build up manufactures in the city, purchase and cultivate farms in the county. This will secure our permanent inheritance, and prepare the way for the gathering of the poor. This is agreeable to the order of heaven, and the only principle on which the gathering can be effected. Let the rich, then, and all who can assist in establishing this place, make every preparation to come on without delay, and strengthen our hands, and assist in promoting the happiness of the Saints. This cannot be too forcibly impressed on the minds of all, and the Elders are hereby instructed to proclaim this word in all places where the Saints reside, in their public administrations, for this is according to the instructions we have received from the Lord.

The Temple of the Lord is in process of erection here, where the Saints will come to worship the God of their fathers, according to the order of His house and the powers of the Holy Priesthood, and will be so constructed as to enable all the functions of the Priesthood to be duly exercised, and where instructions from the Most High will be received, and from this place go forth to distant lands. Let us then concentrate all our powers, under the provisions of our magna charta granted by the Illinois legislature, at the "City of Nauvoo" and surrounding country, and strive to emulate the action of the ancient covenant fathers and patriarchs, in those things which are of such vast importance to this and every succeeding generation.

The "Nauvoo Legion" embraces all our military power, and will enable us to perform our military duty by ourselves, and thus afford us the power and privilege of avoiding one of the most fruitful sources of strife, oppression, and collision with the world. It will enable us to show our attachment to the state and nation, as a people, whenever the public service requires our aid, thus proving ourselves obedient to the paramount laws of the land, and ready at all times to sustain and execute them.

The "University of the City of Nauvoo" will enable us to teach our children wisdom, to instruct them in all the knowledge and learning, in the arts, sciences, and learned professions. We hope to make this institution one of the great lights of the world, and by and through it to diffuse that kind of knowledge which will be of practicable utility, and for the public good, and also for private and individual happiness. The Regents of the University will take the general supervision of all matters appertaining to education, from common schools up to the highest branches of a most liberal collegiate course. They will establish a regular system of education, and hand over the pupil from teacher to professor, until the regular gradation is consummated and the education finished.

This corporation contains all the powers and prerogatives of any other college or university in this state. The charters for the University and Legion are addenda to the city charter, making the whole perfect and complete. . . .

From the kind, uniform, and consistent course pursued by the citizens of Illinois, and the great success which has attended us while here, the natural advantages of this place for every purpose we require, and the necessity of the gathering of the Saints of the Most High, we would say—let the brethren who love the prosperity of Zion, who are anxious that her stakes should be strengthened and her cords lengthened, and who prefer her prosperity to their chief joy, come and cast in their lots with us, and cheerfully engage in a work so glorious and sublime, and say with Nehemiah, "We, His servants, will arise and build." It probably would hardly be necessary to enforce this important subject on the attention of the Saints, as its necessity is obvious, and is a subject of paramount importance; but as watchmen to the house of Israel—as shepherds over the flock which is now scattered over a vast extent of country, and the anxiety we feel for their prosperity and everlasting welfare, and for the carrying out the great and glorious purposes of our God, to which we have been called, we feel to urge its necessity, and say—Let the Saints come here; this is the word of the Lord, and in accordance with the great work of the last days. It is true, the idea of a general gathering has heretofore been associated with the most cruel and oppressing scenes, owing to our unrelenting persecutions at the hands of wicked and unjust men; but we hope that those days of darkness and gloom have gone by, and, from the liberal policy of our state government, we may expect a scene of peace and prosperity we have never before witnessed since the rise of our Church, and the happiness and prosperity which now await us, is, in all human probability, incalculably great. By a concentration of action, and a unity of effort, we can only accomplish the great work of the last days which we could not do in our remote and scattered condition, while our interests, both temporal and spiritual, will be greatly enhanced, and the blessings of heaven must flow unto us in an uninterrupted stream; of this, we think there can be no question.

The greatest temporal and spiritual blessings which always flow from faithfulness and concerted effort, never attended individual exertion or enterprise. The history of all past ages abundantly attests this fact. In addition to all temporal blessings, there is no other way for the Saints to be saved in these last days, as the concurrent testimony of all the holy Prophets clearly proves, for it is written—"They shall come from the east, and be gathered from the west; the north shall give up, and the south shall keep not back." "The sons of God shall be gathered from far, and His daughters from the ends of the earth."

It is also the concurrent testimony of all the Prophets, that this gathering together of all the Saints, must take place before the Lord comes to "take vengeance upon the ungodly," and "to be glorified and admired by all those who obey the Gospel." The fiftieth Psalm, from the first to the fifth verse inclusive, describes the glory and majesty of that event.

"The mighty God, and even the Lord hath spoken, and called the earth from the rising of the sun unto the going down thereof. Out of Zion, the perfection of beauty, God hath shined. Our God shall come, and shall not keep silence; a fire shall devour before Him, and it shall be very tempestuous round about Him. He shall call to the heavens from above, and to the earth (that He may judge the people). Gather my Saints together unto me; those that have made covenant with me by sacrifice."

We might offer many other quotations from the Scriptures, but believing them to be familiar to the Saints, we forbear.

We would wish the Saints to understand that, when they come here, they must not expect perfection, or that all will be harmony, peace, and love; if they indulge these ideas, they will undoubtedly be deceived, for here there are persons, not only from different states, but from different nations, who, although they feel a great attachment to the cause of truth, have their prejudices of education, and consequently, it requires some time before these things can be overcome. Again, there are many that creep in unawares, and endeavor to sow discord, strife, and animosity in our midst, and by so doing, bring evil upon the Saints. These things we have to bear with, and these things will prevail either to a greater or less extent until "the floor be thoroughly purged," and "the chaff be burnt up." Therefore, let those who come up to this place be determined to keep the commandments of God, and not be discouraged by those things we have enumerated, and then they will be prospered—the intelligence of heaven will be communicated to them, and they will, eventually, see eye to eye, and rejoice in the full fruition of that glory which is reserved for the righteous.

In order to erect the Temple of the Lord, great exertions will be required on the part of the Saints, so that they may build a house which shall be accepted by the Almighty, and in which His power and glory shall be manifested. Therefore let those who can freely make a sacrifice of their time, their talents, and their prosperity, for the prosperity of the kingdom, and for the love they have to the cause of truth, bid adieu to their homes and pleasant places of abode, and unite with us in the great work of the last days, and share in the tribulation, that they may ultimately share in the glory and triumph.

We wish it likewise to be distinctly understood, that we claim no privilege but what we feel cheerfully disposed to share with our fellow citizens of every denomination, and every sentiment of religion; and therefore say, that so far from being restricted to our own faith, let all those who desire to locate themselves in this place, or the vicinity, come, and we will hail them as citizens and friends, and shall feel it not only a duty, but a privilege, to reciprocate the kindness we have received from the benevolent and kind-hearted citizens of the state of Illinois.

From *Times and Seasons* (1841)

7. Eliza R. Snow, "The Female Relief Society"

Women participated richly in the life of the early church, fulfilling spiritual as well as domestic functions. Many women recorded visions and dreams, on occasion both spoke and sang in tongues, and exercised the gift of healing. As the temple rose on the Nauvoo skyline in 1842, some women decided to participate actively in this most tangible emblem of Zion-building and gathering. Sarah Granger Kimball and others organized a "Ladies' Society of Nauvoo" to coordinate efforts to clothe the temple workmen better. Eliza R. Snow wrote a constitution, which they presented to Joseph Smith for approval. Their efforts were the catalyst to his recognition that "the Church was never perfectly organized until the women" were organized, but he believed it needed to be done "under the priesthood after the pattern of the priesthood."[3] Accordingly, on March 17, 1842, Smith met with some twenty women to coordinate the formation of the Female Relief Society of Nauvoo. A month later, Joseph Smith proclaimed to them that he was turning "the key to you in the name of God and this Society shall rejoice and knowledge and intelligence shall flow down from this time."[4] The organization rapidly grew to over a thousand and soon extended its ministry to include the assessment of needs and the distribution of resources within local congregations (or wards). The society met for exactly two years before dissolving in the maelstrom of events leading up to Smith's martyrdom and the church's fragmentation and exodus. President Brigham Young waited until 1866 before reorganizing the Relief Society under the direction of Eliza R. Snow and under the old pattern. In subsequent decades, the society achieved substantial autonomy, running a silk industry, coordinating extensive grain storage, and sponsoring the training of Mormon women in eastern medical schools; they also published their own magazine from 1915 to 1970. Today, though with less autonomy, the society continues as a potent force for good, with some six million members in more than 170 countries.

According to authentic testimony, an organization, of which the present Female Relief Society is a facsimile, has always existed when the Church of Jesus Christ has been fully organized. "Elect lady," as it occurs in the New Testament, has direct reference to the same—alluding to one who presided over this Institution. See 2d Epistle of John, 1st verse.

The first organization of this Society, in the present dispensation, was effected on the 17th of March, 1842, by Joseph Smith, President of the Church of Jesus Christ of Latter-day Saints, assisted by other prominent Elders. His apology for deferring the organization till that period, was the great pressure of duties, labors and responsibilities, which devolved upon him. By his suggestion a meeting was appointed in the Masonic Hall, and a limited number invited.

Perhaps a few extracts from the "Minutes of the Organization," would be interesting,—they being too lengthy for insertion in full:

NAUVOO LODGE ROOM
MARCH 17, 1842

Elder John Taylor was called to the chair, and Elder Willard Richards appointed secretary.

Meeting commenced by singing "The spirit of God like a fire is burning," etc. Prayer by Elder Taylor.

When it was moved by Pres. Smith, and seconded by Mrs. Cleveland, that a vote be taken to know if all are satisfied with each female present, and are willing to acknowledge them in full fellowship and admit them to the privileges of the Institution about to be formed. Vote unanimous.

Prest. Smith addressed the meeting to illustrate the objects of the Society; that the Society of sisters might provoke the brethren to good works, in looking to the wants of the poor, searching after objects of charity, etc., to assist, by correcting the morals and strengthening the virtues of the female community, and save the Elders the trouble of rebuking, etc. He proposed that the sisters elect a presiding officer to preside over them, and let that presiding officer choose two counselors; that he would ordain them, and let them preside over the Society, just as the Presidency preside over the Church; and if they need his instruction—ask him—he will give it from time to time.

Let this Presidency serve as a Constitution. If any officers are wanted to carry out the designs of the Institution, let them be appointed and set apart, as Deacons, Teachers, &c., are among us.

The minutes of your meetings will be precedents for you to act upon.

He then suggested the propriety of electing a Presidency to continue in office during good behavior, or so long as they shall fill the office with dignity, &c.

Motioned by Mrs. Whitney, and seconded by Mrs. Packard, that Mrs. Emma Smith be chosen President; passed unanimously.

On suggestion of Prest. Smith, the Presidentess Elect made choice of Mrs. Sarah M. Cleveland and Mrs. Elizabeth Ann Whitney for Counselors.

After which the ceremony of ordination was performed: "When Prest. Smith resumed his remarks, giving instruction how to govern themselves in their meetings, what order to observe, how to regulate discussions, &c., &c., and concluded by saying, "Do not injure the character of any one; if members of the Society shall conduct improperly, deal with them, and keep all your doings within your own bosoms, and hold all characters sacred."

It was them proposed that Elder Taylor vacate the chair. Prest. Emma Smith and her counselors took the chair; and

Elder Taylor moved, seconded by Prest. J. Smith, that we go into an investigation respecting what this Society shall be called; which was carried unanimously.

∙ [*The discussion, which was lengthy and interesting, is wholly omitted.*]

By unanimous vote, Miss Eliza R. Snow was appointed Secretary, and

Miss Phebe M. Wheeler Assistant Secretary, and

Miss Elvira A. Coles, (the late Mrs. Holmes) Treasurer.

Prest. J. Smith said, "I now declare this Society organized with President and Counselors, &c., according to Parliamentary usages, and all who shall hereafter be admitted into this Society must be free from censure, and received by vote."

Elder Taylor addressed the meeting by saying that he is much gratified in seeing a meeting of this kind in Nauvoo; his heart rejoices when he sees the most distinguished characters stepping forth in a cause which is calculated to bring into exercise every virtue, and give scope to the benevolent feelings of the female heart; he rejoices to see this Institution organized according to the law of Heaven;

his prayer is, that the blessings of God and the peace of Heaven may rest on this Institution, henceforth.

After singing "Come let us rejoice," &c., the meeting adjourned for one week. Dismissed by prayer.

Before retiring, each gentleman present gave a liberal donation to commence the funds of the Institution.

The following lines were found written on a scrap and lying on an open Bible in the room where, and at the time when, the Society was organized; which have been carefully preserved and transcribed as an appropriate frontispiece to the F. R. S. Book of Records.

"*O Lord, help our widows and fatherless children! So mote it be. Amen. With the SWORD and the WORD of TRUTH, defend Thou them. So mote it be. Amen.*"

When organized, the Society consisted of nineteen members, exclusive of its officers. This number augmented from time to time, until at the close of the fiscal year it amounted to 1158. The meetings were so large that the largest hall in the city was densely crowded and it became necessary to adjourn to the Grove, the usual place in the Summer for holding Sabbath meeting, which was provided with a suitable stand and a supply of seats for large assemblies.

The Society soon became so popular that even those of doubtful character in several instances applied for admission, and to prevent imposition by extending membership to such ones inadvertently, stricter rules were adopted than seemed requisite at first. Each one wishing to join the Society was required to present a certificate of her good moral character, signed by two or more responsible persons.

The meetings were opened and closed by singing and prayer, and systematic order was observed throughout. In each meeting reports were given by those whose duty it was to visit from house to house and inquire into the circumstances of the sick and destitute—donations were received and those subjects discussed which appertain to woman's duties, influence, responsibilities, etc., etc.—whatever has a tendency to benefit and elevate society at home and abroad.

Frequently President Joseph Smith, Bishop N. K. Whitney and brethren of the Twelve met with the sisters, and through the inspiration of the Spirit of God, imparted rich counsel and intelligence; instructing, not only in duties concerning the poor, but also in all the relations of life, as wives, mothers, daughters, sisters, and, as saints of the Most High, our duties to one another and our responsibilities as examples to the world, etc.

The first winter after the Society was organized, was exceedingly cold and severe. Many, in consequence of exposure and hardship in their expulsion from the State of Missouri, and the unhealthiness of the climate of Nauvoo, had been reduced by sickness to destitution, and had it not been for the timely aid of the F. R. Society would have suffered very much, and probably some would have perished.

About the last of July, 1842, when some of the officials of Missouri were taking measures to drag President Joseph Smith from Illinois by an illegal process, the F. R. Society sent a petition to Thomas Carlin, Governor of Illinois, in behalf of Pres. Smith, claiming his protection as chief magistrate. The petition was signed by every member of the Society, and presented by its President, Mrs. Emma Smith, accompanied by Mrs. Amanda Smith and Miss E. R. Snow. The Governor's residence was in Quincy, fifty miles south from Nauvoo.

The following is transcribed from my journal, written after my return: "The Governor received us with as much cordiality and politeness as His Excellency was master of, assuring us of his protection by saying that the laws and Constitution of our country shall be his polar star in case of any difficulty. He manifested much friendship, and it remains for time and circumstance to prove the sincerity of his professions."

We subsequently ascertained that at the very time that the ladies of Nauvoo were visiting him, presenting the petition and listening to his protestations of friendship and love for legal right and justice, his emissaries were engaged in secret plotting in his behalf, against the rights and safety of Pres. Smith, and aiding the unprincipled bloodhounds of Missouri. But whatever the result, the F. R. Society had made a noble effort, and it was compensated by knowing that the great, good man, Joseph Smith, appreciated it.

The city of Nauvoo was divided into four wards, and after the Society became too numerous to convene in one assembly, it was decided to meet alternately in the different wards from week to week so as to give equal opportunities to all.

Pres. Joseph Smith donated a city lot to the Society for the purpose of making homes for the homeless, and also to furnish work to those who were able to work and were out of employment, which he proposed deeding to the Treasurer and her successors in office, for the use of the Society. He also donated the frame of a house, and made arrangements for it to be moved on the aforesaid lot, for a commencement of the establishment. But this benevolent and judi-cious project, with many others which were designed for the amelioration of the condition of suffering humanity, was blasted in the bud by the blighting hand of religious persecution, and through which the once beautiful city of Nauvoo became a desolation, and its inhabitants exiled to Mexico.

God, who makes the wrath of man praise Him, has overruled, as He ever does in all things, for the good of them who put their trust in Him. In having been driven from a city, we have become a Territory—should have been a State—and here, the Female Relief Society, more amply developed than in Nauvoo, has extended its branches to every ward, and settlement from Bear lake in the North to Santa Clara in the South, and yet, as seen in prospective, it has but little more than emerged from its embryo state in comparison to its great future.

From *Woman's Exponent* (1872)

8. William Clayton, "All Is Well"

"Come, Come, Ye Saints" is the anthem of the Mormon exodus, a poignant ballad of subdued triumph. Camped on the Iowa plains, between flight from Nauvoo, Illinois, and refuge in the West, English convert William Clayton received word that a wife still living in Nauvoo had given birth to a healthy son. In celebration, Clayton com-posed this hymn, borrowing an old tune, but using words that more than any other lyrics capture the essence of pioneer perseverance in the face of trial. Several features contribute to the enduring popularity of the hymn, while some other period pieces have not worn as well. The hymn is void of rancor or militarism or defiance in the face of persecution; rather the words invoke a joyful embrace of the lot that has befallen the Latter-day Saints and enjoin courage in the face of a pilgrimage that is both spiritual metaphor and all too real ordeal. It holds out the promise of a refuge in Zion, which again reverberates with both timeless appeal and a moment of real historical sanctuary. The knowledge that thousands of Latter-day Saints lie buried along the trail and at journey's end makes the hymn, for Mormons, a reverential paean to the faithful dead. The hymn appeared in the Mormon hymnal published in 1851 and is near enough to canonical status to ensure immortality in the Mormon tradition. At one time it was even published in two public school music series and called one of the ten best American hymns.[5]

Come, come, ye Saints, no toil nor labor fear;
But with joy wend your way.
Though hard to you this journey may appear,
Grace shall be as your day.
'Tis better far for us to strive
Our useless cares from us to drive;
Do this, and joy your hearts will swell—
All is well! all is well!

Why should we mourn or think our lot is hard?
'Tis not so; all is right.
Why should we think to earn a great reward,
If we now shun the fight?
Gird up your loins; fresh courage take;
Our God will never us forsake;
And soon we'll have this tale to tell—
All is well! all is well!

We'll find the place which God for us prepared,
Far away in the West,
Where none shall come to hurt or make afraid;
There the Saints will be blessed.
We'll make the air with music ring,
Shout praises to our God and King;
Above the rest these words we'll tell—
All is well! all is well!

And should we die before our journey's through,
Happy day! all is well!
We then are free from toil and sorrow, too;
With the just we shall dwell!

But if our lives are spared again
To see the Saints their rest obtain,
O how we'll make this chorus swell—
All is well! all is well!

From *Hymns of The Church of Jesus Christ of Latter-day Saints* (1846)

9. Brigham Young, "A Revelation Given Dated Winter Quarters Camp of Israel [Doctrine and Covenants 136]"

After the murder of Joseph Smith in a Carthage, Illinois, jail cell in June 1844, the Quorum of the Twelve Apostles was sustained by the majority of Latter-day Saints to lead the church. As president of the Twelve, Brigham Young became the chief executive, though he would not assume Smith's title of president of the church for another three years. In the ensuing months, the first priority of Young and the Mormons was the completion of the Nauvoo Temple, at which they labored unceasingly even as they prepared for a western exodus. Negotiations with Illinoisans had resulted in a spring 1846 deadline for the Mormon departure, but mob harassment and fears of federal interference with their plans led Brigham Young to lead the early groups across the Mississippi in February. Torrential rains, inexperience, and inadequate preparation made the trek across the 265 miles of Iowa lowlands the slowest and most wretched phase of the whole migration. Young set up camp at Council Bluffs, Iowa, in June. Over the summer, Brigham Young led most of the 2,500–3,000 refugees across the Missouri River, where they established a permanent staging base at Winter Quarters. They built several hundred cabins and sod houses, as well as a grist mill and waited out the winter. In January, Young dictated a revelation that established the principles of organization by which the emigration would proceed in the spring. Before the coming of the transcontinental railroad 22 years later, some 70,000 Saints had participated in the largest and most orderly migration of American citizens in history.

The word and will of the Lord concerning the camp of Israel In their journeyings to the west.

Let all the people of the Church of Jesus Christ of Latter day Saints, and those who journey with them, be organized into Companies with a covenant and promise to keep all the commandments and Statutes of the Lord our God: Let the companies be organized with Captains of Hundreds, Captains of Fifties, and captains of Tens with A President & his two councillors at their head, under the direction of the Twelve Apostles. And this shall be our Covenant that we will walk in all the ordinances of the Lord.

Let each Company provide themselves with all the Teams, waggons provisions, Clothing, and other necessaries for the journey that they can. When the companies are organized let them go to with their might to prepare for those who are to tarry.

Let each Company with their Captains, And Presidents, decide how many Can go next spring; then Choose out a sufficient number of able bodied and expert men, to take teams, Seeds, and Farming utensils, to go as Pioneers, to prepare for puting in spring crops.

Let each company bear an equal proportion, according to the dividend of their property, in taking the poor, the widows, the Fatherless, and the families of those who have gone into the Armey, that the Cries of the widow and the Fatherless come not up into the ears of the Lord against this people.

Let each company prepare houses, and fields for raising grain, for those who are to remain behind this season. And this is the will of the Lord concerning his people; Let every man use all his influence and property &c to remove this people to the place whare the Lord shall locate a stake of Zion; And if ye do this with a pure heart in all faithfulness, ye shall be blessed. You shall be blessed in your flocks, and in your herds, and in your fields, and in your houses, and in your families.

Let my servents Ezra T. Benson and Erastus Snow organize a Company, and let my servants Orson Pratt and Wilford Woodruff organize A Company: Also let my Servants Amasa Lyman and George A. Smith organize a company and Appoint Presidents and Captains of hundreds and of fifties and of tens; And let my servants that have been Appointed go and teach this my will to the Saints that they may be ready to go to a land of peace.

Go thy way and do as I have told you; and fear not thine enemies for they shall not have power to stop my work. Zion shall be redeemed in mine own due time, and if any man shall seek to build up himself and seeketh not my council he shall have no power, and his folley shall be made manifest. Seek ye and keep all your pledges one with another and covet not that which is thy brothers.

Keep yourselves from evil to take not the name of thy God in vane, for I am the Lord your God even the God of your Fathers, the God of Abraham and of Isaac and of Jacob. I am he who led the children of Israel out of the Land of Egypt and my arm is streched out in the last days to save my people Israel.

Cease to contend one with another. Cease to speak evil one of another. Cease drunkenness, and let your words tend to edefying one another. If thou borrowest of they neighbor, thou shalt restore that which thou hast borrowed. And if thou Canst not repay, then go straitway, and tell thy neighbor lest he condemn thee.

If thou shalt find that which thy neighbor has lost, thou shalt make diligent search, till thou shall deliver it to him again. Thou shall be diligent in preserving what thou hast, that thou mayest be a wise steward; for it is the free gift of the Lord thy God, and thou art his steward.

If thou art merry, praise the Lord with singing, with music, with dancing and with a prayer of praise and thanksgiving. If thou art sorrowful call on the Lord thy God with supplication, that your souls may be Joyful.

Fear not thine enemies for they are in mine hands and I will do my pleasure with them. My people must be tried in all things, that they may be prepared to recieve the glory that I have for them, even the glory of Zion. And he that will not bear Chastizment, is not worthy of my Kingdom.

Let him that is ignorant learn wisdom by humbling himself, and Calling upon the Lord his God, that his eyes may be opened that he may see, and his ears opened that He may hear, for my spirit is sent forth into the world to enlighten the humble And Contrite, and to the condemnation of the ungodly.

Thy brethren have rejected you and your testimony, even the Nation that has driven you out; and now Cometh the day of their Calamity, even the days of sorrow like a woman that is taken in travel; and their sorrow shall be great, unless they spedily repent! /Yea very spedily./

For they killed the prophets, and they that were sent unto them. And they have shed innocent Blood, which crieth from the ground against them.

Therefore marvel not at these things, for ye are not yet pure: thou canst not yet bear my glory, But thou shalt behold it, if ye are faithful in keeping all my words that I have given you from the days of Adam to Abraham; from Abraham to Moses, from Moses to Jesus and the Apostles and from Jesus and his Apostles to Joseph Smith, whom I did Call upon by mine Angels, my ministering servents and by mine own voice out of the Heavens, to bring forth my work, which foundation he did lay, and was faithful and I took him to myself.

Many have marvelled because of his death, but it was needful that He should seal his testimony with his blood, that he might be honored and the wicked might be condemned.

Have I not deliverd you from your enemies, ownly in that I have left a witness of my name? Now, therefore, harken O ye people of my church; and ye Elders, listen together. You have recieved my kingdom. Be diligent in keeping all my Commandments, lest judgment come upon you, and your faith fail you, and your enemies triumph over you. So no more at present. Amen and Amen.

From *Wilford Woodruff's Journal* (1847)

10. William Atkin, "Handcart Experience"

The first waves of Mormon pioneers traveled principally by covered wagon, but the cost of a wagon and the oxen to pull it was prohibitive for the thousands of pioneers arriving in America from the British Isles and Europe. Initially, a Perpetual Emigrating Fund provided no-interest loans to assist the poor, but funds were so depleted by 1855 that the pragmatic Brigham Young proposed a novel solution: immigrants to Utah would pull or push wooden, single-axle carts of simple and cheap construction. Essentially a three-foot by four-foot box, they sported large, five-foot-diameter wheels and seven-foot pulling shafts ending with a three-foot crossbar. They were light but sturdy and could hold hundreds of pounds. The first three handcart companies departed Iowa City in summer 1856 and arrived successfully in Utah less than four months later. Two later companies totaling nearly a thousand Saints left too late in the season, using carts that were poorly constructed of green wood. Blizzards and depleted supplies brought upon the companies horrific suffering, and more than two hundred perished. A heroic rescue effort launched from Salt Lake City prevented the costliest tragedy in the history of the Mormon migration from total catastrophe. Even with improvements in design and planning, handcarts had little future. Uncertainty surrounding the 1857–1858 "Utah War" brought a temporary halt to Mormon immigration; by 1860, Mormons were using a more efficient system of wagon trains. Like most handcart pioneers, William Atkin was a British convert who made the first leg of his journey by sailing to an American port—in his case New York City—before making his way to the handcart staging grounds in the Midwest.

The latter end of May, 1859, we were in Florence, a place situated on the banks of the Missouri River, in connection with a number of Latter-day Saints preparing to cross the plains with the Hand Cart company. We often sang the Hand Cart song.

A young man by the name of Frank Pitman took great pleasure in singing that song. We would sit around our camp fire, and he would sing it for any one who would ask him to, and it being new to most people, he was asked to sing it quite often.

We were finally provided with our carts and on a lovely afternoon in June we started out with our little all in our carts and traveled out four miles where we were to stop one day to be organized for our journey over the plains. In leaving Florence we had a little steep hill to pull up and this gave us a little insight to what we might expect when we came to the mountains. We arrived in camp and even four miles had its effect on one of our company, as quite a number were from the English Factories and knew nothing of the hardships they were now starting out to undergo. When we arrived I asked our little Frank, as he was by far the smallest man in the company, to sing the Hand Cart song, which he did, and quite a number joined in the chorus. We stayed one day and was organized, with George Rowley as our captain. We had one wagon and two yoke of oxen for the use of the Captain's family, five wagons and ten yoke of cattle to hall part of our provisions, as also to accommodate those who might be sick and some freight, 60 carts, 235 souls, about 75 of them were men, the others women and children.

On the 10th of June, 1859, having rested one day we made a regular start for the plains and traveled 16 miles, and the most of us were tired when we camped at night, and some were already getting foot-sore. Again we asked our little brother Frank to sing the Hand Cart song, but he very reluctantly complied, and I think this was the last time he ever sang it, and there were less who joined in the chorus than before.

The next day we made about 22 miles, and a good many of our feet were sore and a number had their feet blistered, and we were all tired, indeed.

One brother more hardy than many others, asked our little Frank to again sing the Hand Cart song, and methinks I now see him stamp his little feet and wring his hands and yell at the top of his voice, saying "I will never sing it again," and I think he kept his word.

We traveled on and came to large streams of water as the snows were melting very fast, in the distance hills, and we had to wade and carry our children, and some of us, also carried our wives across the streams, and pull our carts through; and thus we traveled on, four or five days, till our captain believed we were in a country where there were plenty of buffalo, so we camped for a day in order to hunt for buffalo. There was a grove of timber along a stream, not far off, and our hunters started out. Their outfit consisted of six shotguns and a few pistols, and we traveled on shanks ponies, but of this, I need not say much, only, when I saw parties from other camps who were well provided with rifles, ammunition, and good horses, I could but laugh at our folly in attempting to hunt buffalo on foot and with such an out fit as that which we had, but we had the best we could procure, under circumstances, and it was all we had to either hunt with or protect ourselves from the red men of the plains, who, in those days, were not very pleasant companions. . . .

This was in a prairie country where you could see as far as the eye could discern, and we could see great numbers of buffaloes feeding. Some of the Indians mounted their horses and killed a buffalo and brought the meat to our camp and traded it to our people, in small pieces, for sugar, coffee, tobacco and other things.

At night we put on a double guard and longed for morning to dawn, as we were filled with fear.

It was a dark night and we dare not make fires for fear it would give the Indians a good opportunity to see us, so we remained in the dark and drew our carts closer together then at other times. Some went to bed and when all was perfectly still, we were startled by one of the most unearthly noises we had ever heard, not far from our camp. It was the Indians.

It was the Indians, some of whom had made their way to our camp without our hearing a sound of any kind, and yet we had been listening and watching very carefully. Two of them had on buckskin suits that were covered with bells and it was curious how they came in without being noticed. They sang, jumped, and made night hideous indeed to us, and in the mischief they knocked down one of our tents while it was full of people, which made them scream and yell, and it was a time with us long to be remembered, for we thought they were having one of their war dances which we had heard of and supposed it would not be long before we would be doomed to die, as they could see our situation and had proposed to take advantage of it. It was, indeed, a pleasure to us to see day light the next morning. We hastened on our journey as soon as daylight did arrive, hoping to be free from them, but lo, our trouble was not at an end, for we had not gone over a mile or two, when a number of the natives came just as fast as they could ride, with their long hair floating in the air behind them, and shouting like demons, and they rode up beside our carts and threw their lassoes to us and showed us that they wanted us to tie them onto the carts, and where there were young women at the carts they seemed determined to tie their ropes to the carts; and thus they followed us and tormented us for hours, and thus our first Indian experience was a terror to us in very deed; and we in our very souls desired that that band of Indians would be the last we would be troubled with. For awhile they had their own fun.

We were now between two and three hundred miles on our journey and our very hard work gave us keen appetites and we had used up a good deal more of our provisions than the distance we had traveled justified, and although our provisions were rationed out to us, yet we had our minds set that we would make the journey in much less time than we had provisions for, as we had 70 pounds of flour for each person, which was one pound a day for ten weeks. When we would receive four days rations, some would eat it in two days and then plead for more, and we all know that no man with a soul in him could deny them, so they would get a little more, and in all this we had a little merriment. We had with us some young men who had worked on farms in England and were large overgrown fellows with keen appetites, who would eat the most of their flour as a rule in half the time, and then they would say they would make starch to stick their ribs together, but this soon ended, as it became too serious to be fun any longer, for we all had to make our rations hold out its time, and thus we began to suffer, but the time we were between three and four hundred miles on our journey and we could not hunt as every one had to pull his cart, and we had four persons to a cart, and myself and wife, two small children, one only three months old, and the other under two years of age, when we started on the plains, thus we had only two of us to pull our cart, and we had a very hard time to pull it and our two children, but the Lord blessed us thus far remarkably, and now when our provisions were very short as we were traveling along I saw a sheep some distance from the road.

Although it looked unreasonable in me to expect to catch a sheep on the prairie, yet I started out, and at the same time I offered up a fervent prayer to my Heavenly Father and asked Him to assist me, and the Lord really heard my prayer, and the consequence was, it was not long before I was back to my cart, having the sheep with me, and it proved to be a very fair mutton. Thus the Lord heard and answered my prayer and gave us the meat we so much needed, and I gave thanks to Him for this great blessing to us in this time of need. As our provisions were not of the kind to give us proper strength to perform our arduous labor, many of us became very weak and the consequence was that some would get behind, but at evening the willing ones would go and assist them to camp. We were more or less scattered, on this account, and some would be away from camp all night. The Lord blessed me with good health, but my wife's health about this time, began to fail, she having a nursing babe, under three months old when we started. As my wife and I were all we had to pull our cart, her failing health made it exceedingly hard for us indeed. This is the year that the Pikes Peak Mines were discovered, at what is now known as the city of Denver in Colorado, and a great many adventurers were rushing for the mines. A company of them passed us at this time, being well provided with horses and rifles to hunt with. They were ahead of us and they killed a very large buffalo. They took one quarter of it and covered up the three quarters carefully with the hide, and put up a notice that read "This is for the hand-carts." We found it in very good condition and it was divided out, giving us from one to two pounds each. Although we were in the midst of buffalo, this was the only good mess of fresh meat of this kind that we had obtained for, as I have before stated, we had neither horses nor other means to obtain it.

From *Union* (1896)

11. Valborg Henrietta Louise Rasmussen, "My Conversion to Mormonism"

In 1849, King Frederik VII of Denmark signed a new constitution that guaranteed freedom of religion to Danish citizens. Less than a year later, Mormon missionaries arrived in Copenhagen, where they met with immediate success. In 1857, one group of converts sailed from that city via Britain to Philadelphia, and went on to constitute a company of handcart pioneers that arrived in Utah that fall. The high point of emigration, however, was in the years 1861–1891. Though missionaries also met with success in Norway and Sweden, most of their Scandinavian converts hailed from Denmark; enough Scandinavian immigrants came to Utah over the next decades that one survey concluded that 45 percent of church membership was at least of partial Scandinavian descent.[6] By the late nineteenth century, the LDS principle of "gathering" was still in full force, and the lure of economic opportunity in America, added to the call of the prophet to "come to Zion," created a powerful motivation. It was unusual, but far from unheard of, for children to make the journey without family. Born in Copenhagen in 1875, Valborg Henrietta Louise Rasmussen was a highly spirited and independent-minded youth converted through church meetings that failed to persuade her mother. Months later, Valborg accepted a missionary's invitation to accompany him to Zion, and after overcoming her mother's objections, she sailed for Zion in 1888 at the age of thirteen. Spurning offers to stay in Denmark and study "home economics" on scholarship, Valborg went on to graduate from the University of Utah, attend Northwestern University, and become a party activist in Utah politics. She died in Ogden, Utah, in 1957.

How peculiar it was that at this time, and in these circumstances, I should meet two young schoolmates who were Mormons. A few months had passed since Mother had moved, so I was beginning to make friends at Hindagal, the school I was attending. Among those friends were Hilda and Oscar Winkler, who lived only a block from our home. They were attractive children, near my own age of twelve.

On Sundays Mother worked at the hospital, and my job was to empty the toilets in the building where we lived. There was no indoor plumbing, so they had to be emptied daily by hand. It was not a pleasant job, but it had to be done. After I finished my chores I would be quite alone; so when Oscar and Hilda invited me to visit their Mormon Sunday School, I was happy to go.

The Latter-day Saints met at Krystalgade on the second floor of a little building inside a court yard. We walked through a portal to get to the yard inside. There were many steps to climb, but at the top was a hall full of children and young people.

After I heard that first lesson I wanted to go again and again. Every Sunday I would hurry to complete my duties by ten o'clock so that I would be ready when my two friends called for me. My Sunday School teacher, Mrs. Thor Nielson, was a convert. I liked her, and we became good friends. Of course, I learned a lot from Oscar and Hilda. Mother was working, so I usually spent the whole day at their home, and we would talk about the morning's lesson. I will always be grateful to my two young friends. But the overall change that eventually took place in my life would never have occurred had it not been for the concern that Elder Willard Hansen showed for me. . . .

My ears and heart had been opened by the messages I had heard on Sundays in the humble hall at Krystalgade. The Mormon faith brought a whole new life to me, even as a child. The missionaries spoke from the Bible; that is what really converted me. I knew what the Bible said, and the Mormon elders proved the truth of the gospel from the Bible. Fortunately, I had not yet reached the years of schooling where a child is taught the Lutheran interpretation of the Bible. During the two years before a child reaches the age of fourteen, he prepares to meet the Lutheran priest. During this "priest period" a student learns those scriptures and interpretations that he will be called upon to recite before the priest, promising to forsake the devil and all his wrong doings and thereby becoming a confirmed member of the Lutheran Church.

At twelve, I was the right age to hear the gospel. I had never learned the lessons or doctrines of the Lutheran Church or any other church but I had learned the lessons of the Bible. I knew that everything Elder Hansen taught Mother and me was true.

That spring brought a beautiful Easter morning, and I, as usual, was on my way to Sunday School. I had finished my chores and had to run to get there by ten o'clock. I was singing all the way. After Sunday School I saw Elder Hansen, and out of the clear blue sky he asked me, "How would you like to go to Zion with me?" From all the events of the past weeks and all I had learned of the gospel, I felt this was a direct call from God to be gathered with his people. I knew the chance would never present itself again. It was not going to be easy, but I was determined to persuade Mother to let me go.

Elder Hansen had undoubtedly made an investigation into our circumstances, because shortly after he invited me to return with him to Zion, the mission president, Niels C. Flygare, hired Mother to cook for the elders in the mission home. She was given a maid's room and was allowed to have me with her. It was a wonderful situation for her. The five mission officials lived on ordinary, decent food, and she was able to save enough money for little things she needed, including a set of artificial teeth. These circumstances softened Mother's attitude toward the Mormons; but she was still not converted to the gospel nor to the idea of my going to Utah.

At spring conference President Teasdale came and spoke. His words were inspired. To me the spirit bore a marked interpreted message. I was fully converted to every truth he spoke. I talked with the elders and was not a bit frightened when Elder Hansen baptized me in the waters of "Langelinge."

But I had a hard task ahead of me. I begged Mother every day and tried to make her see how important it was that I go to Utah. I would listen to no argument from her. I would tell her she didn't know what she was talking about. I'd make her come and kneel down with me each morning before she went to work.

I had really never had anything so important to pray about before this object now in view. Oh, I had had my small everyday wishes, but never a need so great that it required more than just a few minutes of prayer. This was different. I constantly asked my Heavenly Father to help Mother see the truthfulness of the gospel. It was the truth. I knew it was. It was a gift from God. I couldn't have been more convinced of anything in my life than I was of that. And God was calling me to Zion. I preached all summer to my mother, my schoolmates—anyone who would listen: "he who is not willing to leave father, mother, for my name's sake, is not worthy of me." This was the scripture I quoted to substantiate my point of view. So many children didn't have a chance to go, and I did. Somehow I knew that I would go and that Mother would know it was the right thing for me to do.

After six weeks of prayer and meeting and talks with Elder Hansen, Mother gave her consent. After that, all the King's men couldn't have stopped me from going. Our neighbors thought it was a shameful thing for a mother to allow her daughter to do. All the people who had not cared at all if we had no food to eat or clothes to wear now shook their heads in horror at the thought of my leaving with those awful Mormons.

The schools offered me a scholarship if I would stay. Of course, I turned them down. All it amounted to was a course in home economics.

"That poor little Mormon girl," they would say. "And she's such a good student." I did ask my teacher if I could have a character book to take with me to Utah. (That word Utah was a terrible thing to mention to anybody.) She wouldn't give me the book; instead, she set me up before the class and told them I would soon be entering into polygamy and all the other shameful things in the Mormon society. I felt like a heroine. The whole family thought Mother had lost her mind. Karl and his wife, a fine girl from Dresden, came to Copenhagen when they heard I was going to Utah. Aunt Amalie came down from Middlefort. Both of them offered me homes with them if I would not go with Elder Hansen. They could not understand. Had I been looking for a better home I'm sure I would have enjoyed Germany or the Danish isles, but *I was about my Father's business.*

One day the police knocked on our door and served Mother with a summons. She and I went to the police court to be questioned. I was so frightened my heart stood still. Could they stop me from going? They tried. They asked us many questions and attempted to show that I was not my mother's child. No one could believe that any mother would let her youngest child leave home on such an incredible journey. But there was nothing they could do once Mother gave indisputable proof that she had given birth to me. I'm sure it was my relatives who instigated the police investigation. But they couldn't stop me. Karl even refused to shake hands with me when he left, and the disgust of the rest of the family amounted to more attention than they had ever shown before.

I shall never forget the last Sunday School. All the children sang "Farewell." I bore my testimony full of spirit. My eyes had been opened. I knew Christ lived and with the surety of this knowledge I would ever be obedient to his teachings.

I crossed King's Square in Copenhagen that August morning, going toward the harbor where the ship lay on which I would leave in a few moments. Wearing a thin dress and a little black jacket that I had bought with my postal savings, I kissed my mother goodbye at our home while I still had the courage to do so without weeping. I walked down to the harbor alone. I was frightened, but I felt deeply the ultimate triumph of good over evil. I saw clearly how the way had been prepared in the first twelve years of my life for this spiritual adventure. It will always seem miraculous to me how one situation built upon another until that day of departure: the death of my father, the foster homes, hard work, scripture study in the Danish schools until I was twelve, Oscar and Hilda taking me to their Mormon Sunday School, and finally Elder Willard Hansen from Brigham City, Utah, picking me out of several hundred children to return with him to Zion—it had all been preparing me for this day.

Now that glorified moment for which I had fought and struggled had arrived. Yet mine was still the power to choose between the flesh and the spirit. I was still with my mother. I still could stay with her. But I would not falter now; only a coward turns back. It was a decision of immense importance.

I swung myself up the gangplank amidst the waving handkerchiefs of my schoolmates who were bidding me goodbye.

I remember standing still, holding on to the railing as the boat glided out into the wide, soft darkness. I stood my ground without a tear until I saw a sweet, tear-stained face come into view. It was my mother. As she squeezed through the crowds, the heat and confusion almost overcame me. I remember whispering through the dark and stillness, "Oh God, be with us that we may meet again in that land out West, as thou hast promised those who are faithful." It was a child's prayer, and through the whispering of the spirit I felt complete consolation. I was assured that I had done God's will.

serve dinner to the ladies. By that time I was so starved I hurt clear through to my back. I asked Maria if I could have just a crust of bread. She could see how hungry I was, and she fed me. All I ate was a piece of bread and some milk. She would have given me more, but that's all I wanted. It was enough to stop the hunger. I have never been as hungry, before or since, as I was that day.

Being a child, I had not known what to expect when I reached Utah. I had fought to come and had been anxious to arrive in my new home; but I had never seen an American city or town and had no idea what to expect.

My first impression of Brigham City was wonderful. It was beautiful. Every home had a little reed organ. To me that was grand. No matter how poor the family, or how bad the adobes looked, the songs of Zion could be heard drifting out of the little houses.

From *Valborg: An Autobiography of Valborg Rasmussen Wheelwright* (1945)

12. First Presidency (Joseph F. Smith, John R. Winder, and Anthon H. Lund), "Christmas Greeting to Saints in the Netherlands"

Almost from the moment of their church's founding, Latter-day Saints have physically congregated in designated centers in accordance with the principle of gathering. Kirtland, Ohio; Jackson County, Missouri; Nauvoo, Illinois; and Salt Lake City, Utah, served in turn as places where church members assembled by the hundreds and then thousands, started schools and universities, and built (or dreamed of building) their temples. Responding to decades of conflict and expulsions, President Brigham Young was determined not just to reassemble in Utah, but to there achieve economic and cultural autonomy. Eventually forced to make peace with an antagonistic and powerful U.S. federal government, Mormons entered a transitional period of "Americanization." During the same era in which statehood was granted in 1896, effectively ending the political isolation of Utah, some church leaders began to rethink the principle of the gathering. Apostle E. James Talmage noted in 1900 that "the practice of gathering its proselytes into one place prevents the building up and strengthening of foreign branches."[7] In 1902, President Joseph F. Smith enumerated the blessings of the gathering and the consequent "force that has bound the Saints together."[8] He repeated in a May 1907 address "adopted by vote of the Church" in General Conference that "the gathering of scattered Israel" was a principal object of the church.[9] That December, however, the First

*Presidency chose the occasion of a Christmas greeting to Dutch Latter-day Saints
to redefine dramatically the concept of gathering in terms that prevail to this
day in the church. Missionaries continue to fan out throughout the world, but
converts are encouraged to stay in their own areas and "build Zion" locally. The
gathering is to the wards and stakes wherever the Latter-day Saints live.*

We feel that we can say of the Saints in the Netherlands, that we esteem them
as among the very best citizens. They can be nothing else and be true to their
faith, for that teaches them to be loyal to their government wherever they may
dwell. A doctrine that is most emphatically enjoined upon the Saints is that
"We believe in being subject to kings, presidents, rulers and magistrates, in
obeying, honoring, and sustaining the law." Moreover "we believe in being
honest, true, chaste, benevolent, virtuous, and in doing good to all men." Our
mission is one of peace and good will; and through obedience to the doctrine
of Christ the Saints are of necessity honest, chaste, industrious, frugal, peaceful and law-abiding citizens. Live so that you may have fellowship with God;
keep the commandments of your Redeemer and teach others to walk after your
example, and you will have the respect and favor of honest, unprejudiced men.

The policy of the Church is not to entice or encourage people to leave their
native lands; but to remain faithful and true in their allegiance to their governments, and to be good citizens. We desire that the members of the Church
should continue diligent in learning the truth and their duties in the Church
toward God and man, and in increasing their faith in the Gospel of Jesus
Christ. Our Elders should carefully avoid holding out to the Saints temporal
advantages or worldly gain, admonishing them that our object is not to hold
out temporal advantages or inducements, but above all other things to hold
out to them their spiritual and temporal welfare, leaving them to receive such
other admonitions and promptings as the Spirit of the Lord may impress upon
their minds.

The Dutch people who gather to Zion have invariably been treated with
great kindness and consideration by the people of this country and especially
by the Latter-day Saints, and have been shown every courtesy due to all worthy people whether native or foreign born; and in many instances have been
elevated to positions of honor and responsibility in the communities to which
they belong, and we bespeak for the Elders of the Church in the Netherlands

and elsewhere and those who embrace the truth and adhere to their counsel, the same kind treatment and fair consideration that we so cheerfully give to people who sojourn with us.

And we desire also to express our gratitude to an abiding love for the people of the Netherlands for the measure of religious freedom that prevails throughout their land, and to thank them for their fair and hospitable treatment of the Elders of the Church who labor without worldly gain for their good and the Saints who dwell among them. We hold the people of the Netherlands in the highest esteem for their many deeds of kindness. We feel sure that the seed of Israel abounds among them and know they have descended from a noble race of men.

From *Der Stern* (1907)

13. Bruce R. McConkie, "Come: Let Israel Build Zion"

Under the dynamic administration (1973–1985) of President Spencer W. Kimball, the church experienced a growth surge that almost doubled the missionary force and the membership (17,000 to 30,000 and 3.3 million to 6 million, respectively). The church began its transition from an American institution centered in Utah to a truly international body. Convert rates exploded in Latin America, and with the 1978 extension of the priesthood to men of all races, missionary work commenced in Africa. As the church center of gravity shifted, Bruce R. McConkie— perhaps the most influential apostle of his era—reaffirmed and elaborated the new paradigm of gathering introduced by President Joseph F. Smith and his counselors earlier in the century. Gathering was not only now defined as congregating in local units; the Zion that had been geographically defined for most of the church's history was now equated with "the pure in heart" (in accordance with Doctrine and Covenants 97:21). But metaphorical readings of Mormon Zionism had their limits; McConkie also made a point of reaffirming Mormon belief in the millennium, which would be accompanied by Christ's literal return, and the construction of a New Jerusalem on the North American continent.

As is well known, ancient Israel was scattered among all the nations of the earth because they forsook the Lord and worshipped false gods. As is also well known, the gathering of Israel consists of receiving the truth, gaining again a true knowledge of the Redeemer, and coming back into the true fold of the Good Shepherd. In the language of the Book of Mormon, it consists of being "restored to the true church and fold of God," and then being "gathered" and "established" in various "lands of promise" (2 Nephi 9:2). "When they shall come to the knowledge of their Redeemer, they shall be gathered together again to the lands of their inheritance" (2 Nephi 6:11).

Two things are accomplished by the gathering of Israel: First, those who have thus chosen Christ as their Shepherd; those who have taken upon themselves his name in the waters of baptism; those who are seeking to enjoy his Spirit here and now and to be inheritors of eternal life hereafter—such people need to be gathered together to strengthen each other and to help one another perfect their lives.

And second, those who are seeking the highest rewards in eternity need to be where they can receive the blessings of the house of the Lord, both for themselves and for their ancestors in Israel who died without a knowledge of the gospel, but who would have received it with all their heart had opportunity afforded.

Manifestly in the early days of this dispensation, this meant gathering to the mountain of the Lord's house in the tops of the mountains of North America. There alone were congregations strong enough for the Saints to strengthen each other. There alone were the temples of the Most High where the fulness of the ordinances of exaltation are performed.

However, in the providences of Him who knoweth all things, in the providences of Him who scattered Israel and who is now gathering that favored people again, the day has now come when the fold of Christ is reaching out to the ends of the earth. We are not established in all nations, but we surely shall be before the second coming of the Son of Man.

As the Book of Mormon says, in the last days, "the saints of God" shall be found "upon all the face of the earth." Also: "The saints of the church of the Lamb and . . . the covenant people of the Lord"—scattered as they are "upon all the face of the earth"—shall be "armed with righteousness and with the power of God in great glory" (1 Nephi 14:12, 14).

We are living in a new day. The Church of Jesus Christ of Latter-day Saints is fast becoming a worldwide church. Congregations of Saints are now, or soon will be, strong enough to support and sustain their members no matter where they reside. Temples are being built wherever the need justifies. We can foresee many temples in South America in process of time.

Stakes of Zion are also being organized at the ends of the earth. In this connection, let us ponder these truths: A stake of Zion is a part of Zion. You cannot create a stake of Zion without creating a part of Zion. Zion is the pure in heart; we gain purity of heart by baptism and by obedience. A stake has geographical boundaries. To create a stake is like founding a City of Holiness. Every stake on earth is the gathering place for the lost sheep of Israel who live in its area.

The gathering place for Peruvians is in the stakes of Zion in Peru, or in the places which soon will become stakes. The gathering place for Chileans is in Chile; for Bolivians it is in Bolivia; for Koreans it is in Korea; and so it goes through all the length and breadth of the earth. Scattered Israel in every nation is called to gather to the fold of Christ, to the stakes of Zion, as such are established in their nations.

Isaiah prophesied that the Lord "shall cause them that come of Jacob to take root; Israel shall blossom and bud, and fill the face of the world with fruit." The Lord's promise is: "Ye shall be gathered one by one, O ye children of Israel" (Isaiah 27:6, 12).

That is to say—Israel shall be gathered one by one, family by family, unto the stakes of Zion established in all parts of the earth so that the whole earth shall be blessed with the fruits of the gospel.

This then is the counsel of the Brethren: Build up Zion, but build it up in the area where God has given you birth and nationality. Build it up where he has given you citizenship, family, and friends. Zion is here in South America and the Saints who comprise this part of Zion are and should be a leavening influence for good in all these nations.

And know this: God will bless that nation which so orders its affairs as to further his work.

His work includes the building up of Zion in the last days. He has commissioned us to do that work for him. The foundations of Zion have already been laid in North America, in South America, in Europe, in Asia, in the South Pacific and in every place where there are stakes of Zion. But Zion is not yet perfected in any of these places. When she is perfected, it will be as it was with Zion of old—the Lord will come and dwell with his people.

Our tenth Article of Faith says, "We believe in the literal gathering of Israel." This gathering occurs when the lost sheep of Israel come into the Church. It occurs when their sins are washed away in the waters of baptism, so that once again they have power to become pure in heart; and Zion is the pure in heart.

Our Article of Faith says that "We believe . . . in the restoration of the Ten Tribes." This is in the future. It will occur when the Lord brings again Zion, according to the promises.

Our Article of Faith says "that Zion (the New Jerusalem) will be built upon this [the American] continent." This also is future and will occur after the Lord's people have gained strength and influence and power in all the nations whither he hath scattered them.

Our Article of Faith says "that Christ will reign personally upon the earth; and, that the earth will be renewed and receive its paradisiacal glory." This also is future, a day which we devoutly desire and seek (Articles of Faith 1:10).

Each one of us can build up Zion in our own lives by being pure in heart. And the promise is, "Blessed are the pure in heart: for they shall see God" (Matthew. 5:8). Each one of us can extend the borders of Zion by gathering our friends and neighbors into the fold of Israel.

From *Ensign* (1977)

FOUR

GOVERNMENT AND POLITICS

T HE CHURCH OF JESUS CHRIST of Latter-day Saints has the distinction of being the religious group most systematically persecuted by state and federal governments in America's history. Ironically, Mormons are also generally seen as among the nation's most patriotic citizens in the twenty-first century. This paradox is a function of their history and theology alike. Joseph Smith and subsequent Mormon leaders were emphatic in considering the U.S. Constitution an inspired document and the American experiment in liberty a providential preparation for the restoration of the gospel. Time and again they saw their sufferings as revealing inadequate regard for constitutional principles on the part of their fellow citizens, not deficiency in those principles themselves. At the same time, the extraordinary influence that Smith, as prophet, exerted over his followers led some of them, not just outsiders, to protest the blurring of religious obligation and political liberties. In 1835, Joseph Smith's close associate Oliver Cowdery enunciated a clearly defined separation of church and state, to assuage his own apprehensions as much as that of non-Mormons, and Smith acceded to the canonization of the statement though he had no hand in its composition. Fears of Mormon theocratic tendencies would nonetheless become even more pronounced through the church's Illinois and Utah periods and have waxed and waned to this day.

At the very moment when Latter-day Saints were engaged in a forced exodus from the United States, drenched in pain and suffering, the U.S. Army recruited five hundred of them for the 1846 war with Mexico. Though economic self-interest was the principal motive for LDS enlistments, the Mormon Battalion nonetheless embodied the paradox of an American flag that was for Latter-day Saints a symbol of both hope and oppression. A decade later, however, any dreams of peaceful coexistence, even from their remote desert fastness, were shattered by a U.S. federal policy of subjugating the theocratic, polygamous dissenters to mainstream (meaning Protestant and Republican) values. A U.S. federal expeditionary force marched on Utah after Latter-day Saints struggled to recognize the authority of federally commissioned officials. Once again, Mormons contemplated the specter of armed oppression and prepared to abandon Salt Lake City. Just in time, warfare was narrowly averted. The U.S. government later adopted legislative means to eradicate plural marriage, forcing large numbers of LDS leaders, as well as rank and file polygamists of both genders, into the Mormon underground.

By the final decade of the nineteenth century, the Protestant establishment (the mainline Christian denominations who effectively controlled American society) had successfully pressured Mormon leaders to abandon their long-held hope of establishing a theocratic Zion in Deseret. Along with the practice of plural marriage, which they began to abandon in 1890 with the issuance of the "Manifesto" by President Wilford Woodruff, church leaders finally submitted to American political pluralism in a bid for Utah statehood in 1896. Even on the cusp of statehood, a scandal erupted when the church sanctioned two leaders for seeking office without permission of the leadership. Woodruff refused to cede what he saw as the church's responsibility to safeguard the sanctity of both ecclesiastical and political duties by managing their competing claims. The church weathered the storm, and statehood was granted as the church disbanded its own political party, promised to remain politically neutral as an ecclesiastical institution and encouraged its members to participate in government policy-making on both sides of the political aisle. Within a decade, however, church leaders found themselves embroiled in the U.S. Senate confirmation hearings of Apostle Reed Smoot, when a petition drive held up his official seating. Mormon critics pressed charges of post-1890 Manifesto plural marriages and a reemergence of theocracy in Utah against Smoot and his colleagues. Reed Smoot's congressional testimony reveals much about the evolving character of the church and its increasingly successful attempts to assimilate into the American mainstream.

Meanwhile, those same women whom Americans had been struggling to liberate from Mormon patriarchy were engaged in another struggle: to re-secure the right to vote that those patriarchs had given them in 1870, only to have it revoked by the more paternalistic U.S. Congress in 1887 when LDS women did not use it to vote out polygamy. The topsy-turvy history of female suffrage in Utah is a striking instance of how inadequate simplistic labels—progressive or reactionary, feminist or chauvinist—can be when applied to the Mormon case.

For much of the remaining twentieth century, the church assumed a low-key political profile. Apostle (and later church president) Ezra Taft Benson became the first of many Latter-day Saints to serve prominently in high political office, as President Dwight D. Eisenhower's secretary of agriculture. But leery of res-urrecting old concerns about undue political influence, the church kept largely under the radar. When political issues cut too deeply into the moral fabric of the church, as with abortion, leaders made public statements, while most, but not all, Latter-day Saints fell in line. In the 1970s, Mormon dissenters made their opposition public when they believed it was the church, not the political mainstream, which was on the wrong side of shifting moral tides. Feminist Sonia Johnson became the church's most outspoken proponent of the pending Equal Rights Amendment, in direct opposition to official church policy. Her post-excommunication interview and Judith Dushku's reflections on abortion highlight the limits of dissent within American Mormonism and the dilemma of many church members who struggle to reconcile the twin ideas of faithful obedience and intellectual independence.

By the new millennium, public perception was widespread that Latter-day Saints were overwhelmingly conservative and Republican. In 2007, two of the most prominent politicians in the country were Mormon but came from oppo-site ends of the political spectrum, giving the lie to any one party's political monopoly on the Mormon membership. In that year, Senate Majority Leader Harry Reid and former Massachusetts Governor Mitt Romney described in different contexts how their Mormon faith affects their political views. Reid, a Democrat, explained why his conversion to the church has had such an impact on his liberal policy making, while Romney, a Republican, attempted to convince Evangelical Christians that his presidential candidacy should not be thwarted on the basis of his religious beliefs and affiliation, referencing the constitutional separation of church and state in America.

1. Oliver Cowdery, "Governments and Laws in General [Doctrine and Covenants 134]"

Oliver Cowdery was Joseph Smith's closest associate in the early days of the church, serving as principal scribe for the Book of Mormon translation and as one of the original three witnesses to the gold plates. He was the only participant with Smith in receiving the Aaronic Priesthood at the hands of the resurrected John the Baptist and the Melchizedek Priesthood from Peter, James, and John. Cowdery served as second elder of the church at its organization and as assistant president of the church from 1834 to 1838. In 1829, Cowdery drafted the "Articles of the Church of Christ," laying the groundwork for Joseph Smith's "Articles and Covenants of the Church" (Doctrine and Covenants 20). Then, after a mob-aborted effort to publish a collection of Smith's revelations in 1833, Cowdery was appointed part of a committee to prepare a new compilation. In August 1835, he presided at a general conference (Joseph Smith was absent) where the volume received the church's approval. At the same time, and apparently on his own initiative, Oliver Cowdery presented for inclusion a document he authored, "Of Governments and Laws in General." In an earlier 1833 revelation (Doctrine and Covenants 98), Smith had affirmed the church's support of constitutional principles, in the face of persecutions Mormons were suffering in Missouri. Months later, Joseph Smith declared that the U.S. Constitution in fact bore the imprint of divine inspiration (Doctrine and Covenants 101:80). In the document, Cowdery, who was particularly passionate about maintaining—and separating—political and religious liberties, expanded upon Smith's earlier pronouncements. The assembly accepted Oliver Cowdery's statement of belief, and Joseph Smith later endorsed the decision.

We believe that governments were instituted of God for the benefit of man, and that he holds men accountable for their acts in relation to them, either in making laws or administering them, for the good and safety of society.

We believe that no government can exist, in peace, except such laws are framed and held inviolate as will secure to each individual the free exercise of conscience, the right and control of property and the protection of life.

We believe that all governments necessarily require civil officers and magistrates to enforce the laws of the same, and that such as will administer the law in equity and justice should be sought for and upheld by the voice of the people, (if a Republic,) or the will of the Sovereign.

We believe that religion is instituted of God, and that men are amenable to him and to him only for the exercise of it, unless their religious opinion prompts them to infringe upon the rights and liberties of others; but we do not believe that human law has a right to interfere in prescribing rules of worship to bind the consciences of men, nor dictate forms for public or private devotion; that the civil magistrate should restrain crime, but never control conscience; should punish guilt, but never suppress the freedom of the soul.

We believe that all men are bound to sustain and uphold the respective governments in which they reside, while protected in their inherent and inalienable rights by the laws of such governments, and that sedition and rebellion are unbecoming every citizen thus protected, and should be punished accordingly; and that all governments have a right to enact such laws as in their own judgments are best calculated to secure the public interest, at the same time, however, holding sacred the freedom of conscience.

We believe that every man should be honored in his station: rulers and magistrates as such being placed for the protection of the innocent and the punishment of the guilty: and that to the laws all men owe respect and deference, as without them peace and harmony would be supplanted by anarchy and terror: human laws being instituted for the express purpose of regulating our interests as individuals and nations, between man and man, and divine laws given of heaven, prescribing rules on spiritual concerns, for faith and worship, both to be answered by man to his Maker.

We believe that rulers, states and governments have a right, and are bound to enact laws for the protection of all citizens in the free exercise of their religious belief; but we do not believe that they have a right, in justice, to deprive citizens of this privilege, or proscribe them in their opinions, so long as a regard and reverence is shown to the laws, and such religious opinions do not justify sedition nor conspiracy.

We believe that the commission of crime should be punished according to the nature of the offence: that murder, treason, robbery, theft and the breach of the general peace, in all respects, should be punished according to their criminality and their tendency to evil among men, by the laws of that government in which the offence is committed: and for the public peace and tranquility, all men should step forward and use their ability in bringing offenders, against good laws, to punishment.

We do not believe it just to mingle religious influence with civil government, whereby one religious society is fostered and another proscribed in its spiritual privileges, and the individual rights of its members, as citizens, denied.

We believe that all religious societies have a right to deal with their members for disorderly conduct according to the rules and regulations of such societies, provided that such dealing be for fellowship and good standing; but we do not believe that any religious society has authority to try men on the right of property or life, to take from them this world's goods, or put them in jeopardy, either life or limb, neither to inflict any physical punishment upon them, they can only excommunicate them from their society and withdraw from their fellowship.

We believe that men should appeal to the civil law for redress of all wrongs and grievances, where personal abuse is inflicted, or the right of property or character infringed, where such laws exist as will protect the same; but we believe that all men are justified in defending themselves, their friends and property, and the government, from the unlawful assaults and encroachments of all persons, in times of exigencies, where immediate appeal cannot be made to the laws, and relief afforded.

We believe it just to preach the gospel to the nations of the earth, and warn the righteous to save themselves from the corruption of the world; but we do not believe it right to interfere with bond servants, neither preach the gospel to, nor baptize them, contrary to the will and wish of their masters, nor to meddle with, or influence them in the least to cause them to be dissatisfied with their situations in this life, thereby jeopardizing the lives of men: such interference we believe to be unlawful and unjust and dangerous to the peace of every government allowing human beings to be held in servitude.

From *Messenger and Advocate* (1835)

2. Joseph Smith, *General Smith's Views of the Powers and Policy of the Government of the United States* (1844)

In 2012, Governor Mitt Romney took his run for presidential office further than any other Mormon. Joseph Smith never won a party endorsement, but he ran as an independent candidate in the 1844 presidential election. His people had suffered violent expulsion from Missouri in 1838 and spent the next years seeking redress at the state and then federal level. Smith attempted to parley the influence

he wielded over a significant voting block into a weapon to find political support
for his people among sitting presidents and candidates alike, as Mormon troubles
continued in Illinois. In fall 1843, he wrote five presidential candidates (Lewis
Cass, Richard Johnson, Henry Clay, Martin van Buren, and John Calhoun) ask-
ing "What will be your rule of action, relative to us, as a people?" With no com-
mitment of intervention or protection forthcoming, Smith decided that January
to run for the high office himself.

Critics saw in Joseph Smith's gesture megalomania at the best, and a dangerous
extension of his theocratic designs at the worst. He already commanded a militia
of thousands and ran Nauvoo as a virtual city-state; his political designs played
into the hands of his enemies and may have contributed to his death months
later. Smith lacked a national constituency, and it is unlikely he considered his
candidacy viable. However, the campaign gave him what his movement needed
at the moment: a national spotlight. He would use the platform to draw attention
to their plight as a persecuted people, to promulgate his views on a host of timely
political issues, all while spreading missionaries and the message of the restora-
tion nationwide. Hundreds of elders volunteered to canvass the country, distribut-
ing fifteen hundred copies of his Views, *which was probably authored largely by*
William W. Phelps, with assistance from John Bernhisel. On the two major issues
of the day, Smith took a position on the national bank that pleased neither party
and advocated national abolition, consistent with his liberal leanings: "Educate
[the slaves] and give them their equal rights," he had said years earlier.

Born in a land of liberty, and breathing an air uncorrupted with the sirocco
of barbarous climes, I ever feel a double anxiety for the happiness of all men,
both in time and in eternity. My cogitations, like Daniel's, have for a long time
troubled me, when I viewed the condition of men throughout the world, and
more especially in this boasted realm, where the Declaration of Independence
"holds these truths to be self-evident, that all men are created equal; that they
are endowed by their Creator with certain unalienable rights; that among these
are life, liberty, and pursuit of happiness," but at the same time some two or
three millions of people are held as slaves for life, because the spirit in them
is covered with a darker skin than ours; and hundreds of our kindred for an
infraction, or supposed infraction, of some over wise statute, have to be incar-
cerated in dungeon glooms, or suffer the more moral penitentiary gravitation

of mercy in a nut-shell, while the duelist, the debauchee, and the defaulter for millions, and other criminals, take the upper-most rooms at feasts, or, like the bird of passage find a more congenial clime by flight.

The wisdom which ought to characterize the freest, wisest, and most noble nation of the nineteenth century, should, like the sun in his meridian splendor, warm every object beneath its rays; and the main efforts of her officers, who are nothing more nor less than the servants of the people, ought to be directed to ameliorate the condition of all, black or white, bond or free; for the best of books says, "God hath made of one blood all nations of men for to dwell on the face of the earth."

. . . . No honest man can doubt for a moment, but the glory of American Liberty, is on the wane, and that calamity and confusion will sooner or later destroy the peace of the people. Speculators will urge a national bank as a savior of credit and comfort. A hireling pseudo priesthood will plausibly push abolition doctrines and doings, and "human rights," into Congress and into every other place, where conquest smells of fame, or opposition swells to popularity. — Democracy, Whiggery, and Cliquery, will attract their elements and foment divisions among the people, to accomplish fancied schemes and accumulate power, while poverty driven to despair, like hunger forcing its way through a wall, will break through the statutes of men, to save life, and mend the breach of prison glooms.

A still higher grade, of what the "nobility of nations" call "great men," will dally with all rights, in order to smuggle a fortune at "one fell swoop"; mortgage Texas, possess Oregon, and claim all the unsettled regions of the world for hunting and trapping; and should an humble, honest man, red, black, or white, exhibit a better title, these gentry have only to clothe the judge with richer ermine, and spangle the lawyer's finger with finer rings, to have the judgment of his peers, and the honor of his lords as a pattern of honesty, virtue, and humanity, while the motto hangs on his nation's escutcheon: "Every man has his price!"

Now, oh! people! people! turn unto the Lord and live; and reform this nation. Frustrate the designs of wicked men. Reduce Congress at least one half. Two Senators from a state and two members to a million of population, will do more business than the army that now occupy the halls of the National Legislature. Pay them two dollars and their board per diem; except Sundays, that is more than the farmer gets, and he lives honestly. Curtail the offices of government in pay, number and power; for the Philistine lords have shorn our nation of its goodly locks in the lap of Delilah.

Petition your state legislatures to pardon every convict in their several penitentiaries, blessing them as they go, and saying to them, in the name of the
Lord, go thy way and sin no more. Advise your legislators when they make laws
for larceny, burglary or any felony, to make the penalty applicable to work upon
roads, public works, or any place where the culprit can be taught more wisdom and more virtue; and become more enlightened. Rigor and seclusion will
never do as much to reform the propensities of man, as reason and friendship.
Murder only can claim confinement or death. Let the penitentiaries be turned
into seminaries of learning, where intelligence, like the angels of heaven, would
banish such fragments of barbarism. Imprisonment for debt is a meaner practice than the savage tolerates with all his ferocity. "Amor vincit amnia." Love
conquers all.

Petition, also, ye goodly inhabitants of the slave states, your legislators to
abolish slavery by the year 1850, or now, and save the abolitionist from reproach
and ruin, infamy and shame. Pray Congress to pay every man a reasonable
price for his slaves out of the surplus revenue arising from the sale of public
lands, and from the deduction of pay from the members of Congress. Break off
the shackles from the poor black man, and hire him to labor like other human
beings; for "an hour of virtuous liberty on earth, is worth a whole eternity of
bondage!" Abolish the practice in the army and navy of trying men by court
martial for desertion; if a soldier or marine runs away, send him his wages,
with this instruction, that his country will never trust him again; he has forfeited his honor. Make HONOR the standard with all men: be sure that good is
rendered for evil in all cases; and the whole nation, like a kingdom of kings and
priests, will rise up with righteousness; and be respected as wise and worthy
on earth; and as just and holy for heaven; by Jehovah, the author of perfection.
More economy in the national and state governments, would make less taxes
among the people; more equality through the cities, towns & country, would
make less distinction among the people; and more honesty and familiarity in
societies, would make less hypocrisy and flattery in all branches of the community; and open, frank, candid, decorum to all men, in this boasted land
of liberty, would beget esteem, confidence, union, and love; and the neighbor
from any state, or from any country, of whatever color, clime or tongue, could
rejoice when he put his foot on the sacred soil of freedom, and exclaim: the
very name of "American" is fraught with friendship! Oh! then, create confidence! restore freedom! — break down slavery! banish imprisonment for debt,
and be in love, fellowship and peace with all the world! Remember that honesty

is not subject to law: the law was made for transgressors: wherefore, a Dutchman might exclaim: "Ein ehrlicher name ist besser als Reichthum" (a good name is better than riches).

For the accommodation of the people of every state and territory, let Congress shew their wisdom by granting a national bank, with branches in each state and territory, where the capital stock shall be held by the nation for the mother bank: and by the states and territories, for the branches; and whose officers and directors shall be elected yearly by the people with wages at the rate of two dollars per day for services; which several banks shall never issue any more bills than the amount of capital stock in her vaults and the interest. The net gain of the mother bank shall be applied to the national revenue, and that of the branches to the states and territories' revenues. And the bills shall be par throughout the nation, which will mercifully cure that fatal disorder known in cities as brokerage; and leave the people's money in their own pockets.

Give every man his constitutional freedom, and the president full power to send an army to suppress mobs; and the states authority to repeal and impugn that relic of folly, which makes it necessary for the governor of a state to make the demand of the president for troops, in case of invasion or rebellion. The governor himself may be a mobber and, instead of being punished, as he should be, for murder and treason, he may destroy the very lives, rights, and property he should protect. Like the good Samaritan, send every lawyer as soon as he repents and obeys the ordinances of heaven, to preach the gospel to the destitute, without purse or scrip, pouring in the oil and the wine; a learned priesthood is certainly more honorable than an "hireling clergy."

As to the contiguous territories to the United States, wisdom would direct no tangling alliance. Oregon belongs to this government honorably, and when we have the red man's consent, let the union spread from the east to the west sea; and if Texas petitions Congress to be adopted among the sons of liberty, give her the right hand of fellowship; and refuse not the same friendly grip to Canada and Mexico; and when the right arm of freemen is stretched out in the character of a navy for, the protection of rights, commerce and honor, let the iron eyes of power, watch from Maine to Mexico, and from California to Columbia; thus may union be strengthened, and foreign speculation prevented from opposing broadside to broadside.

Seventy years have done much for this goodly land; they have burst the chains of oppression and monarchy; and multiplied its inhabitants from two to twenty millions; with a proportionate share of knowledge; keen enough to circumnavigate the globe; draw the lightning from the clouds; and cope with all the crowned heads of the world.

Then why? Oh! why! will a once flourishing people not arise, phoenix like, over the cinders of Martin Van Buren's power; and over the sinking fragments and smoking ruins of other catamount politicians; and over the windfalls of Benton, Calhoun, Clay, Wright, and a caravan of other equally unfortunate law doctors, and cheerfully help to spread a plaster and bind up the burnt, bleeding wounds of a sore but blessed country? The southern people are hospitable and noble: they will help to rid so free a country of every vestige of slavery, whenever they are assured of an equivalent for their property. The country will be full of money and confidence, when a national bank of twenty millions, and a state bank in every state, with a million or more, gives a tone to monetary matters, and makes a circulating medium as valuable in the purses of the whole community, as in the coffers of a speculating banker or broker.

The people may have faults, but they should never be trifled with. I think Mr. Pitt's quotation in the British Parliament of Mr. Prior's couplet for the husband and wife, to apply to the course which the king and ministry of England should pursue to the then colonies of the now United States, might be a genuine rule of action for some of the breath made men in high places, to use towards the posterity of this noble, daring people:

> Be to her faults a little blind;
> Be to her virtues very kind.

We have had democratic presidents; whig presidents; a pseudo democratic whig president; and now it is time to have a president of the United States; and let the people of the whole union, like the inflexible Romans, whenever they find a promise made by a candidate, that is not practised as an officer, hurl the miserable sycophant from his exaltation, as God did Nebuchadnezzar, to crop the grass of the field, with a beast's heart among the cattle.

Mr. Van Buren said in his inaugural address, that he went "into the presidential chair the inflexible and uncompromising opponent of every attempt, on the part of Congress, to abolish slavery in the District of Columbia, against the wishes of the slave holding states; and also with a determination equally decided to resist the slightest interference with it in the states where it exists." Poor little Matty made this rhapsodical sweep with the fact before his eyes, that the state of New York, his native state, had abolished slavery, without a struggle or a groan. Great God, how independent! From henceforth slavery is tolerated where it exists; constitution or no constitution; people or no people; right or wrong; Vox Matti; vox Diaboli: "the voice of Matty" — "the voice of the devil;" and peradventure, his great "Sub-Treasury" scheme was a piece of the same mind; but the man and his measures have such a striking resemblance to the anecdote of the Welshman and his cart-tongue, that when the constitution was so long that it allowed slavery at the capitol of a free people, it could not be cut off; but when it was so short that it needed a Sub-Treasury, to save the funds of the nation, it could be spliced! Oh, granny, what a long tail our puss has got! As a Greek might say, hysteron proteron; (the cart before the horse); but his mighty whisk through the great national fire, for the presidential chestnuts, burnt the locks of his glory with the blaze of his folly!

In the United States the people are the government; and their united voice is the only sovereign that should rule; the only power that should be obeyed; and the only gentlemen that should be honored; at home and abroad; on the land and the sea. Wherefore, were I president of the United States, by the voice of a virtuous people, I would honor the old paths of the venerated fathers of freedom; I would walk in the tracks of the illustrious patriots, who carried the ark of the government upon their shoulders with an eye single to the glory of the people and when that people petitioned to abolish slavery in the slave states, I would use all honorable means to have their prayers granted; and give liberty to the captive; by paying the southern gentleman a reasonable equivalent for his property, that the whole nation might be free indeed! When the people petitioned for a national bank, I would use my best endeavors to have their prayers answered, and establish one on national principles to save taxes, and make them the controllers of the ways and means; and when the people petitioned to possess the territory of Oregon or any other contiguous territory; I would lend the influence of a chief magistrate to grant so reasonable a request, that they might extend the mighty efforts and enterprise of a free people from the east to the west sea; and make the wilderness blossom as the rose; and when a neighboring realm petitioned to join the union of the sons of liberty, my voice would be, come: yea, come, Texas; come Mexico; come Canada; and come all the world — let us be brethren, let us be one great family, and let there be a universal peace.

Abolish the cruel custom of prisons (except in certain cases,) penitentiaries, and court martials for desertion; and let reason and friendship reign over the ruins of ignorance and barbarity; yea I would as the universal friend of man, open the prisons, open the eyes; open the ears and open the hearts of all people, to behold and enjoy freedom, unadulterated freedom; and God, who once cleansed the violence of the earth with flood; whose Son laid down his life for the salvation of all his father gave him out of the world; and who has promised that he will come and purify the world again with fire in the last days, should be supplicated by me for the good of all people.

From *General Smith's Views of the Powers and Policy of the Government of the United States* (1844)

3. Letter from Margaret L. Scott to Her Brother J. Allen Scott

A peculiar confluence of competing interests produced in 1846 one of the most unlikely collaborations in the history of the American Republic. The Mormons were in the midst of an exodus from Illinois, culminating bitter and increasingly violent conflict between the Latter-day Saints and their neighbors that spanned almost fifteen years and two states—a conflict in which the U.S. federal government repeatedly refused to intervene. Summer 1846 found thousands of Mormons scattered across the plains of Iowa, congregating primarily at Council Bluffs and across the Missouri River in Winter Quarters (modern day North Omaha, Nebraska), preparing for a march to the West. At the same time, the administration of President James K. Polk had goaded Mexico into armed conflict, as a pretext for annexing New Mexico and California. Latter-day Saints were canny enough, at this critical moment, to raise the specter of an alliance with the British, ostensibly in order to secure permission to emigrate to Vancouver Island. However sincere Mormon intentions in that regard, it gave them some leverage with a U.S. federal government nervous about British designs on California. With the helpful mediation of the influential social reformer and aspiring politico Thomas L. Kane, an agreement was reached beneficial to both Latter-day Saints and Polk. Mormon leaders would provide a battalion of five hundred volunteers to march to California as an occupying force. Polk would secure that area and forestall Mormon defection to a competing foreign power; Mormons, for their part, would receive monetary resources at a time of acute need, even as a battalion of Latter-day Saints was funded on its trek westward. The infantry march of two thousand was one of the longest in American history. Margaret Scott's letter captures some of the bewilderment and pathos of the wives, sisters, and children left behind at a time of dire need. The cost in Scott's case was supreme: her brother James died along the route of the battalion's march.

Dear brother I received your letter bearing the dates of July 16 to August the 5th on the 25th inst and with mingled emotions of sorrow and admiration I perused its content. I would have written by the next mail, but my mind was too much agitated to write. James you are aware that it is a hard trial, but I have no alternative, but to submit and calmly resign myself and my beloved brother, into the arms of our heavenly father for protection, and preservation. You speak correctly when you say, that I do not understand the present movements of the church (would that I did) they are indeed strange to me. For the Church to start to leave the U.S. and stop on the way, and send 500 of her members, to bear privations, and encounter danger, in the service of this government, is, I acknowledge, beyond my comprehension. As to protecting the church, perhaps she [the government] will, and perhaps she will not. You know how she has acted in that regard. But, not withstanding my ignorance on the subject, I have confidence enough in your judgment to believe that you have good reasons for acting as you have done. Nevertheless I wish it were otherwise. When you write again can't you put some of the whys and where-fores on a scrap so as to give me some insight. You promise to come back after me when you are discharged. I should like to know how the matter can be arranged, won't the emigrants be all gone from their present station before that time. I have seen an item from the Hancock eagle stating that the church would collect all her scattered members that wished to go this fall and winter and continue their journey next spring. . . .

The winter is coming be sure to procure under clothing if possible and take good care of your health as circumstances will admit of, be temperate in all things. You know that nature has her laws which if transgressed you will be punished—I rejoice in what H. C. Kimball has told you and hope it will prove true. . . . I have been reading Josephus lately and he gives an account of some pious Jews that the whole company was preserved—And I pray our heavenly father that his choicest blessings may rest on your Battalion collectively and on you individually. I am much pleased that you have prayers so regularly in your Crowd. If prayer is attended to throughout the campaign in faith and humility I think you *will* be preserved—

I peruse your letters with satisfaction and profit. I am pleased with the manner in which you write. But my dear brother the more I see to admire the harder it is to part with you but I am determined with the aid of the holy spirit to try and bear up under it, hoping that it will be all for the best, though I can't understand it now. . . .

Sarah has continued firm and has been looking for your posts, but like me is doomed to disappointment. When I consider the dangers to which you are exposed and the hardships you must undergo and the length of time before you are free, it is almost insupportable, but when I reflect whose you are, a gleam of hope inspires me with courage, and I feel like we'll meet again and spend some happy hours together; if you write often it will help to support me.

Next to your God endeavor to gain the good will of your officers if they try to be good men and obey them you must whether good or bad. Are your Captains all Elders. I want a particular account of your captain. May our heavenly father direct and protect and in due time return to safe home is the prayer of your sister who loves you with undimmed affection—

From *Army of Israel: Mormon Battalion Narratives* (1846)

4. Brigham Young, "Proclamation by the Governor" (1857)

In 1852, Apostle Orson Pratt publicly acknowledged and defended the church practice of plural marriage. Preachers, politicians, and novelists immediately launched a moral crusade against Mormonism that gained widespread American support. In 1856, the new Republican Party organized their platform around the eradication of those "twin relics of barbarism," slavery and polygamy. The next year, three federally appointed U.S. judges, feeling insulted and rebuffed in their efforts to exercise authority in Utah, returned to Washington, D.C., and complained that the territory was in a state of virtual rebellion, instigated by the despotic Brigham Young, the territorial governor and church president. Coming soon after reports of intransigence and disloyalty made in Washington, D.C., by a thwarted surveyor general and suspicious Indian agents, these depictions convinced U.S. President James Buchanan that federal intervention was called for. In July 1857, Buchanan ordered a federal army of 2,500 to invade the Utah Territory, seat a new governor (Alfred Cummings), and restore order. After Young's announcement of martial law, Mormon raiders harassed the troops along their western march, torching grazing land, scattering their cattle, blocking routes, and burning baggage trains. The federal army, under the command of Colonel Albert S. Johnston, was forced to winter well short of Salt Lake Valley. The next spring, Johnston was still intent on occupying Salt Lake City to humble the Mormons, avenge his army's own humiliation, and establish incontestable federal control. At this point, Brigham Young proposed to the Salt Lake City Latter-day Saints that if necessary, they would move their families and belongings south and burn their homes and destroy their orchards so that federal invaders would inherit nothing of value. Thousands of refugees were soon moving southward, but further conflict was narrowly avoided in part by the timely intervention of a skilled negotiator and friend to the Latter-day Saints, Thomas L. Kane.

We are invaded by a hostile force who are evidently assailing us to accomplish our overthrow and destruction.

For the last twenty-five years we have trusted officials of the Government, from Constables and Justices, to Judges, Governors and Presidents, only to be scorned, held in derision, insulted and betrayed. Our houses have been plundered and then burned, our fields laid waste, our principle men butchered while under the pledged faith of the government for their safety, and our families driven from their homes to find that shelter in the barren wilderness and that protection among hostile savages, which were denied them in the boasted abodes of Christianity and civilization.

The Constitution of our common country guarantees unto us all that we do now or have ever claimed.

If the Constitutional rights which pertain unto us as American citizens were extended to Utah, according to the spirit and meaning thereof, and fairly and impartially administered, it is all that we could ask, all that we have ever asked.

Our opponents have availed themselves of prejudice existing against us because of our religious faith, to send out a formidable host to accomplish our destruction. We have had no privilege, no opportunity of defending ourselves from the false, foul and unjust aspersions against us before the nation. The government has not condescended to cause an investigating committee or other persons to be sent to inquire into and ascertain the truth, as is customary in such cases.

We know those aspersions to be false, but that avails us nothing. We are condemned unheard and forced to an issue with an armed, mercenary mob, which has been sent against us at the instigation of anonymous letter writers ashamed to father the base, slanderous falsehoods which they have given to the public; of corrupt officials who have brought false accusation against us to screen themselves in their own infamy; and of hireling priests and howling editors who prostitute the truth for filthy lucre's sake.

The issue which has been thus forced upon us compels us to resort to the great first law of self preservation and stand in our own defense, a right guaranteed unto us by the genius of the institutions of our country, and upon which the government is based.

Our duty to ourselves, to our families, requires us not to tamely submit to be driven and slain, without an attempt to preserve ourselves. Our duty to our country, our holy religion, our God, to freedom and liberty, requires that we should not quietly stand still and see those fetters forging around, which are calculated to enslave and bring us in subjection to an unlawful military despotism such as can only emanate (in a country of constitutional law) from usurpation, tyranny and oppression.

Therefore I, Brigham Young, Governor and Superintendent of Indian Affairs for the Territory of Utah, in the name of the People of the United States in the Territory of Utah,

> 1st—Forbid all armed forces, of every description, from coming into this Territory under any pretense whatever.
>
> 2d—That all the forces in said Territory hold themselves in readiness to march, at a moments notice, to repel any and all such invasion.
>
> 3d—Martial law is hereby declared to exist in this Territory, from and after the publication of this Proclamation; and no person shall be allowed to pass or repass into, or through, or from this Territory, without a permit from the proper officer.

Proclamation by the Governor, Church History Library (1857)

5. Letter from Martha Hughes Cannon to Husband Angus M. Cannon

Martha Hughes Cannon, second of three daughters from a Welsh family of Mormon converts, embodied much that was paradoxical about polygamy. A precocious youth, she was a schoolteacher by fourteen, then earned a chemistry degree from the University of Deseret (University of Utah), a medical degree from the University of Michigan by the age of twenty-three, and studied pharmacy at the University of Pennsylvania as the only female out of seventy-five students. While a resident physician at Deseret Hospital, she became in 1884 the fourth plural wife among Angus Cannon's eventual six wives. Angus was arrested for practicing polygamy after the marriage, and Martha fled to a series of Utah towns, then to England, Switzerland,

and Michigan—largely to avoid having to testify against her husband or others liv-
ing "the principle." The following letter, written shortly after her return to Utah, con-
veys the wrenching agony both men and women experienced in an underground
practice that denied them both physical proximity and emotional fulfillment on the
one hand and the respect of peers and a wider public on the other. Her commitment
to plural marriage coexisted with passionate devotion to women's suffrage and a
feminist sensibility. She campaigned vigorously for the restoration of Utah women's
suffrage (polygamists were disenfranchised in 1882 and all Utah women in 1887).
Her political involvement in both state and national suffrage movements led to her
election as senator in the Utah legislature. She was the first women to hold such a
state office in America, defeating her husband in the process.

My Own Loved "A":— Your letter of 19th ult. with one enclosed from dear
Mother came duly to hand but I had just written so did not answer immediately.
I was glad to hear of your safe arrival home, as I feared you might be caught in
the "Cold Wave" of the North West. I was also relieved to hear of the improvement in dear little Maude's health. Mother has had a sore ordeal in the little girl's
illness. Your letter of the 26th ult. with Mother's, Lottie's, Birdie's, Clara's, Mary
W[oolley]'s, the R.R. Tickets and the book for Lizzie arrived here yesterday and
I had a "feast of fat things" in their perusal. Dearest, you have not had that experience yet; I mean the eagerness with which we look for news from home, after
being an exile for a time, and limited to but few correspondents. Mother writes
cheerfully, and tells me what a kind friend you have been to them the past two
years for which I feel very grateful to you, while the thought also occurs to me
how much longer will he be able to stand under the ever increasing burden that
is placed upon him from so many sources. I was pained to see that you had aged
rapidly since I last saw you—but I suppose I would not be surprised at your ag-
ing were I acquainted with all you have and are doing. I am sorry to hear you
are suffering from a cold and trust you will soon be relieved, and do try and
take good care of yourself for the sake of those who love you. What should we
do without you? There is no one in the wide world could fill your place in our
heart. I am pained to hear of your daughter's distress. I am assured her trials
must be very great, unless she has a thorough knowledge from God, that the
principle for which we are battling and striving to maintain in purity upon the
earth is ordained by Him, and that we are chosen instruments in His hands to

engage in so great a calling. Even with this assurance grounded in one's heart, we do not escape trials and temptations, grievous at times in their nature. I can recall many families with which I have become acquainted during my sojourn among the Gentiles. Several with whom I am associated with more or less at the present time, whose marriage relations are a joy and comfort to witness. Where the wife and mother is proud and happy in the devotion of a noble husband, while he in turn is equally contented and happy in the possession of the partner he has chosen for life; while at home in each other's association, is where their greatest joys are centered. Witnessing scenes like these, my mind then reverts to my own peculiar wedded experience of the past three years and more, where a few stolen interviews thoroughly tinctured with the dread of discovery, is all that has constituted our married felicity. Looking at the thing from a human standpoint, it is a deplorable situation. But thank God we view the plan through different goggles than those of mere human invention. Otherwise I fear some of us would only stand it long enough for the legal arrangements to be made to dissolve the unnatural relationship. Dear One, do not think from this I am dissatisfied with my lot. To the contrary, I am thankful that God so ordained my destiny to embrace the celestial principle of marriage when I did. And now in it, my energies shall be bent towards its continuance, but I greatly feel my weakness at times, and know not how long I will hold out in the great Cause. And [I] feel certain, that had my movements towards marriage been left or deferred until the present time, and that I had merely human instincts to guide me, I should have given the whole plural system a wide berth, so far as going into it anyway but [as a] first [wife] was concerned. I should have made it a point to [have] been first wife, while at the same time I should have been perfectly willing for my husband to take others who were sufficiently ignorant to sense the situation, or sufficiently heroic to make martyrs of themselves. But why burden you with these boorish soliloquies? Simply to let you know that although I do not talk as much as some people do, still at the same time I strongly sense my situation at the present time—and were it not for daily petitions to God for strength, the adversary would make me feel and believe that it is really a condition of degradation instead of one of honorable wifehood. If you only knew the subterfuges one has to resort to, in order to make any movements appear reasonable to sensible people with whom I meet, while occupying the position I do, you would not wonder at a sense of degradation stealing over me at times. But darling do not misunderstand me and think I blame you for this—for I strongly realize that you, much more than myself, are weighted and clogged & depressed by the conditions that our enemies are subjecting us to, and while I greatly wish for the good of our whole people that the situation was other than it is, still I shall be found with others striving to do my part, thankful to our Heavenly Father that I have you for my husband. For I would rather spend one hour in your society, than a whole life time with any other man I know of. I suppose after all, things with me are just as they should be, for I should certainly be too happy for this testing scene of earth were I permitted to be near you always. 'Tis this very devotion that makes me jealous of you, and our separation so hard. Still when I think if we do right here, that we will associate in the eternities as only those who have passed their ordeal successfully will be permitted to associate, then my mind takes a restful turn, and the perplexities of human existence sink into insignificance. . . .

I will now close by assuring you I love you more than ever, because you are such a good-natured noble fellow and took & take all my scoldings in such good part. Good by and write immediately & accept a thousand kisses from your own Little Maria.

From *Letters From Exile: The Correspondence of Martha Hughes Cannon and Angus M. Cannon, 1886–1888* (1888)

6. First Presidency and Quorum of the Twelve Apostles (Wilford Woodruff, George Q. Cannon, Joseph F. Smith, et al.), "To the Saints [Political Manifesto]"

The perception of President Brigham Young's theocratic control over Utah Territory, combined with the practice of plural marriage, had resulted in the imposition of U.S. federally appointed governors and the refusal of numerous petitions for statehood. To achieve that political end, subsequent Mormon leaders took a number of actions to assure the American public of their readiness to be integrated into American political and religious culture. President Wilford Woodruff issued the Manifesto in 1890 that set in motion the beginning of the end of polygamy. Months later, he disbanded the Utah People's Party, which had been the Mormons' defiant alternative to participation in national party politics. At that time, Woodruff encouraged Latter-day Saints to join both parties, though most avoided the Republican Party, which from its inception had opposed the church and polygamy. In 1894–1895, Utah produced a state constitution that formally disallowed the practice of plural marriage. As a consequence of these steps, Utah finally became an American state in January 1896, but there was still difficult terrain to negotiate in the church's accommodation to a thoroughly secular state. That year, two high-ranking Latter-day Saints, Apostle Moses Thatcher and Seventy Brigham H. Roberts, accepted Democratic Party nominations for the U.S. Senate and Congress, respectively. The Mormon leadership censured both men for presuming to run for high office without consulting them, which had formerly been the practice for members of the church's leadership core. Subsequently, Wilford Woodruff prepared a political manifesto to require Mormon ecclesiastical leaders officially to obtain the church's permission before running for office. He defended the policy as an important guarantee that attention to religious duties remained paramount among the leadership. Woodruff's insistence that its provisions compromised neither individual rights nor the separation of church and state reflects the view of skeptics that it did both.

On behalf of the Church of which we are leading officers, we desire again to state to the members and also to the public generally, that there has not been, or is there, the remotest desire on our part or on the part of our co-religionists to do anything looking to a union of Church and State.

We declare that there has never been any attempt to curtail individual liberty—the personal liberty of any of the officers or members of the Church. The First Presidency and other leading officers did make certain suggestions to the people when the division on party lines took place. That movement was an entirely new departure, and it was necessary, in order that the full benefit should not be lost which was hoped to result from this new political division, that people who were inexperienced should be warned against hasty and ill-considered action. In some cases they were counseled to be wise and prudent in the political steps they were about to take, and this with no idea of winning them against their will to either side. To this extent, and no further, was anything said or done upon this question, and at no time and under no circumstances was any attempt made to say to voters how they should cast their ballots. Any charge that has been made to the contrary is utterly false.

Concerning officers of the Church themselves, the feeling was generally expressed in the beginning of the political division spoken of that it would be prudent for leading men not to accept of office at the hands of the political party to which they might belong. This counsel was given to men of both parties alike—not because it was thought that there was any impropriety in religious men holding civil office, not to deprive them of any of the rights of citizenship, but because of the feeling that it would be better under all the circumstances which had now arisen to avoid any action that would be likely to create jealousy and ill-feeling. An era of peace and good-will seemed to be dawning upon the people, and it was deemed good to shun everything that could have the least tendency to prevent the consummation of this happy prospect. In many instances, however, the pressure brought to bear upon efficient and popular men by the members of the parties to which they belonged was of such a character that they had to yield to the solicitation to accept nomination to office, or subject themselves to the suspicion of bad faith in their party affiliations. In some cases they did this without consulting the authorities of the Church; but where important positions were held, and where the duties were of a responsible and exacting character, some did seek the counsel and advice of the leading Church authorities before accepting the political honors tendered them. Because some others did not seek this counsel and advice, ill-feeling was engendered, and undue and painful sensitiveness was stimulated; misunderstanding readily followed, and as a result the authorities of the Church were accused of bad faith and made the subjects of bitter reproach. We have maintained that in the case of men who hold high positions in the Church, whose duties are well defined, and whose ecclesiastical labors are understood to be continuous and necessary, it would be an improper thing to accept political office or enter into any vocation that would distract or remove them from the religious duties resting upon them, without first consulting and obtaining the approval of their associates and those who preside over them. It has been understood from the very beginning of the Church that no officer whose duties are of the character referred to, has the right to engage in any pursuit, political or otherwise, that will divide his time and remove his attention from the calling already accepted. It has been the constant practice with officers of the Church to consult or, to use our language, to "counsel" with their brethren concerning all questions of this kind. They have not felt that they were sacrificing their manhood in doing so, nor that they were submitting to improper dictation, nor that in soliciting and acting upon the advice of those over them, they were in any manner doing away with their individual rights and agency, nor that to any improper degree were their rights and duties as American citizens being abridged or interfered with. They realized that in accepting ecclesiastical office they assumed certain obligations; that among these was the obligation to magnify the office which they held, to attend to its duties in preference to every other labor, and to devote themselves exclusively to it with all the zeal, industry and strength they possessed, unless released in part or for a time by those who preside over them. Our view, and it has been the view of all our predecessors, is that no officer of our Church, especially those in high standing, should take a course to violate this long-established practice. Rather than disobey it, and declare himself by his actions defiantly independent of his associates and his file leaders, it has always been held that it would be better for a man to resign the duties of his Priesthood: and we entertain the same view today.

In view of all the occurrences to which reference has been made, and to the diversity of views that have arisen among the people in consequence, we feel it to be our duty to clearly define our position, so there may be no cause hereafter for dispute or controversy upon the subject:

First—We unanimously agree to and promulgate as a rule that should always be observed in the Church and by every leading official thereof, that before accepting any position, political or otherwise, which would interfere with the proper and complete discharge of his ecclesiastical duties, and before accepting a nomination or entering into engagements to perform new duties, said official should apply to the proper authorities and learn from them whether he can, consistently with the obligations already entered into with the Church upon assuming his office, take upon himself the added duties and labors and responsibilities of the new position. To maintain proper discipline and order in the Church, we deem this absolutely necessary; and in asserting this rule, we do not consider that we are infringing in the least degree upon the individual rights of the citizen. Our position is that a man having accepted the honors and obligations of ecclesiastical office in the Church cannot properly of his own volition make those honors subordinate to or even coordinate with new ones of an entirely different character; we hold that unless he is willing to counsel with and obtain the consent of his fellow-laborers and presiding officers in the Priesthood, he should be released from all obligations associated with the latter, before accepting any new position.

Second—We declare that in making these requirements of ourselves and our brethren in the ministry, we do not in the least desire to dictate to them concerning their duties as American citizens, or to interfere with the affairs of the State; neither do we consider that in the remotest degree we are seeking the union of Church and State. We once more here repudiate the insinuation that there is or ever has been an attempt by our leading men to trespass upon the ground occupied by the State, or that there has been or is the wish to curtail in any manner any of its functions.

From *Deseret Weekly News* (1896)

7. Reed Smoot, Speech Before the United States Senate (1907)

The Mormon practice of plural marriage is shrouded in mystery and ambiguity, particularly as regards its inauguration and its cessation. Joseph Smith apparently was practicing plural marriage in Kirtland in the 1830s and began secretly to teach the principle to close associates in Nauvoo in the early 1840s. During this period, the church's official position was stated in Doctrine and Covenants 101, titled "marriage." There, a statement authored by Oliver Cowdery and approved in Smith's absence in 1835 affirmed that "inasmuch as this church of Christ has been reproached with the crime of fornication, and polygamy: we declare that we believe, that one man should have one wife; and one woman, but one husband." Cowdery opposed the practice and likely hoped to forestall it and safeguard the church's reputation; Joseph Smith, knowing public knowledge would exacerbate both dissent and persecution, did nothing to remove the declaration from subsequent editions. Not until 1852 did the church officially acknowledge the unorthodox marriage practice, from the relative safety and isolation of their Utah home. Under mounting U.S. federal pressure culminating in draconian measures that imprisoned polygamists, disenfranchised Utah Latter-day Saints, and appropriated Mormon assets, President Wilford Woodruff announced a cessation to the practice in his Manifesto of 1890. However, leaders and members alike were deeply committed to a practice integral to their faith and for which they had sacrificed so much. Accordingly, many Mormons interpreted the Manifesto to be largely for American public consumption. For a generation after, confusion prevailed in the church as to how the leadership's injunction against contracting further plural marriages or cohabiting with plural wives from pre-Manifesto marriages was to be understood. Recognizing that some Latter-day Saints were persisting in the practice with apparent collusion of their leaders, the U.S. Senate convened hearings in 1903 on whether or not to seat the newly elected senator from Utah, Apostle Reed Smoot. Hearings continued until 1907, when a majority—but not the required two-thirds—voted to exclude him.

Mr. President, in what I shall say to the Senate I do not intend to analyze the voluminous testimony taken before the committee or to make an argument thereon. The greater part of this testimony has been before the Senate for more than two years, and all of it for nearly one year. It has been fully argued by the distinguished Senators who have already spoken upon this question.

My own testimony, covering more than 125 pages of the record, is before you, and I do not feel that I should trespass upon your time by indulging in any extended discussion. Indeed, I should have been content to submit the case upon the record and speeches made by others, without saying anything myself at all, except that there are certain matters which can be known only to myself; and I think that the Senate is entitled to a frank statement from me as to my personal attitude respecting those matters. The Senate is entitled to know my personal attitude upon the subject of polygamy and upon the subject of loyalty to this Government. Upon these two matters I shall express myself briefly, but with entire candor.

First, I desire to state as I have repeatedly heretofore stated, to the Senate and to the country that I am not and never have been a polygamist. I never have had but one wife, and she is my present wife, and I deem it proper to further state that I have never taught polygamy.

There has been a more or less prevalent opinion that the doctrine of polygamy was obligatory upon the members of the Mormon Church, whereas, in truth and fact, no such obligatory doctrine has ever existed. The revelation concerning polygamy, as originally made and as always interpreted, is permissible, and not mandatory. As a matter of fact, only a small percentage of the adherents of that faith have ever been polygamists. The vast majority of the adult members of the church, from its foundation to the present time, have been monogamists.

The Mormon people, however, regarded this doctrine, although permissible in character, as part of their religious faith, and when the law was passed denouncing its practice the execution of the law was resisted on the ground that it was unconstitutional as being an interference with their religious liberty. Appeals were taken to the highest courts of the land, every phase of the subject was tested in the courts, and the law was upheld. Then the church adopted the Manifesto against polygamy, which was ratified by the general conference of the people, and thereupon the practice of polygamy for the future was abandoned.

This Manifesto, adopted in 1890, discontinuing plural marriage, has been presented and discussed in church conferences repeatedly, sent out in the church book, The Articles of Faith, and in many other publications issued by the church, such as text-books for the various quorums, manuals for the mutual improvement associations, Sunday schools, primaries, conference proceedings, etc., and in that way has been much more widely circulated than the original revelation on marriage. Consequently its text, tenor, and purpose in prohibiting marriages violative of law are known to every member of the church in every part of the world.

But the practice, which had prevailed in the period previous to 1890, left a heritage for the succeeding period that was a grave problem. There were in 1890 about 2,451 male members of the Mormon Church who had polygamous families. That these were placed in a position of difficulty was recognized by all who were familiar with conditions. The present conditions in reference to polygamous cohabitation have grown out of past conditions, and both must be considered together to fully understand the toleration exercised by most of the people of Utah, Mormon and non-Mormon alike.

The status of the men who had entered into the plural marriage relation before the issuance of the manifesto had been fixed before that time. There was no power in the church or in the law to change that existing fact. What had been done had been irrevocably done. The only question was as to the future. What should be the attitude of the people toward the future relations of those who had entered into the polygamous status before the manifesto? This problem was a serious and perplexing one.

At that time all the machinery of the courts in the Territory was in the hands of non-Mormon officials who had been vigorous in the prosecution of polygamous relationships. These recognized the vexed nature of the situation and extended the olive branch, as it were. As a relief in this dilemma came an exercise of forbearance on the part of prosecuting officers. The three assistant United States district attorneys for that period were E. B. Critchlow, Frank B. Stephens, and William M. McCarty. Judge McCarty was inclined to continue prosecutions in some cases, but the United States district attorney refused to allow his accounts therefore and he ceased. Mr. Critchlow was the writer of the principal protest in this case and one of its signers. All of these and other Government prosecuting officers testified before the committee to the cessation of prosecutions against then existing polygamous relations, and of the general sentiment among the non-Mormon population that that was the best and quickest way to get rid of the whole question—to let the old-time relations naturally end in death. There was a general acquiescence by the people, both

Mormon and non-Mormon, in this method of solving the problem. And this method is working out a complete and final solution.

At the time the manifesto was adopted there were 2,451 polygamous households in the church. Careful statistics have been taken and preserved, and will be found in the testimony, which show that this number has gradually decreased until there was at the time the testimony closed not to exceed 500 such households in existence.

There are twenty-six general authorities of the Mormon Church, including the first presidency, patriarch, apostles, first council of seventies, and presiding bishopric. In 1890 this list of officials was composed of twenty-three polygamists and three monogamists.

The first presidency and council of apostles, prior to my selection as an apostle in 1900, was composed of ten polygamists and five monogamists. In 1906 these same quorums comprised five polygamists and ten monogamists. Of the fourteen general authorities chosen since 1890, only two were polygamists, the other twelve being monogamists.

Of the seven apostles chosen since April, 1900, when I was named, only one was a polygamist, the other six being monogamists. The only polygamist chosen an apostle since 1897 is now 75 years of age, and entered into that relationship before the manifesto. At the time of his selection as an apostle his youngest child was 22 years of age. He has been a member of the church for over half a century, performing faithful and distinguished church service during most of this long period. It was on account of his long, faithful service that I voted for him to be an apostle. Nothing would have induced me to have voted for him if he had been guilty of taking a plural wife since the manifesto.

Of the 96 members of presidencies of stakes (ecclesiastical subdivisions) in 1890, 47, or about one-half, were polygamists. Of 165 such prominent church officials in 1906—the increase in number being because of the creation of new "stakes"—only 16, or less than 10 percent, were polygamists.

But, Mr. President, it is claimed that there have been new cases of polygamous marriage since the manifesto, and this presents altogether a different question.

I have no hesitation, Mr. President, in declaring to the Senate and to the American people that, in my opinion, any man who has married a polygamous wife since the manifesto should be prosecuted, and if convicted, should suffer the penalties of the law; and I care not who the man might be or what position he might hold in the church, he should receive the punishment pronounced by the law against his crime.

The testimony taken before the committee tends to show that there have been some polygamous marriages since the manifesto. I believe sincerely, Mr. President, that such cases have been rare. They have not received the sanction or the encouragement of the church. They have been sporadic and not systematic in their occurrence.

In respect to the thoroughness of the search made by the committee for such violations of the law, a witness before the committee testified that he had been employed since 1898 in hunting down such cases; that he "had undoubtedly the closest information possible" on this matter. This witness gathered and presented all the rumors, intimations, and suspicions he could discover of new polygamous relations in the United States, Canada, Mexico, or elsewhere, and the whole number thus suggested, though not proved, is less than an average of two cases for each year since the manifesto in all these communities, numbering over 300,000 people.

In most of the cases where rumor attached to persons a violation of the law, such persons are and have been fugitives from justice, and the alleged marriages have none of them been charged to have occurred within the jurisdiction of the United States. In but one instance was there direct proof of the plural marriage, and this, it was testified, occurred in Mexico, where the parties, after importuning an apostle then in charge of the Mexican mission to marry them and being refused, went 75 miles to another apostle, who was visiting the mission, and, as far as the testimony shows (the apostle is dead), without his knowledge that there was a previous marriage and a living wife of the man, secured his consent to marry them.

If any of these cases, resting as they do at the present time upon rumor and suspicion, are actually cases of attempted assumption of polygamous relations, such attempt is not only without the sanction and approval of the Mormon Church, but is in the face of, and in defiance of, its most solemn protest and admonition.

The forbearance displayed toward old relations does not apply to persons who might seek to form new relations; toward the latter there is the most determined hostility and aversion.

The Mormon church has stopped plural marriages, and no polygamous relation assumed subsequent to 1890 is with the permission, sanction, or approval of the church; that is final and fixed. Every such violation of the law has the express condemnation of the church. The manifesto of 1890 was submitted to and approved by the conference of the church—which means by the body of the members of the church—and it remains the law of the church, binding upon every officer thereof, however high. It cannot be repealed, modified, or suspended except by the same power that enacted it.

Reference has been made to an alleged treasonable obligation which it is sought to claim is a part of the Mormon endowment ceremonies. The Senate will understand that these ceremonies are of a sacred character to those participating in them and are therefore not divulged. They were instituted in the Mormon Church by Joseph Smith, sometime prior to his death, and are yet given as part of the temple ceremonies; being of a religious, spiritual character, they are for the living and for the dead, a part of the Mormon belief being vicarious performance of ordinances and ceremonies.

There does not exist in the endowment ceremonies of the Mormon Church the remotest suggestion of hostility or of antagonism to the United States or to any other nation. They are of a purely religious nature, wholly between the person taking them and his God, and, as with the ritual of various fraternal organizations, regarded as sacred and secret.

Comment has been made on the fact that upon one occasion, before the year 1890, a single district judge in Utah—one of four such judges, Judge T. J. Anderson—refused to naturalize several Mormons because of an alleged endowment oath. But your attention was not then called to the significant fact, shown by undisputed testimony before the committee, that not only did the other judges not agree with him, but that within a month after rendering the decision referred to the same judge admitted to citizenship Mormons who had received the endowment ceremonies, and he never again refused them.

It is also significant that this decision was rendered in Salt Lake City shortly before an important and bitterly contested municipal election—the contest being between pro-Mormon and anti-Mormon parties. And never again during the six years before Utah was admitted as a State, was it attempted to prevent the naturalization of a Mormon on these grounds.

Adverting to the religious and spiritual character of those ceremonies, it is conceded that such character in ceremonies often has an influence on the conscience and conduct of the persons concerned. There is not a solitary instance where that influence in the endowment ceremonies has been displayed in an act of hostility to the Government. If any effect has been wielded, it has been for the most devoted loyalty to our own nation.

The application in this respect, as to the loyalty of the Mormon people, can be brought home readily by an illustration within our own knowledge.

We will pass by the incident of the Mormon exiles from Nauvoo furnishing a battalion for the United States Army in the war with Mexico; the action of the Utah pioneers in raising the American flag in the Salt Lake Valley when that was Mexican soil; the fidelity of Utah to the Union during the civil war. Come to the period of the Spanish American war and the insurrection in the Philippines—all, within our personal recollection.

Mr. President, we are grateful to the men who, on the field of battle, offer their lives, a noble sacrifice for the honor of the nation and the glory of the flag. Whether they pass unscathed amid the storms of shot and shell to ultimate victory; whether they return with maimed and scarred bodies; or whether they meet the angel of death in facing their country's foe, we give to them unstinted praise for their heroism which has made the American flag respected in every nation upon the globe and has placed our own America the foremost of earth's Governments in maintaining the sacred principles of freedom and human rights. Such actions on the part of American soldiers are a proof of fidelity, of loyalty, that is beyond controversy; and well it may be.

The State of Utah came into the Union eleven years ago.

Scarce two years had passed when there appeared on our national horizon the cloud of war with Spain. You all know the causes and the results. When the nation's chief, the late President McKinley, called for volunteer's to uphold the honor and dignity of the American flag in the struggle which was at hand. Utah was neither last nor least in the ranks of patriotic response. Side by side, shoulder to shoulder, with every other State in the Union, she furnished her full quota of American soldiers and offered more.

There was no question of religious distinction or dispute then. The Utah Light Artillery was composed of men of differing religious beliefs, including orthodox Mormons who had partaken of their church rites known as the "endowment ceremonies." Maj. Richard W. Young, the commanding officer of the Utah Light Artillery, was one of these. Sergt. Harry A. Young and others who gave up their lives for the flag were of this number. And in so far as these endowment ceremonies may have relation to this Government, an unreserved and indisputably accurate interpretation is given by the record of the Mormons mustered into the Utah Light Artillery, which served in the war with Spain and during the subsequent Philippine insurrection. No man has a right to question that interpretation; no true American will do it; it is inscribed in letters of fire by the history of many a battlefield.

It is not my province to describe the operations of the Utah Light Artillery in the Philippine Islands during 1898 and 1899. There is no hint or suggestion on my part that they were better than any other organization. They were the same as the men from Pennsylvania, California, or the States of the mountains and the plains. The reports of the commanding general have an oft-repeated expression: "As usual the Utah battery did most excellent service."

A high meed of praise has been given to all those Army organizations which fought successfully through the Philippine campaign, and it was well deserved. Like the organizations from other States, the Utah Light Artillery had its losses. The frequent official report was: "These casualties occurred while serving their guns."

In the face of an accusation of an "oath of hostility," what is the reply of those men of the Utah Light Artillery who had received of the Mormon Church endowment ceremonies? It is given in the roar of battle at Malate, before Manila came into possession of our troops; at Caloocan, when the Filipino insurrection burst forth in its fury; along the Pasig, searching out the ambuscades of a fierce and bloodthirsty foe; in the personal privation, the nerve-racking strain of scores of hard-fought engagements, and the unswerving loyalty of those American soldiers, who never shrank from duty or wavered in the face of the enemy; it is given in the mutilated and lifeless remains of those brave boys whom our Government brought back home to Utah, to be placed at rest by their loving relatives and friends. And here in the Senate of their countrymen, upon the incontrovertible witness borne by the brave survivors and the heroic dead of the Utah Light Artillery, I hurl back the charge of the defamer that there ever was a word or breath of hostility or disloyalty in the sacred religious ceremonies which they or any other persons participated in as members of the Mormon Church.

It is not an infrequent occurrence, Mr. President, for somebody, often a person of prominence, to come out with a declaration that this or the other thing is "menacing" the life of the Republic; that we are following the path which brought ancient world powers to decay; that our wealth, our industrial combinations, our free speech, are crowding the nation to destruction. Notwithstanding all these dire predictions, none of which is more absurd than the myth of Mormon "hierarchal" domination, the American Union is going to stand. It will continue a free and enlightened Government. It is founded on the popular will of a liberty-loving people. It discusses its public questions and decides them according to rules of tolerance, humanity, and justice. It is builded on the undying principles of human rights and human freedom. As such it will advance. It will grow. It will increase. It will progress. No other nation will prevail against it. It has the favor of God and the gratitude of its own people to perpetuate it along the centuries to come, as they have maintained it in the century that is past.

Those who lament its possible overthrow or shiver in apprehension at its being swept away will not live long enough to view as a reality the fancied cause of their lamentations and apprehensions, nor will their children or their children's children. The Government of the United States is here to stay and to win over every obstacle. And so far as I am concerned, I formally and solemnly aver that in every vote and action as United States Senator I shall be governed in the future, as I have been in the past, only by my convictions of what is best for the whole people of the United States, under my oath to support the Constitution and laws of this nation.

In closing, let me say, under my obligation as a Senator that what I have said under oath before the committee, that I have never taken any oath or obligation, religious or otherwise, which conflicts in the slightest degree with my duty as a Senator or as a citizen. I owe no allegiance to any church or other organization which in any way interferes with my supreme allegiance in civil affairs to my country—an allegiance which I freely, fully, and gladly give.

United States Congressional Record (1907)

8. Susa Young Gates, "The History of Woman Suffrage in Utah, 1900–1920"

Latter-day Saints have been remarkably progressive in some areas of women's issues, even while remaining one of few Christian denominations to preserve church leadership and the priesthood as exclusively male domains. To outsiders, the institution of polygamy seemed egregious evidence of an oppressive gender inequality. American suffragist leaders of the nineteenth century deplored plural marriage but nevertheless found unlikely allies among Mormon women. For while it was easy to see polygamy and political equality as incompatible, LDS women actually found in their religion a basis for aspirations to full equality and self-realization. Plural marriage by its very nature engendered great independence and resilience on the part of women who were frequently charged with running households, farms, and sometimes businesses, while the husband attended to other families. President Brigham Young actively encouraged Mormon women to secure an education and develop careers not typically open to women in the nineteenth century, including business, accounting, medicine, and law. In addition, Mormon women had long administered with virtual independence their own organization, the Relief Society, and in 1872 they inaugurated their own journal, the Woman's Exponent, *unabashedly feminist in its orientation. Anticipating much of the twentieth century feminist agenda, the* Exponent *proclaimed gender equality and lobbied for gender equity in pay. It was therefore natural that after securing their own suffrage in 1870, Mormon women should ally with the national movement to secure the same right for all American women. In addition to her work advocating for suffrage, Susa Young Gates founded and edited two church periodicals, established the music department at Brigham Young Academy, authored both novels and historical works, and participated in several national Republican conventions.*

The results of equal suffrage in Utah for fifty years—1870–1920—with an unavoidable interim of eight years, have demonstrated the sanity and poise of women in the exercise of their franchise. The Mormon women had had long training, for from the founding of their church by Joseph Smith in 1830 they had a vote in its affairs. Although the Territory of Wyoming was the first to give the suffrage to women—in November, 1869—the Legislature of Utah followed in January, 1870, and the bill was signed by Governor S. A. Mann on February 12. Women voted at the regular election the next August and there was no election in Wyoming until September, so those of Utah had the distinction of being the pioneer women voters in the United States and there were over five times as many women in Utah as in Wyoming. The story of how their suffrage was taken away by an Act of Congress in 1887 and how it was restored in full by the men of Utah when they made their constitution for statehood in 1895 and adopted it by a vote of ten to one is related in detail in Volume IV of the *History of Woman Suffrage*. The women have voted since then in large numbers, filled many offices and been a recognized political influence for the benefit of the State.

The large and active Territorial Woman Suffrage Association held annual conventions until after it succeeded in gaining the franchise. In 1899, during a visit of Mrs. Carrie Chapman Catt to Salt Lake City, a meeting was called and steps taken to form a Utah Council of Women to assist the suffrage movement in other States and Mrs. Emily S. Richards was made president.

This Council, composed of Mormons and non-Mormons, continued in existence for twenty years. For the first ten years there were monthly meetings and also special and committee meetings and prominent speakers addressed the annual gatherings, eulogizing and commemorating the lives and labors of the suffrage pioneers throughout the Union. Whenever the National American Suffrage Association called for financial aid it responded liberally. The suffrage having been gained it was hard to keep up the interest and after 1910 meetings were held only at the call of the president for the purpose of carrying out the wishes of the National Suffrage Association, at whose conventions the Council was always represented by delegates. In 1909–10, when the association was collecting its monster petition to Congress, the Council obtained 40,000 names as Utah's quota.

The official personnel remained practically the same from 1900. That noble exponent of the best there is in womanhood, Mrs. Emily S. Richards, preserved the spirit and genius of the Council, which recognized no party and whose members cast their votes for good men and measures without undue partisan bias. She was sustained by its capable and resourceful secretary, Mrs. Elizabeth M. Cohen, and both maintained a non-partisan attitude in the conduct of the Council. The officers were: Emmeline B. Wells, member national executive committee; Elizabeth A. Hayward, Mrs. Ira D. Wines, Dr. Jane Skolfield and Mrs. B. T. Pyper, vice-presidents; Anna T. Piercey, assistant secretary; Hannah S. Lapish, treasurer.

As Territory and State, every county, every town, every precinct has been served faithfully and well by women in various positions. It would be impossible to name all who have done yeoman service during the past years but the three women who have meant more than all others to the suffrage cause are Mrs. Sarah M. Kimball, who was appointed by Brigham Young and Eliza R. Snow as the standard bearer of that cause in the late '60s and who maintained her active hold upon politics until about 1885, when her able first lieutenant, Mrs. Emmeline B. Wells, took up the work dropped by the aged hands of Mrs. Kimball. She in turn carried the banner of equal civic freedom aloft, assisted by Mrs. Richards, until she relinquished it in 1896 and Mrs. Richards became the standard bearer. Many other splendid women have labored assiduously in this cause.

In legislative matters a committee from the Council has worked during every session since 1911 with associated committees from the other large organizations of women, the powerful Relief Society, the Young Ladies' Mutual

Improvement Association and the Federated Clubs leading in all good movements. Results in the enactment of welfare laws for women and children have been very gratifying. The women's committees of the various organizations meet at the State Capitol during the legislative sessions and go over very carefully every bill in which they are interested. If after investigation a bill meets with their approval it is endorsed and every effort is made to secure its passage. From 1911 to 1917 the women's legislative committee secured copies of laws already in successful operation in other States and framed bills to meet their own needs. These were always submitted to two young lawyers, Dan B. Shields and Carl Badger, who corrected any flaws which might jeopardize their constitutionality. Among the women who comprise these committees are Mrs. Cohen, chairman, Miss Sarah McLelland of the Relief Society; Mrs. Adella W. Eardley and Mrs. Julia Brixen of the Y. L. M. I. A.; Mrs. Richards and Mrs. Hayward of the Suffrage Council; Mrs. C. M. McMahon, president, Mrs. Peter A. Simpkin, Mrs. A. V. Taylor and Mrs. Seldon I. Clawson, members of the Federation of Women's Clubs.

In many Legislatures since statehood there have been women members and their work has been along expected lines. In 1896, the year Utah was admitted to the Union, Dr. Martha Hughes Cannon was elected to the State Senate, the first woman in the United States to receive that honor. Several women were elected to the Lower House then and others in the years following. Needed reform measures were secured by Mrs. Mary G. Coulter, who sat in the Lower House and was made chairman of the Judiciary Committee in 1903. There was a long interim when no women were sent to the Legislature but in 1913 four were elected, Mrs. Annie Wells Cannon, Dr. Skolfield, Mrs. Elizabeth Ellerbeck Reid and Mrs. Annie H. King. They were instrumental in securing the Mothers' Pension Law and the Minimum Wage Law and through Mrs. Cannon the bureau of emigration labor was provided with a woman deputy to look after the women and children workers. Utah already had an equal guardianship law but largely through the efforts of Mrs. Cannon it was improved and is now regarded as a model and has been copied by other States. She is a representative daughter of Mrs. Wells.

In 1915 Mrs. Elizabeth A. Hayward and Mrs. Lily C. Wolstenholme were elected and to the former the improved child labor law must be credited. In 1917 she was re-elected and Dr. Grace Stratton Airy and Mrs. Daisy C. Allen became members of the Lower House. During 1915–1917 laws raising the age of protection for girls to 18 and requiring equal pay for equal work were enacted.

Mrs. Hayward, at the request of the women's Legislative Council, introduced the resolution calling on Congress to submit the Federal Amendment. In 1918 she was elected State Senator. In 1919 Dr. Airy was re-elected and Mrs. Anna G. Piercy and Mrs. Delora Blakely were elected to the Lower House. Altogether there have been thirteen women members of the Legislature. No State has better laws relating to women and children than Utah.

It has been difficult to persuade the women to stand for important offices. The modern furious pace set by campaigners and the severance of home ties for long periods are not alluring to wives and mothers but they find many public activities through which to exercise their executive abilities. They sit on the boards of many State and local institutions and serve on committees for civic and educational work. A considerable number have filled and are now filling city and county offices. Mrs. L. M. Crawford has a responsible position in the office of the State Land Board. Mrs. McVickar was State Superintendent of Schools. In 1917 a new department was added to the office of the Adjutant General to secure pensions for those veterans who had served in the early Indian wars of Utah. Mrs. Elizabeth M. Cohen was given custody of the old Indian War Records and was named Commissioner of Pensions. In order to prove the claims of these men and women she cooperated with the Pension Bureau at Washington, D.C. Up to date out of a possible 1,500 whose claims have merit nearly 700 pensions have been granted, bringing into the State the sum of $400,000.

When Brigham Young established those monuments to his name, the Brigham Young University of Provo and the Brigham Young College of Logan in 1874 he placed women on their boards. Mrs. Martha J. Coray of Provo served ten years for the former and Professor Ida M. Cook for the latter. Mrs. Gates was made a trustee of the university in 1891, which position she still occupies, while her sister, Mrs. Zina Young Card, has been a trustee since 1914. Mrs. Gates was on the board of the State Agricultural College 1905–1913. Mrs. A. W. McCune was on this board ten years, seven of them its vice-president. Mrs. Rebecca M. Little, Mrs. Antoinette B. Kinney and Dr. Belle A. Gummel have been regents of the university. Professor Maude May Babcock has been dean of physical education and expression since 1892 and a trustee since 1897. Her culture and personality have left an indelible impress on the history of this State.

From the beginning women have allied themselves with the different political parties, occasionally uniting on a great issue like that of Prohibition. From the time they were enfranchised by the State constitution they have received the recognition of the parties. In 1900 women were sent as delegates and alternates to both national presidential conventions and Mrs. Cohen seconded the nomination of William Jennings Bryan. A number were sent in following years. In 1908 Mrs. Margaret Zane Cherdron was a delegate and a presidential elector, carrying the vote to Washington. She was one of the two received by President Taft and was royally entertained while in the capital. Among other women who have acted as delegates and alternates since 1900 are Mrs. William H. Jones, Mrs. Hayward, Mrs. Sarah Ventrees, Mrs. Gates, Mrs. Lucy A. Clark, Mrs. B. T. Pyper, Mrs. L. M. Crawford, Mrs. Alice E. Paddison.

Women have their representation on all political committees—Mrs. Hayward is a member of the Democratic National Committee—and their participation in politics is accepted without question. There are about 10,000 more women voters than men voters. As a rule about 90 per cent. of the women vote and about 86 per cent. of the men, as some of the latter are in the mines or out of the State for various reasons. Among the Republican leaders are Mrs. Wells, Mrs. Gates, Mrs. Cherdron, Mrs. Jannette A. Hyde, Mrs. Cannon, Mrs. Wolstenholm, Mrs. Loufborough, Mrs. William Spry, Mrs. Reed Smoot; Mrs. Martha B. Keeler of Provo and Mrs. Georgina G. Marriott of Ogden. The Democratic party has had among its leading women Mrs. Richards, Mrs. Alice Merrill Horne, Mrs. Cohen, Mrs. Hayward, Gwen Lewis Little, Mrs. Piercy, Mrs. S. S. Smith, Mrs. Annice Dee, Mrs. Inez Knight Allen and Miss Alice Reynolds.

No State exceeded Utah in the proportion of the work done by women during the World War. Mrs. Clarissa Smith Williams was the unanimous choice for chairman of the State branch of the Woman's Council of National Defense. She was eminently fitted for this position through her long experience as first counsellor to Mrs. Emmeline B. Wells, head of the Relief Society, and every demand of the Government was fully met.

RATIFICATION. At the request of the Suffrage Council and without urging, Governor Simon Bamberger called a special session of the Legislature for Sept. 30, 1919, to ratify the Federal Suffrage Amendment submitted the preceding June. The resolution was presented by Senator Elizabeth A. Hayward and was ratified unanimously by both Houses within thirty minutes. The Governor signed it without delay. The women and the Legislature had helped in every possible way to secure the Amendment and the entire Utah delegation in Congress had voted for it.

A striking event in the train of possible fruitful activities left behind was the visit of the great leader, Mrs. Carrie Chapman Catt, president of the National

American Suffrage Association, with her able young assistants, who came to Utah for Nov. 16–18, 1919. She was accompanied by Dr. Valerie Parker and Mrs. Jean Nelson Penfield, chairmen in the National League of Women Voters, and Miss Marjorie Shuler, director of publicity for the National Association. The convention, held in the Assembly Hall, was in charge of the Suffrage Council, its president, Mrs. Richards, assisted by Mrs. Cohen and Mrs. E. E. Corfman. A long and valuable program was carried out. Mrs. Catt spoke in the Tabernacle on Sunday afternoon, introduced by President Charles W. Penrose with a glowing tribute to her power as a leader, to the sincerity and womanliness of her character and to the catholicity of her vision and sympathy. There were banquets, teas and receptions.

At the close of the convention the Suffrage Council, which had rendered such splendid service for the past twenty years, was merged into the State League of Women Voters and Mrs. Richards willingly resigned her leadership to its chairman, Mrs. Clesson S. Kinney.

On Feb. 12, 1920, a jubilee celebration was held in honor of the fiftieth anniversary of the signing of the woman suffrage bill by the Territorial Governor S. A. Mann. There was also celebrated the granting of the complete franchise by the immense majority of the voters in 1895.

Utah celebrated in Salt Lake City August 30, with a great demonstration, the triumph of woman suffrage in the United States through the ratification of the Federal Amendment, which had been proclaimed August 26. It was introduced with an impressive parade led by bands of music and the program of ceremonies was carried out on the steps of the State Capitol. Governor Bamberger, former Governor Heber M. Wells, Congressman E. O. Leatherwood and Mayor C. Clarence Neslen joined the women in congratulatory addresses. Mrs. Richards, Mrs. Hannah Lapish and Mrs. Lydia Alder, veteran suffragists, told of the early struggles and Mrs. Beulah Storrs Lewis appealed to women to keep high the standard in order to lead men out of the darkness of war into the light of brotherly love and make ready for world peace. Mrs. Annie Wells Cannon and Mrs. Susa Young Gates were appointed to send a telegram of congratulation to Mrs. Catt. The celebration was under the auspices of the League of Women Voters, whose chairman, Mrs. Kinney, presided. The most impressive figure on the platform was President Emmeline B. Wells, 92 years old, who had voted since 1870 and who had labored all these years for this glorious achievement. What those dim eyes had seen of history in the making, what those old ears had heard and what that clear brain had conceived and carried out only her close associates knew. She was the incarnate figure of tender, delicate, eternally determined womanhood, arrived and triumphant.

From *The History of Woman Suffrage* (1922)

9. J. Reuben Clark, General Conference Address

In social welfare as in so many other areas, Mormons brought the spiritual and the earthly into juxtaposition. In 1905, President Joseph F. Smith taught that "a religion which has not the power to save people temporally and make them prosperous and happy here on earth, cannot be depended upon to save them spiritually and exalt them in the life to come."¹ Virtually since its founding, the church had administered material assistance through the bishops' storehouses, where tithing in kind and goods procured through fast and other offerings were maintained for the relief of the poor. However, these resources were depleted by the severity of the Great Depression, where Mormons living in Utah suffered as deeply as almost any of their fellow Americans. Seeking a solution in 1933, Pioneer Stake president Harold B. Lee began experimenting with cooperatively managed farms in an area that was particularly devastated by unemployment. The two key ingredients to its success were the providing of dignified labor for those in need and the distribution throughout the stake of goods produced. Church president Heber J. Grant admired the formula and made the decision to implement a church-wide version of Lee's welfare program in 1936.

One-half century after the centralization of the welfare system, the church held 172,000 acres of farmland, 199 agricultural production projects, 51 canneries, and 63 grain storage facilities feeding into 113 central, regional, and branch storehouses.² Mormons are justly famous for the efficiency of their operations and their commitment to taking care of their own. But in addition to their welfare program, which looks inward, more than 2,400 humanitarian missionaries serve in Welfare Services worldwide, extending the reach of LDS relief efforts to Mormons and non-Mormons alike in more than 150 countries.

As promised at the last April [1936] Conference, we inaugurated a Church Security Plan. To facilitate the putting into effect of the Plan, we organized a General Committee whose functions were to represent the Presiding Bishopric in the detailed administrative work of coordinating and supervising the labors of the various regularly established Church organizations in their large and important security operations.

The Security Plan contemplated no new Church machinery for this work, but provided for the use of all the existing Church organizations—the Stake and Ward organizations, the Priesthood quorums, the Relief Society, and the various auxiliary organizations of which was to render the maximum service it could furnish in the interest of the general welfare of the Church.

OBJECTIVE TO PROVIDE NECESSITIES

The announced objective set for the Church under this Program was to provide by October 1, 1936, by a wholly voluntary system of gifts in cash or in kind, sufficient food, fuel, clothing, and bedding to supply through the coming winter, every needy and worthy Church family unable to furnish these for itself, in order that no member of the Church should suffer in these times of stress and emergency.

WORK TO REPLACE IDLENESS

Our primary purpose was to set up, in so far as it might be possible, a system under which the curse of idleness would be done away with, the evils of a dole abolished, and independence, industry, thrift and self respect be once more established amongst our people. The aim of the Church is to help the people to help themselves. Work is to be re-enthroned as the ruling principle of the lives of our Church membership.

Our great leader, Brigham Young, under similar conditions, said:

> Set the poor to workout orchards, splitting rails, digging ditches, making fences, or anything useful, and so enable them to buy meal and flour and the necessities of life.

This admonition is as timely today as when Brigham Young made it.

CONTRIBUTIONS IN LABOR

The harvests not having been yet fully completed, it is not possible to make a final report upon our present situation under the Plan, but we are happy to make the following preliminary statement:

In accordance with the Plan, everything that has been done has been accomplished by the purely voluntary gift or labor of members of the Church as well as the gifts of many non-members who have contributed most generously of their substance to aid the Church in its efforts. We wish especially to thank these for their help.

More than 15,000 persons have performed labor on various Stake and Ward projects in connection with this Plan. Many of these have contributed their work gratis; others have received for their services, work certificates entitling them to help during the coming winter. Hundreds of thousands of work hours have been furnished by the people to this necessary and praiseworthy purpose.

The Church Security Plan contemplates that those now on WPA projects shall continue on these projects, making sure to give a full day's work for value received but they are expected to contribute of their time when not so employed to the carrying out of the plan.

The Church aims to help provide for the care and sustenance of those on direct relief, State and County, as also for those for whom the Church has heretofore cared. The exact number of such persons cannot now be certainly given but they may be as many as 15,000. We have strongest reasons for believing we shall be able to give these the aid they need.

REPORTS FROM STAKES

Oct. 1st, the date set on which reports were to be made, 98 stakes out of a total of 117 had reported on their organizations and achievements, and 83 answer that they are prepared to supply food, clothing, bedding, etc., to every person in need.

We commend the presidencies of stakes and bishoprics of wards for this outstanding record of promptness and efficiency.

It is also contemplated that under this plan work shall be sought and obtained for the unemployed in private industries, thus relieving both the government and the Church. To this time upwards of 700 persons have been so placed by the Security agencies. Efforts along this line will be steadily pursued.

RESULTS ITEMIZED

As already stated the harvests are not yet completed and so returns are necessarily incomplete, but data available show as to food-stuffs actually now on hand the following items:

Wheat, over 4,000 bushels. Beans, over 13,000 pounds. Dried fruits, over 23,000 pounds. Meat, over 10,000 pounds. Vegetables, over 14,000 pounds. Potatoes, over 6,000 bushels. Shelled corn, over 3,000 pounds. Flour, over 62,000 pounds. Canned fruit and vegetables, almost 300,000 cans.

There are numbers of other items of foodstuffs of lesser amounts.

There are over 23,000 articles of men's, women's and children's clothing, including dresses, underwear, coats, suits, stockings, socks and shoes.

There are more than 2,000 quilts already made; and other bedding is being accumulated in substantial quantities.

Arrangements are under way for the supply of fuel as needed. The foregoing partial summary will indicate what the people have done in the short space of time of five months only. It is a glowing promise of what the people are able to do when they put their wills and hearts to this work.

WARDS AND STAKES TO HELP EACH OTHER

Every ward and stake is expected to face the necessity, not only of providing for its own, but of helping other wards and stakes. In no other way would it be possible to do the work which the Church is aiming to do. But few stakes and wards are in a position where they may be rightfully satisfied by merely caring for their own.

This great work must continue unabated during the winter months along all lines and activities possible in that inclement season. When spring comes, the measures taken to supply foodstuffs must be redoubled.

We shall then easily be able to do better than this year because we can begin our work when the planting season begins. We must not contemplate ceasing our extraordinary efforts until want and suffering shall disappear from amongst us.

The responsibility of seeing that no one is hungry or cold or insufficiently clad rests upon the bishops, each one for the members of his own ward. He will use every Church organization of his ward to help him in his work. For help outside his ward, he will look for necessary assistance to his Stake Presidency, they to their regional organization, and these to the Presiding Bishopric of the Church whose primary responsibility it is to look after the poor of the Church as a whole.

From *Conference Report* (1936)

10. Sonia Johnson and Karen S. Langlois, "All on Fire: An Interview with Sonia Johnson"

The American feminist movement of the 1960s somewhat influenced Mormon culture, registering on the pages of some of the independent Mormon journals, such as Dialogue, *and more particularly in the founding in 1974 of* Exponent II, *a quarterly magazine targeting readers who share "a connection to the Mormon Church and a commitment to women" (the original* Woman's Exponent *publication had ceased in 1914). But church leaders confronted feminism directly and dramatically in 1976, when the First Presidency issued a statement opposing passage of the Equal Rights Amendment. The document cited the amendment's encouragement of a "unisex society" and its potential to threaten the family as an institution by ignoring traditional gender roles and differences. The next year, fifth-generation Mormon Sonia Johnson organized "Mormons for ERA" with three other women. Increasingly vocal in her criticism of the church's political involvement opposing the amendment, Johnson gave testimony in Senate hearings and spoke out publicly and fiercely to the press and professional conventions. In 1979, the church excommunicated her, allegedly citing her efforts to damage the church's missionary program (she implored Americans to shut the doors to missionaries) and her teaching of false doctrines. Negative reaction to the church's position increased with her excommunication, which she parleyed as a public relations success by arguing her beliefs, rather than her public attacks on church leaders and Mormon missionary work, were the basis for church sanctions. Ultimately, the church's ability to mobilize member opposition to the amendment was seen as decisive in its 1982 defeat, though widespread support for passage was by then waning nationally. Johnson went on to run for the American presidency in 1984 as a Citizens Party candidate.*

In an interview you gave us a year ago January, the word had just come out about the divorce. You said something about how you had been too busy looking at the trees to see the forest. What did you mean by that?

The divorce took me totally by surprise. It happened very fast to him, too. It was a great shock, but as far as losing anything, I still have all the Church's teachings, and I have gained a lot of self-knowledge besides. I feel a deep, inner peace and serenity. It wasn't that I was particularly lacking this before, but I just feel better about me. I feel confident about the future. I feel that there isn't much that can harm me now. I have faced the worst and it didn't break me. I feel good about myself and about human nature. . . .

Do you feel bitter?

I don't think "bitter" is the word. I am angry, but "bitter" connotes that I wish the Church ill as an institution. I don't. I am still angry about the Church's right-wing politics which is anti-women. This makes me angry as the dickens, and I hope I don't ever stop being angry about that. Somebody from a radio station in Arizona called me to ask that question, and I said, I wish the Mormon Church well, but I feel very little interest in it anymore as a religious institution.

So you don't feel any need to come back into the Church?

No, I don't think I will ever come back.

What if the Church changed its mind on the ERA?

Oh, they would have to change their minds on too many other things. Half the apostles would have to become women. Women would have to be called to decision-making bodies.

You would like a husband-wife bishop team?

If the wife could be called "bishop" and the husband "assistant bishop!" Somehow or other, women have got to be given their due. I just don't think that will happen in my time. I do feel a need for something, though, and more so lately. Mostly for the children's sake. They miss the ritual of going to church on Sunday and the structure of it, so I am going to have to think of something to do about that. Last Sunday was the first time I really felt this. I would like to find a Quaker meeting. I am attracted to that not because it is the only true Church—the Only True Church concept has left my thinking altogether. But the Quakers are my kind of people—decent people who care about issues like war and peace and poverty and are not hierarchical. There is no bullying in the ranks; there is no punishment idea—conforming or being zapped by God. But I don't think the children would find enough structure there. If it were just me, I would gravitate toward a congregation where people think like me. The Unitarian Church has good things for children. I will go to see what they have, but obviously, the main thing I will have to do is teach them myself. We talk now about everything: how we live and how to live with integrity—what we owe other people. But they need to be able to discuss these things with other young people in a place where there is intellectual freedom and they can come home and talk about them afterwards.

If you were going to write your own Articles of Faith, what would you add to what you have just said?
I think we just have to care about other people more than we do. We must be more concerned that people are living and dying in poverty. I think if we are not concerned about that, then we will not be whole. Even though we are middle-class and never see this kind of suffering, we must do something.

Poverty seems to be uppermost in your mind.
Especially among women. It is incredible. The women's movement—and I know the leaders personally, I know Gloria Steinem personally; I know Bella Abzug personally, I know Ellie Smeal personally—these mothers of the woman's movement care about the suffering of women. Whenever the husbands are out of work, or have left or died, it all devolves upon the women. Economic crisis! Women are in it all the time! These are the women who are not articulate about it, who feel powerless, and there are millions of them in this country. All you have to do is go to the places where they come, and my gosh, the misery that is afoot in this land. Sometimes you can't face it.

The reason people don't want to know about it is because it is so heartbreaking. Often when I visit cities, I visit projects like battered wives' shelters. I often ask to visit these places so I can find out what it is I mean when I talk about justice for women.
One of Beverly Campbell's arguments is that laws are not worded in a way that they can be enforced. She says women must learn to write good laws themselves.

That's true.
She says that laws protecting battered wives and others cannot be enforced because they are not written well.
They are not enforced because the American people don't care enough. People still believe, and the Church still believes, that whatever happens in the home is sacrosanct. If a woman is being exploited there, no one has a right to interfere. It's patriarchy—male rule—and if women suffer, it's too bad because God ordained it. It makes us think that it doesn't really matter to God if a women is being beaten and killed in her own home. It's patriarchy, the belief that men are supreme, and once women get equality, then men cannot exploit them. When I say women are in slavery, people

say to me, oh well, those are strong words. The United Nations put out these statistics when I was in Copenhagen: Women do two-thirds of the world's work. For that they make one-tenth of the world's money. Now, that's slavery! . . .

In a telephone conversation a few months ago, just after the last LDS Conference, you said, "Mormon women now have the upper hand. Men are now in a precarious position." What did you mean by that?
How long can men keep up the nonsense that only men should make decisions about how the Church—how the world is run? The whole attitude of the world is changing. It is obvious that women are just as bright, that they can run institutions, and that they ought to have a say in the Church that demands all their time and love. When they fought the ERA, they didn't ask women; they assumed they could speak for women. I think we are coming to the point where women aren't going to let men do that anymore. God would never expect people who are total non-experts on this subject to give advice to experts. Women are the experts on being women, but we are told who we are and what we are and what we must feel by men who haven't a clue—who haven't even had a menstrual cycle! Women aren't going to take that anymore. How can they tell me when I am feeling fulfilled? We are all different! We are not clones!

God made us as various as men. Women are as different from one another as men are different from one another. All men don't want to be farmers. Neither do all women want to bake bread or whatever. Women are to the point where it is harder for men only to invoke God because it makes God look so foolish. And God is not foolish!

Women in the Mormon Church are as safe as in their mothers' wombs right now. This is the time for them to move.

Are there any other hopeful signs? Like BYU Women's Conferences, where there has been emphasis on different lifestyles?
Yes, even Beverly Campbell says that! Beverly Campbell is a frustrated feminist! She would like to be on our side, and she may someday be because she says the things we say, and then she has to backtrack and try to make them fit in to the way men meant them. You know, she can't do that forever. Well, maybe she can, but anyway, *Exponent II* finally seems to be saying things without being so fearful. Women are losing their fear. They feel the rightness of it. They are not stopping to equate men and God.

The new managing editor at the *Deseret News* is a woman. She is a popular choice, apparently, a single woman who has worked hard at her career.

That is a hopeful sign. I wish Mormon women understood their power.

Senator Paula Hawkins appears in the *Church News* with her husband who says he is not threatened and has even joined the Congressional Wives Club.

Very good. When are the women of the Church going to recognize that the women being held up for them as models are the women they are told not to emulate?

It's a double message: These women who are telling them to behave certain ways are women who are not like that themselves. Beverly Campbell, Elaine Cannon, not a one of them is a woman with millions of kids staying home and baking bread. I think women are beginning to figure that out. The women the men honor are not the women in the home. If they really want to keep women in the home, I don't think their actions show those are the women they really think are terrific.

Are Mormon men beginning to understand?
The only Mormon men I associate with anymore are the Mormons for ERA—about 400 or so of them. There are about 1,200 members of the Mormons for ERA altogether. . . .

If women had the priesthood, wouldn't that mean the demise of the priesthood? Who would have authority then?
Yes, then you would have to consider ordinary people's views and feelings. We would all be considered equally important.

People could get together and divide up duties and roles? You could just draw lots every time? From what I've read, that's not the way to keep a group going.

If you traded off on jobs, it wouldn't get to be hierarchical. Now, whoever controls the money is at the top.

So economics is what lies at the bottom of it? Ownership of property?
Yes, we need an economic revolution. People say to me, why do you think the ERA is so important? It won't do anything. But they fight it anyway. There are little powerless, poverty-stricken women fighting the richest

institutions we have, including organized religion. What I would like to say to Beverly Campbell, if I had a chance, when she talks about how the Church wants women to have equality, I would like her to tell me what the Church is doing about that. I would like to ask her if she believes in patriarchy, and if she does, how she can believe in patriarchy and equality at the same time.

It's another compartmentalized Mormon thing. Patriarchy means that if you are male, you are born into the ruling class. Rulers are always higher, and they keep the money for themselves. This is patriarchy: the men on top the women underneath, economically and every other way. Mormons have splits right down the middle of their heads. "Of course I believe in equality; Of course I believe in patriarchy." I mean schizophrenic as the dickens. They don't know what patriarchy means; they don't know what equality means. They haven't even thought through it enough to understand that they are believing in two ideas that are antithetical. Patriarchy is antithetical to equality, absolutely, totally. Therefore, you can't have God believing in patriarchy and equality at once. If God, the Deity, believes in equality of human beings, then he would not set up one sex above the other.

Is it possible to have the gospel without the patriarchy?
Yes. We can still believe in baptism, the Holy Ghost, the laying on of hands, faith, repentance, even the Articles of Faith without patriarchy. I think the Church will change eventually. It will have to.

What good does civil disobedience do, especially in a church setting where certain civil laws don't apply?
It dramatizes and symbolizes and helps bring people to accountability. If a person is committed enough to risk and to sacrifice, this helps society change. Because the Church entered the political arena with both feet, it deserves to be treated like any other political body. And if the larger society changes, the Church will have to change too. If there develops too great a dissonance between church and society, then the pews will be empty, and the Church will have to change.

If people finally come to believe that women are truly equal, the churches will all have to change their politics. Now my father, for instance, doesn't believe the Mormon Church could survive if it were not built on patriarchy, that the gospel itself is founded on patriarchy. I, for one, don't care whether or not the Church gives the priesthood to women so long as we get our legal rights.

One last question: If the ERA had not become an issue in the Church, would you have stayed in the Church, or do you think you might have found yourself in other kinds of trouble?
I like to think I would still have cared enough about women's rights to want to help them. It might have taken another ten years. I used to care a lot about the blacks but remained quiet about them. Even without the ERA, though, I was getting very disquieted by certain happenings in the Church and religious problems were piling up on me.

Do you think you have changed? Have you acquired any non-Mormon habits?
Yes, in fact, I have. I have acquired the habit of free thought.

From *Dialogue: A Journal of Mormon Thought* (1981)

11. Judith Rasmussen Dushku, "A Time of Decision"

Few faith traditions are as steeped in the expression of choice and accountability as Mormonism. Satan is the fallen angel who "sought to destroy the agency of man" before the earth was even created. "Know this, that every soul is free," proclaimed the first hymn anthologized in the church's 1835 hymnal. Humans are "agents unto themselves," not one but four scriptures declare (Doctrine and Covenants 29:39; 58:28; 104:17; Moses 6:56). At the same time, few churches are as emphatically opposed to abortion as the church. One theological basis for this position can be found in the revelation warning members not to "kill, nor do anything like unto it" (Doctrine and Covenants 59:6). In addition, Mormon belief that all humans existed as pre-mortal spirits in God's presence means that life begins even before conception (though no doctrine on the moment of embodiment exists). Finally, procreative powers are associated in Mormon theology with opportunities for endless posterity for those who are saved in the Celestial Kingdom, thereby endowing these powers with special sanctity and responsibility. Church leaders routinely denounce the practice of abortion, and church policy mandates ecclesiastical discipline for those who even encourage an abortion, and exceptions for the most grievous circumstances—rape, incest, and danger to a mother's life—are possible but not automatic. Latter-day Saints tend to largely obey their prophet's mandates, and abortion is no exception; they engage in abortion at levels far below the national average. Nonetheless, some church members struggle to reconcile agency with legal prohibition, and personal morality with political position. One such person is Judith Dushku, a self-described Mormon feminist and academic.

"You are 'Pro-Choice' aren't you?" mumbled the young legislator at his desk as he pored over my application. Anticipating my response, he wrote the label boldly across the front page. I asked why the label had to be so prominently displayed on my application for a seat on the Massachusetts Delegation to the White House Conference on Families.

"Come on," he replied sarcastically. "You know this game. When we had the state elections, the Pro-Lifers were so well organized they walked all over the delegate selection process. They bused in hundreds of voters every day. Almost all the delegates were from their slates. We checked them out. Some are reasonable people—an asset to the state—but some are real crazies. The Governor is upset. He is a Pro-Lifer, as you know, but he is embarrassed by this mob. Even he admits that the delegation needs balance. So now he wants a list to choose his appointees from. Probably he will name more Pro-Lifers, but he would like a list of decent minorities and decent Pro-Choice types to pick from. I just heard you were pregnant. Can I tell him? Pro-Choice and pregnant is easier to take than just Pro-Choice." He took a quick breath and began again.

"These right-wingers are so prepared for battle they had their buses loaded while we were still putting a staff together. I give them credit for enthusiasm, but they are the scariest people I've ever met. I'm a good Catholic with a clean Pro-Life record, but they call me names because I talk to people like you. Sorry—

"Anyway, that is why I have to know where you stand and I have to make it public." I started to protest but he went on. "Yeah, it's too bad. I know some people like to keep their thoughts on abortion to themselves. It's a heavy issue. But these days you have to take a stand—publicly.

"Hey, what's the matter? I thought you were a Pro-Choice person. Someone from NOW and from your university said you are a real civil-liberties type and a supporter of the State Women's Caucus. No?"

Of course I am Pro-Choice, I reminded myself. Hadn't I always believed in freedom and agency for all? I had been teaching civil liberties to my political science classes for thirteen years, working hard to impress upon students the value of guaranteeing this freedom. It was a philosophy that had never embarrassed me. Although it is a hard principle to apply in all situations, I have never questioned it as a good and right goal. Moreover, it is a basic tenet of my religion. Growing up a Mormon I had been taught the principle of free agency, and I have always taken it seriously. People—all people—have the right and the responsibility to choose.

Yes, I had read President Kimball's strong statement on abortion, and I felt that I understood his counsel. A society that encourages abortions does tend to lose sight of the value of human life and does begin to feel less responsibility for the conceiving and the bearing of children. But I had never understood his counsel to negate individual agency.

"Of course," I responded firmly to the legislator. "Put my name on the top of your 'recent Pro-Choice' list!"

Although I was not appointed by the Governor of Massachusetts, I was picked by a White House team from a pool of at-large nominees and sent to the Conference on Families in Baltimore in May 1980, where I associated myself with the Pro-Choice faction.

I liked most of them. They were good people, seemingly dedicated to improving institutions that affect family life. Although this group constituted a clear numerical majority at the Conference, it incurred the constant wrath of the vocal and critical "minority representing the Moral Majority" who claimed mistreatment at the hands of everyone else.

I met several Mormons at the Conference. They were tentatively friendly but suspicious of my lack of the identifying buttons or banners of the Moral Majority. I had counted on my maternity dress to endear me to them. When two fervent women asked me how I could possibly refrain from endorsing a like-minded people committed to "all" the same things "we" were, I replied, "I don't believe that they are committed to all of the goals of the Church. In fact, I see some of their efforts as conflicting with the goals of my church." One woman shook my hand and left. Another discussed points of disagreement for a few minutes, frowned as if she were sure the Spirit had departed my soul, then backed away with a promise to send me some literature. I was left to my thoughts.

My thoughts had to do with choosing—choosing the best as opposed to the better, the bad as opposed to the worst, choosing the great over the simply worthwhile.

Speakers at the Conference clarified some of my thoughts and confused others. Each proclaimed some policy as essential, and each was convincing. Once preliminary policy recommendations had been agreed to, I and the other delegates had to mark ballots showing whether or not we "agreed strongly," "agreed moderately," "disagreed strongly" or "disagreed moderately." At first I tried to imagine myself in the place of those making the proposals, but I soon gave up on that. It was hard enough to decide what I would do for myself.

The more I thought about these choices, the more agonizing the process seemed. I began to favor policies that enlarged the scope of choice. It seemed important that each human being have the right to make his or her own choices without interference.

A handicapped delegate took the floor to propose that the conference go on record as supporting laws in all states that would keep a handicapped person from being institutionalized, even temporarily, against his will. That seemed right. Handicapped people also have the right to choose. But the parent of a severely handicapped child spoke in opposition. He described his difficulties in rearing a family of six children with most of the money and energy spent on the one handicapped child. Because of the problems of transporting this child, the family had never taken a trip together, had never found a suitable place to leave the child or a suitable person to care for him.

"We need a break," this father said desperately. "Our child will never agree to stay in an institution, even for a few weeks. We need someone to take him—against his will—and we need the option of a family vacation!" That too was reasonable. I felt so sympathetic that I formulated a standard in my head: "The greatest number of choices for the greatest number of people."

Feeling comfortable with this, I realized that it would require decent, even inspired people to make right choices. In any system allowing a large number of options there will be selfish, careless people who will insist on hurting themselves and others. But I wanted to believe in the people with imagination and compassion who were capable of doing great things for themselves and others. But I also believed that all the creativity and good will in the world are useless without the freedom to exercise them.

Our group decided to vote against the proposal on the handicapped because it would destroy too many options.

As I had expected, many speakers raised abortion issues. Since in Massachusetts the subject had been part of a long and angry debate, I thought I had heard all arguments both for and against it. But the tough questions I thought

I had answered long ago were before me again. Listening to the speakers, I secretly prayed I would never have to make the decisions some of them had faced. I was to remember that prayer. . . .

During the rest of my time at the Conference, certain truths came to me forcefully and unexpectedly, with new and deeper meaning. In the past I had heard and had repeated to myself a whole set of judgments on the importance of having children, the greatness of blessings bestowed upon women who participate in the sacred process of giving birth. Somehow, however, my experience seemed rather routine. To be sure, I had regarded the birth of a child, mine or someone else's, as miraculous, but I had never given the event the reverence I was now realizing it deserved. The addition of each child to our family had never required significant sacrifice on anyone's part, I thought. Imagining other circumstances was shocking me into a new level of awareness. The preparation—physical and spiritual—that must often accompany the bringing of a helpless child into a hostile world can be arduous. It is important to use wisdom in choosing if and when to have a child at any time or place. Granted the standards for making wise judgments may change, wisdom must prevail. For the first time I realized that part of being a wise and a good mother was choosing when to have a child and how many children to have. . . .

I was exhausted. From childhood I had anticipated a time when I might be challenged to step over a line and be counted. I had imagined myself bounding boldly to the Right Side, confident and proud, firm in my convictions. At this conference, I had taken a stand consistent with my deepest convictions. But the dramatic stepping over the line was far less satisfying than I had imagined. I found myself longing for the comfort of my private life.

Five days later I was home. Instead of comfort, however, I found a stormier scene than the one I had left in Baltimore. After a week with the children and a week away from me, my husband had confirmed for himself what he had hinted at earlier. We must not under any circumstances add the baby I was expecting to our large and demanding family. He was sure he could not take it. He was sure I could not take it. "Make an appointment with the doctor immediately and terminate the pregnancy," he insisted. "Neither you nor I can possibly devote the time and energy to our other children nor to each other that is required if we have another baby. You must do this for the family." Although my husband is not LDS, he reminded me that a basic principle of my faith is the preeminence of the family. I was ignoring that principle.

I burst into tears as he went on. "What about the position you so boldly defended at the Family Conference?" he demanded. "You have spent all this time and energy fighting for the right of a woman to an abortion. Now you have the chance to take advantage of that right."

What followed were the most agonizing days of my life. I spent hours examining doctrines, arranging priorities, trying to understand fears and to analyze anxieties. Since I am not one to suffer in silence, I shared my ambivalence with others, men and women, friends in and outside the Church. Often my cries brought demonstrations of support. Just as often I was censured for even thinking about aborting a fetus which some claimed was like "killing a child." These friends trusted me with a large number of confidences, their tales only adding to my unrest. Some had chosen to abort, others had chosen birth; some seemed sad or angry. Most of them were caring people with whom I felt real kinship of spirit.

I spent intense hours in prayer and intense hours with my bishop. I discussed my dilemma with two therapists and several doctors and nurses. My sympathetic bishop thought I was worrying in the right way. The Lord, the Prophet, and he, my bishop, were concerned with nothing less than my eternal welfare and that of my husband—indeed of my whole family, born and unborn. President Kimball's strongly worded cautions against aborting a fetus without careful, even agonizing thought and prayer, reminded me of my responsibilities. I was accountable. I could not abrogate that accountability.

Assuming that the problem of whether or not we could "handle another baby" might be less complicated if we could be assured of a normal one, I decided to undergo amniocentesis. This was intended to relieve my husband of anxiety about a handicapped child. While I found the test an intellectual delight (I am impressed with the technology of modern science), and the results delightful (I was carrying a healthy girl, our first after three sons)—my husband was not comforted. For him the issue was not the health of the child but the fact of the child itself. He and I are both forty years old. I teach full time at a university, and he teaches and counsels inner-city children who make enormous demands upon him. We have always been committed to doing as much as we can not only for own children but for the students we daily serve. He could not be the parent he wanted to be and still fulfill his commitments at school. I could not argue; his reasoning was sound, but I was realizing openly what I had always known secretly: I could not abort this child. Why? I certainly did not believe that to abort a fetus was murdering a child. Yet it was clear that I had already projected a lifetime of dreams, of mother-daughter intimacies upon it, calling it by name and talking to it. Was it because this would be my first daughter after three sons? Was it because of my age and the feeling that the end of my child-bearing years was near? Did I want one final chance to savor and cling to this ability? Obviously one cannot equate the long, involved problems of child-rearing with the self-contained glories of childbirth. Was I responding to fantasies of ghostly pioneer role models? Was my eternal optimism getting the better of me, leading me to disaster? Occasionally I felt inspired. My daughter was to fill a special mission in life, a mission that had been entrusted to my stewardship.

But more often I just felt unsure. It was hard to insist to my husband that the Lord was influencing me. Was I simply afraid of abortion? Yes, but not extremely so. In one ambivalent moment, I even decided to make an appointment for abortion. When I went in to see the doctor about it, the nurse asked me why. I explained that my husband felt strongly about it. She wanted to know how I felt. I admitted that I was not exactly thrilled with the idea. But it had to be; I was resigned. After describing the details of the procedure, she said, "You are a poor candidate for an abortion—at least this one. My experience has convinced me that women should not choose abortion to please their husbands or anyone else. It ruins relationships." My mouth dropped open as she went on. "It builds future resentments. You would be setting your husband up as the thief, the one who deprived you of your joy."

"Does my joy show so much?" I whispered.

"It certainly does. And your feelings of happiness are an important reason to reconsider." Although she went on to apologize for interfering, she ended with an emphatic, "Don't do it!"

By then I was sobbing. I seemed to feel several emotions at once: sadness for my husband, guilt and remorse for our relationship, terror at what I had almost done.

And joy! I realized then that I adored my unborn child in ways I could not name. I felt sure that the next few years would be harder than the last year had been, but in a strange way I was glad.

Ambivalence was to return and sleepless nights, but the clarity of that moment was to sustain me. And as an LDS woman, I desperately wanted to know whether that moment was the result of the inspiration of the Holy Spirit. I earnestly prayed for this assurance.

Although my husband had always accompanied me to the delivery room and supported me there, he was not present for the birth of our little girl. For a few weeks after she and I returned from the hospital, he felt no genuine happiness in her presence. He finally warmed to her, though, and over the past months has fallen sincerely in love with her. But our year of animosity has left deep scars on our marriage, and I worry about our daughter, indeed about our sons as well. Can we parents provide them with the spiritual sustenance they need?

Recently I met a man from the Massachusetts delegation to the White House Conference. "Ah, I remember you," he said. "You are the Pro-Choice lady."

Am I? I asked myself. Certainly I am a far different woman from the one he met in Baltimore, bruised and battered, but tougher, less naive yet less cynical.

Yes, I am still "Pro-Choice," I told him, but I now know that I am also "Pro-Life" and have been ever since that faraway time when I stood in the councils of heaven and actually volunteered for the suffering and the ambiguity of this earth.

From *Dialogue: A Journal of Mormon Thought* (1981)

12. Harry Reid, "Faith, Family, and Public Service" (2007)

Given the Republican Party's founding platform, which aimed to eliminate from America the twin relics of barbarism, black slavery and Mormon polygamy, it is ironic that a majority of Latter-day Saints today gravitate toward the Republican Party. That preference is a recent phenomenon, fueled in part by the culture wars of the 1960s and 1970s. The Democrat Party's assimilation of countercultural elements, associated with sexual promiscuity, drug use, and rebelliousness, alienated large numbers of Mormons wed to "traditional" values. The national legalization of abortion in 1973 and the ongoing efforts to redefine marriage have further driven a wedge between mainstream Latter-day Saints and the Democrat Party. Many Mormons, however, including a number of church leaders, have nonetheless publicly espoused a preference for the Democrat Party, pointing to its greater harmony with church teachings in the areas of environmentalism, care for the poor, concern for other marginalized constituencies, and less strident militarism. The 2008 and 2012 U.S. presidential elections held out a unique prospect in American politics: with the Republican candidacy of Mitt Romney, it was possible that Americans would see two of the most powerful political posts in the country occupied by Mormons, but church members belonging to opposite parties. Harry Reid had served as U.S. Senate Majority Leader since January 2007. In this piece, he gives a defense of his political affiliation, while making a strong argument for the religious obligation that Latter-day Saints, members of a frequently insular culture, have to be proactive in public service.

It is not uncommon for members of the Church to ask how I can be a Mormon and a Democrat. Some say my party affiliation puts me in the minority of our Church members. But my answer is that if you look at the Church membership over the years, Democrats have not always been the minority, and I believe we won't be for long. I also say that my faith and political beliefs are deeply inter-twined. I am a Democrat because I am a Mormon, not in spite of it.

Growing up in Searchlight, my mother always had on our wall a small pillowcase—royal blue with gold fringe, with the words we can, we will, we must. And the name on the bottom in large gold letters—Franklin Delano Roosevelt. President Roosevelt was the closest we had to a worshipful figure as I grew up. For my economically challenged parents, even though a man of great wealth and privilege, Roosevelt represented them. He fought for the workers of America. President Roosevelt is the basis of my political direction. Social secu-rity is the most successful social program in the history of the world. A govern-ment program that helps the old, the handicapped, widows and orphans. The Works Progress Administration and the Civilian Conservation Corps programs that put hundreds of thousands of unemployed people to work. Not handouts, but jobs. Roosevelt tackled our greatest economic crisis with the 3 R's: relief, recovery, and reform. And let's not forget—he was commander-in-chief of the greatest military ever assembled at a time of great crisis in the world.

As we learned in the man-made tragedy of September 11th, 2001, during a crisis people have only three places to look for help: family, government, and God. I say government can be our friend. Some say it is never our friend. I say working people are the cornerstone of our economy. Some say that if you help the wealthy, they will create jobs and it will trickle down and help all. I say unions are responsible for the forty-hour work week, decent wages, and safe working conditions. Some say unions are unnecessary, that employers in an open market will take good care of their employees.

I say global warming is here and is an environmental emergency. Some say it is only nature's cycle and our free enterprise system will deal with it. I say our country using 21 million barrels of oil each day and millions of tons of coal must stop. Some say it is too costly to switch to solar, wind, and geo-thermal energy.

I say the invasion of Iraq was the worst foreign policy blunder in our country's history. Some say this war of choice was our only reasonable alternative. I say our diplomatic army should be stronger than our military army. Some say the war on terror must be won militarily.

On the topic of abortion, let me say I am pro-life and for the twenty-five years I have been in Congress have always been pro-life. Some say Democrats can't be pro-life, but I am proof that we can. During my first year in the Senate, there was an abortion issue that came up for a vote. It was a very close vote. My vote mattered; it could well have been the difference. In the well of the Senate, senators were explaining the importance of my vote and how important it was. Senator Barbara Mikulski, at that time the only woman in the Senate and one of the nation's feminist leaders, told everyone to leave me alone, my vote was a matter of character. I have been left alone for more than two decades, but there are other Democratic senators who share my pro-life position.

I'm not getting involved in the Democratic primary for president, because there are four Democratic senators running and many other friends. But regarding the Republican primary, let me say in passing, I hope that Mitt Romney's presidential bid is determined by his political stands and not his religion.

People say I started life without much. But because of America, it didn't matter the economic station of my parents, the color of my skin, my non-religion, or the size or place of my home. I am fortunate and now have what I believe to be the world's best job. Education was the equalizer in my life—it must be for you and for all of us.

Those today here assembled come from all backgrounds, all races, from all over our wonderful country and some from countries beyond our borders. The vast majority of you are bound by a common religious belief. With the many blessings you enjoy, including the benefits of this unique, world famous university, you must also accept the responsibility to go a little further than others. Many have chosen to pursue an educational direction pointed toward a lucrative field of endeavor.

There is nothing wrong with seeking a career that will bring you financial success. But never forget the clarion call of King Benjamin: "When you are in the service of your fellow beings you are only in the service of your God." As I have proceeded through life, I have witnessed many who have made monetary fortunes but have hated their work. I have seen many of modest means who love their profession of occupation. In short, work to be productive. To be happy. As Montaigne said more than three hundred years ago, "Living is my job and my art."

To what then, was King Benjamin referring? I believe in today's context he would of course have in mind a bishop, an elder's quorum president, a missionary, and of course a home or visiting teacher. But I suggest that King Benjamin would consider the Peace Corps, Teach for America, work in a non-profit to help the poor or the sick as commendable service.

Let me give you an example of public service. Senator Jay Rockefeller—rich, very rich. In fact, while getting on the subway to go from the Hart Office Building to the Capitol was asked, what was in the attache case he was carrying? And he responded—my spending money. Jay was wealthy, well educated and from New York, when as a young man he volunteered to be part of the Volunteers in Service to America—he became a Vista Volunteer in West Virginia. After his contact with the poor of Appalachia he never returned to New York and became secretary of state of West Virginia, governor, and now a multiterm United States senator. That's public service.

I propose King Benjamin then was referring to public service, running for elective office, serving in an appointed government board or commission. Within the Church there are hundreds and hundreds of examples from Ezra Taft Benson, while an apostle serving in President Eisenhower's cabinet, or Reed Smoot while an apostle serving in the United States Senate, or David Kennedy serving as secretary of the treasury, or Rex Lee as U.S. solicitor general, or the recently departed Elder James Faust serving in the state legislature, or Elder Oaks serving as a member of the Utah State Supreme Court, or the late Elder Haight, who served as mayor of Palo Alto, California.

Public service is a broad field you owe it to your state, your country, and yourself. Jewish tradition declares—"Ingratitude to man is ingratitude to God." President Monson has said, "What an exciting life is available for each of us today. We can be explorers in spirit with a mandate to make this world better by discovering improved ways of living. God left the world unfinished for man to work his skill upon."

James Fallows, one of America's exemplary journalists, author, commentator, publisher of *US News and World Report* and much more. Fallows was interviewed on public radio after having been a correspondent in the Far East for many years and was asked "who represents America in the most positive terms overseas?" Fallows responded, "members of the Foreign Service, that is, our diplomatic corps. They speak the language and they understand the culture." Peace Corps volunteers, they speak the language, help the poor, the very poor and the underprivileged. And finally, this non-Mormon said, Mormon missionaries. They speak the language, are cleanly dressed and live with the people, not away from the people. These are examples. They show the beauty and strength of public service by helping others.

"Faith, Family, and Public Service" (2007)

13. Mitt Romney, "Faith in America" (2007)

Latter-day Saints in Utah weathered decades of hostility, legal oppression, and suspicion before they finally overcame their marginalized status to achieve statehood in 1896. In 1898, the U.S. Congress refused to seat the elected polygamist and Mormon leader Brigham H. Roberts. A few years later, in 1903, the Senate moved to do the same after the election of (non-polygamist) Apostle Reed Smoot, but after years of contentious hearings he took his place. For a hundred years, church membership seemed to be no impediment to participation in the American political process. Then in 2007, Mitt Romney announced his candidacy for the Republican nomination for U.S. president. With troubling echoes of the early twentieth century, even nationally respected journalists and other public figures questioned the fitness of a Mormon for the highest political office. Some alleged that assent to the founding stories of the church, including angels, gold plates, and seerstones, called into question Romney's judgment. More commonly, objections were raised about the perceived conflict between a president's constitutional duties and a Latter-day Saint's loyalty to the Mormon prophet. Even when not making direct challenges, pundits and other candidates raised questions about esoteric Mormon teachings and beliefs. It became increasingly clear that Mitt Romney would need to make a public statement in response to public concern about his faith. John F. Kennedy had powerfully and effectively assuaged similar anxiety about the divided loyalty issue when he addressed Protestant ministers in 1960. Romney's speech may not have soared to Kennedyesque heights, but he adroitly differentiated what he considered legitimate inquiry into his constitutional commitments from what he deemed irrelevant questions about the content of his religious faith. Whether lingering suspicions played a decisive role in the subsequent campaign is impossible to determine. Romney mounted a strong, but ultimately unsuccessful, campaign for both the 2008 and 2012 U.S. presidency.

Today, I wish to address a topic which I believe is fundamental to America's greatness: our religious liberty. I'll also offer perspectives on how my own faith would inform my presidency, if I were elected.

There are some who may feel that religion is not a matter to be seriously considered in the context of the weighty threats that face us. If so, they are at odds with the nation's founders, for they, when our nation faced its greatest peril, sought the blessings of the Creator. And further, they discovered the essential connection between the survival of a free land and the protection of religious freedom. In John Adams's words: "We have no government armed with power capable of contending with human passions unbridled by morality and religion. . . . Our Constitution," he said, "was made for a moral and religious people."

Freedom requires religion just as religion requires freedom. Freedom opens the windows of the soul so that man can discover his most profound beliefs and commune with God. Freedom and religion endure together or perish alone.

Given our grand tradition of religious tolerance and liberty, some wonder whether there are any questions regarding an aspiring candidate's religion that are appropriate. I believe there are. And I'll answer them today.

Almost fifty years ago another candidate from Massachusetts explained that he was an American running for president, not a Catholic running for president. Like him, I am an American running for president. I do not define my candidacy by my religion. A person should not be elected because of his faith nor should he be rejected because of his faith.

Let me assure you that no authorities of my church, or of any other church for that matter, will ever exert influence on presidential decisions. Their authority is theirs, within the province of church affairs, and it ends where the affairs of the nation begin.

As governor, I tried to do the right as best I knew it, serving the law and answering to the Constitution. I did not confuse the particular teachings of my church with the obligations of the office and of the Constitution—and of course, I would not do so as president. I will put no doctrine of any church above the plain duties of the office and the sovereign authority of the law.

As a young man, Lincoln described what he called America's "political religion"—the commitment to defend the rule of law and the Constitution. When I place my hand on the Bible and take the oath of office, that oath becomes my highest promise to God. If I am fortunate to become your president, I will serve no one religion, no one group, no one cause, and no one interest. A president must serve only the common cause of the people of the United States.

There are some for whom these commitments are not enough. They would prefer it if I would simply distance myself from my religion, say that it's more a tradition than my personal conviction, or disavow one or another of its precepts. That I will not do. I believe in my Mormon faith and I endeavor to live by it. My faith is the faith of my fathers. I will be true to them and to my beliefs.

Some believe that such a confession of my faith will sink my candidacy. If they are right, so be it. But I think they underestimate the American people. Americans do not respect respecters—excuse me—believers of convenience.

Americans tire of those who would jettison their beliefs, even to gain the world. There is one fundamental question about which I often am asked. What do I believe about Jesus Christ? I believe that Jesus Christ is the son of God and the savior of mankind. My church's beliefs about Christ may not all be the same as those of other faiths. Each religion has its own unique doctrines and history. These are not bases for criticism but rather a test of our tolerance. Religious tolerance would be a shallow principle indeed if it were reserved only for faiths with which we agree.

There are some who would have a presidential candidate describe and explain his church's distinctive doctrines. To do so would enable the very religious test the founders prohibited in the Constitution. No candidate should become the spokesman for his faith. For if he becomes president he will need the prayers of the people of all faiths.

I believe that every faith I have encountered draws its adherents closer to God. And in every faith I have come to know, there are features I wish were in my own: I love the profound ceremony of the Catholic Mass, the approachability of God in the prayers of the evangelicals, the tenderness of spirit among the Pentecostals, the confident independence of the Lutherans, the ancient traditions of the Jews, unchanged through the ages, and the commitment to frequent prayer of the Muslims. As I travel across the country and see our towns and cities, I am always moved by the many houses of worship with their steeples, all pointing to heaven, reminding us of the source of life's blessings.

It's important to recognize that while differences in theology exist between the churches in America, we share a common creed of moral convictions. And where the affairs of our nation are concerned, it's usually a sound rule to focus on the latter, on the great moral principles that urge us all on a common course. Whether it was the cause of abolition, or civil rights, or the right to life itself, no movement of conscience can succeed in America that cannot speak to the convictions of religious people.

We separate church and state affairs in this country, and for good reason. No religion should dictate to the state nor should the state interfere with the free practice of religion. But in recent years, the notion of the separation of church and state has been taken by some well beyond its original meaning. They seek to remove from the public domain any acknowledgment of God. Religion is seen as merely a private affair with no place in public life. It's as if they are intent on establishing a new religion in America—the religion of secularism. They are wrong.

The founders proscribed the establishment of a state religion, but they did not countenance the elimination of religion from the public square.

We are a nation "under God," and in God we do indeed trust.

We should acknowledge the Creator as did the Founders in ceremony and word. He should remain on our currency, in our pledge, in the teaching of our history, and during the holiday season, nativity scenes and menorahs should be welcome in our public places. Our greatness would not long endure without judges who respect the foundation of faith upon which our Constitution rests. I will take care to separate the affairs of government from any religion, but I will not separate us from "the God who gave us liberty."

Nor would I separate us from our religious heritage. Perhaps the most important question to ask a person of faith who seeks a political office is this: Does he share these American values—the equality of human kind, the obligation to serve one another and a steadfast commitment to liberty?

They are not unique to any one denomination. They belong to the great moral inheritance we hold in common. They're the firm ground on which Americans of different faiths meet and stand as a nation, united.

We believe that every single human being is a child of God—we're all part of the human family. The conviction of the inherent and inalienable worth of every life is still the most revolutionary political proposition ever advanced. John Adams put it that we are "thrown into the world all equal and alike."

The consequence of our common humanity is our responsibility to one another, to our fellow Americans foremost, but also to every child of God. It's an obligation which is fulfilled by Americans every day, here and across the globe, without regard to creed or race or nationality.

Americans acknowledge that liberty is a gift of God, not an indulgence of government. No people in the—No people in the history of the world have sacrificed as much for liberty. The lives of hundreds of thousands of America's sons and daughters were laid down during the last century to preserve freedom, for us and for freedom-loving people throughout the world. America took nothing from that century's terrible wars—no land from Germany or Japan or Korea, no treasure, no oath of fealty. America's resolve in the defense of liberty has been tested time and again. It has not been found wanting, nor must it ever be. America must never falter in holding high the banner of freedom.

These American values, this great moral heritage, is shared and lived in my religion as it is in yours. I was taught in my home to honor God and love my neighbor. I saw my father march with Martin Luther King. I saw my parents provide compassionate care to others, in personal ways to people nearby, and in just as consequential ways in leading national volunteer movements. I am moved by the Lord's words: "For I was an hungered, and ye gave me meat. I was thirsty, and ye gave me drink. I was a stranger, and ye took me in. Naked, and ye clothed me."

My faith is grounded on these truths. You can witness them in Ann and my marriage and in our family. We're a long way from perfect and we have surely stumbled along the way, but our aspirations, our values, are the self-same as those from the other faiths that stand upon this common foundation. And these convictions will indeed inform my presidency.

Today's generations of Americans have always known religious liberty. Perhaps we forget the long and arduous path our nation's forebears took to achieve it. They came here from England to seek freedom of religion. But upon finding it for themselves, they at first denied it to others. Because of their diverse beliefs, Anne Hutchinson was exiled from Massachusetts Bay, Roger Williams founded Rhode Island, and two centuries later, Brigham Young set out for the West. Americans were unable to accommodate their commitment to their own faith with an appreciation for the convictions of others to different faiths. In this, they were very much like those of the European nations they had left.

It was in Philadelphia that our founding fathers defined a revolutionary vision of liberty, grounded on self evident truths about the equality of all, and the inalienable rights with which each is endowed by his Creator.

We cherish these sacred rights, and secure them in our Constitutional order. Foremost do we protect religious liberty, not as a matter of policy but as a matter of right. There will be no established church, and we are guaranteed the free exercise of our religion.

I'm not sure that we fully appreciate the profound implications of our tradition of religious liberty. I've visited many of the magnificent cathedrals in

Europe. They are so inspired, so grand and so empty. Raised up over generations, long ago, so many of the cathedrals now stand as the postcard backdrop to societies just too busy or too "enlightened" to venture inside and kneel in prayer. The establishment of state religions in Europe did no favor to Europe's churches. And though you will find many people of strong faith there, the churches themselves seem to be withering away.

Infinitely worse is the other extreme, the creed of conversion by conquest: violent jihad, murder as martyrdom, killing Christians, Jews, and Muslims with equal indifference. These radical Islamists do their preaching not by reason or example, but in the coercion of minds and the shedding of blood. We face no greater danger today than theocratic tyranny, and the boundless suffering these states and groups could inflict if given the chance.

The diversity of our cultural expression, and the vibrancy of our religious dialogue, has kept America in the forefront of civilized nations even as others regard religious freedom as something to be destroyed.

In such a world, we can be deeply thankful that we live in a land where reason and religion are friends and allies in the cause of liberty, joined against the evils and dangers of the day. And you can be—You can be certain of this: Any believer in religious freedom, any person who has knelt in prayer to the Almighty, has a friend and ally in me. And so it is for hundreds of millions of our countrymen: We do not insist on a single strain of religion—rather, we welcome our nation's symphony of faith.

Faith in America, Associated Press (2007)

14. First Presidency (Thomas S. Monson, Henry B. Eyring, and Dieter F. Uchtdorf), "Preserving Traditional Marriage and Strengthening Families" (2008)

While the church maintains official political neutrality and does not endorse candidates, like other churches it campaigns actively for issues it considers to cut across religious and moral lines. Defining marriage is one such issue. Even the church's participation in the anti–Equal Rights Amendment initiative did not arouse the internal divides and the external hostility provoked when Mormon leaders urged members to contribute time and money to the passage of California Proposition 8. Passed on November 2008, the ballot initiative was called The California Marriage Protection Act, designed to restrict marriage to opposite-sex couples. The initiative passed 52 to 48 percent but was overturned as unconstitutional by a three-judge panel of the Ninth Circuit Court of Appeals.

It is likely that the considerable outlays of Mormon money turned the tide in favor of the proposition, even though Mormons are a small minority in the state (less than 2 percent), and were in coalition with Orthodox Jewish, evangelical, and Catholic groups. They quickly became the most visible factor in the contentious debate, and consequently LDS temples, meetinghouses, and individuals suffered a disproportionate backlash of violence and vandalism. In spite of reams of negative press, surveys indicate that Latter-day Saints have about the same favorability ratings in 2012 as they did at the height of the controversy.

Mormon theology does place heterosexual marriage at the summit of its salvation scheme, teaching that those who inherit eternal life will enjoy a continuing marriage relation and "a continuation of the seed forever"; that is, the capacity for eternal procreation. However, Mormon opposition to gay marriage is based on the same logic cited by the lone dissenter in the proposition's defeat on appeal: Judge Randy Smith argued that "The family structure of two committed biological parents—one man and one woman—is the optimal partnership for raising children." Since the Proposition 8 battle, the church supported gay rights legislation in Salt Lake City, Utah, that banned discrimination in housing and employment. Some within the church, in the younger generation especially, follow the larger social trends generally of supporting such rights in the domain of marriage as well.

The following letter was sent from the First Presidency to California Church leaders to be read to all congregations on June 29, 2008, in the months leading up to the November vote.

Preserving Traditional Marriage and Strengthening Families

In March 2000 California voters overwhelmingly approved a state law providing that "Only marriage between a man and a woman is valid or recognized in California." The California Supreme Court recently reversed this vote of the people. On November 4, 2008, Californians will vote on a proposed amendment to the California state constitution that will now restore the March 2000 definition of marriage approved by the voters.

The Church's teachings and position on this moral issue are unequivocal. Marriage between a man and a woman is ordained of God, and the formation of families is central to the Creator's plan for His children. Children are entitled to be born within this bond of marriage.

A broad-based coalition of churches and other organizations placed the proposed amendment on the ballot. The Church will participate with this coalition in seeking its passage. Local Church leaders will provide information about how you may become involved in this important cause.

We ask that you do all you can to support the proposed constitutional amendment by donating of your means and time to assure that marriage in California is legally defined as being between a man and a woman. Our best efforts are required to preserve the sacred institution of marriage.

"Preserving Traditional Marriage and Strengthening Families,"
The Church of Jesus Christ of Latter-day Saints (2008)

FIVE

RACE AND ETHNICITY

From the founding of The Church of Jesus Christ of Latter-day Saints in 1830, its membership perceived the world and its ethnic groups in terms of the Bible and Book of Mormon narratives. Related nineteenth-century Mormon conceptions of lineage played a major role in Latter-day Saint self-understanding and evangelism priorities. The origin of the Native Americans had long been a subject of speculation in the New World, with many writers positing a connection to the House of Israel. The Book of Mormon made the case explicitly—tying them not to the Ten Tribes lost with the Assyrian conquest, as many popular accounts did, but making them exiles from the tribe of Manasseh at the time of the later Babylonian captivity. With their place in providential history scripturally affirmed, the Native Americans became an early focus of Mormon missionary labors.

During the early twentieth century, church leaders like Apostle Orson F. Whitney continued to expound upon the lineal descent of Latter-day Saints from the chosen House of Israel and affirmed the missionary priority to gather scattered Israel. Combining inherited Christian racial beliefs with a unique Mormon anthropology of the spirit, Apostle Joseph Fielding Smith took these ideas a step further in his book *The Way to Perfection*. In this account, some biblical lineages were blessed, while others—in particular those of African descent—were apparently cursed based on their pre-mortal disobedience. Thus ran one Mormon narrative explaining a church practice that, hovering ambiguously between policy and doctrine, had banned men of African descent from the priesthood since the early 1850s. Joseph Smith had raised no such barriers and welcomed free blacks into the church, as Jane Elizabeth Manning James's account reveals. He was if anything personally progressive on the question of race. A revelation declared as early as 1833 that "it is not right that any man should be in bondage to another" (Doctrine and Covenants 101:79), and Smith eventually advocated emancipation. The situation changed abruptly with the Mormons' removal to Utah. President Brigham Young made no specific claim of revelation to support his prohibition against blacks receiving the priesthood. It seems to have been rather inherited Christian beliefs regarding the curse of Cain, reinforced by his own reading of biblical scripture and Joseph Smith's writings, which spurred his decision.

Native Americans, in contrast, believed by Latter-day Saints to be "Lamanites," or descendants of the "children of Lehi" of Book of Mormon fame, continued to factor prominently in Mormon culture. Apostle (and future church president) Spencer W. Kimball regularly taught that this downtrodden group was to be the beneficiaries of great spiritual and temporal blessings in the last days, as they were of "royal blood." Latter-day Saints even created a placement program in 1947 to give American Indian youth school-year residence with white Mormon families to afford them better educational opportunities. The program was disbanded in 1996 in response to a shifting American political climate that saw the program as paternalistic and destructive of Native American culture. As the twentieth century progressed, the "blood of Israel" came to assume a significance more metaphorical than literal; at the same time, Mormon readings of the Book of Mormon that saw the scripture as a local rather then hemispheric history gained ascendance, even as scientific challenges arose to the American Indian–Israelite connection. As a result, the meaning of the term *Lamanite* became unstable, with unsettling repercussions for some Mormons of Native American ancestry.

Meanwhile, the Mormon policy of excluding blacks from the priesthood came under increasing attack in the 1960s, during the Civil Rights era in America. The church weathered the storm and then, when it had passed, made a momentous announcement. Even as most American baby boomers still recall where they were when they learned of President John F. Kennedy's assassination, their Mormon counterparts can remember what they were doing when they heard of President Spencer W. Kimball's 1978 revelation extending the rights of the priesthood to all worthy males, regardless of race or lineage. Later canonized in the Doctrine and Covenants (Official Declaration 2), this prophetic pronouncement marked a new day for blacks within the church. The Mormon experience of Joseph Freeman reveals how some black Latter-day Saints have navigated their membership in a historically white church in North America.

As the church entered the new millennium, it was faced with dramatic demographic shifts that involved several ethnicities beyond the African American and American Indian. Like Christianity generally, the church was becoming increasingly a southern hemispheric membership, with growth most pronounced in Africa and Latin America, and with Asian mission fields yet to be fully reaped. Within the United States, the administration and assimilation of a variety of ethnic and language groups remains a challenge. Rounding out this section are firsthand accounts of what it means to be an Asian American in a church still predominantly Western and of a Latina who has experienced, and herself embodies, the challenges of language-specific branches in North America.

1. Parley P. Pratt, "Mission to the Lamanites"

Parley P. Pratt was a young seeker and itinerant preacher when he happened upon a Book of Mormon just months after its publication in 1830. He had long harbored a dream of taking the gospel to the Native Americans and was an ardent millennialist. The Book of Mormon, which declared itself to be both a record of ancient American derivation and a herald of the Second Coming, powerfully spoke to Pratt's interests, and he requested baptism in the Mormon faith almost immediately. About this same time, U.S. President Andrew Jackson signed the Indian Removal Act, accelerating the process of relocating American Indians to lands west of the Mississippi. That development seemed to Parley Pratt to coincide with Book of Mormon predictions of the gathering of the remnant of the tribe of Joseph (which Latter-day Saints interpreted as Native Americans, or "Lamanites"). Joseph Smith announced a mission to the Lamanites to depart that October and commissioned his scribe Oliver Cowdery and another Book of Mormon witness, Peter Whitmer Jr., to head west. Pratt implored Smith to be included, and a few days later he and Ziba Peterson were called to go along. The foursome, who would be joined en route by another member, Frederick G. Williams, were given polite hearings by tribes along the way and in the Indian Territory, but the mission yielded no Native American converts. Two enormously important consequences nonetheless followed from their efforts. Stopping midway in the Kirtland,

Ohio, area, Parley Pratt converted his friend and mentor Sidney Rigdon, who had been a powerful preacher in the Campbellite movement. Aided by Rigdon's influence, the Mormons baptized more than 120 converts, almost tripling the size of the fledgling church. In addition, their success in Kirtland and pioneering labors among the settlers in northwestern Missouri created the template for the two major gathering places of the early church.

It was now October, 1830. A revelation had been given through the mouth of this Prophet, Seer and Translator, in which Elders Oliver Cowdery, Peter Whitmer, Ziba Peterson and myself were appointed to go into the wilderness, through the western States, and to the Indian territory. Making arrangements for my wife in the family of the Whitmers, we took leave of our friends and the church late in October, and started on foot.

After travelling for some days we called on an Indian nation at or near Buffalo; and spent part of a day with them, instructing them in the knowledge of the record of their forefathers. We were kindly received, and much interest was manifested by them on hearing this news. We made a present of two copies of the Book of Mormon to certain of them who could read, and repaired to Buffalo. . . .

We now pursued our journey for some days, and at length arrived in Sandusky, in the western part of Ohio. Here resided a tribe, or nation of Indians, called Wyandots, on whom we called, and with whom we spent several days. We were well received, and had an opportunity of laying before them the record of their forefathers, which we did. They rejoiced in the tidings, bid us God speed, and desired us to write to them in relation to our success among the tribes further west, who had already removed to the Indian territory, where these expected soon to go. . . .

We halted for a few days in Illinois, about twenty miles from St. Louis, on account of a dreadful storm of rain and snow, which lasted for a week or more, during which the snow fell in some places near three feet deep. Although in the midst of strangers, we were kindly entertained, found many friends, and preached to large congregations in several neighborhoods.

In the beginning of 1831 we renewed our journey; and, passing through St. Louis and St. Charles, we travelled on foot for three hundred miles through vast prairies and through trackless wilds of snow—no beaten road; houses few and far between; and the bleak northwest wind always blowing in our faces with a keenness which would almost take the skin off the face. We travelled for whole days, from morning till night, without a house or fire, wading in snow to the knees at every step, and the cold so intense that the snow did not melt on the south side of the houses, even in the mid-day sun, for nearly six weeks. We carried on our backs our changes of clothing, several books, and corn bread and raw pork. We often ate our frozen bread and pork by the way, when the bread would be so frozen that we could not bite or penetrate any part of it but the outside crust.

After much fatigue and some suffering we all arrived in Independence, in the county of Jackson, on the extreme western frontiers of Missouri, and of the United States.

This was about fifteen hundred miles from where we started, and we had performed most of the journey on foot, through a wilderness country, in the worst season of the year, occupying about four months, during which we had preached the gospel to tens of thousands of Gentiles and two nations of Indians; baptizing, confirming and organizing many hundreds of people into churches of Latter-day Saints.

This was the first mission performed by the Elders of the Church in any of the States west of New York, and we were the first members of the same which were ever on this frontier.

Two of our number now commenced work as tailors in the village of Independence, while the others crossed the frontier line and commenced a mission among the Lamanites, or Indians.

Passing through the tribe of Shawnees we tarried one night with them, and the next day crossed the Kansas river and entered among the Delawares. We immediately inquired for the residence of the principal Chief, and were soon introduced to an aged and venerable looking man, who had long stood at the head of the Delawares, and been looked up to as the Great Grandfather, or Sachem of ten nations or tribes.

He was seated on a sofa of furs, skins and blankets, before a fire in the center of his lodge; which was a comfortable cabin, consisting of two large rooms.

His wives were neatly dressed, partly in calicoes and partly in skins; and wore a vast amount of silver ornaments. As we entered his cabin he took us by the hand with a hearty welcome, and then motioned us to be seated on a pleasant seat of blankets, or robes. His wives, at his bidding, set before us a tin pan full of beans and corn boiled up together, which proved to be good eating; although three of us made use alternately of the same wooden spoon.

There was an interpreter present and through him we commenced to make known our errand, and to tell him of the Book of Mormon. We asked him to call the council of his nation together and give us a hearing in full. He promised to consider on it till next day, in the meantime recommending us to a certain Mr. Pool for entertainment; this was their blacksmith, employed by government.

The man entertained us kindly and comfortably. Next morning we again called on Mr. Anderson, the old chief, and explained to him something of the Book. He was at first unwilling to call his council; made several excuses, and finally refused; as he had ever been opposed to the introduction of missionaries among his tribe.

We continued the conversation a little longer, till he at last began to understand the nature of the Book. He then changed his mind; became suddenly interested, and requested us to proceed no further with our conversation till he could call a council. He despatched a messenger, and in about an hour had some forty men collected around us in his lodge, who, after shaking us by the hand, were seated in silence; and in a grave and dignified manner awaited the announcement of what we had to offer. The chief then requested us to proceed; or rather, begin where we began before, and to complete our communication. Elder Cowdery then commenced as follows:

"Aged Chief and Venerable Council of the Delaware nation; we are glad of this opportunity to address you as our red brethren and friends. We have travelled a long distance from towards the rising sun to bring you glad news; we have travelled the wilderness, crossed the deep and wide rivers, and waded in the deep snows, and in the face of the storms of winter, to communicate to you great knowledge which has lately come to our ears and hearts; and which will do the red man good as well as the pale face.

"Once the red men were many; they occupied the country from sea to sea— from the rising to the setting sun; the whole land was theirs; the Great Spirit gave it to them, and no pale faces dwelt among them. But now they are few in numbers; their possessions are small, and the pale faces are many.

"Thousands of moons ago, when the red men's forefathers dwelt in peace and possessed this whole land, the Great Spirit talked with them, and revealed His law and His will, and much knowledge to their wise men and prophets. This they wrote in a Book; together with their history, and the things which should befall their children in the latter days.

"This Book was written on plates of gold, and handed down from father to son for many ages and generations.

"It was then that the people prospered, and were strong and mighty; they cultivated the earth; built buildings and cities, and abounded in all good things, as the pale faces now do.

"But they became wicked; they killed one another and shed much blood; they killed their prophets and wise men, and sought to destroy the Book. The Great Spirit became angry, and would speak to them no more; they had no more good and wise dreams; no more visions; no more angels sent among them by the Great Spirit; and the Lord commanded Mormon and Moroni, their last wise men and prophets, to hide the Book in the earth, that it might be preserved in safety, and be found and made known in the latter day to the pale faces who should possess the land; that they might again make it known to the red man; in order to restore them to the knowledge of the will of the Great Spirit and to His favor. And if the red man would then receive this Book and learn the things written in it, and do according thereunto, they should cease to fight and kill one another; should become one people; cultivate the earth in peace, in common with the pale faces, who were willing to believe and obey the same Book, and be good men and live in peace.

"Then should the red men become great, and have plenty to eat and good clothes to wear, and should be in favor with the Great Spirit and be his children, while he would be their Great Father, and talk with them, and raise up prophets and wise and good men amongst them again, who should teach them many things.

"This Book, which contained these things, was hid in the earth by Moroni, in a hill called by him, Cumorah, which hill is now in the State of New York, near the village of Palmyra, in Ontario County.

"In that neighborhood there lived a young man named Joseph Smith, who prayed to the Great Spirit much, in order that he might know the truth; and the Great Spirit sent an angel to him, and told him where this Book was hid by Moroni; and commanded him to go and get it. He accordingly went to the place, and dug in the earth, and found the Book written on golden plates.

"But it was written in the language of the forefathers of the red man; therefore this young man, being a pale face, could not understand it; but the angel told him and showed him, and gave him knowledge of the language, and how to interpret the Book. So he interpreted it into the language of the pale faces, and wrote it on paper, and caused it to be printed, and published thousands of copies of it among them; and then sent us to the red men to bring some copies of it to them, and to tell them this news. So we have now come from him, and here is a copy of the Book, which we now present to our red friend, the chief of the Delawares, and which we hope he will cause to be read and known among his tribe; it will do them good."

We then presented him with a Book of Mormon.

There was a pause in the council, and some conversation in their own tongue, after which the chief made the following reply:

"We feel truly thankful to our white friends who have come so far, and been at such pains to tell us good news, and especially this new news concerning the Book of our forefathers; it makes us glad in here"—placing his hand on his heart.

"It is now winter, we are new settlers in this place; the snow is deep, our cattle and horses are dying, our wigwams are poor; we have much to do in the spring—to build houses, and fence and make farms; but we will build a council house, and meet together, and you shall read to us and teach us more concerning the Book of our fathers and the will of the Great Spirit."

We again lodged at Mr. Pool's, told him of the Book, had a very pleasant interview with him, and he became a believer and advocate for the Book, and served as an interpreter.

We continued for several days to instruct the old chief and many of his tribe. The interest became more and more intense on their part, from day to day, until at length nearly the whole tribe began to feel a spirit of inquiry and excitement on the subject.

We found several among them who could read, and to them we gave copies of the Book, explaining to them that it was the Book of their forefathers.

Some began to rejoice exceedingly, and took great pains to tell the news to others, in their own language.

The excitement now reached the frontier settlements in Missouri, and stirred up the jealousy and envy of the Indian agents and sectarian missionaries to that degree that we were soon ordered out of the Indian country as disturbers of the peace; and even threatened with the military in case of non-compliance.

We accordingly departed from the Indian country, and came over the line, and commenced laboring in Jackson County, Missouri, among the whites. We were well received, and listened to by many; and some were baptized and added to the Church.

Thus ended our first Indian Mission, in which we had preached the gospel in its fulness, and distributed the record of their forefathers among three tribes, viz: the Catteraugus Indians, near Buffalo, N. Y., the Wyandots of Ohio, and the Delawares west of Missouri.

We trust that at some future day, when the servants of God go forth in power to the remnant of Joseph, some precious seed will be found growing in their hearts, which was sown by us in that early day.

From *The Autobiography of Parley Parker Pratt* (1874)

2. Jane Elizabeth Manning James, "Autobiography" (n.d.)

Ethnicity is a subject of central importance to the history and theology of the church. Latter-day Saints were themselves represented and culturally constructed into an identifiable ethnic group, with enduring consequences to the present. (The "only indigenously derived ethnic community in America" according to some.) At the same time, while the Christian world largely saw the New Testament as replacing a covenant based on blood affiliation with one based on adoption, Latter-day Saints returned to particularistic conceptions of chosenness and cursedness based on literal descent. Native Americans, for example, have been seen in whole or in part by Mormons as literal descendants of ancient Israel and heirs of biblically grounded promises. Persons of African descent have had a variable place in Mormon thought and culture. Initially, Latter-day Saints were largely progressive on the issue of race. Intemperate Mormon praise for "the wonderful events of this age," in which "much is doing towards abolishing slavery" fueled anti-Mormon violence in Missouri, and Joseph Smith himself campaigned for U.S. president in 1844 on a platform that advocated a federal buyout of all slaves by 1850.[1] Jane Elizabeth Manning was born a free black in Connecticut in 1822. Converted at nineteen, she led her family to Nauvoo, where she was welcomed into the Mormon community. After Smith's martyrdom, she made the difficult trek to Utah, where church policy toward black members soon shifted to one of exclusion from full participation. Manning lived and died a faithful member, even though she suffered the humiliating consequences of the church's new "negro policy." Asking to be vicariously "sealed" to the Joseph Smith family in accordance with the prophet's earlier invitation, she was allowed to do so: but only in the status of servant.

When a child only six years old, I left my home and went to live with a family of white people. Their names were Mr. and Mrs. Joseph Fitch. They were aged people and quite wealthy. I was raised by their daughter.

When about fourteen years old, I joined the Presbyterian Church—yet I did not feel satisfied. It seemed to me there was something more that I was looking for. I had belonged to the Church about eighteen months when an Elder of The Church of Jesus Christ of Latter-day Saints, [who] was traveling through our country, preached there. The pastor of the Presbyterian Church forbade me going to hear them as he had heard I had expressed a desire to hear them; nevertheless I went on a Sunday and was fully convinced that it was the true gospel he presented and I must embrace it. The following Sunday I was baptized and confirmed a member of The Church of Jesus Christ of Latter-day Saints.

One year after I was baptized, I started for Nauvoo with my mother, Eliza Manning, my brothers Isaac Lewis, and Peter, my sisters, Sarah Stebbins and Angeline Manning, my brother-in-law Anthony Stebbins, Lucinda Manning (a sister-in-law), and myself in the fall of 1840 [sic]. We started from Wilton, Connecticut, and traveled by canal to Buffalo, New York. We were to go to Columbus, Ohio, before our fares were to be collected, but they insisted on having the money at Buffalo and would not take us farther. So we left the boat and started on foot to travel a distance of over eight hundred miles.

We walked until our shoes were worn out, and our feet became sore and cracked open and bled until you could see the whole print of our feet with blood on the ground. We stopped and united in prayer to the Lord; we asked God the Eternal Father to heal our feet. Our prayers were answered and our feet were healed forthwith.

When we arrived at Peoria, Illinois, the authorities threatened to put us in jail to get our free papers. We didn't know at first what he meant, for we had never been slaves, but he concluded to let us go. So we traveled on until we came to a river, and as there was no bridge, we walked right into the stream. When we got to the middle, the water was up to our necks but we got safely across. Then it became so dark we could hardly see our hands before us, but we could see a light in the distance, so we went toward it. We found it was an old Log Cabin.

Here we spent the night. The next day we walked for a considerable distance, and stayed that night in a forest out in the open air.

The frost fell on us so heavy, it was like a light fall of snow. We arose early and started on our way walking through that frost with our bare feet, until the sun rose and melted it away. But we went on our way rejoicing, singing hymns, and thanking God for his infinite goodness and mercy to us—in blessing us as he had, protecting us from all harm, answering our prayers, and healing our feet.

In course of time, we arrived at La Harpe, Illinois—about thirty miles from Nauvoo. At La Harpe, we came to a place where there was a very sick child. We administered to it, and the child was healed. I found after [that] the elders had before this given it up, as they did not think it could live.

We had now arrived to our destined haven of rest: the beautiful Nauvoo! Here we went through all kinds of hardship, trial and rebuff, but we at last got to Brother Orson Spencer's. He directed us to the Prophet Joseph Smith's mansion. When we found it, Sister Emma was standing in the door, and she kindly said, "Come in, come in!"

Brother Joseph said to some white sisters that was present, "Sisters, I want you to occupy this room this evening with some brothers and sisters that have just arrived." Brother Joseph placed the chairs around the room and then he went and brought Sister Emma and Dr. Bernhisel and introduced them to us.

Brother Joseph took a chair and sat down by me and said, "You have been the head of this little band, haven't you!" I answered, "Yes sir!" He then said, "God bless you! Now I would like you to relate your experience in your travels."

I related to them all I have above stated—and a great deal more minutely, as many incidents has passed from my memory since then.

Brother Joseph slapped Dr. Bernhisel on the knee and said, "What do you think of that, Dr.? Isn't that faith?" The Dr. said, "Well I rather think it is. If it had have been me, I fear I should have backed out and returned to my home!" [Joseph Smith] then said, "God bless you. You are among friends now and you will be protected."

They sat and talked to us awhile, gave us words of encouragement and good counsel. We all stayed there [the mansion house] one week. By that time, all but myself had secured homes. Brother Joseph came in every morning to say good morning and {see] how we were. During our trip I had lost all my clothes—they were all gone. My trunks were sent by canal [boat] to the care of Charles Wesley Wandell. One large trunk full of clothes of all descriptions—mostly new!

On the morning that my folks all left to go to work, I looked at myself—clothed in the only two pieces I possessed—[and] I sat down and wept. Brother Joseph came into the room as usual, and said, "Good morning. Why—not crying, [are you]?" "Yes sir. The folks have all gone and got themselves homes and I have got none." He said, "Yes you have. You have a home right here, if you want it. You mustn't cry; we dry up all tears here." I said, "I have lost my trunk and all my clothes." He asked how I had lost them. I told him I put them in care of Charles Wesley Wandell and paid him for them and he has lost them. Brother

Joseph said, "Don't cry. You shall have your trunk and clothes again." Brother Joseph went out and brought Sister Emma in and said, "Sister Emma, here is a girl that says she has no home. Haven't you a home for her?" "Why yes, if she wants one." He said, "She does." And then he left us. Sister Emma said, "What can you do?" I said, "I can wash, iron, cook, and do housework." "Well," she said, "when you are rested, you may do the washing, if you would just as soon do that." I said, "I am not tired." "Well," she said, "you may commence your work in the morning."

. . . I had to pass through Mother Smith's room to get to mine, [and] she would often stop me and talk to me. She told me all Brother Joseph's troubles, and what he had suffered in publishing the Book of Mormon. One morning I met Brother Joseph coming out of his mother's room. He said, "Good morning!" and shook hands with me. I went to his mother's room. She said, "Good morning. Bring me that bundle from my bureau and sit down here." I did as she told me. She placed the bundle [in] my hands and said, "Handle this and then put it in the top drawer of my bureau and lock it up." After I had done it she said, "Sit down. Do you remember that I told you about the Urim and Thummim when I told you about the Book of Mormon? I answered yes ma'am. She then told me I had just handled it. "You are not permitted to see it, but you have been permitted to handle it. You will live long after I am dead and gone and you can tell the Latter-day Saints that you was permitted to handle the Urim and Thummim."

Sister Emma asked me one day if I would like to be adopted to them as their child. I did not answer her. She said, "I will wait awhile and let you consider it." She waited two weeks before she asked me again. When she did, I told her, "No Ma'am," because I did not understand or know what it meant. They were always good and kind to me but I did not know my own mind; I did not comprehend.

Soon after, they broke up the mansion and I went to my mother. There was not much work because of the persecutions, and I saw Brother Joseph and asked him if I should go to Burlington and take my sister Angeline with me. He said, "Yes. Go and be good girls, and remember your profession of faith in the everlasting gospel, and the Lord will bless you." We went and stayed three weeks and then returned to Nauvoo. It was during this time that the prophet Joseph and his brother Hyrum was martyred. I shall never forget that time of agony and sorrow. I went to live in the family of Brother Brigham Young. I stayed there until he was ready to immigrate to this valley.

From *Journal of Discourses* (1855)

3. Parley P. Pratt, "The Standard and Ensign for the People"

The very term New Testament places the Christian canon into relation with the Jewish and, by implication, the Christian religion into relation with Judaism. How Christians have perceived that relationship has conditioned their history of interaction—and plays an important role in Christian theology—from the crusades to the present. Does the "New" suggest that the text and the gospel covenant are a supplement, a replacement, or something else? Historically, Christians embraced supersessionism, the theology that Israel lost its covenantal privileges through its rejection of Christ or, at the least, was superseded by the Christian church after fulfilling its purpose of preparing a core group of people for Christ's advent. In either case, Judaism is viewed as having effectively been replaced by a Christian covenant. What this means for salvation history is that Jews must yet accept Jesus the Christ if they are not to find themselves excluded from God's plan. In more recent years, liberal Christians have adopted a dual-covenant theology, which allows a kind of "two-track" system, with neither covenant relationship privileged over the other.

LDS theology takes a rather novel approach to its relationship with the original Abrahamic covenant. In Joseph Smith's teachings, the Christian dispensation does not represent the first full flowering of the gospel. In Smith's revision of the Old Testament, the Lord expressly forgives Adam for his "transgression," teaches Adam about Christ's future atonement, and baptizes him with water and the Holy Ghost. Furthermore, Smith read the covenant with Abraham as incorporating the fullness of God's promises to humankind, including not just eternal life but also an eternal posterity, that is, a continuation of the family in the worlds to come. In an important sense, then, the restoration that Joseph Smith effected was his attempt to recuperate the original covenant God had made with Israel. In this sense, at least, one could say that to receive the blessings of salvation, the Christians must become Israel, and not the other way around. The following discourse was given by Apostle Parley P. Pratt, the most influential theologian of first-generation Latter-day Saints.

We are told, by the Prophet . . . Isaiah . . . that the Lord would, some time, "lift up a standard for the people," "an ensign for the nations," and that He would not only do this, but do it as a manifestation which should result in the great restoration of all things spoken of by the Prophets, in the restoration of the twelve tribes of Israel from the four quarters of the earth, to their own country, nationality, institutions, and religion; that they might again be nationalized, established, and reinstated in their covenant renewed unto them, as in days of old, and have their own Priesthood, rulers, governors, and consequently their own blessings. I say, we are told, by one of the greatest Prophets, whose prophecies are on record, that a standard would be lifted up or manifested, in order to bring about that great restoration. What is that standard? . . .

I do not understand the prediction to which I refer as exclusively pertaining to a book, but rather to a religion, to a set of principles developed, to a covenant established, or, to carry it out more fully, to a people organized, gathered together, and established in one, having one faith, one spirit, one baptism, one God, one eternal and everlasting covenant by which they are all united, and one set of principles by which they are governed. . . . Nothing short of this, if I understand the prediction of Isaiah, would be considered by the Jews, and by the other tribes of Israel, wherever they were found, and finally by the whole of the Gentile world that might live to see it, as a "standard." This would be something worthy to be called a standard, something to which they could look, and come to, and be organized, consolidated, nationalized, and governed by, politically and religiously; or more truly and consistently speaking, religiously, because that includes all the political governments that are worth naming or striving for in heaven or on earth . . .

Then with this view of the subject, such a system introduced, even among a few men, they being organised upon it, and acting it out in a good measure, we should call this a "standard." The Jews could look to it and call it a "standard." The ten tribes, and the scattered remnants, and all that appertain to the lineage of Abraham, Isaac, and Jacob, scattered through the world, waiting for the redemption, and the restoration of the kingdom to Israel, could look to such a "standard," to the people organised upon these principles developed from heaven, and carrying them out in all their points, for they are capable of governing a world, or a million of worlds; to this they could look and say, there is a "standard." . . .

"Well, but," you say, "let the Jews take their own standard." Then they will neither have the Christian dispensation, nor that of Moses and the Prophets, because both of these had power in them that the Jews do not profess to have. The Christian religion had its inspired men, Apostles and Prophets. Those the Jews have not got. Moses and the Prophets had their miracles, gifts, powers, and oracles, men who were raised up by heaven, to direct, make laws and governments, and organise a kingdom among the Jews; they have not got these either. The most they pretend to have is a Book that gives the history of their fathers, and of Moses and the Prophets; showing that they lived under a dispensation of Priesthood, revealed from heaven, and handed down from the fathers, from generation to generation, which Priesthood held the Urim and Thummim, and the charge of the holy place, containing the holy things, and power to inquire of God, and to instruct the people in what was for their peace, defence, welfare, government, judgment, and law. The Jews cannot say they have these things now. Moses and the Prophets had the ministering of angels. The Jews at this day have not. Moses and the Prophets had living oracles from heaven. The Jews have not. Moses and the Prophets had power to control the elements, and work mighty wonders in the name of the Lord, some of them even rolled the earth back on its axis. Have the Jews this power? No. To restore them to Palestine, and let their own institutions be a standard, would be to put there what neither resemble Moses and the Prophets, nor Jesus and the Prophets.

"But suppose we try to convert them to the present Christian institutions," says one. Well, where is the "standard?" Who has got it? The Christian institution consisted of Apostles and Prophets, ministers whose Priesthood was after the order of the Son of God, and ordained by himself, for he says, "As my Father hath sent me, even so send I you;" "ye have not chosen me, but I have chosen you, and ordained you." Connected with the Apostleship are the keys and powers of government, the administration of ordinances, and the gifts and powers of the Holy Spirit. This is a "standard," which the Jews, and the ten tribes would all acknowledge, and it is a Christian one, yet such a one all Christendom cannot present. They can present a book, like the Jews; the one is a book that testifies that Moses and the Prophets had this power, the other that Jesus and his Apostles had it, but neither of these books can be the "standard," because the mere history that somebody had this power would not be a living "standard." If the Christians present the Jews with the New Testament, the Jews will present the Christians with the Old Testament, and the writers of both of them had the power. The Jew would have to admit, that the power and "standard" that his book was the key of, had passed away; and the Christian, that the angels, gifts, and blessings that his book gave an account of, had also passed away.

. . . To take the republican form of government, and set it up as a standard, would be to set the Jews and the Ten Tribes, when they get home, to creating their own government, religion, and officers. They would say, "This is not a restoration of all things to the order of the fathers. . . . The Jews and the Ten Tribes know better than to bow to such an order of things, for no rule, prec- edent, or example, can be found in the history of the fathers to substantiate such a course; they would either conclude that God had changed, or that such proceedings were an imposition, and pertained to no real government from heaven at all. "Well, then," says the Lord, "I will set up a standard for my people, and lift up my hand to the Gentiles. A system shall be developed from heaven, by which the people are to be planted in one, that is, those who embrace it; . . . it would be a principle of government developed in all its parts, not differing so much from the old one either. "Do you mean the law of Moses?" Yes, but only so far as the same eternal principles existed in that law. There were many prin- ciples given in that law which pertained not to the eternal kingdom of God; they had to be fulfilled in Christ, and then have an end. . . .

Hence the kingdom of God had to be set up twice, . . .—at two distinct times, or else the whole matter is a mistake from the beginning to the end, because John the Baptist said it was at hand in his day, Jesus Christ said the same, the Apostles and Seventies said, in their days, that it was right at the door. And then Jesus Christ predicted a whole string of events, including the destruction of Jerusalem, and the dispersion of the Jews. He then predicted signs that were to be seen in the sun, moon, and stars, and said, lo! "the king- dom of God is nigh at hand." Just as sure as the sun shines, the kingdom had to be set up twice, or there is no meaning to the Book, ...

Hence the gathering of the Saints; the organization of the kingdom of God, religiously and politically, if you will; the revelation of the law of God, and the new and everlasting covenant made to Abraham of old and his seed, which has never been altered by the Lord, only lost to the people. Paul said that the law given upon Mount Sinai, four hundred and thirty years after that covenant was made, might not disannul it. Jesus Christ was that man spoken of when God said, "In thee and in thy seed shall all nations of the earth be blessed." Thus, Paul and Jesus, in so many words, confirmed the covenant made with Abra- ham, that neither the law of Moses nor Jesus Christ ever disannulled. What was it? A great many things, but the principal thing was, "I will greatly multiply thy seed"; in short, a law was given him by which he and his posterity should be regulated and governed, with regard to matrimony and posterity. Now, then,

to restore the new and everlasting covenant made with Abraham, and not disannulled by Moses, the Prophets, Jesus Christ, and the Apostles; to restore an
organization of principles, of law; a development that would make a standard
to regulate families, households, and kingdoms in every respect; that would be
to fulfil the words of Isaiah, where he says, I will "set up my standard to the
people"; then I will gather you. Going to work to gather them to a standard set
up by modern professors would be nonsense, for it would not chime in with
the law that governed Abraham and his family matters, when he and a great
many others should come together and sit down in the kingdom of God. Such
a standard would be lame in some points.

If I were a Jew, you might cry to me and preach to me until doomsday, and
then take a sword, and hold it over me to sever my head from my body, but I
should say, "I will not move one step to the standard that is not Abraham's, nor
from the everlasting covenant in which my fathers Abraham, Isaac, and Jacob,
and all the holy Prophets will come and sit down in the presence of God, upon
the same principles with their modern children. I am a Jew, and my hope is
in the covenants of the fathers. If you nations who are not numbered in that
covenant wish to be blessed, it must be in that covenant, and in no other way;
and you cannot bring me any other standard that is a lawful one. You may
teach me Christianity, as you call it; you may try to govern me by a republican
government, as you call it; and ten thousand other things; but when you have
taught them all to me, neither for your fire, your sword, your government, your
religion, your threats, nor anything else will I ever embrace any other system
but the standard, the covenant, in which all my nation, all the Ten Tribes and
the scattered remnants can be blessed; a covenant that will look them up, with
all the Gentile world; and raise all the ancients from the dead, and by which
all can sit down together in the same kingdom, and be governed by the same
principles, covenants, laws, and ordinances for ever." That is the stubbornness
I should have in my nature, if I were a Jew. And the blood that flows quick
through my veins tells me I am not one whit behind the Jew; it tells me I am
of the seed of Abraham, Isaac, and Jacob; therefore I am just about as hard as
they are to believe in anything but a full and complete standard, a development of that system which will organize me and my house, and all the people,
whether Jew or Gentile, that will embrace it, in all the world, if they will repent.
I read it, in so many words of the good old Prophet, that "the nation and kingdom that will not serve thee shall perish; yea, those nations shall be utterly
wasted." I would say to king Agrippa, if he were here to-day, "Believest thou

the Prophets?" If the world would believe, then, the whole of their kingcraft, and priestcraft, and confused systems would soon pass away, and the covenant made with Abraham, Isaac, and Jacob, and to which the Prophets, Jesus, and the Apostles looked forward, would be established. . . .

Here we are, and, thank God for it, a small government, you may call it a republican government, or what you please; but the spirit, and Gospel, and law, and principles of union are here, and nobody can help it. . . . We find ourselves a government organized upon these great principles, and a government in peace. This government has to maintain its character, and become a standard, having developed in it every principle for the salvation of the living and the dead; to hold the keys of the Priesthood that bear rule in heaven, on earth, and in hell, and maintain a people built upon it, which is all necessary in order to become a standard. To this the Ten Tribes will look, to this will look the scattered remnants that are aware of the promise to Abraham, that in his seed, and not in some other Priesthood and lineage, shall all the nations and people of the earth be blessed. Where should they look, if we were to be scattered abroad, if we should come to a standstill, and stick our stakes, and say to the Almighty and to His servants—"We will do this, and that, and that is what we will not do, but we will go our own way?" Suppose now the spirit of prophecy should descend upon the Ten Tribes of Israel, and they smite the mountains of ice by the word of God, and the mountains flow down, and their Prophets travel abroad to search the world through, for they have seen the signs in the heavens, and they feel like the wise men of the east as they inquired for the Saviour; suppose the Ten Tribes come and inquire—"Where is the Temple of God, for we have seen the signs in the heavens; where shall we find it?" and we were to scatter and divide, and lose the Spirit of God, and become sectarians, or something worse; the Ten Tribes would then have to search with a lighted candle, and could not find the Temple here, and I defy them to find it anywhere else.

From *Journal of Discourses* (1853)

4. Brigham Young, "Spiritual Gifts—Hell—The Spirit World—The Elders and the Nations—The Lamanites—The Temple"

Four years after entering the Salt Lake Valley, the Mormon-led Utah Territorial Legislature met for the first time. In the opening session, Brigham Young, in his capacity as Territorial Governor, addressed the body. There, for the first recorded time, Young established a course change from Joseph Smith's practice of according black members all rights and privileges in the church and of ordaining black men to the priesthood along with their white brethren. "Any man having one drop of the seed of [Cain] . . . in him cannot hold the priesthood, and if no other prophet ever spake it before I will say it now."² Associating black skin with Cain's posterity and slavery with Ham's posterity was commonplace in nineteenth-century religious thinking (to be "a servant of servants" was the seeming destiny decreed for Canaan, the son of Ham, who was the son of Noah in Genesis 9:25; see also Abraham 1:21–26). In further remarks given in 1854, Young put the racial prohibition in the broader context of what he couched as a liberal, quasi-universalist vision that accorded to different peoples different standards, expectations, blessings, curses, and time tables, apportioned to their level of preparation. Latter-day Saints, in particular, were generally considered to be literal descendants of the House of Israel. Their congregating upon conversion was in the Mormon view a fulfillment of the prophesied gathering of Israel in the latter days. So were Native Americans (through Manasseh) members of that lineage, who on that basis and on account of their lesser wickedness, Brigham Young taught, will be restored to their promised inheritance before the descendants of Judah.

Many people believe that the Spirit of the Lord has not been upon the earth when the Gospel was not among men in its purity; they believe the Spirit of the Lord has been entirely taken from the earth since the apostacy of the Church. I do not believe for one moment that there has been a man or woman upon the face of the earth, from the days of Adam to this day, who has not been enlightened, instructed, and taught by the revelations of Jesus Christ. "What! the ignorant heathen?" Yes, every human being who has possessed a sane mind. I am far from believing that the children of men have been deprived of the privilege of receiving the Spirit of the Lord to teach them right from wrong. No matter what the traditions of their fathers were, those who were honest before the Lord, and acted uprightly, according to the best knowledge they had, will have an opportunity to go into the kingdom of God. I believe this privilege belonged to the sons and daughters of Adam, and descended from him, and his children who were contemporary with him, throughout all generations.

Men who are under the influence of their traditions and former notions, will desire to ask scores of questions upon this subject, but I think I can relieve your minds.

The Spirit of the Lord, in teaching the people, in opening their minds to the principles of truth, does not infringe upon the laws God has given to mankind for their government; consequently, when the Lord made man, He made him an agent accountable to his God, with liberty to act and to do as he pleases, to a certain extent, in order to prove himself. There is a law that governs man thus far; but the law of the celestial kingdom, as I have frequently told you, is, and always will be, the same to all the children of Adam. When we talk of the celestial law which is revealed from heaven, that is, the Priesthood, we are talking about the principle of salvation, a perfect system of government, of laws and ordinances, by which we can be prepared to pass from one gate to another, and from one sentinel to another, until we go into the presence of our Father and God. This law has not always been upon the earth; and in its absence, other laws have been given to the children of men for their improvement, for their education, for their government, and to prove what they would do when left to control themselves; and what we now call tradition has grown out of these circumstances.

There is so much of this, that I hardly dare to commence talking about it. It would require a lengthy discourse upon this particular point. Suffice it to say, the Lord has not established laws by which I am compelled to have my shoes made in a certain style. He has never given a law to determine whether I shall have a square-toed boot or a peaked-toed boot; whether I shall have a coat with the waist just under my arms, and the skirts down to my heels; or whether I shall have a coat like the one I have on. Intelligence, to a certain extent, was bestowed both upon Saint and sinner, to use independently, aside from whether they have the law of the Priesthood or not, or whether they have ever heard of it or not. "I put into you intelligence," saith the Lord, "that you may know how to govern and control yourselves, and make yourselves comfortable and happy on the earth; and give unto you certain privileges to act upon as independently in your sphere as I do in the government of heaven."

No matter whether we are Jew or Gentile, as the two classes of people are called; though Gentile signifies disobedient people; no matter whether we believe in the Koran as firmly as we now believe in the Bible; no matter whether we have been educated by the Jews, the Gentiles, or the Hottentots; whether we serve the true and the living God, or a lifeless image, if we are honest before the God we serve.

Brother George Q. Cannon brought me a god from the Sandwich Islands, made out of a piece of wood. If all the people bow down to such a god as that, it is in accordance with their laws and ordinances, and their manner of dealing among themselves; the Lord permits them to do as they please with regard to that matter, and this illustration will apply to all the nations upon the face of the earth. People who fall down beneath the wheels of Juggernaut, and are crushed to death; who sacrifice their children in the worship of idols; if they act according to the best of their knowledge, there is a chance for their salvation, as much as there is for the salvation of any other person.

"Do you suppose the Hindoos have the light of the Spirit of Christ?" I know they have; and so have the Hottentots, and so has every nation and kingdom upon the face of the earth, even though some of them may be cannibals, indulging in a practice the most repugnant to our refined feelings of any we know of among any people; yet that is a practice which the religious, refined, and polished inhabitants of our lovely country shudder at. But let me place any member of this congregation, or the whole of them, in such a state of suffering, from year to year, that they shall never see one day or one hour's comfort, nor satisfaction of human life; when compared with a condition of that kind, the sin of killing and eating a human being would not be as great as many sins committed by the so-called Christian nations.

Can I refer your minds to circumstances of this kind among the people of our lovely country? Yes, brethren and sisters, ladies and gentlemen, scores of them. When a man has power over his neighbour, over his fellow-being, and puts him in torment, which is like the flames of everlasting fire, so that he never dares to speak his mind, or walk across the street, or attend to any branch of business without a continual fear of his oppressor, and of the rod hanging over him for punishment, it is worse than to kill and eat him. That is as the torment of hell, do you know it? Now do not be scared when you hear of the heathen engaging in loathsome practices, for I defy you to bring up a meaner or more degraded set than now exists among the so-called civilized nations of the earth.

When I heard brother George Q. Cannon speak about the traditions of the people where he has been, I thought that some of their traditions were no worse than some of ours. They believe that no one is better capable of teaching the inhabitants of the earth than they; and I defy them to believe that stronger than we believe it of ourselves. It is what we have been taught, and what we verily believe; they have been taught the same idea, and believe it with all their hearts; then don't cast them down to hell for their honest belief.

But when the light of the knowledge of God comes to a man and he rejects it, that it is his condemnation. When I have told all I have been authorized to declare to him in the name of the Lord, if he does not have the visions of eternity, it is all nonsense to him. To know the truth of my testimony he must have the visions and revelations of God for himself. And when he gets them, and turns aside, becoming a traitor to the cause of righteousness, the wrath of God will beat upon him, and the vengeance of the Almighty will be heavy upon him. This comes, not because their fathers lived in darkness before them, and the ancestors of their fathers before them; not because the nations have lived and died in ignorance; but because the Lord pours the spirit of revelation upon them, and they reject it. Then they are prepared for the wrath of God, and they are banished to another part of the spirit world, where the devil has power and control over them. . . .

Cain conversed with his God every day, and knew all about the plan of creating this earth, for his father told him. But, for the want of humility, and through jealousy, and an anxiety to possess the kingdom, and to have the whole of it under his own control, and not allow any body else the right to say one word, what did he do? He killed his brother. The Lord put a mark on him; and there are some of his children in this room. When all the other children of Adam have had the privilege of receiving the Priesthood, and of coming into the kingdom of God, and of being redeemed from the four quarters of the earth, and have received their resurrection from the dead, then it will be time enough to remove the curse from Cain and his posterity. He deprived his brother of the privilege of pursuing his journey through life, and of extending his kingdom by multiplying upon the earth; and because he did this, he is the last to share the joys of the kingdom of God.

Here are the Lamanites, another example. Their wickedness was not so great as those who slew the Son of God. Jesus revealed himself to them after he was slain, preached to them the Gospel. But in the fourth generation the Priesthood was driven from their midst, and after that, the laws, ordinances, and power of the Gospel ceased to be with them. Is their curse as great as that of those in Palestine? No, it is light, in comparison. They began to thirst for each other's blood, and massacred each other, from generation to generation, until they sunk into wickedness, and evil principles the most degrading, and have become loathsome and vile. Still, the curse will be removed from them before it will be removed from the children of Judah; and they will become "a white and delightsome people."

———————————

From *Journal of Discourses* (1854)

5. Joseph Fielding Smith, "Appointment of Lineage"

Joseph Smith intimated the doctrine of pre-mortal existence as early as 1830 but definitively announced the doctrine with an 1833 revelation, which stated that "man was also in the beginning with God. Intelligence, or the light of truth, was not created or made, neither indeed can be" (Doctrine and Covenants 93:29). Pre-mortal existence was maintained by many Jewish and early Christian authorities but deemed heretical in the sixth century. The idea persisted among many philosophers, poets, and religious thinkers, though it had little acceptance in antebellum America. Smith and his contemporaries did very little to develop the doctrine, though historically it had been a powerful idea to resolve an array of difficult issues, from the justice of God, to the problem of human freedom, to the soul's origins, to spiritual recognition of truth. Apostle (and later president) Joseph Fielding Smith was one of the most influential—and doctrinaire—church leaders of the twentieth century. His essay on lineage is one of the fullest Mormon expositions ever of the array of implications that follow from a belief in pre-mortal existence. Among these inferences, most potentially troubling was the correlating of pre-mortal behavior with present circumstance. But Joseph Fielding Smith's suggestion that blacks were less faithful in the pre-mortal realm proved appealing in two regards. It seemed to explain an otherwise unfathomable history of oppression and disadvantage; and it made sense ex post facto of Brigham Young's prohibition of the priesthood to those of African descent. However, in August 1978, just months after President Spencer W. Kimball announced that all worthy male church members—regardless of race—could hold the priesthood, Apostle Bruce R. McConkie (Joseph Fielding Smith's son-in-law) publically encouraged Latter-day Saints to abandon past racial views and embrace new prophetic realities. "There are statements in our literature by the early Brethren which we have interpreted to mean that the Negroes would not receive the priesthood in mortality. I have said the same things, and people write me letters and say, 'You said such and such, and how is it now that we do such and such?' And all

I can say to that is that it is time disbelieving people repented and got in line and believed in a living, modern prophet," McConkie declared. "Forget everything that I have said, or what President Brigham Young or President George Q. Cannon or whomsoever has said in days past that is contrary to the present revelation. We spoke with a limited understanding and without the light and knowledge that now has come into the world."[3]

PRE-MORTAL SPIRITS GRADED

We have learned through the word of the Lord to Abraham that spirits in the pre-existence were graded. That is, some were more intelligent than others, some more faithful, while some actually rebelled and lost their standing and the privilege of receiving the second estate. This is the word of the Lord:

If there be two spirits, and one shall be more intelligent than the other, yet these two spirits, notwithstanding one is more intelligent than the other, have no beginning; they existed before, they shall have no end, they shall exist after, for they are gnolaum, or eternal. And the Lord said unto me: These two facts do exist, that there are two spirits, one being more intelligent than the other; there shall be another more intelligent than they; I am the Lord thy God, I am more intelligent than they all.—Abraham 3:18–19.

It is also made known that one-third of the hosts of heaven rebelled and followed Lucifer. "* * * for behold, the devil was before Adam, for he rebelled against me, saying, Give me thine honor, which is my power; and also a third part of the hosts of heaven turned he away from me because of their agency; and they were thrust down and thus came the devil and his angels."—D.C. 29:36–37.

THOSE NOT VALIANT DEPRIVED OF GREATEST PRIVILEGES

Among those who fell there must have been some superior intelligences. Lucifer, himself, was of this kind, and it was because of this that he was able to influence so many of his fellow spirits. How many were almost persuaded, were indifferent, and who sympathized with Lucifer, but did not follow him, we do not know. The scriptures are silent on this point. It is a reasonable conclusion however, that there were many who did not stand valiantly with Michael in the great battle for the protection of the free agency and the plan for the merited exaltation of mankind, although they may not have openly rebelled. We may justify ourselves in this conclusion by several passages of scripture which seem to have a bearing on this thought. Man had his agency and because of it one-third of the hosts rebelled. We naturally conclude that others among the two-thirds did not show the loyalty to their Redeemer that they should. Their sin was not one that merited the extreme punishment which was inflicted on the devil and his angels. They were not denied the privilege of receiving the second estate, but were permitted to come to the earth-life with some restrictions placed upon them. That the negro race, for instance, have been placed under restrictions because of their attitude in the world of spirits, few will doubt. It cannot be looked upon as just that they should be deprived of the power of the Priesthood without it being a punishment for some act, or acts, performed before they were born. Yet, like all other spirits who come into this world, they come innocent before God so far as mortal existence is concerned, and here, under certain restrictions, they may work out their second estate. If they prove faithful in this estate, without doubt, our Eternal Father, who is just and true, will reward them accordingly and there will be in store for them some blessings of exaltation.

SOME SINNED BEFORE BIRTH

This doctrine that man could, and did in many instances, sin before he was born, was well understood in ancient times. We have the instance of the question put to the Savior regarding the man born blind. If this question had been an improper one, and the doctrine false, the Savior would have corrected it by saying, "Ye do err, for no man could sin before he was born." This the Lord did not do, but by implication seemed to confirm the doctrine in his answer: "Neither hath this man sinned, nor his parents; but that the works of God should be made manifest in him."

NO SCRIPTURAL PROOF OF PRE-MORTAL CHOOSING

We have no scriptural justification, however, for the belief that we had the privilege of choosing our parents and our life companions in the spirit world. This belief has been advocated by some, and it is possible that in some instances it is true, but it would require too great a stretch of the imagination to believe it to be so in all, or even in the majority of cases. Most likely we came where those in authority decided to send us. Our agency may not have been exercised to the extent of making choice of parents and posterity.

ECHOES OF ETERNITY

An interesting phase of this question is discussed by Elder Orson F. Whitney. I quote his words:

> Why are we drawn towards certain persons, and they to us, as if we had always known each other? Is it a fact that we always have? Is there something, after all, in that much abused term "affinity" and is this the basis of its claim? At all events, it is just as logical to look back upon fond associations, as it is to look forward to them. We believe that ties formed in this life, will be continued in the life to come; then why not believe that we had similar ties before we came into the world, and that some of them at least, have been resumed in this state of existence?
>
> After meeting someone whom I had never met before on earth, I have wondered why that person's face seemed so familiar. More than once, upon hearing a noble sentiment expressed, though unable to recall that I had ever heard it until then, I have found myself in sympathy with it, was thrilled by it, and felt as if I had always known it. The same is true of some strains of music; they are like echoes of eternity. I do not assert pre-acquaintance in all such cases, but as one thought suggests another these queries arise in the mind.
>
> When it comes to the Gospel, I feel more positive. Why did the Savior say: "My sheep know my voice?" Did a sheep ever know the voice of its shepherd if it had never heard that voice before? They who love the Truth, and to whom it most strongly appeals—were they not acquainted with it in a previous life? I think so. I believe we knew the Gospel before we came here, and that is what gives to it a familiar sound.

PREVIOUS EXPERIENCES GUIDE OUR PREFERENCES IN LIFE

President Joseph F. Smith said to Elder Whitney:

> I heartily endorse your sentiments respecting congeniality of spirits. Our knowledge of persons and things before we came here, combined with the divinity awakened within our souls through obedience to the Gospel powerfully affects, in my opinion, all our likes and dislikes, and guides our preferences in the course of this life, provided we give careful heed to the admonitions of the Spirit.
>
> All those salient truths which come so forcibly to the head and heart seem but the awakening of the memories of the spirit. Can we know anything here that we did not know before we came? Are not the means of knowledge in the first estate equal to those of this? I think that the spirit, before and after this probation,

possesses greater facilities, aye, manifold greater, for the acquisition of knowledge, than while manacled and shut up in the prison house of mortality. I believe
that our Savior possessed a foreknowledge of all the vicissitudes through which
He would have to pass in the mortal tabernacle.

If Christ knew beforehand, so did we. But in coming here, we forgot all, that
our agency might be free indeed, to choose good or evil, that we might merit
the reward of our own choice and conduct. But by the power of the Spirit, in the
redemption of Christ, through obedience, we often catch a spark from the awakened memories of the immortal soul, which lights up our whole being as with the
glory of our former home.—Era 23:101 and Gos. Doc. 15–16.

PRE-ASSIGNMENT TO NATION OR TRIBE

Our place among the tribes and nations evidently was assigned to us by the
Lord. That there was an assignment of this kind before earth-life began, is a
declaration in the Scriptures. Certain spirits were chosen to come through the
lineage of Abraham, and this choice was made in the beginning. Other selections were also made and the nations determined upon by the councils in the
heavens. When Paul was speaking on Mars' Hill he said to the Athenians:

Ye men of Athens, I perceive that in all things ye are too superstitious.

For as I passed by, and beheld your devotions, I found an altar with this
inscription, TO THE UNKNOWN GOD. Whom therefore ye ignorantly worship, him declare I unto you.

God that made the world, and all things therein, seeing that he is Lord of
heaven and earth, dwelleth not in temples made with hands:

Neither is worshipped with men's hands, as though he needed anything, seeing he giveth to all life, and breath, and all things;

And hath made of one blood all nations of men, for to dwell on all the face of
the earth; and *hath determined the times before appointed, and the bounds of their
habitation.*—Acts 17: 22–26.

If the Lord appointed unto the nations the bounds of their habitations, then
there must have been a selection of spirits to form these nations. In greater
clearness Moses has declared the same thing:

Remember the days of old, consider the years of many generations; ask thy father,
and he will shew thee; thy elders, and they will tell thee.

When the Most High divided to the nations their inheritance, when he separated the sons of Adam, he set the bounds of the people according to the number
of the children of Israel.

For the Lord's portion is his people; Jacob is the lot of his inheritance.—Deut.
32:7–9.

If bounds were set according to the number of the children of Israel, and
they were the Lord's portion (i.e., those with whom he made covenant), when
the Lord divided the sons of Adam, it must have been done before this earth-
life began. For in these days of old when this division was made, the nation of
Israel had not been brought into existence on the earth.

CHOICE SPIRITS GIVEN THE FAVORED LINEAGE

Is it not a reasonable belief, that the Lord would select the choice spirits to come
through the better grades of nations? Moreover, is it not reasonable to believe
that less worthy spirits would come through less favored lineage? Does this not
account, in very large part, for the various grades of color and degrees of intelligence we find in the earth? Is not the Lord doing the best that can be done in
accordance with the laws of justice and mercy for the people of the earth? For in
his mercy he has a salvation, with some degree of exaltation, even for the heathen
and for those who die without law. However, we must not be unmindful of the
fact, that these world conditions have also been brought about in large degree by
rebellion and disregard of the laws of God in this life. Retrogression has come
upon mankind because they have rejected the counsels and commandments of
the Almighty. Advancement has come largely because men have been willing to
walk, in part at least, in the light of divine inspiration. Moreover, notwithstanding the fact that the Lord chose a certain nation as his "portion" and that Jacob
became the "lot of his inheritance," the Almighty also was kind to other nations
and leavened them by scattering the blood of Israel among them. In this and
other ways the nations became blessed as the seed of Abraham.

From *The Way to Perfection: Short Discourses on Gospel Themes* (1931)

6. Helen Sekaquaptewa, "My Church"

*Much of the interest surrounding the Book of Mormon in the church's first genera-
tion was the light it shed on Native American origins. "Do you wish to purchase a*

history of the Indians" was the pitch of Samuel Smith, the church's first ordained missionary. Since the seventeenth century, numerous writers had linked them to the Lost Tribes of the Old Testament, and the idea was a commonplace in antebellum America. The novelty of the Book of Mormon was that it claimed to be actually written by Israelite descendants (of a sixth-century BCE Manassehite), with the intention of bringing to their latter-day posterity the knowledge that "they are not cast off forever" from the Lord and the covenant made with Abraham. With limited success, Latter-day Saints focused some early proselytizing missions among Native Americans, hoping they would recognize in the Book of Mormon echoes of either spiritual or tribal memory. Once settled in Utah, the Mormons had to learn to coexist with, as well as evangelize, the Native American inhabitants of the west. Mormon lore highlights Brigham Young's progressive policy, captured in his dictum that it was cheaper to feed Indians than fight them, and the example of the kindly "apostle to the Indians," Jacob Hamblin. Recent scholarly appraisals suggest that while Young and the Mormons in general were more enlightened in their dealings with the Native Americans than most Americans of their era, they fell well short of the modern ideal.

While the ritual part of the Hopi religion had no appeal to me . . . the things my parents taught me about the way to live were good. When we were living in Hotevilla, my father was often in our home. During the long winter evenings he would explain the teachings of the kiva saying, "You are young now and may not be interested, but I must teach you now while I am here with you. As you grow older, then you will learn to understand and know it is the truth." This has come to pass.

He said:

"The white man has kept a written record of the history of the people from the beginning, while the Hopis have passed their history from one generation to another by word of mouth. With the telling over the years, some of it has been omitted or misunderstood, and changes have been made. The written record is more accurate and true. There will come a time when the written record will be brought to the Hopis by the white man. There will be many religions taught. You will need to be wise to recognize and choose the right church. It will teach you to be humble and will not try to force you into it. When that time comes we should all forsake our native religion and join this true church. There will come a time when all the people of the earth will belong to the one true church, and we will all speak the same language and be as one people."

He said this many times, and at the end he would say, "I tell you this because you are my own blood. I want you to take it to heart and teach it to your children. I want you and your children to live by those teachings and benefit by what I have said."

Both Emory and I heard him say this long before we ever heard of the Book of Mormon. He *did* say it in our presence. The Traditionals would now deny that this is what their fathers used to teach. When we heard of and read the Book of Mormon it sounded like a familiar story. Reading the Bible and the Book of Mormon has helped us to understand the Hopi traditions, and the Hopi traditions help us to understand these books of scripture. . . .

During the 1860's and 1870's, Jacob Hamblin led several scouting parties of Mormons to the Hopi villages, their object being to make friends and to teach their religion. This was the very first contact that the Hopis had with the religious group. Of course, this was before my time, but I do remember hearing my elders talk of "Jee-co-ba." There are still a few of the ancient ones who remember and tell of Jacob, his policy of honesty and kindness, in contrast to the abuse and exploitation they had known at the hands of the other *pahanas* who had come.

On one of his trips, Jacob took Tuba, one of the chief men of Oraibi, and his wife Talasnimka—she was known as kachina mana, girl kachina—back to Utah with him where they stayed for a year. It was a goodwill trip; they left in the fall of 1871 and returned in September, 1872. Tuba's wife was my grandmother's sister. She came back wearing a cotton dress and a bonnet, and like Marco Polo, she brought back "things"—yeast, a coffeepot, a dishpan, and a dutch oven. One of the first of the wagons of the settlers to Arizona passed by Oraibi and in it was a cookstove for Talasnimka. It was the very first stove in Oraibi. As a little girl I remember being fascinated with the tiny door that had a slide in it to make a draft. I also remember my great aunt in her old age. After the death of her husband, Tuba, she lived in Bacabi with some of her nieces and later in a little house that was built there for her.

The Hopis always classed the Mormons as different and separate from other whites, especially after Tuba's visit to Utah. They felt that the Mormons were friendly and did not look down on the Indians. They were industrious and would share their food with hungry Indians. The Hopis said, "When we go to their homes they invite us in to sit at the table and eat with them. They do not give us food on a plate to eat outside like dogs."

There is a bone in the neck of the sheep that looks like a hat. That bone is called "mo mon a" or Mormon. We recognized Mormons afar because they wore hats. The first dolls brought in by the trader were called "Mo-mon-ho-ya," or little Mormon.

One afternoon in the 1920's a man drove into Hotevilla and parked his car in my neighbor's yard. He was a stranger and didn't look like a government worker. It was getting late, and he was still sitting in his car; no one had offered him hospitality; they wouldn't ask anybody in. So I went over and asked if he wanted to stay in the village overnight and if he was hungry. He said he had come on a mission to make friends with the Hopi tribe. He accepted my invitation and came over to my house and ate supper and spent the evening with us. He slept in his car, as I had a big family to sleep.

He told me that he was a Mormon Elder and was thankful to be invited into our house since no one else seemed to want him. He had come to see the Chief and find out if the church could open a mission there. He chopped wood for me. I understood that he stayed in the village taking care of peaches and went back to the ranch the next morning. I never learned if he made a good impression on the Chief.

It was in 1950 that I next heard of the Mormons. Abbott was staying with Aunt Elsie, beginning his first year at Phoenix Union High School, when he was suddenly stricken with acute arthritis. He was in great pain and unable to move. They carried him out on a stretcher and took him home to Elsie. He was in hospitals in Phoenix and Winslow, bedfast for a year. After three years he was released from hospitals but was rigid from the waist down. Wayne took his books on radar to him, and Abbott learned how to repair radios by studying while he was in bed. He wrote home about some Mormon Elders coming to visit him in the hospital. He said, "Here is a religion we should get interested in and try to learn more about." Of course I wanted to do what Abbott wanted because he had been sick so much, and I went along with him.

Once when one of my babies was born, I was in Hotevilla, when quite a crowd of Mormons from around "Joe" City and Snowflake came there. They called the people together in front of the store and talked to us, giving us a sermon. I listened with interest, but none of them ever came back again for a long time. The first full-time missionaries came to Oraibi in 1951. The first ones to come to our house were Brother Virgil Bushman and his wife Ruth.

Emory Jr. had come home from West Point, having been given a medical discharge after being there for a few months. He was very disappointed and discouraged but had decided that he wanted to go to college and was considering the Brigham Young University at Provo, Utah. I don't know how they found it out, but the Bushmans drove out to the ranch one day. They stayed with me all day until Emory Jr. came in from riding the range. Brother Bushman rode a horse with Emory all the next day and talked him into going to Brigham Young University. Emory left right away.

Virgil and Ruth Bushman then started coming out regularly once a week teaching Emory, Abbott, and me the Gospel in a systematic way. What they taught sounded good to me, like a familiar philosophy, like the teachings we were used to, like the Hopi way. I was really converted the first week and believed everything, although I was not baptized right soon. I read the Book of Mormon. It sounded exactly like Hopi tradition.

When the young missionaries first came to Hotevilla they had a hard time. A villager would see them coming and go from door to door saying, "Don't let them in. Don't listen to them." When I saw the doors slammed in the faces of the missionaries, I felt like it was slammed in my face even before I became interested. So I often invited them to my house to eat and sleep, and they were happy to accept. Emory and I sometimes went with them to visit the Navajos, and he acted as their interpreter.

When the Mormon missionaries came to Second Mesa, they taught the first chapters of the Book of Mormon, telling of a prophet named Lehi who was told by the Lord to take his family, a wife and four sons, and leave Jerusalem because that city was going to be destroyed because of the wickedness of the inhabitants (this in the year 600 B.C.), how they journeyed many days in the wilderness on their way to the sea, how Lehi sent his sons back to Jerusalem to get their records of their forefathers and the teachings of their prophets, how they were led to a land that was choice above all other lands, having crossed the mighty waters and landed in America.

The head priests of the Hopis at Second Mesa, hearing these things, accosted the Elders and angrily said, "How come you know these things? You are not old enough to know it. Who told you these things? Only older men, high in the priesthood, know that. You keep your mouths shut."

My son Wayne was living in Phoenix, and he had been converted and baptized into the Church of Jesus Christ of Latter Day Saints, commonly called "Mormons." I felt that I should go ahead and be baptized and that I wanted my son to baptize me. I went to Phoenix to attend Allison's graduation from high school in May, 1953. While there, I told the Bishop I wanted to be baptized by my son Wayne, which event transpired on May 3, 1953. Edward and Marlene were baptized at the same time. I have no doubt I did right. I have never been sorry. It has made a better woman of me, and I have surely been happy in my church.

From *Me and Mine: The Life Story of Helen Sekaquaptewa* (1969)

7. Lacee A. Harris, "To Be Native American—and Mormon"

Mormon rhetoric about American Indians, or "Lamanites," has always been ambiguous. In the Book of Mormon narrative, the original Israelite colony fragments into the righteous, peaceable Nephites, and the wicked, warlike Lamanites. After centuries of conflict, the Nephites fall into spiritual corruption and are completely annihilated in a genocidal war by the far more numerous Lamanites. So in the Mormon mind, the Lamanites are inevitably associated with apostasy and rebellion. However, as sole survivors of a remnant of Israel, they are heirs to great promises and special favor in the latter days. Compounding confusion over their identity is the shifting meaning of the term Lamanite *in both the Book of Mormon and in Mormon history. At the time of Christ's New World, post-resurrection appearance narrated in the book's climactic chapters, the designations Nephite and Lamanite become indicative of Christian discipleship or disbelief, respectively, not of tribal affiliation. As a result, the terms cease to correlate completely with any Israelite descent. In Mormon history, Joseph Smith and subsequent leaders understood the Book of Mormon history to encompass the Western Hemisphere and accordingly used the term Lamanite to refer to any person with Native American ancestry. More careful attention to the Book of Mormon text in recent years has resulted in revisionist conceptions of Book of Mormon geography and of the designation Lamanite. A revised, official introduction to the American scripture now refers to Lamanites not as "the principal ancestors of the American Indians" but as "among the ancestors." Finally, recent DNA studies (though widely criticized as both conceptually and methodologically flawed, and largely moot in light of those latest developments) have further undermined the traditional self-understanding of Mormon American Indians as having an Israelite connection. Below is one Native American's perspective on what it is like to live in both the Mormon and Indian worlds.*

"Lamanite! I am not a Lamanite. They are a wicked people. I am not a wicked person." I can well remember my father, Albert H. Harris, saying this, both in church and to anyone else who would listen. Born on the Northern Ute Reservation in 1920, he was mixed blood. His father, Muse K. Harris, was Ute and my grandmother, Ivy Mae Harris, was anglo, a second-generation Latter-day Saint of pioneer stock. My father's grandmother, Great-grandmother Mary Reed Harris, said her own grandmother had been baptized by Brigham Young. Thus, the LDS Church had had a seven-generation impact on my family by the time I was born.

Although I remember my father's protest at being classified as a Lamanite, I never inquired about his background or youth, or his other feelings about the Church. He had served as president of the Fort Klamath Branch of the Klamath Falls Oregon Stake, on the high councils in Roosevelt, Utah, and Billings, Montana, and had held other stake positions. Still, by the time I was twenty-eight, he was dead in his Salt Lake City home, just before his fifty-first birthday, of alcohol-related causes. I don't remember what his bishop said at the time of his death. I remember that the Ute elders on the reservation spoke highly of his efforts to keep the traditional ways alive. As I look at the pattern of his life, I wonder if it was the strenuousness of that struggle to live in both worlds that moved him toward his early death. . . .

My childhood memories of religion are of Sunday meetings, not of home discussions or activities. I remember very long Sundays of getting dressed, sitting in long meetings listening to speakers talk about subjects I didn't understand, watching the big boys passing the sacrament and wishing I could too. When I was about seven years old, we moved to Roosevelt, only eight miles but a whole world away. I enjoyed being in the Cub Scouts and Boy Scouts, but I don't recall any lessons that made an impact. Being an Indian, being a Mormon were never mentioned. My Indianness, like my Mormonness, was just there.

My father was a realty officer for the Bureau of Indian Affairs and we moved relatively often. When I was ten or eleven, we moved to Klamath Agency on the Klamath-Modoc Reservation just north of Klamath Falls, Oregon, lived in agency housing, and went to church in a small branch about twelve miles away. None of the other LDS children were my age so all my friends were non-LDS. After a year, I returned to Roosevelt, Utah, to live with my grandparents.

Soon afterwards, I had my first disappointment at Church functions. At Scout camp where Order of the Arrow candidates were to be chosen, all the other boys assumed that I would be chosen for this "Indian" group. So did I.

I was crushed when I wasn't and began losing interest in Scouting, even though I continued going because most of my friends were active. . . .

During ninth grade, I was junior high band vice president, ninth grade seminary class president, and junior high student body vice president. I don't think being either LDS or Indian had anything to do with either position, even though many of my schoolmates were LDS. At the end of the school year, I rejoined my parents who, by now, were in Muskogee, Oklahoma. I attended school there until half-way through my junior year. My main interests in the Muskogee branch were Scouting and MIA. There was only one boy my age and we didn't have a great deal in common, although we were friends and home teaching companions. The LDS students from Basone Junior College, an Indian junior college, however, were very helpful and so were some of the missionaries in the area. I was called to my first Church teaching position—teaching the Blazer class—at age fourteen. I really enjoyed that.

However, in retrospect, although I met with a great deal of kindness and was included in many activities that were happening, I don't recall any adult leader—teacher, Scout leader, priesthood quorum advisor, or MIA instructor—who seemed interested in establishing a personal relationship with me or who seemed concerned about my personal spirituality. The lessons, as I recall, did not seem aimed toward action.

I was starting to feel different. I knew I wasn't a Lamanite because my father said we weren't. I knew I was an Indian but I didn't know how that fit into the Mormon system of anglos and Lamanites. The more I grew to understand my Indianness, the less I understood how I fit into the Church. In Oklahoma, surrounded by Indians of many tribes and nations, I was conscious of real pride in being an Indian. It was also in Oklahoma that my sense of being Mormon sharpened, thanks to the loving sacrifice of James C. and Della Watkins. My "foster father"-to-be, James C. Watkins, was a safety engineer for the Corps of Engineers, U.S. Army, stationed briefly at Muskogee. They had two girls, Carol and Sharon, and one boy, James. Carol was two years older than I, Sharon was six months older and James at that time was four years old. I am not really sure why they invited me to live with their family. I am not even sure why my parents agreed. I was fifteen years old. I'm glad that both did agree, for I wonder sometimes where I would be today without the Watkins family and all the help and sacrificing they did for me. This was not a part of the Church's formal placement program. When they moved on to Salina, Kansas, they asked me to go with them.

I accepted on a lark, more or less, as an adventure. My father said, "Take him, if you think you can handle him." My mother said, "Okay. . . ." It is only in retrospect that I sense my mother's pain and hurt that I would so casually leave the family. . . .

I had never looked farther ahead than being out of high school. I didn't date much—we were on the move too much and we usually lived out of town or on-base. But fortunately, Carol began attending BYU and mentioned its Indian Education program. The school sent the forms, I filled them out, and meanwhile my family had moved to Palm Springs, California, about the time we moved to Alaska. I had already lived among the Klamath, Modoc, Navajo, Creek, Sioux, Cherokee, and other Oklahoma tribes. Now I added the Agua Caliente Indians of Palm Springs.

I was accepted by BYU and, in 1962, moved into Taylor Hall in Helaman Halls with forty other fellows, all anglos, on my floor. There were only thirty-five Indians on campus that year. While I stayed with my foster parents, my parents helped out by sending money, clothes, and letters which didn't get answered too often. I am still a poor letter writer. I had been given lots of freedom to make my own choices—given lots of information about the effect of those choices—but was allowed to choose. So when I chose to go to BYU, my parents were happy that I had decided to go to college after high school. The fact that it was BYU was even better. The fact that it had an Indian Education program made it even better for them. . . .

As a first-semester freshman, I took a mandatory Book of Mormon class and really began to learn about the Lamanites. The more I learned, the more I felt that the Church really had no place for us as "Indians." We only belonged if we were Lamanites.

I felt that the teachings of the Church were excellent and I did not doubt the teachings of the Book of Mormon about the Lamanites as apostate survivors of great nations, but taking that story personally was too much for me. Were those Lamanites my Indian people? My people were good, deeply spiritual, in tune with the rhythms of the earth and with their own needs. How could we be descended from a wicked people? How could I be a descendant of wickedness and still be good without repudiating the heritage that made it possible for me to accept Mormon goodness?

These were difficult questions for a college freshman, and I found myself avoiding more and more the all-anglo ward. I was drawn to the BYU Indian Education Tribe of Many Feathers, the Indian club on campus, with its warmly welcoming activities. Our club advisors sincerely cared about us but I still felt, uneasily, that they were trying to make us into something we weren't.

My nineteenth birthday had passed. Everyone assumed I would go on a mission, and I routinely sent in my papers, asking for the Southwest Indian Mission, then the only Indian mission in the United States. Six months before I left, in January of 1964, the Southwest Indian mission was divided into the Northern Indian and the Southwest Indian and I was sent to headquarters in Holbrook, Arizona. That meant I had to learn the Navajo language and culture.

I had expected to enjoy my mission experience and I did. I had two mission presidents, J. Edwin Baird and Hal Taylor. In Arizona, I started in Pinon, and went on to Chinle, Many Farms, Lukachukai, Dennchutso, the Gap, Tuba City, Inscription House, and Chichinbitso with a stint in Cortez, Colorado, among the Ute Mountain Utes. We worked hard. No one had quite found the right set of lesson plans for Navajos, and we went through four or five during my two years. Some of the Navajo elders helped translate the lessons into Navajo and we learned to read, write, and speak the language.

Although there are inevitable differences between two people who live together twenty-four hours a day, I liked most of my companions. Six were Anglo and three were Indians, all Navajo. Many of the anglo elders were fine missionaries, good at the language, and hard working. Some of them loved the area and people, leaving only with deep regret. Others never got over the culture shock, waited out their two years with impatience, and contributed little.

Ironically, it was in the mission field, serving the Lord full time that I first became fully aware in the center of my being of some of the cultural differences between Indian and anglo Mormons. Some of my anglo companions left me with bitter memories of patronage, of being left out of decisions, of being told in subtle ways that I wasn't equal in ability or capacity. A pattern of occasional comments and offhand judgments began to take shape about the people we were teaching and working with: "lack of commitment," "Indian standard time," "a reservation Indian." Some of the anglo elders were disappointed that some of the people didn't want to hear our stories, as the lessons were called by the people, and never realized that they were communicating "we know what's best for you" by not listening to what the Indian people were saying. In their eagerness to help, many missionaries unwittingly crossed the line between assistance and taking over.

When I returned to BYU in the fall of 1964, the fifty-eighth Ward, an all-Indian unit, had been organized. We had heard about it in the mission field and were excited about it. I loved the ward but, newly sensitized to paternalism, it bothered me that our bishop was anglo when all the other officers were Indian. One of the events early in that school year of 1964 fall semester was a pre-announced talk by our bishop on interracial dating. It seemed to be an issue for him. A number of us showed up with non-Indian dates and sat on the front row. It was a joke—yet it wasn't. Something in me was starting to feel pushed around, and I wanted to push back.

Another problem that year was our bishop's discouragement of our dances and "ceremonies." Again it seemed to be an issue for the Church, an unwritten issue. Some of us protested. Why would the Church sponsor the Polynesian Center cultural ceremonies and dances, while we couldn't have our own? Policy, our bishop explained briefly. Could he show us where, we wanted to know? He became vague. We pushed harder for an explanation. Several of us were called before one of the university vice presidents to discuss "code violations." We were not violating any rules; but I learned in the session that we were questioning the wisdom of the Church leaders by asking "inappropriate" questions. We only wanted to know why we couldn't be who and what we were—Indians. To us part of being Indian was our dances and ceremonies. They had cultural, not spiritual, significance to us because none of us had the right to practice or conduct any of the real spiritual ceremonies. Many of us went home for those. We all wanted to graduate, so we stopped taking our questions to our bishop.

In retrospect, the difference between our two situations seems clearer. Polynesian dances have become detached from their philosophy and values. Doing them was harmless entertainment—good exercise. Indian dances, on the other hand, had living connections with our past, our values, our other, non-Mormon identities. They could corrupt us. We didn't know how or where, but somehow they would. . . .

My faith in Mormonism is still strong. It is important to me, that both my Indian people and the Mormons believe that the earth was created spiritually before it was created physically, that the purpose of this life is to gain experience, that our lives are to be lived so that our Creator can be proud of us individually and as a people, that the Son of God came among us to teach us how to live. We have traditions around the numbers three, twelve, and thirteen, that are reminiscent of Mormon ways. Ceremonies allow those who are authorized to bless, marry, and heal. Fasting and prayer are ways to spiritual power in both cultures.

Yet many of my questions are still there, too. When people tell me that my traditions develop from the Book of Mormon, I ask, "Then why do I have to give up those traditions to be a Mormon?" When people say, "You don't have to give up anything good. Mormonism just builds on something that is better," I say, "Why must I abandon the foundations to have the rest of the building?"

A problem for me is that I see the LDS culture as a separate structure from LDS teachings. With all my heart I accept those LDS teachings and want them for my children; but the LDS culture has become more alien, not more familiar, as the years have passed. I think sometimes of that LDS culture—of that first generation of Saints, all of them converted to a shockingly radical new religion, trying in faith to build together a new community. From their efforts, ironically, have come the culture that now tells us that we are not converted unless we accept the culture as well as the teachings—or even seems to urge us to accept the culture, never mind about the teachings. As I have talked to many Indians, they, too feel that the culture of the Mormons gets in the way of the teachings.

I may be wrong. I have been wrong before. I know that all people must abandon parts of their culture to accept the gospel. Many of my Indian brothers and sisters have given up their cultures to become Mormon—to be acceptable to their anglo Mormon brothers and sisters. How long do they last? The teachings of the Church allow us to be both Indian and Mormon, but to expect Indians to be anglo Mormons puts an enormous strain on some of the Indian people. Some feel they must choose between being Mormon and being Indian. Yet those who abandon their roots and their heritage altogether, trying to be white except for their skins, do not seem to be either happier or more successful.

It shouldn't be a conflict. We shouldn't have to choose. In both my ward and among my people, I am called "brother." I feel that responsibility in both settings. I feel the potentiality of that reward. And I remember my grandmother, the first Indian member of the Relief Society in the Uintah Basin. After years of faithful service, she went back to the traditional ways. For her, the gap got wider and wider until she had to choose. Surely, four generations later for me and my children, it should be possible to retain the beauty and the blessedness in both ways.

From *Dialogue: A Journal of Mormon Thought* (1985)

8 and 9. First Presidency (Spencer W. Kimball, N. Eldon Tanner, and Marion G. Romney), "Revelation Extends Blessings of Gospel"; and Joseph Freeman, "A Momentous Weekend"

Judged by the number of its full-time missionaries, the church is the most missionary-minded of all contemporary Christian denominations. But Mormon evangelizing has long labored under twin albatrosses. Even before its public acknowledgment of plural marriage in 1852, rumors of unorthodox marriage practices undermined efforts to win widespread public respectability. The church's prohibition against ordination of people of African descent to the priesthood, dating to the same year, became a serious impediment to missionary work—and a source of discomfort among many Latter-day Saints—only in the more racially enlightened post–Civil Rights era. Mormon doctrines and practices are almost always rooted in canonized scripture or revelations to the church prophet. The priesthood ban apparently had a foundation in neither one, paving the way for a variety of mythologies and speculations to arise by way of explanation. Compounding the uncertainties surrounding the ban was the fact that it hovered ambiguously somewhere between revealed doctrine and simple historical policy. A church president attuned to the possibilities of the church to transition to a truly worldwide body was Spencer W. Kimball, who was a relatively dynamic innovator in a conservative institution. Protests against the church practice erupted in the 1960s, and Mormon scholars prompted leaders to re-examine the historical bases of the ban. The most decisive developments, however, were taking place in Africa and South America. Congregations of thousands in Nigeria and elsewhere had arisen without an official Mormon presence or even recognition. Missionary work was also surging in Brazil, where a temple was under construction in 1978. Kimball was disturbed especially by the prospect of thousands of Brazilian Saints, many of whom had African ancestry, being denied access to a temple they had sacrificed so much to build. That June, he announced he had divine authorization to remove a painful barrier with nineteenth-century roots. In this section, we present two documents: Spencer W. Kimball's official announcement of the ban's reversal and the reaction of Joseph Freeman, the first Mormon of African descent to receive the priesthood under the new policy.

DOCUMENT 8

As we have witnessed the expansion of the work of the Lord over the earth, we have been grateful that people of many nations have responded to the message of the restored gospel, and have joined the Church in ever-increasing numbers. This, in turn, has inspired us with a desire to extend to every worthy member of the Church all of the privileges and blessings which the gospel affords.

Aware of the promises made by the prophets and presidents of the Church who have preceded us that at some time, in God's eternal plan, all of our brethren who are worthy may receive the priesthood, and witnessing the faithfulness of those from whom the priesthood has been withheld, we have pleaded long and earnestly in behalf of these, our faithful brethren, spending many hours in the Upper Room of the Temple supplicating the Lord for divine guidance.

He has heard our prayers, and by revelation has confirmed that the long-promised day has come when every faithful, worthy man in the Church may receive the holy priesthood, with power to exercise its divine authority, and enjoy with his loved ones every blessing that flows therefrom, including the blessings of the temple. Accordingly, all worthy male members of the Church may be ordained to the priesthood without regard for race or color. Priesthood leaders are instructed to follow the policy of carefully interviewing all candidates for ordination to either the Aaronic or the Melchizedek Priesthood to insure that they meet the established standards for worthiness.

We declare with soberness that the Lord has now made known his will for the blessing of all his children throughout the earth who will hearken to the voice of his authorized servants, and prepare themselves to receive every blessing of the gospel.

From *Church News* (1978)

DOCUMENT 9

When my wife called me to the phone, I didn't mind at all leaving the yard work and that hot June sun for the relative cool of the house. But as I picked up the phone, in my wildest hopes I couldn't have guessed what was going to happen during the next few minutes.

"Hello."

"Brother Freeman, did you hear the announcement?" Was that a suppressed excitement in my friend's voice?

"What announcement?"

"On TV. Have you been watching TV this morning?"

"No, I've been outside working."

"Well, listen! President Kimball has had a revelation—about your people, the blacks."

Instantly the thought flashed through my mind—priesthood! Oh, but it couldn't be so. Was this some foolish joke? I must not get excited.

"Is that right?" I kept my voice calm.

"Yes—about the priesthood. You can hold the priesthood now!"

Again the mixed hope and fear. ("Lord, let it be true!") Again my cautious reply: "Is that right?"

"Brother Freeman," came the frustrated response, "don't you believe me? There will be a special report about it at noon. Turn on the TV and see for yourself. I wanted to be the first to tell you the news."

Instant stupor of thought—instant apprehension. It couldn't be—or could it? My friend must have taken some statement out of context, or maybe he was playing his April Fool's joke a little late.

Even when he repeated the information, I kept outwardly under control. I just couldn't allow myself to get excited about his news. It was unbelievable, too wonderful to hope for, and yet. . . .

It was hard to maintain my poise when I put the phone down, though, because my wife—with her constant stream of "Who is it?" "What's happening?" and "How wonderful!"—had gotten the gist of the conversation. And certainly she was no model of calm and serenity as she danced around clapping her hands. Nevertheless, the thought remained with me—I had to stay quiet, not get excited. I kept thinking, *This is just some misunderstanding*; I feared that to believe it would produce a devastating letdown.

Then the feeling hit the pit of my stomach—maybe it *is* true! And suddenly I had to know right away. I phoned the Church Office Building and was put through to the First Presidency's office. A voice which to me sounded like an angel's spoke those wonderful words: "Yes, Brother Freeman, what you've heard is true. The official announcement that the priesthood is now available to all worthy males of The Church of Jesus Christ of Latter-day Saints will be given over radio and television all day."

As I hung up the phone, little beads of perspiration broke out on my fore-head, and my knees began to shake uncontrollably. It was true! It was really true! I could hold the priesthood!

My lifetime dream of becoming a complete follower and servant of Jesus Christ had come true. The yearning desire I'd had since joining the Church—to be found worthy to act in the name of the Lord, to know that I would have my family forever, to be able to bless and baptize my own children, to lead as a priesthood patriarch in our home—this tremendous blessing was now to be mine!

Meanwhile, involved with her own thoughts, my wife (who could tell by my reaction what the incredible verdict was) sent up a whoop of joy and relief that was heard, I'm sure, throughout the state of Utah. Hugs. Cheers. Tears. Our hearts and home were filled with ecstasy as we tried to express in actions the indescribable exhilaration we felt in our souls.

After we calmed down a little (only a very little), the tremendous implica-tions of what this actually meant began to hit us. In addition to the things which had already flashed through my mind pertaining to holding the priesthood, it suddenly dawned on me that I could now be sealed for time and eternity to my lovely wife and our three precious children in the temple. The temple! The thought took my breath away.

Our personal celebration of the great announcement was soon interrupted, however, and shortly afterward our home began to look like Grand Central Station. Phone calls came, and a steady stream of visitors arrived with excla-mations and congratulations as many friends shared with us the thrill of this occasion.

About an hour after I first heard the news I was brought back to reality by a very special phone call. Those crazy butterflies started to dance in my stomach when I heard my bishop's voice on the other end of the phone. "I'd like to meet with you this evening in my office, Brother Freeman. Can you be over here at ten?"

"Yes, Bishop, I'll be glad to meet you then." My heart was beating so hard I thought it would burst.

The rest of the day went by in a haze as I anticipated the upcoming inter-view. But my nerves were calmed as I sat across the desk from my bishop that night. We talked about many things, including, of course, my feelings about the priesthood. And I can't remember ever having a better feeling in my life than I did after I answered the necessary questions concerning my own personal worthiness. I felt so thankful that, in the bishop's judgment, now that the priesthood could be given to all worthy men, nothing need delay my own ordination. As we concluded the interview, I felt that maybe, just maybe, the Lord was approving of me, too.

As we talked, the bishop also brought up the subject of going to the temple. My first reaction was, "Maybe we shouldn't rush into anything. What will people say?"

"Well, I'm not worrying about what people will say, but about what the Lord has already said. If you're worthy to hold the priesthood, Brother Freeman, you're also ready to go to the temple. If you hold the priesthood today, you can go to the temple tomorrow."

"Wow!" I thought. "When the Lord moves, he doesn't waste any time!"

Two days later I entered the stake president's office, just hoping that somehow I would be able to hold on to my stomach. I'm sure I aged five years during that one weekend. There happened to be a general priesthood meeting in our stake that day, and during the meeting my name was presented to those assembled for approval of my receiving the Melchizedek Priesthood and being ordained an elder. As the hundreds of hands were raised simultaneously in a unanimous show of approval, I felt overwhelmed again. Only three days earlier my life had been so different. My concerns then had often stemmed from personal limitations which I had no ability to change. And now—now I had been found worthy and approved by my priesthood brethren to be ordained a bearer of the Melchizedek Priesthood!

After my bishop and the other elders laid their hands on my head a short while later, many poignant memories flashed through my mind: the days of learning about the Church, my courtship and marriage, the experiences of my childhood and youth—all of which had combined to lead me to this moment. Who would ever have dreamed that I, Joseph Freeman, Jr., of Vanceboro, North Carolina, would one day be found worthy to hold the royal priesthood of God!

But it was so. With my dear wife present, and feeling the influence of the Spirit in abundance and power, I received the holy priesthood and was ordained an elder in The Church of Jesus Christ of Latter-day Saints on Sunday, June 11, 1978.

It would be impossible to describe adequately my thoughts and feelings on that occasion and during that momentous weekend. I was well acquainted with the scriptural story. I knew that since the beginning of the black race, when the world was new and fresh and Father Adam still walked the earth in youthful vigor, the priesthood of God had been denied my race. I was aware that the first pharaoh of Egypt, a man of righteousness and wisdom, earnestly followed the patriarchal order of government established by Adam and greatly longed for the priesthood which normally accompanied it, but that his racial origins prohibited him from bearing the priesthood. How many other good men of the same lineage had throughout the ages lived and died with the same yearning desire was an unanswerable question, but their number could have been considerable.

I knew that after Abraham's writings scripture says little on the subject. I had wondered to what extent the primitive Christian Church was affected—probably not much, since within a generation or two of its founding it succumbed to apostasy anyway. Then, after a millennium and a half of darkness, the gospel light burst forth again, this time initially in North America, where some of the millions of the black inhabitants would in due time gladly accept the gospel message. After some initial uncertainties the principle had been set forth in this dispensation, too: blacks could still not hold the priesthood.

Like other black converts, I had recognized and accepted this position. What the Church offered me in terms of truth and salvation was in any case so far above any other church's concepts that I could live with even this limitation.

To determine the true reason why the priesthood was denied—other than that the Lord had commanded it—was something else, for LDS speakers and writers on the subject did not seem able to clearly establish a specific reason. As to whether (and, if so, when) the limitation would be removed, the general assumption was that it would be removed one day, but probably few expected the limitation to be lifted before the Millennium at the earliest.

Yet now it had actually come to pass—the Lord had spoken, and all the previous whys and wherefores no longer mattered. Under this further acceleration of God's purposes in the last days, the full blessings of the gospel would now be available without limitation to all who would truly accept Christ and faithfully follow his commandments. And I, Joseph Freeman, Jr., had now received the holy priesthood, the gateway to those unlimited blessings.

Moreover, by some coincidence, I was the first of my race to receive the priesthood following the announcement that ordination of Negroes was now permitted. Obviously that fact had no significance as regards worthiness—many of my black brethren in the Church were just as worthy as I, or more so; and many of them, having been Church members longer, had waited longer than I had for this great privilege. Yet luck had cast me in the role of a symbol, so to speak—a "first."

Suffice it to say that, after my ordination, I reflected a great deal on my position. I now held the priesthood of God. I could mentally look back over the nearly six thousand years since my race was begun and feel myself to be at the beginning of an era, so to speak. And I held the priesthood with the same power and authority as any other elder. I am sure that my black brethren who received the priesthood in 1978 had similar reflections. In the entire history of the world we were the first generation for our people to receive the power and authority to act for God. This represented a great challenge and an awesome responsibility.

These were humbling thoughts to me on that Sunday in June 1978. They frequently recur, and they have lost none of their power to move me to deep appreciation and renewed commitment.

From *In the Lord's Due Time* (1979)

10. Chieko N. Okazaki, "Baskets and Bottles"

To many outsiders, the Utah-headquartered church continues to represent a white, North American religious movement. But years before the Mormons began their settlement of the American West, they had begun to evangelize in the Pacific world, including Australia in 1840 and Tahiti in 1844. During the 1850s, church leaders sent missionaries to Hawaii, Siam, China, and even India. Thus, the Pacific Basin has been a crucial part of LDS history for nearly the entire life span of the church. Exploring Mormonism in the Pacific world allows us to see features of the past that aren't as visible from Salt Lake City. The Mormons settled in Utah, but in the Pacific, they were in motion, interacting with native peoples, European and American merchants and missionaries, and voyagers from eastern Asia. A close look at the early growth and development of the Mormon faith and its activities in the Pacific reveals a great deal about the early history of the church as well as American history more generally. Just as the United States "came of age" as an international power by the end of the nineteenth century, so the church transformed itself after 1900 from an insular religious community into a world presence. Chieko N. Okazaki, the daughter of Hawaii-born Japanese parents and a convert from Buddhism to Mormonism, eventually served as a counselor in the Relief Society general presidency. She often referred to her own formative experiences in the Pacific world and cultures to illuminate and explicate her understanding of Mormon doctrines and practices. Okazaki became well known for her inclusive worldview and ability to help church members around the world feel like full participants in the global church.

My dear brothers and sisters, aloha! In February, I rejoiced with you when the number of members outside the United States edged ever so slightly past the number of members inside the United States. That slight shift is an important symbol of the international nature of the Church. I thought of Paul's statement to the Galatians: "There is neither Jew nor Greek, there is neither bond nor free, there is neither male nor female: for ye are all one in Christ Jesus" (Gal. 3:28). This week I celebrate the 54th anniversary of my baptism. People like me who are converts know the promise of Paul: "For by one Spirit are we all baptized into one body" (1 Cor. 12:13).

Brothers and sisters, today I want to talk about the beautiful oneness that we share in the gospel. I just returned from the Philippines, Australia, New Zealand, Tonga, and Fiji three weeks ago, where Sister Susan Warner and I participated in leadership training. Earlier assignments have taken me to Mexico, Honduras, Guatemala, Samoa, Korea, and Japan.

In all these places we worked hard and long. People have said, "Oh, you must have been so tired." On the contrary, there was a feeling of being borne up "as on eagles' wings" (Doctrine and Covenants 124:18), because we have seen the daughters of Zion "awake, and arise . . . and put on [their] beautiful garments" (Moro. 10:31) in response to the good news of the gospel. We taught but—and this is the point I want to stress—we also learned.

The most important lesson was that we are truly all one in Christ Jesus. We are one in our love of the Savior. We are one in our testimonies of the gospel. We are one in faith, hope, and charity. We are one in our conviction that the Book of Mormon is the inspired word of God. We are one in supporting President Hinckley and the other General Authorities. We are one in loving each other.

Are we perfect in any of these things? No. We all have much to learn. Are we exactly the same in any of these things? No. We are all at different points on our journey back to our Father in Heaven. Did the Jews and Greeks whom Paul addressed in his epistle to the Galatians stop being Jews and Greeks when they were baptized? Did the men stop being men and the women stop being women? No. But they had all "been baptized into Christ" and had "put on Christ" (Gal. 3:27).

Nephi explains the same principle in these terms: [The Savior] "inviteth . . . all to come unto him and partake of his goodness; and he denieth none that come unto him, black and white, bond and free, male and female . . . and all are alike unto God" (2 Ne. 26:33).

God has given us many gifts, much diversity, and many differences, but the essential thing is what we know about each other—that we are all his children. Our challenge as members of the Church is for all of us to learn from each other, that we may all love each other and grow together.

The doctrines of the gospel are indispensable. They are essential, but the packaging is optional. Let me share a simple example to show the difference between the doctrines of the Church and the cultural packaging. Here is a bottle of Utah peaches, prepared by a Utah homemaker to feed her family during a snowy season. Hawaiian homemakers don't bottle fruit. They pick enough fruit for a few days and store it in baskets like this for their families. This basket contains a mango, bananas, a pineapple, and a papaya. I bought these fruits in a supermarket in Salt Lake City, but they might have been picked by a Polynesian homemaker to feed her family in a climate where fruit ripens all year round.

The basket and the bottle are different containers, but the content is the same: fruit for a family. Is the bottle right and the basket wrong? No, they are both right. They are containers appropriate to the culture and the needs of the people. And they are both appropriate for the content they carry, which is the fruit.

Now, what is the fruit? Paul tells us: "The fruit of the Spirit is love, joy, peace, longsuffering, gentleness, goodness, faith, meekness, [and] temperance" (Gal. 5:22–23). In the sisterhood of Relief Society, in the brotherhood of priesthood quorums, in the reverent coming together to partake of the sacrament, the fruit of the Spirit unites us in love, joy, and peace whether the Relief Society is in Taipei or Tonga, whether the priesthood quorum is in Montana or Mexico, and whether the sacrament meeting is in Fiji or the Philippines.

All over the world, as brothers and sisters in the gospel, we can learn from each other, grow closer together, and increase in love for each other. Our unity grows from what we have in common all around the world. They are the doctrines and ordinances of the gospel, our faith in the Savior, our testimonies of the scriptures, our gratitude for guidance from living prophets, and our sense of ourselves as a people striving to be Saints. These are the principles of the gospel.

Let us be sensitive to the unchanging and powerful core principles of the gospel. Let us understand that they matter most. Let us build firm foundations on these principles. Then when the rains fall and the floods come, our house will be "founded upon a rock" and it will not fall (Matt. 7:25).

Then, building on that firm foundation, let us rejoice with each other, listen to each other, learn from each other, and help each other apply those principles as we deal with our different circumstances, different cultures, different generations, and different geographies.

For six years now, I have been listening to the Relief Society women of the Church. I have learned from all of them. I have learned from divorced mothers who are struggling to raise their children alone. I have learned from women who long to be married but are not, from women who yearn for children but cannot bear them, from women who are at risk from emotional and physical abuse in their homes. I have learned from women who work in their homes and women who work outside their homes. I have learned from women who endure chemical dependencies, experiences of childhood sexual abuse, and chronic illness.

Not many of these women thought they were giving me a gift. Most of them thought they were asking for help. But all of them blessed me as I listened and learned from them.

When I was called to the Relief Society general presidency six years ago this month, President Hinckley counseled me: "You bring a peculiar quality to this presidency. You will be recognized as one who represents those beyond the borders of the United States and Canada and, as it were, an outreach across the world to members of the Church in many, many lands. They will see in you a representation of their oneness with the Church." He gave me a blessing that my tongue might be loosed as I spoke to the people.

President Hinckley, I want to bear witness to the Lord before you and this congregation that your counsel and your blessing have been literally fulfilled.

I do not speak Korean or Spanish or Tongan. But when I received my assignment to go among the Relief Society sisters and their priesthood leaders in lands where those languages were spoken, I was filled with a great desire to speak to them in their own language. I drew strength from President Hinckley's words of comfort and blessing. With the help of the Church Translation Department and good coaches who spent hours working with me, I was blessed to deliver my addresses in Spanish, Korean, and Tongan as I went among those people. I could feel the Spirit carrying my words to their hearts, and I could feel "the fruit of the Spirit" (Gal. 5:22) bringing back to me their love, their joy, and their faith. I could feel the Spirit making us one.

Brothers and sisters, whether your fruits are peaches or papaya, and whether you bring them in bottles or in baskets, we thank you for offering them in love. Father in Heaven, may we be one and may we be thine (see Doctrine and Covenants 38:27), I pray in the sacred name of our Savior Jesus Christ, amen.

From *Ensign* (1996)

11. Esmeralda Meraz Amos, "El Evangelio"

Like much of Christianity in general, Mormonism is fast becoming a southern hemispheric religious movement. Deriving from upstate New York, and fueled largely by a convert base in England and Scandinavia, the church was long a primarily Anglo-Saxon institution nestled in the relative isolation of Utah. The church's priesthood ban on those of African descent further solidified the church's monochromatic constitution for generations. In the second half of the twentieth century, the demographic of Latter-day Saints dramatically shifted. Conversions in North America and Europe have slowed, while membership growth in Africa and especially Latin America has been explosive. In addition, within the American church, there are increasing numbers of Hispanics, African Americans, and Asian Americans. At the present day and for the foreseeable future, Spanish is spoken by a faster growing number of Latter-day Saints than is English. A recurring problem faced in every point of cross-cultural contact is the problem of assimilation versus cultural continuity. In the United States, with a sizeable Hispanic population, the church has experimented with both linguistic accommodation and ethnic autonomy. Increasingly, in areas of high ethnic density within the American church, the trend is toward independent branches where services are conducted in the native language. Weighed against the advantages of cultural and linguistic integration are the benefits of members being able to feel ownership for their own religious community and for those who are not yet bilingual to participate fully and not self-consciously in worship. In this selection, Esmeralda Amos surveys her own experience as an insider/outsider Hispanic Mormon, finding she operated comfortably in both worlds.

In October, 1979, when I was nine, our family moved to El Centro, California, from Mexicali, Mexico. Learning a new language was difficult for me. I was lonely at school and hated it. I had few friends, and to make matters worse, my two younger siblings and I were all sent to different schools. My youngest sister was not old enough to attend school. I didn't know a soul. I looked forward to the end of the school day, when the bus drove by my brother's school and picked him up.

Unfortunately, our [LDS] Church experience was not too different. Because of the language barrier, we attended a small Spanish branch. I remember not enjoying Sundays very well. Our Primary class consisted of myself, my brother and sister, and sometimes two or three other children. We all had the same teacher. It was not like it used to be when we lived in Mexicali, and so I resented it. One thing I did enjoy greatly was singing time. The sister who taught us was kind and patient. She taught us to sing the beautiful Primary songs that today I sing to my own children. When I got older, I tried to avoid attending seminary. I never felt that I belonged, and truly I guess that I didn't. My seminary classmates lived in the same town as I did and attended the same high school as I did, but because we never saw each other at church, we didn't really know one another. They were mean and delighted in poking fun at the Mexicans who were not part of their class. The spirit of unity and love did not exist.

Our small Spanish branch in El Centro, however, did grow stronger. My dad was called as branch president, and church seemed to be going better. I guess we were getting used to life in the United States. I'm not sure how long we attended the branch, but before I left Primary, the El Centro Branch was asked by the stake to join the Calexico Spanish Branch.

It was truly a disappointment to the entire Spanish-speaking group living in El Centro. Calexico is about twelve miles from El Centro. It seems as if twelve miles would not be a significant distance to travel, but it is when there is no car in the home or public transportation from one town to the other. When the stake asked our branch to combine with the Calexico Branch, we were told that our support was needed so that the branch in Calexico would not have to be dissolved. The stake presidency also told us that the move would be temporary. As I look back I think that the stake presidency may have thought that it was better to have one Spanish-speaking group instead of two in such close proximity. The members in Calexico had their own building. English-speaking members living in Calexico had been attending one of the English-speaking wards in El Centro for many years, so they were not affected by the change. Our faith was tested by the stake presidency's request. Many of our members became less active, and many of us who remained active became discouraged.

Although our numbers with members from both towns were greater, our leadership was weak. The Primary was bigger and a bit more organized, but the teachers lacked dedication to their callings and were often absent.

I never heard my parents complain about the situation, although they expressed surprise at the sudden change. My parents supported the missionary work effort and were active in their callings in the Calexico branch. I continued to be disappointed by the instructors, who seemed to lack interest, gospel knowledge, and general church experience. Perhaps I expected to be uplifted or truly inspired, but most of the time I felt that I could have taught the lesson with more fervor. My arrogance was partly a result of the gospel knowledge I had gained at that age through weekly family home evening lessons.

All this changed when I turned fifteen and my family moved to Watsonville, California.

Attending church in Watsonville was different. Spanish- and English-speaking members met together during sacrament meeting, with translation provided for those who only spoke Spanish. Sunday School was held in Spanish for adults, as was Relief Society and priesthood. Primary-age children and youth joined the English-speaking ward. While we lived in Watsonville I began attending regularly. I noticed that the youth of the Watsonville Ward were different. Were they different because we first got to know each other in Sunday School? I don't know. I'll never know, but I will say that for the first time in many years, I felt included among my English-speaking peers at church. They were my friends at church and at school. It gave me confidence to be treated with respect by other youth who professed to believe in loving one another.

This was the beginning of a series of wonderful experiences. In October of my high school junior year my family moved one more time because of my dad's job. This time we went to Santa Maria, California. My whole family loved Santa Maria. It was the place that influenced my testimony the most, other than my home. School was challenging, but I enjoyed it. The students seemed friendlier than at any other school I had attended. In my band class, which consisted of fewer than twenty students, I became acquainted with Jenny, who was also a member of the Church. Her friendship was very meaningful to me. Jenny's dad was bishop of a ward in our stake.

Santa Maria, like most other areas I had lived in, had arranged for its Spanish-speaking members. Sacrament meeting was held in Spanish, as were all adult meetings. The children and youth joined with the English-speaking ward for Sunday School, Primary, and youth classes after sacrament meeting.

Although I enjoyed attending sacrament meeting in Spanish, I often skipped out on our Spanish-speaking service to attend Santa Maria's Fourth Ward sacrament meeting. My parents consented to my wishes most of the time. I learned many things by visiting the English-speaking sacrament meeting. Most important, I learned gospel terminology. Also, by attending the English-speaking sacrament meeting I avoided having to translate the high council member's talk, and I could see and talk with the cute boys in the ward.

Seminary became one of my favorite weekday activities. It was during a seminary class that my teacher, sister Nidens, challenged our class to read and pray about the truthfulness of the Book of Mormon. I took her challenge seriously, and I read the Book of Mormon. Throughout the course of my reading and praying I came to learn for myself that prophets of God wrote the Book of Mormon. I gained a testimony that year in seminary. I gained new friends and the knowledge that the gospel is for all regardless of race, color of skin, or language. My church friends in Santa Maria taught me what it meant to show love for others. I will always be grateful to them for loving my family and me.

During my senior year in high school, one of my friends encouraged me to apply to Brigham Young University. Until that point I had not given much thought to what I was going to do after graduating from high school. I took college-prep courses all four years in high school, but it seemed almost too sudden to think about college. I decided to apply to BYU and hope for the best. I was accepted. I could not believe it. I often wonder how life would be today if my friend Maryann had not encouraged me to apply to BYU.

I attended BYU for three years, went on a mission, and then returned to BYU to finish my major. While I was at BYU I never attended a Spanish-speaking ward.

My parents moved back to El Centro the summer after I graduated from high school. They were once again attending church in Calexico. My brother and sisters experienced many of the same negative things brought about by their church peers that I had gone through when I had attended high school there. At that age it is difficult to separate home, school, and general life from church since church takes up such a large chunk of a person's life.

After graduating from BYU I moved back home for about six months while I waited to hear from graduate schools. I attended the Calexico Branch with my family while I lived there. Things had not changed much in Calexico, except that the branch had grown large enough to get a small building. I was accepted by the Graduate School of Political Management at George Washington

University, and despite my mother's wishes for me to not study far away from home, I enrolled in the program in the fall of 1994.

That's where I met Marc Amos in the Langley Singles Ward. Marc was a student at George Mason University School of Law. Marc and I were married in the Washington D.C. Temple on December 28, 1994.

I now live in a suburb of Richmond, California. My family and I attend the Gayton Ward, and its Spanish-speaking membership has grown significantly. What started out three years ago as only a handful of Hispanic members has now grown to over one hundred Spanish-speaking members who are part of the ward. This is a unique ward, and in my opinion it is a role model for other areas working with Spanish-speaking members.

First, the Gayton Ward during the three years I have been here has had one hundred percent visiting teaching and well over sixty percent home teaching. In addition, the former and current bishop and bishoprics have been able to speak Spanish. The elders quorum president and his counselors have also been able to communicate in Spanish. The former and current Relief Society presidents, although not fluent in Spanish, have made every attempt possible to communicate with the Spanish-speaking sisters. Both presidents have appointed a Spanish-speaking sister as an additional counselor to their presidencies to better serve the needs of all the sisters in the ward. Our former bishop is now our stake president, so I can say that the stake president, too, is able to speak and understand every Spanish-speaking member of our stake.

The Gayton Ward is truly a unique ward. We are blessed to have in our ward and stake leadership positions members who have been on Spanish-speaking missions or who are life-long Hispanic church members.

Another unique aspect of our ward is that in the past three years our bishops have tried to unify the ward. Everyone, regardless of language, attends sacrament meeting together, and Spanish translation is provided for those who need it. Sunday School is available in Spanish, as are gospel principles, temple preparation, and the teacher development class. Opening exercises for Relief Society and elders quorum are in English, but Spanish translation is also available. The groups then separate to listen to the lesson in the language of their choice. Primary and youth Sunday School classes and Young Men and Young Women programs are taught only in English.

Every member who is worthy and willing has a calling. It may seem insignificant to be a greeter or perhaps the person responsible for collecting the Spanish song books, but it makes everyone feel valued. I'm sure our ward is not perfect, but it comes as close to it as earthly possible. But beyond the programs, love is what creates the success in the Gayton Ward.

I have attended many wards and have experienced every type of arrangement possible. It is my opinion that practicality, diligence, and love are the ingredients necessary to making a Spanish/English-speaking ward successful no matter what the arrangement. Although I favor the arrangement that the Gayton Ward is implementing, if love had been present in the wards I attended earlier, more missionary and retention success could have resulted.

From *All God's Children: Racial and Ethnic Voices in the LDS Church* (2004)

SIX

SEXUALITY AND GENDER

I N A 2007 PEW FORUM ON RELIGION AND PUBLIC LIFE national survey, Americans offered "polygamy" and "family values" as their leading impressions of The Church of Jesus Christ of Latter-day Saints.[1] The paradoxical juxtaposition of these seemingly conflicting comments is not lost on insider and outsider observers of the Mormon tradition. An examination of twentieth-century Mormon attitudes toward gender characteristics and roles, alternative household structures, sanctity of family life, homosexuality, feminism, and the role of sexuality within marriage sheds light on important ways in which Latter-day Saints both mirror and depart from mainstream American culture.

Although Joseph Smith apparently took his first plural wife in the 1830s, his practice of polygamy did not become known to a wider public—or even his close associates—until the Nauvoo period of the 1840s. Only in 1843 did Smith pronounce the much earlier received revelation (Doctrine and Covenants 132) that invoked divine authorization for its practice, even as it articulated a doctrine of eternal, or death-transcending, marriage. Mormon reassignment of marriage to an eternal status cannot help but reshape Mormon conceptions of deity as well. Latter-day Saints are more literalist in regard to the *imago Dei*, the idea of man being in God's image, than perhaps any other major Christian denomination. "In God's image and likeness" means for them that as man is an eternal spirit in a body of flesh and bones, so is God—though his body is glorified and immortal. It also suggests that as there is a God, Father of our spirits, so must there be an eternal Mother in heaven. Though seldom spoken of from the pulpit in the twenty-first century church, the idea of a feminine deity is frequently affirmed in one of the Latter-day Saints' most popular hymns, which was written by "Zion's poetess," Eliza R. Snow.

Eliza R. Snow was herself a plural wife of both Joseph Smith and Brigham Young. The experience of polygamy is far too diverse to portray in any one selection. Perhaps 20 to 25 percent of Mormon adults were members of polygamous households during its practice.[2] The essence of its nineteenth-century practice may best be captured, perhaps, by the remark of a contemporary that it was designed to "try the women even to nearly tear their heart strings out of them."[3] (It was soul-wrenching for most men as well, popular characterizations to the contrary notwithstanding). Annie Clark Tanner's experiences poignantly capture the disillusionment and bruised heart of one young plural bride. By 1890, threatened with the effective destruction of the church at the hands of the federal government on the one hand and a desire to acquire the privileges of statehood on the other, President Wilford Woodruff publicly directed the Saints to no longer enter into new plural marriages. As it turned out, Mormon polygamy cessation became a long, painful process, rather than an event, but his Manifesto was the formal beginning of the end.

While marriage had been rewritten to extend into an endless future in 1843 by Joseph Smith, Apostle James E. Talmage extended the concept of gender into an eternal past in 1914. Since the 1950s, scholars have emphasized the socially constructed nature of gender, in differentiation from sex, or biological difference. By contrast, Mormon theology largely has opted, and continues, to conflate the two. Before every child was tabernacled in flesh in this life, Talmage taught, they lived in a pre-mortal world as a male or a female spirit. Moreover, when they leave this earthly existence at death, they will continue in their identity as men and women throughout the eternities, capable of producing "eternal increase," or spiritual offspring. The eternity of gender was reaffirmed in the 1995 Proclamation on the Family. Thus, gender plays an indispensable role in the exaltation of mankind, according to Mormon theology. The precise nature of those eternal gender roles appears to be in process of negotiation. For example, Mormon leadership has shown itself increasingly open to women pursuing educational and professional satisfactions commensurate with their male counterparts, and the model of family government is now routinely described in terms of parents "co-presiding" over the home.

If polygamy, eternal marriage, and pre-mortal gender placed Latter-day Saints at the periphery of the American mainstream, by the 1930s they were moving toward the center. In those years, Mormons found comfortable accommodation with early versions of a national sex education agenda, and while rejecting the sexual revolution of the 1960s, a best-selling Mormon publication reveals that Latter-day Saints may be conservative, but they are not Victorians. Stephen E. Lamb and Douglas E. Brinley discuss intimacy in the context of Mormon marriage, exploding in the process some myths about LDS sexuality in the new millennium.

Not all self-identified Latter-day Saints fit comfortably within the social, sexual, and theological boundaries that church leaders constructed in the proclamation on the family. Issues surrounding homosexuality and the gay rights movement have shaken up every Christian denomination in America, including the church. In "My God, My God, Why Hast Thou Forsaken Me?" one American Mormon describes his anguishing struggle to reconcile his homosexual orientation with his LDS faith. Church leaders have become increasingly sensitive to the needs of gay congregants, while at the same time holding the line against homosexual practices. In 2006, Elders Dallin H. Oaks and Lance B. Wickman addressed the moral and theological issues surrounding same-gender attraction during an official interview that was subsequently posted in cyberspace. Like their Catholic counterparts, some LDS women feel disenfranchised and marginalized in a church that does not extend the right to the priesthood to females—a dilemma made more poignant by the Mormon practice of granting that authority to all worthy males twelve years of age and older. Maxine Hanks provides an illuminating overview of feminist perspectives on the role of women and authority within Mormon history. Finally, Emily Milner shares her struggles to reconcile the competing demands of motherhood, professional potential, and self-fulfillment. Their differing perspectives document the diversity of female perspectives within the Mormon faith.

1. Joseph Smith, "Revelation [on Plural Marriage]"

No one knows when Joseph Smith first considered the idea of a plurality of wives, but it almost certainly occurred to him in his reworking of the Old Testament in 1831, if not earlier when he translated the Book of Mormon (Jacob 2:24–29). It is likewise unknown when Smith first entered into a relationship with a plural wife, though it was most likely in the mid-1830s with Fanny Alger. He seems to have subsequently desisted in the practice, until the early 1840s, when he was secretly sealed to some thirty women, according to what he said was a divine command to do so. Joseph's wife Emma alternately resisted and acceded to his conduct, while his close brother Hyrum disbelieved the growing rumors. Under pressure from both to justify the practice with a revelation, Joseph Smith dictated one on July 12, 1843. Given the incendiary nature of the practice, and the church's already fraught relationship with American society, the doctrine would not be made public and widely printed until 1852 when the Saints were safe in their Utah refuge or published in Mormon scripture until 1876.

Doctrine and Covenants Section 132 is one of those seminal texts that is read in very different ways even today. Confusion arises from the fact that the revelation ranges over a few interrelated principles, using vocabulary that is fraught with ambiguity and multiple meanings. The plurality introduced in the opening verses transitions almost immediately to discussion of "the new and everlasting covenant," understood by most then and by many today to refer to the doctrine of plural wives. However, the revelation also speaks specifically to the eternal duration of marriage bonds, and that is the sense in which church leaders in the twentieth and twenty-first centuries have understood that "new and everlasting covenant."⁴ Joseph Smith believed that only he had the priesthood keys to authorize the practice of plural marriage, and he did so to a limited extent during his lifetime. The principle proved to be highly controversial not just to other Christians, but even to Smith's followers. Not until 1852 was the practice publicly acknowledged, by which time it had found general acceptance, though it never found universal practice, in the church.

Verily thus saith the Lord, unto you his servant Joseph, that inasmuch as you have enquired of my hand, to know and understand wherein I the Lord justified my servants, Abraham, Isaac, and Jacob; as also Moses, David, and Solomon, my servants, as touching the principle and doctrine of their having many wives, and concubines: Behold! and lo, I am the Lord thy God, and will answer thee as touching this matter. Therefore, prepare thy heart to receive and obey the instructions which I am about to give unto you; for all those, who have this law revealed unto them, must obey the same; for behold! I reveal unto you a new and an everlasting covenant, and if ye abide not that covenant, then are ye damned; for no one can reject this covenant, and be permitted to enter into my glory; for all who will have a blessing at my hands, shall abide the law which was appointed for that blessing, and the conditions thereof, as was instituted from before the foundations of the world: and as pertaining to the new and everlasting covenant, it was instituted for the fulness of my glory; and he that receiveth a fulness thereof, must, and shall abide the law, or he shall be damned, saith the Lord God.

And verily I say unto you, that the conditions of this law are these: All covenants, contracts, bonds, obligations, oaths, vows, performances, connections, associations, or expectations, that are not made, and entered into, and sealed, by the Holy Spirit of promise, of him who is anointed, both as well for time and for all eternity, and that too most holy, by revelation and commandment, through the medium of mine anointed, whom I have appointed on the earth to hold this power, (and I have appointed unto my servant Joseph to hold this power in the last days, and there is never but one on the earth at a time, on whom this power and the keys of this priesthood are conferred,) are of no efficacy, virtue, or force, in and after the resurrection from the dead; for all contracts that are not made unto this end, have an end when men are dead.

Behold! mine house is a house of order, saith the Lord God, and not a house of confusion. Will I accept of an offering, saith the Lord, that is not made in my name! Or, will I receive at your hands, that which I have not appointed! And will I appoint unto you, saith the Lord, except it be by law, even as I and my Father ordained unto you, before the world was! I am the Lord thy God, and I give unto you this commandment, that no man shall come unto the Father, but by me, or by my word which is my law, saith the Lord; and everything that is in the world, whether it be ordained of men, by thrones, or principalities, or powers, or things of name, whatsoever they may be, that are not by me, or by my word, saith the Lord, shall be thrown down, and shall not remain after men are dead, neither in nor after the resurrection, saith the Lord your God: for whatsoever things remaineth, are by me; and whatsoever things are not by me, shall be shaken and destroyed.

Therefore, if a man marry him a wife in the world, and he marry her not by me, nor by my word; and he covenant with her, so long as he is in the world, and she with him, their covenant and marriage is not of force when they are dead, and when they are out of the world; therefore, they are not bound by any law when they are out of the world; therefore, when they are out of the world, they neither marry, nor are given in marriage, but are appointed angels in heaven, which angels are ministering servants, to minister for those, who are worthy of a far more, and an exceeding, and an eternal weight of glory; for these angels did not abide my law, therefore they cannot be enlarged, but remain separately and, singly, without exaltation, in their saved condition, to all eternity, and from henceforth are not Gods, but are angels of God forever and ever.

And again, verily I say unto you, if a man marry a wife, and make a covenant with her for time, and for all eternity, if that covenant is not by me, or by my word, which is my law, and is not sealed by the Holy Spirit of promise, through him whom I have anointed and appointed unto this power, then it is not valid, neither of force, when they are out of the world, because they are not joined by me, saith the Lord, neither by my word; when they are out of the world, it cannot be received there, because the angels and the Gods are appointed there, by whom they cannot pass; they cannot, therefore, inherit my glory, for my house is a house of order, saith the Lord God.

And again, verily I say unto you, if a man marry a wife by my word, which is my law, and by the new and everlasting covenant, and it is sealed unto them by the Holy Spirit of promise, by him who is anointed, unto whom I have appointed this power, and the keys of this priesthood, and it shall be said unto them, ye shall come forth in the first resurrection; and if it be after the first resurrection, in the next resurrection; and shall inherit thrones, kingdoms, principalities, and powers, dominions, all heights, and depths, then shall it be written in the Lamb's Book of Life, that he shall commit no murder, whereby to shed innocent blood; and if ye abide in my covenant, and commit no murder whereby to shed innocent blood, it shall be done unto them in all things whatsoever my servant hath put upon them, in time, and through all eternity; and shall be of full force when they are out of the world, and they shall pass by the angels, and the Gods, which are set there, to their exaltation and glory in all things, as hath been sealed upon their heads, which glory shall be a fulness and a continuation of the seeds forever and ever.

Then shall they be Gods, because they have no end; therefore shall they be from everlasting to everlasting, because they continue; then shall they be above all, because all things are subject unto them. Then shall they be Gods, because they have all power, and the angels are subject unto them.

Verily, verily I say unto you, except ye abide my law, ye cannot attain to this glory; for strait is the gate, and narrow the way, that leadeth unto the exaltation and continuation of the lives, and few there be that find it, because ye receive me not in the world, neither do ye know me. But if ye receive me in the world then shall ye know me, and shall receive your exaltation, that where I am, ye shall be also. This is eternal lives, to know the only wise and true God, and Jesus

Christ whom he hath sent. I am He. Receive ye, therefore, my law. Broad is the gate, and wide the way that leadeth to the death; and many there are that go in thereat, because they receive me not, neither do they abide in my law.

Verily, verily I say unto you, if a man marry a wife according to my word, and they are sealed by the Holy Spirit of promise, according to mine appointment, and he or she shall commit any sin or transgression of the new and everlasting covenant whatever, and all manner of blasphemies, and if they commit no murder, wherein they shed innocent blood—yet they shall come forth in the first resurrection, and enter into their exaltation, but they shall be destroyed in the flesh, and shall be delivered unto the buffetings of Satan, unto the day of redemption, saith the Lord God.

The blasphemy against the Holy Ghost, which shall not be forgiven in the world, nor out of the world, is in that ye commit murder, wherein ye shed innocent blood, and assent unto my death, after ye have received my new and everlasting covenant, saith the Lord God, and he that abideth not this law, can in no wise enter into my glory, but shall be damned, saith the Lord.

I am the Lord thy God, and will give unto thee the law of my Holy Priesthood, as was ordained by me, and my Father, before the world was. Abraham received all things, whatsoever he received, by revelation and commandment, by my word, saith the Lord and hath entered into his exaltation, and sitteth upon his throne.

Abraham received promises concerning his seed, and of the fruit of his loins—from whose loins ye are, viz, my servant Joseph—which were to continue, so long as they were in the world; and as touching Abraham and his seed, out of the world, they should continue; both in the world and out of the world should they continue as innumerable as the stars; or, if ye were to count the sand upon the sea-shore, ye could not number them. This promise is yours, also, because ye are of Abraham, and the promise was made unto Abraham, and by this law are the continuation of the works of my Father, wherein he glorifieth himself. Go ye, therefore, and do the works of Abraham—enter ye into my law, and ye shall be saved. But if ye enter not into my law, ye cannot receive the promises of my Father, which he made unto Abraham.

God commanded Abraham, and Sarah gave Hagar to Abraham, to wife. And why did she do it? Because this was the law, and from Hagar sprang many people. This, therefore, was fulfilling, among other things, the promises. Was Abraham, therefore, under condemnation? Verily, I say unto you, Nay; for I the Lord commanded it. Abraham was commanded to offer his son Isaac;

nevertheless, it was written thou shalt not kill. Abraham however, did not refuse, and it was accounted unto him for righteousness.

Abraham received concubines, and they bare him children, and it was accounted unto him for righteousness, because they were given unto him, and he abode in my law: as Isaac also, and Jacob did none other things than that which they were commanded; and because they did none other things than that which they were commanded, they have entered into their exaltation, according to the promises, and sit upon thrones; and are not angels, but are Gods. David also received many wives and concubines, as also Solomon, and Moses my servant; as also many others of my servants, from the beginning of creation until this time; and in nothing did they sin, save in those things which they received not of me.

David's wives and concubines were given unto him, of me, by the hand of Nathan, my servant, and others of the prophets who had the keys of this power; and in none of these things did he sin against me, save in the case of Uriah and his wife; and, therefore, he hath fallen from his exaltation, and received his portions; and he shall not inherit them out of the world; for I gave them unto another, saith the Lord.

I am the Lord thy God, and I gave unto thee, my servant Joseph, an appointment, and restore all things; ask what ye will, and it shall be given unto you, according to my word; and as ye have asked concerning adultery, verily, verily I say unto you, if a man receiveth a wife in the new and everlasting covenant, and if she be with another man, and I have not appointed unto her by the holy anointing, she hath committed adultery, and shall be destroyed. If she be not in the new and everlasting covenant and she be with another man, she has committed adultery; and if her husband be with another woman, and he was under a vow, he hath broken his vow, and hath committed adultery; and if she hath not committed adultery, but is innocent, and hath not broken her vow, and she knoweth it, and I reveal it unto you, my servant Joseph, then shall you have power, by the power of my Holy Priesthood, to take her, and give her unto him that hath not committed adultery, but hath been faithful, for he shall be made ruler over many; for I have conferred upon you the keys and power of the priesthood, wherein I restore all things, and make known unto you, all things, in due time.

And verily, verily I say unto you, that whatsoever you seal on earth, shall be sealed in heaven; and whatsoever you bind on earth, in my name, and by my word, saith the Lord, it shall be eternally bound in the heavens; and whosesoever sins you remit on earth, shall be remitted eternally in the heavens; and whosesoever sins you retain on earth, shall be retained in heaven.

And again, verily I say, whomsoever you bless, I will bless; and whomsoever you curse, I will curse, saith the Lord; for I, the Lord, am thy God.

And again, verily I say unto you, my servant Joseph, that whatsoever you give on earth, and to whomsoever you give any one on earth, by my word, and according to my law, it shall be visited with blessings, and not cursings, and with my power, saith the Lord, and shall be without condemnation on earth, and in heaven; for I am the Lord thy God, and will be with thee even unto the end of the world, and through all eternity: for verily, I seal upon you, your exaltation, and prepare a throne for you in the kingdom of my Father, with Abraham, your father. Behold, I have seen your sacrifices, and will forgive all your sins; I have seen your sacrifices, in obedience to that which I have told you: go, therefore, and I make a way for your escape, as I accepted the offering of Abraham, of his son Isaac.

Verily I say unto you, a commandment I give unto mine handmaid, Emma Smith, your wife, whom I have given unto you, that she stay herself, and partake not of that which I commanded you to offer unto her; for I did it, saith the Lord, to prove you all, as I did Abraham; and that I might require an offering at your hand, by covenant and sacrifice: and let mine handmaid, Emma Smith, receive all those that have been given unto my servant Joseph, and who are virtuous and pure before me; and those who are not pure and have said they were pure, shall be destroyed, saith the Lord God; for I am the Lord thy God, and ye shall obey my voice; and I give unto my servant Joseph, that he shall be made ruler over many things, for he hath been faithful over a few things, and from henceforth I will strengthen him.

And I command mine handmaid, Emma Smith, to abide and cleave unto my servant Joseph and to none else. But if she will not abide this commandment, she shall be destroyed, saith the Lord, for I am the Lord thy God, and will destroy her if she abide not in my law; but if she will not abide this commandment, then shall my servant Joseph do all things for her, even as he hath said; and I will bless him, and multiply him, and give unto him an hundred fold in this world, of fathers and mothers, brothers and sisters, houses and lands, wives and children, and crowns of eternal lives in the eternal worlds. And again, verily I say, let mine handmaid forgive my servant Joseph his trespasses, and then shall she be forgiven her trespasses, wherein she hath trespassed against me; and I the Lord thy God will bless her, and multiply her, and make her heart to rejoice.

And again, I say, let not my servant Joseph put his property out of his hands, lest an enemy come and destroy him, for Satan seeketh to destroy; for I am the Lord thy God, and he is my servant; and behold! and lo, I am with him, as I was with Abraham, thy father, even unto his exaltation and glory.

Now, as touching the law of the priesthood, there are many things pertaining thereunto. Verily, if a man be called of my Father, as was Aaron, by mine own voice, and by the voice of him that sent me, and I have endowed him with the keys of the power of this priesthood, if he do anything in my name, and according to my law, and by my word, he will not commit sin, and I will justify him. Let no one, therefore, set on my servant Joseph; for I will justify him; for he shall do the sacrifice which I require at his hands, for his transgressions, saith the Lord your God.

And again, as pertaining to the law of the priesthood—if any man espouse a virgin, and desire to espouse another, and the first give her consent; and if he espouse the second, and they are virgins, and have vowed to no other man, then is he justified, he cannot commit adultery, for they are given unto him; for he cannot commit adultery with that, that belongeth unto him, and to none else: and if he have ten virgins given unto him by this law, he cannot commit adultery; for they belong to him; and they are given unto him—therefore is he justified. But if one, or either or the ten virgins, after she is espoused, shall be with another man, she has committed adultery, and shall be destroyed; for they are given unto him to multiply and replenish the earth, according to my commandment, and to fulfil the promise which was given by my Father before the foundation of the world; and for their exaltation in the eternal worlds, that they may bear the souls of men; for herein is the work of my Father continued, that he may be glorified.

And again, verily, verily I say unto you, if any man have a wife who holds the keys of this power, and he teaches unto her the law of my priesthood, as pertaining to these things; then shall she believe, and administer unto him, or she shall be destroyed, saith the Lord your God; for I will destroy her; for I will magnify my name upon all those who receive and abide in my law. Therefore, it shall be lawful in me, if she receive not this law, for him to receive all things, whatsoever I the Lord his God will give unto him, because she did not believe and administer unto him, according to my word; and she then becomes the transgressor, and he is exempt from the law of Sarah, who administered unto Abraham according to the law, when I commanded Abraham to take Hagar to wife. And now, as pertaining to this law—verily, verily I say unto you,

I will reveal more unto you, hereafter; therefore, let this suffice for the present. Behold, I am Alpha and Omega.—AMEN.

———————

From *Deseret News* (1852)

2. Eliza R. Snow, "My Father in Heaven"

The logical corollary of faithful humans eventually becoming gods, men and women eternally married and siring spirit children, would be a Mother in Heaven, companion of a literally envisioned Father in Heaven. Joseph Smith apparently taught that principle to close associates, though never publicly. The idea became widely promulgated with the publication in 1845 of Eliza R. Snow's poem, "My Father in Heaven." It was put to music and is a beloved hymn today in the church, though now titled "On My Father." Snow very likely heard the doctrine from Joseph Smith personally. Known to her fellow Saints as "Zion's Poetess," Snow was a prolific author of poetry and other writings, an accomplished intellectual, and a leader and role model for Mormon women. In 1842, she participated in the founding of the Relief Society (the church's women's organization) in Nauvoo; in 1867, under Brigham Young's direction, she reorganized the program and served as its president until her death. In the early twentieth century, the First Presidency issued a formal statement affirming that just as human infants derive from "an earthly father and mother," so are we as eternal beings "the undeveloped offspring of celestial parentage." Nevertheless, church leaders have in recent years tended to avoid elaborating upon the belief or even general mention of it, probably for two reasons. First, they have labeled the topic too sacred and delicate a matter to expose to public speculation or sensationalization. Second, Mormon feminists latched onto the principle as a way of furthering a feminist theology in the church, and LDS leaders have censured as heretical related feminist initiatives aimed at encouraging prayer to a female deity.

At the same time, many Mormon women espouse a variety of feminism entirely compatible with Mormon theology. Emphasizing the heroic role of Eve, the necessary co-participation of man and woman in the process of exaltation, and the reality of a heavenly mother, these feminists counter the notion of socially constructed and oppressive gender identity with a view of femaleness that is both essentialist and empowering. In addition to the Eliza R. Snow hymn, members were reminded of the doctrine of a heavenly Mother in the First Presidency's 1995 proclamation: "The Family."

O my Father, thou that dwellest
In the high and glorious place;
When shall I regain thy presence,
And again behold thy face?
In thy holy habitation
Did my spirit once reside?
In my (first) primeval childhood
Was I nurtur'd near thy side?

For a wise and glorious purpose
Thou hast plac'd me here on earth,
And withheld the recollection
Of my former friends and birth:
Yet oft times a secret something
Whispered you're a stranger here;
And I felt that I had wandered
From a more exalted sphere.

I had learn'd to call thee father
Through thy spirit from on high;
But until the key of knowledge
Was restor'd, I knew not why.
In the heav'ns are parents single?
No, the thought makes reason stare;
Truth is reason—truth eternal
Tells me I've a mother there.

When I leave this frail existence—
When I lay this mortal by,

Father, mother, may I meet you
In your royal court on high?
Then, at length, when I've completed
All you sent me forth to do,
With your mutual approbation
Let me come and dwell with you.

From *Times and Seasons* (1845)

3. Annie Clark Tanner, "Marriage in Polygamy"

Although Mormon women strenuously defended plural marriage against the general public's condemnation and the federal government's attempts at eradication, they considered the practice more of a sacred obligation and duty than an appealing marital arrangement. As this excerpt makes painfully clear, women who became plural wives knew they were sacrificing the aspiration to be the sole focus of another human being's love and affection. Most LDS women never entered into a plural marriage, and of those who did, the great majority were one of two wives. In all cases, first wives could be heartbroken by the appearance of a wife often younger and unworn by years of childbearing and domestic chores. Second wives for their part could be apprehensive about upsetting the harmony of an established union and about their status as a "junior" wife. While some women in polygamy found happiness and harmony as sister wives, Annie Clark Tanner's story is also instructive, insofar as she never experienced the emotional intimacy she came to believe only monogamy could offer, compensated only slightly by her development of "an independence that women in monogamy never know." She was the second plural wife (of an eventual three) of Joseph Tanner, who rose to prominence as a university president and superintendent of church schools. The marriage took place in 1883, as the anti-polygamy crusade was crescendoing. Consequently, Annie Clark Tanner went into hiding from federal authorities in 1888, when pregnant with her first child.

In the early part of the nineteenth century many new religions sprang up in the frontiers of an expanding America. It was a period of strong religious fervor.

SEXUALITY AND GENDER | 290 |

The Bible was the one rock upon which many of these faiths were founded. Here was the literal Word of God. Within its pages man could find the salvation and security so desperately sought by those frontier peoples.

As the young Prophet Joseph Smith turned its pages, among the other things he found therein, was the practice of polygamy by the ancient Patriarchs of Israel. He believed it to be a part of the Gospel Plan taught by the servants of God in an earlier dispensation. Now, *this* dispensation which he inaugurated was to be the one of the Fullness of Times, wherein all principles and practices of former dispensations were to be restored. God, who was the same yesterday, today, and forever, had once sanctioned, indeed, commanded polygamy. Why not today? What greater authority than the precedent of Abraham, Isaac, and Jacob? Had they not walked and talked with God? Such reasoning was the theological basis of polygamy in Mormonism. I have frequently reflected that Joseph Smith was influenced considerably more by the Old Testament than by the New. So with earnest prayer on the subject he felt that he too was commanded of the Lord to advocate and practice this principle.

I was not only born and reared in the institution of Celestial Marriage (as we referred to it), but I also received the above instructions from sacred scriptures, both ancient and modern, for its Divine sanction. The girlhood religious impressions already related will amply reveal the strength of my determination to follow the path approved by these teachings. Indeed, when I received an offer of plural marriage, I was so determined upon a course of duty at any price that I was afraid to consider so serious a thing without a prayerful mind and heart. Had not Brother Maeser taught that each one of us had some special mission to fill in this life? Perhaps this mission, this destiny, was to be mine.

That was nearly sixty years ago. My grandchildren now receive a different training. I have read their school lessons with them and I appreciate in some measure the new world into which they are born and reared.

The Bible tells us quite another story now. That "Great Book" is seen today as a history which begins with a primitive people. Our first picture of these ancient Israelites sees them wandering as Nomads of the desert. Here was a low cultural and spiritual level indeed. Abraham was making history for Israel by his revolt against human sacrifice. From these low beginnings we find a long evolutionary story lasting through centuries as these desert wanderers settled down in Palestine to achieve gradually higher levels of culture. The real story contained in the Word of God is not one of an earlier Golden Age, as once was taught. Its beginnings were primitive. Its story has a time-span of all evolutionary periods. A long history had passed before one of the prophets could express the exalted spiritual answer of Micah: ". . . what doth the Lord require of thee, but to do justly, and to love mercy, and to walk humbly with thy God?"

Polygamy in the Bible was a practice of the very earliest period in Hebrew history. So far as we know today, the very earliest historical character accepted by most Biblical scholars would be that of Abraham. Even his story is one shrouded by tradition and legend. One of the stories told of him was a command he received of God to take Hagar as a plural wife. This was the earliest Biblical approval. Later stories of David and Solomon reveal more extreme practices, though still with Divine approval. Yet King David's time was quite early, so far as the generally accepted history of the Hebrew people is concerned. With the Old Testament's period of truly great religious teachings, the age of the prophets, polygamy is not so sanctioned. In the New Testament it is not even mentioned; though I remember as a girl listening many times to sermons by the Church authorities wherein the speculation that Mary and Martha were plural wives of Jesus, was commonly referred to as a probability.

There is another aspect of polygamy that may be mentioned. It concerns the status of women within the social order. Polygamy is predicated on the assumption that man is superior to woman. For example, the Mohammedans practice polygamy today, and we see that among them woman occupies a decidedly inferior status to man. And this was also her position according to the ancient Hebrew standard, as is amply revealed in Old Testament scriptures. The Mormon tradition follows that of the early Hebrews. It teaches woman to honor and obey her husband and to look to him as her lord and master.

It is my opinion that if the practice of polygamy is to be successful, a man must possess privileged rights in domestic affairs that may not be necessary nor desirable in monogamy. My husband used to say: "I've got to have a free hand to direct the affairs of my family."

However, as to whether woman really is inferior is yet another question. It is not surprising that in ages of time, man really thinks himself superior to woman. Dr. Adler, an eminent psychologist, states that "All our institutions, our traditional attitudes, our laws, our morals, our customs give evidence of the fact that they are determined and maintained by the privileged males for the glory of male domination." For ages this masculine dominance has spelled itself out in inheritance rights which have been the sole privilege of the male. Among all peoples of the earth, a boy has been received with greater acclamation than a girl. It suited men in the Church who had confidence in their own judgment to take advantage of this doctrine.

Psychologists now tell us that there is not justification for believing in the superiority of the "manly" over the "womanly" character traits, and modern education has proved the mental equality of the sexes.

However, women in polygamy were converted to the idea of the superiority of men. All men in the Mormon Church held the Priesthood which was not conferred on women. This fact always bothered me a little, and I discussed it with Aunt Zina Young, one of President Young's wives. She settled the question by saying, "I am proud to follow an Adam into the Celestial Kingdom."

The Priesthood is a spiritual power which purports to give man superior wisdom. Because of this superiority in power and authority, a wife was subservient to her husband. It was considered to be to the advantage of the whole family for the husband to take this position. And those men who were ambitious to be among the leaders felt a compulsion to accept and practice this principle. Prominent men were counseled by Church leaders to enter this practice as a qualification for leadership.

And yet, polygamy was not practiced by all men in the Church. I have heard the percentage placed at from three to five percent. As stated, it was promoted and practiced almost exclusively by the Church leaders. This was in part due, perhaps, to the fact that only the more prosperous could afford to assume these added obligations. It was taught at that time that the second wife opened the door of salvation in the Celestial Kingdom not only for herself, but for her husband and his first wife.

The manner of living polygamy most successfully depended upon the integrity and standards of those involved. Perhaps no two cases were alike. At least there were no fixed rules by the Church pertaining to its practice. In my own case, for instance, after going home at the end of the school year, Mr. Tanner, of whom I have written, began a correspondence with me. In one of his first letters, he requested that our correspondence should be through Mrs. Tanner, his first wife. She was two years his senior. They were married when he was nineteen.

"It would be the proper thing," he said, "for your letters to be addressed to her." Consequently, there were no letters. I felt that if polygamy were to begin this way, it would end in failure.

Soon Mr. and Mrs. Tanner came to visit me. When Mr. Tanner proposed that he take me for a walk, I replied, "No, not for the world would I make Mrs. Tanner feel badly. This is her outing and she is my guest."

The next morning she and I went for a buggy ride, which was the customary way to entertain friends in the country. Mrs. Tanner, having observed that I had been comparatively indifferent to her husband, brought up the subject of polygamy. I told her that without her approval, our affair was at an end.

"Why," she answered, "don't you love him?"

"Independent of that," I replied, "without your approval, our interest in each other will go no farther."

She then related her father and mother's miserable experience in the principle, and excused herself for the aversion she felt for it, but concluded, "I have no children although I have been married five years. I can't deprive Marion of a family, and of all the girls I know, you are my choice."

After our return and my guests were leaving the house to take the train, Mr. Tanner noticed a quiver in my face as he indifferently took his departure. He came back and saw that I was brokenhearted. He wrote a letter immediately following their visit, explaining that Mrs. Tanner admired my self-respect, and thereafter nothing more was said about my letters being addressed to her.

He came a few times to see me in the fall, yet when the day was set for our marriage I would gladly have put it off. Perhaps it was because I was so young, having recently passed my nineteenth birthday. I was as happy at home as a girl could be, but Mr. Tanner insisted that a long courtship in cases of polygamy was entirely improper.

On the appointed day I was to come to Salt Lake to meet him and Mrs. Tanner at Apostle Joseph F. Smith's home. Brother Smith later became President of the Mormon Church. From this home I went to the Endowment House with Mrs. Smith. In the late afternoon Mr. Tanner came, and we were married on the 27th day of December, 1883.

After the ceremony, Mr. Tanner and Aunt Jennie, as we familiarly called the first wife, and I took the northbound train. I got off at Farmington and they went on to Ogden. I do not recall any conversation while on the train. Perhaps the feelings of Aunt Jennie accounted for the silence.

It was after dark when the train arrived home and my brother Wilford was at the depot. I remember being so glad that some member of the family was there at the station to meet me. I entered the dear old home, happy to be back again. I recall now of feeling, as I entered the house, that I was glad to be safely there and free, for a while at least, of all the uncertainty that the future might bring.

Mary Elizabeth gave me a hearty welcome with the question, "Did it happen?" She and the others were satisfied with my answer when I cheerfully replied, "Ask me no questions."

The family had finished the evening meal. As I sat down to a glass of bread and milk the thought came to me. "Well, this is my wedding supper." In those few minutes I recalled the elaborate marriage festivals which had taken place in our own family, of the banquets I had helped to prepare and the many lovely brides among my friends. I even began to compare their wedding gowns. I was conscious of the obscurity of my own first evening after marriage.

"What a contrast," I said to myself. "No one will ever congratulate *me*."

Yet I was sure I had taken the right step and recall feeling confident that something really worthwhile had been accomplished. Finally I broke the silence.

"The experience wasn't half bad."

"You haven't half begun yet," father replied.

I realized the truthfulness of his remarks two weeks later, when Mr. Tanner failed to keep his appointment to come to see me. I was so disappointed that it seemed to me that the very angels wept with me.

From *A Mormon Mother: An Autobiography of Annie Clark Tanner* (1941)

4. Wilford Woodruff, "Official Declaration"

With the termination of the Civil War and slavery's end, the United States turned its attention to the great perceived remaining stain on the nation's honor: the Mormon practice of polygamy. Successive legislative assaults made normal life increasingly difficult for Latter-day Saints. The 1862 Morrill Act intended "to punish and prevent the practice of polygamy in the territory"; the 1874 Poland Law federalized some territorial offices and repealed some Utah statutes; the 1882 Edmunds Act declared polygamy a felony, disenfranchised polygamists and revoked their right to jury trial, and federalized all territorial offices. An 1885 Idaho law disenfranchised even non-polygamous Mormons. That same year, church officials went underground to avoid imprisonment. The 1887 Edmunds–Tucker Act required wives to testify against husbands, pushing many of them (like Annie Clark Tanner) into hiding as well. Its provisions also included the disincorporation of the church itself and confiscation of its major assets. By 1890, President Wilford Woodruff realized the very viability of the church and the continuation of its salvific mission for the living and the dead would be precluded by continued resistance to federal pressures. Assuring the Latter-day Saints his decision was divinely sanctioned, he pronounced an end to new plural marriages in late September. The following decade and a half were fraught with confusion about Woodruff's intentions. Americans by and large suspected it was a mere show of conformity to win statehood and relief from harassment. Church members often thought the same, and in fact some church leaders did persist in both authorizing and performing plural marriage for several years. Only in the aftermath of the national controversy and public embarrassment of its leaders resulting from U.S. Senate confirmation hearings (1904–1907) for Apostle Reed Smoot, a monogamist, did the church definitively abandon the practice and cut off recalcitrant members. The ban remains in place, and today polygamy is grounds for summary excommunication.

<hr>

Press dispatches having been sent from Salt Lake City, which have been widely published for political purposes to the effect that the Utah Commission, in their recent report to the Secretary of the Interior, allege that plural marriages are still being solemnized, and that forty or more such marriages have been contracted in Utah since last June or during the past year; also, that in public discourses the leaders of the church have taught, encouraged, and urged the continuance of the practice of polygamy:

I, therefore, as President of the Church of Jesus Christ of Latter-day Saints, do hereby, in the most solemn manner, declare that the charges are false. We are not teaching polygamy or plural marriage, nor permitting any person to enter into its practice; and I deny that either forty or any other number of plural marriages have, during that period, been solemnized in our temples or in any other place in the Territory.

One case has been reported in which the parties alleged that the marriage was performed in the Endowment House in Salt Lake City in the spring of 1889, but I have not been able to learn who performed the ceremony. Whatever was done in this matter was without my knowledge. In consequence of this alleged occurrence the Endowment House was by my instructions taken down without delay.

Inasmuch as laws have been enacted by Congress forbidding plural marriages, which laws have been pronounced constitutional by the Court of last resort, I do hereby declare my intention to submit to those laws, and to use all my influence with the members of the church over which I preside to have them do likewise. There is nothing in my teachings to the church, or in those of my associates, during the time specified which can reasonably be construed to inculcate or encourage polygamy, and when any elder of the church has used language which appeared to convey such teaching he has been promptly reproved; and I now publicly declare that my advice to the Latter-day Saints is to refrain from contracting any marriage forbidden by the laws of the land.

From *Deseret Weekly News* (1890)

5. James E. Talmage, "The Eternity of Sex"

The doctrine of pre-mortal existence, as we have seen, was first laid out by Joseph Smith in the 1830s. In his 1844 King Follett Discourse, pre-mortality was integral to humankind's definition as an eternal being, co-existent with God, and with the potential to share in his divinity. Apostle James E. Talmage discoursed here on pre-mortality in order to establish gender differentiation, as a fact of both human identity and of roles both earthly and eternal. (What he called sex would today be identified with gender.) Like all contemporary faiths, the church and its leaders have had to grapple with the question of the degree to which gender is a social construct and the extent to which it is God-given and essential, as well as the problem of how to reconcile a patriarchal church history with a modern political sensibility. Mormonism, like Catholicism, remains steadfastly committed to a male priesthood, even as it has softened its rhetoric in recent years to characterize women as co-equals and partners rather than as subordinates to men. Like the male priesthood, the doctrine of plural wives makes it difficult to be fully persuasive in this regard. To assist their case, Latter-day Saints frequently invoke a unique reading of the Fall, wherein Mother Eve emerges as a courageous and honorable pioneer of mortality, rather than the architect of our mortal catastrophe. In addition, Mormons emphasize the destiny of righteous women to achieve full divinity and the impossibility of a husband achieving that condition in the absence of his wife. In sum, James E. Talmage was here attempting to situate the political, the cultural, and the theological debates surrounding woman in the context of the church's unique history and human anthropology. His assurance that women will be compensated hereafter for injustices suffered in this life was seemingly progressive in 1914.

The Church of Jesus Christ of Latter-day Saints affirms as reasonable, scriptural, and true, the doctrine of the eternity of sex among the children of God. The distinction between male and female is no condition peculiar to the relatively brief period of mortal life; it was an essential characteristic of our pre-existent state, even as it shall continue after death, in both the disembodied and resurrected states.

That birth or even its antecedent, conception, in no wise marks the creation of a being who before that event did not exist, is abundantly attested by the revealed word; it is positively declared that every child born to earth lived as an individual spirit, male or female, in the primeval world. There is no accident or chance, due to purely physical conditions, by which the sex of the unborn is determined; the body takes form as male or female according to the sex of the spirit whose appointment it is to tenant that body as a tabernacle formed of the elements of the earth, through which means alone the individual may enter upon the indispensable course of human experience, probation, and training.

That the vital distinction of sex characterizes life on earth cannot be questioned; its antemortal and postmortal existence may be thought by some to require demonstration. . . .

These scriptures [Genesis 1:27; 2:4–7; Moses 2:27] attest a state of existence preceding mortality, in which the spirit-children of God lived, doubtless with distinguishing personal characteristics, certainly with the distinction of sex, for "male and female created He them" spiritually, even "before they were [created] naturally upon the face of the earth." It is plain that this spiritual creation of mankind embraced the entire human family and not alone the pair ordained to be the first mortal parents of men; for it is expressly stated that "the Lord God had created all the children of men" before a man had been placed upon the earth "to till the ground"; yea, even before the earth was tillable, or capable of supporting the vegetation necessary for human food.

In passing, one may inquire: Is it not in harmony with the genius of these scriptures to infer that the spirits, since known in their embodied state as the human family, lived, developed, and progressed, as sentient beings of varied degrees of intelligence and capability, within the limitations of that primeval sphere of activity: and that in due time they have been and are yet being sent to earth to gain the experiences incident to mortality? For scriptural affirmation supporting this inference, cons[i]der that marvelous revelation given to Abraham, wherein the Lord God declared that the Divine purpose in forming the earth, from materials before existent but unorganized, was to provide a place whereon His children, then existing as spirits, could dwell, that they might be proved as to integrity and righteous effort; that among those spirit children there were many who were relatively noble and great, and that these were chosen and fore-ordained to labors of special importance in the course of their mundane life. (See Abraham 3:21–26. For special study of the antemortal existence of the human family see the author's "Articles of Faith," pp. 195–199.)

The continuation of individual existence beyond the grave is even more abundantly declared, though perhaps not more specifically attested, in scripture, than is the fact of antemortal life. All Christendom professes belief in life after death, and accepts to some degree, though not infrequently in distorted form, the doctrine of the resurrection. The Church of Jesus Christ of Latter-day Saints proclaims the plain, simple, uncorrupted, scriptural truth of a literal resurrection of the body, by which the spirit that had been disembodied by death will again be clothed with a tabernacle of flesh and bones identical in form with the body that was laid down. This comprises as a necessary condition the continuation of the individual existence of the spirit, as a separate and distinct being, intelligent and progressive, during the interval between death and the resurrection. The literalness of the resurrection is explicitly taught by Alma, a Nephite prophet, in the forceful declaration that in the resurrected body every limb and joint shall be restored to the possession of the spirit, and that "even a hair of the head shall not be lost, but all things shall be restored to their proper and perfect frame." (Alma 40:23; read the entire chapter. For a special treatment of the "Resurrection of the Body," and the literalness thereof, see the author's "Articles of Faith," pp. 391–403.)

With such definite word as to the actuality of a bodily resurrection, which shall come to all, righteous and sinner alike, is it conceivable that the essential differences of sex shall be eliminated? Children of God have comprised male and female from the beginning. Man is man and woman is woman, fundamentally, unchangeably, eternally. Each is indispensable to the other and to the accomplishment of the purposes of God, the crowning glory of which is "to bring to pass the immortality and eternal life of man" (Moses 1:39).

The status of woman in the world is a subject of present-day discussion and an element of current social unrest; it is, however, by no means a new topic. The female sex is not infrequently referred to as the weaker of the two. As gauged by physical standards this classification may be essentially correct. And be it said to the discredit and shame of the stronger sex, man through the centuries gone has been prone to use his superior strength to the oppression of woman. She has suffered the greatest humiliation during periods of spiritual darkness, when the Gospel of Christ was forgotten. Woman occupies a position all her own in the eternal economy of the Creator; and in that position she is as truly superior to man as is he to her in his appointed place. Woman shall yet come to her own, exercising her rights and her privileges as a sanctified investiture which none shall dare profane.

It is part of woman's mission in this life to occupy a secondary position of authority in the activities of the world, both in the home and in the affairs of public concern. Of this condition, explanation and justification may be found in the fact that in every organization, however simple or complex, there must needs be a centralization of authority, in short, a head. The secular law recognizes the husband as the head of the household, and theoretically at least holds hi[m] accountable for his administration. That many men fail in their station, that some are weak and unfit, that in particular instances the wife may be the more capable and in divers ways the better of the pair, should not be considered as evidencing impropriety or unrighteousness in the established order as a general condition. Woman should be regarded, not in the sense of privilege but of right, as the associate of man in the community of the home, and they two should form the governing head of the family institution, while to each separately pertain duties and functions which the other is less qualified to discharge. Weakness or inefficiency on the part of either in specified instances must not be taken to impugn the wisdom by which the organization of the home and of society has been planned.

In the restored Church of Jesus Christ, the Holy Priesthood is conferred, as an individual bestowal, upon men only, and this in accordance with Divine requirement. It is not given to woman to exercise the authority of the Priesthood independently; nevertheless, in the sacred endowments associated with the ordinances pertaining to the House of the Lord, woman shares with man the blessings of the Priesthood. When the frailties and imperfections of mortality are left behind, in the glorified state of the blessed hereafter, husband and wife will administer in their respective stations, seeing and understanding alike, and co-operating to the full in the government of their family kingdom. Then shall woman be recompensed in rich measure for all the injustice that womanhood has endured in mortality. Then shall woman reign by Divine right, a queen in the resplendent realm of her glorified state, even as exalted man shall stand, priest and king unto the Most High God. Mortal eye cannot see nor mind comprehend the beauty, glory, and majesty of a righteous woman made perfect in the celestial kingdom of God.

Through the sure word of revealed truth we learn of the actual relationship between God and man, and that this is the literal relationship of parent to child. The spirits of men are the offspring of Deity, born in the antemortal world and endowed with the Divine birthright of eternal development and progression, in which course of advancement the life on earth is but a stage. The glorious possibilities of man's attainment are indicated in the admonition of the Lord Jesus: "Be ye therefore perfect, even as your Father which is in heaven is perfect" (Matt. 5:48).

To become perfect as God is perfect is to attain the state, power, dignity, and authority of godship. Plainly there is a way provided by which the child of God may follow the footsteps of the Father, and in time—sometime in the distant eternities—be as that Divine Father is. Even as Christ, the Only Begotten Son of God in the flesh, endured the experiences of mortality, passed the portals of death and became a resurrected Being, so the Father before Him had trodden the same path of progression from manhood to Godhood, and today sits enthroned in the heavens by right of achievement. He is the Eternal Father and with Him, crowned with glory and majesty, is the eternal Mother. They twain are the parents of the spirit-children for whose schooling in the lessons of mortality this earth was framed. When God said, "Let us make man in our image, after our likeness," "male and female created He them"; and male and female shall they be, to and beyond the resurrection, forever.

Eternal exaltation is the assured attainment of those who obey in its fulness the whole law of the Gospel of Christ; theirs it is to become like unto their Celestial Parents.

"Then shall they be Gods, because they have no end; therefore shall they be from everlasting to everlasting, because they continue; then shall they be above all, because all things are subject unto them. Then shall they be Gods, because they have all power, and the angels are subject unto them" (Doctrine and Covenants 132:20).

Is there anything inconsistent, unnatural, or even surprising in the fact that offspring may develop to the status and spiritual stature of the parents? Would not the contrary be an exception to the recognized order of life? Such complete achievement, however, is possible only to children who pursue the course of development that the parents have followed,—to those only who resolutely advance, ever obedient, through struggle and strife, endurance and suffering, denial and conquest, as those who went before had to do.

The association of man and woman in marriage may be a union for mortality only, or for this life and the hereafter, according to the authority by which the relationship is sanctioned and solemnized. A marriage contracted under human law alone, while legally binding and valid on earth, is terminated by the death summons. This condition is expressly recognized and specified in the ordinary ritual of marriage, in the pronouncement of the officiating authority to the contracting parties, "Until death do you part."

To be effective and binding in the eternal worlds, the union of man and woman in marriage must be solemnized by an authority greater than any that can be established or invoked through human institutions. This superior authority must of necessity be given from the heavens, wherein its administration is to be recognized. Such is found in the Holy Priesthood only. Marriage covenants authorized and sealed by that God-given power endure, if the parties thereto are true to their troth, not through mortal life alone, but through time and all eternity. Thus the worthy husband and wife who have been sealed under the everlasting covenant shall come forth in the day of the resurrection to receive their heritage of glory, immortality, and eternal lives.

It is the blessed privilege of resurrected beings who attain an exaltation in the celestial kingdom to enjoy the glory of endless increase, to become the parents of generations of spirit-offspring, and to direct their development through probationary stages analogous to those through which they themselves have passed.

Eternal are the purposes of God; never-ending progression is provided for His children, worlds without end.

From *Young Woman's Journal* (1914)

6. Virginia Budd Jacobsen, "Book Review of *New Patterns in Sex Teaching*"

The National Education Association first addressed the topic of sex education in 1892, and the first American public schools began teaching the subject in the early twentieth century. In spite of strong opposition from the Catholic Church and other religious groups, the trend continued, often in the interests—or in the name at least—of public health. By the 1930s, the U.S. Office of Education was involved. In those years before the moral upheavals of the 1960s, most programs advocated hygiene, self-control, and the evils of masturbation and promiscuity. In a progressive action for a conservative religion, the church, as early as 1924, published an article in its official magazine, Improvement Era, *to help teachers in the Mormon educational system "fit in properly to the program of sex education needed for any boy or girl." The writer recommended a three-step curriculum: "the processes of reproduction in plants and lower animals may be taught in later childhood. Second, the opportunities afforded in hygiene and other classes to warn against social diseases should be utilized. Third, when the child reaches the stage of full development and asks questions, 'effective enlightenment' concerning individual sex life should be given."⁶ Otherwise, church leaders said very little pro or contra the subject. In 1931, for example, the church reprinted, but without comment, a notice that a papal encyclical had reaffirmed Catholic teaching on "coeducation, sex education and gymnastics for girls, all of which were roundly disapproved." Given the church's historical attitudes toward Catholicism (which leaned heavily toward the negative), the notice did not suggest approval of the Vatican stand. It was not therefore surprising that when Dr. Frances B. Strain, a non-Mormon, published "a practical guide over the somewhat unfamiliar and often hilly country of the sex life of children," a Latter-day Saint would approve the map it provided in the following book review.*

Parents of today are faced with the serious problem of training children in the matters of sex. Whether we like it or not, the problem is ours, and we must face it. If we do not instruct them in these matters very early, they are sure to get the facts from their playmates or older children in an unwholesome manner.

Even at the age of four, five and six, questions related to sex come into the minds of these youngsters of ours and it is our task and privilege to answer them honestly and frankly. We must be ready to answer their first questions when they arise. But we are handicapped, generally, with a lack of scientific knowledge, presence of mind, and courage to answer truthfully and honestly as we should.

To aid in answering these questions, "every family should have one strong-backed book on the subject of sex training of children—not a leaflet, not a pamphlet, but a dignified volume that can be a lantern in the hand to every intelligent and progressive parent. It should be a part of the family child-guidance bookshelf." Such a book is *New Patterns in Sex Training* by Frances Bruce Strain.

Mrs. Strain, besides being a splendid mother, is widely known as an educator, lecturer, and author. She is a graduate of the University of Iowa, later she became Acting Psychologist of the Children's Clinic of the Colorado Psychopathic Hospital at Denver. From this position she went to the University of Minnesota, where she carried on a long research on the problems and methods of sex training and education. At present, Mrs. Strain is Associate Educational Director of the Cincinnati Social Hygiene Society, lecturing yearly on sex education to thousands of parents and acting as consultant on individual problems.

"New Patterns in Sex Teaching is offered as a practical guide over the somewhat unfamiliar and often hilly country of sex life of children from infancy to adolescence. Its purpose is to take away that feeling of insecurity which most parents suffer in the face of hazards of neighborhood play, questionable companions, street talk, sex activities, occasional immoralities—experiences which sooner or later, directly or indirectly, come into the horizon of most children. It includes ways of meeting these situations, ways of interpreting them, ways of supplanting them, in order that undesirable results may be lessened and parental peace of mind be restored.

"It includes answers to hundreds of the most usual questions in relation to pregnancy, birth, fertilization, mating, which children ask in the early years. . . . The answers are adaptable to the varying ages of children and usable by adults who have little familiarity with biological facts and terms."

How many of us know how to meet these situations? More than that, how many of us know how to meet them in such a way that no injury shall be done to the child nature?

"Modern methods of child guidance and mental hygiene point out the difference between a bad habit corrected and a habit corrected badly. . . . Punishment can leave an injury that is greater than the thing which caused the punishment. . . . More than any other part of our natures, our sex natures have been injured—often irreparably injured—by wrong methods of training. Nobody was to blame. Until recently, nobody knew there was such a nature in childhood to save from injury. That is one of the things we have come to know.

"Most mothers of today have accepted sex education whole-heartedly because back in their minds is the memory of many futile gropings for a few simple facts that were withheld from them."

Mrs. Strain has treated almost every phase of the sex problem as it is related to youth, in this delightful book. She has written it in response to a pressing and repeated demand from parents for a permanent guide in handling this very important problem.

Perhaps a brief outline of the chapter headings will best answer the question "Just what is in the book?"

   I. Introduction.
  II. The Love Impulse.
 III. Making the Right Start.
 IV. Learning Social Standards.
  V. Playground Problems.
 VI. First Questions of Young Children.
VII. A Few Rules of the Game.
VIII. The Questionless Child.
 IX. The Rough and Tumble Age.
  X. Preparation for Maturity.

There are four pages of questions which children ask concerning the sex problem, with the page given whereon the proper answer is given. For example:

Where do babies come from?—Page 95
Where did you get me, Mother?—Page 94
How big is a baby when it starts to grow?—Page 153
How does the baby get out?—Page 98
How can the opening be made big enough?—Page 99
Why must there always be a father?—Page 152
What is menstruation?—Page 192
Why are girls different from boys?—Page 157

These few questions give a fair idea of the breadth of the book. It is truly a valuable handbook. It is frank. It is sincere. It is honest in dealing with the most difficult phase of life to teach to children. The answers to the questions are simple and direct, and given in such a manner as to eliminate any embarrassment for parent or child.

From *Relief Society Magazine* (1936)

7. Stephen E. Lamb and Douglas E. Brinley, "Sexual Intimacy in Marriage"

One group of social scientists has written that "the findings on sexuality appear to differentiate LDS people from non-LDS people more than any other set of variables." They are "more like to practice chastity, [and] less likely to engage in premarital . . . sexual relations."[7] These behaviors are the consequence of a stringent church moral code that condemns not only sexual relations before or outside of marriage, but also pornography and masturbation as sexual sins. In Mormon thought, procreation is a power that pertains to eternal beings and a heaven to come, adding a powerful theological rationale for sexuality's sacred status. The acme of LDS devotional life is attendance at a temple, entered only with a special recommend form. And to qualify for that recommend, members must certify in personal interviews with ecclesiastical leaders that they are in compliance with church teachings on sexual behavior. Youth are also interviewed regularly by church leaders, generally twice yearly. Powerful social pressures are at work as well, as young Mormon men are expected to fulfill two-year missions, and all youth are encouraged to marry in the temple. Persistent or unrepented sexual transgression is a barrier to both opportunities. The upside of higher than average LDS sexual continence and marriage emphasis is far lower incidence of STDs, pregnancy out of wedlock, and, for temple-qualified couples, an extraordinarily low divorce rate. The downside has been less noted. The designation of some sexual sin as second only to murder in grievousness, and a persistent regimen of preaching on the evils of sexual immorality, can impose associations that are hard to overcome even after the transition into a married life. In addition, a family-centered theology and culture, and strict taboos against sexual expression outside of marriage, combine to produce powerful pressures on single Latter-day Saints who have not yet found their eternal partner, as well as on gays within the church.

Sexual intimacy in marriage plays many important roles. President Ezra Taft Benson stated: "Sex was created and established by our Heavenly Father for sacred, holy, and high purposes." Unfortunately, many married individuals are uncertain about sex, and for some, questions remain long into their marriages. They wonder: "Is it normal to have sexual urges?" "Is it truly acceptable to God to have sexual relations with my spouse?" "Is it appropriate to touch my spouse in private areas after we are married?" "Is nudity in front of my companion all right?" One young man wrote, "My wife and I awoke on our first honeymoon morning, looked at each other and said, 'Is what we did last night really okay, or are we in trouble?'"

Statements such as this indicate that some young people are confused about sex. They understand the importance of temple marriage and the need to remain chaste in preparation for marriage, so they steel themselves against Satan's temptations. Much to their credit, they pursue personal purity in spite of their natural curiosity, considerable pressure from peers, and a well-orchestrated effort "in the hearts of conspiring men in the last days," (D&C 89:4) to lead them away from virtue and truth. Simply, they learn to say "no" to sex because they know it is wrong for them, just as they learn to say "no" to drugs, alcohol, and other dangerous things.

It is not surprising, therefore, that some youth approach marriage with uncertainty and internal conflict about sexual matters. They wonder about saying "yes" to their spouse after saying "no" for so long. Perhaps in our attempts to encourage young people to be chaste, we sometimes send an unbalanced message. Have we failed to convey the peace of mind that comes through self-control before marriage and the exultant joy of proper sexual intimacy afterward? Have we not fully explained that God Himself instructed His children to participate in sexual relations as an important aspect of the marriage covenant?

LDS couples, young and old, need to know that sexual relations within marriage are not merely acceptable to the Lord; they are encouraged and ordained by Him. "Husband and wife . . . are authorized, in fact they are commanded to have proper sex," President Kimball said, "when they are properly married for time and eternity." A knowledge of the divinely ordained purposes of sexual intimacy can help individuals approach marriage with less trepidation, allowing them to enjoy the marital union more freely and without inappropriate guilt or concern.

Latter-day church leaders have taught that there are at least four purposes for sexual intimacy in marriage (these are not in any order):

1. To provide a profound expression of love
2. To bring emotional and physical closeness
3. To fulfill God's commandment to have children
4. To experience pleasure and joy

Let's look at each of these more closely.

TO PROVIDE A PROFOUND EXPRESSION OF LOVE

The first purpose of sexual intimacy is to provide an expression of love. It is perhaps the most sublime way for a married couple to say, "I love you." Elder Parley P. Pratt expressed his thoughts on the love to be found in marriage: "Our natural affections are planted in us by the Spirit of God, for a wise purpose; and they are the very main-springs of life and happiness—they are the cement of all virtuous and heavenly society—they are the essence of charity, or love. . . . There is not a more pure and holy principle in existence than the affection which glows in the bosom of a virtuous man for his companion" (Robinson, 52.). . . .

Unfortunately, Satan has intentionally sought to blur the line between sex and love. He would lead people to believe that sex is love and that love can only be expressed through sexual relations. This is a devilish distortion that many people have accepted, much to their eventual disappointment. The truth is that marital love is more profound than sex, although sex is a powerful way for a couple to express their devotion to each other. Physical intimacy is an important part of marriage, but it is only one part. Indeed, any attempt to build a lasting marriage on this element alone will be unsuccessful.

TO BRING EMOTIONAL AND PHYSICAL CLOSENESS

The second purpose of marital intimacy is to foster emotional and physical closeness between spouses. When a man and woman come together as married partners, they bring with them a lifetime of experience and expectations. Soon after the wedding ceremony, they discover that their spouse doesn't share all their cherished views, a fact that was not so apparent during the heady days of dating and courtship. They learn that they have differences that stem from their distinct personalities or cultural and family backgrounds. As a result, husbands and wives often have different approaches to handling problems, making decisions, resolving conflicts, raising children, managing finances, and dealing with other activities. These differences can challenge the fragile stability of their newly formed union.

The Lord designed sexual intimacy as one way for marriage partners to bring emotional closeness back into a relationship that may often become frayed in the tussle of day-to-day married life. Through physical closeness, spirits are buoyed and feelings are soothed. Partners are reassured and commitment is rejuvenated. Through the selfless giving of themselves, a couple learns how dependent they are upon each other for emotional and spiritual sustenance. . . .

The Lord provided marital intimacy as a way for couples who are occasionally pulled apart by the world to come together again and be reminded of their commitments to each other. It is an act of regeneration and healing whereby each spouse is validated anew. If offenses have been committed, it is the final gesture of a repentant heart. Through this sacrament, the husband and wife, in effect, say, "I'm sorry for my part in what happened. I'm glad it's behind us. I will do better. I'm grateful for you. I want you to know I always want to be with you. Thank you for being my dearest friend."

TO FULFILL GOD'S COMMANDMENTS TO HAVE CHILDREN

The third purpose of sexual intimacy in marriage is to provide the means whereby Heavenly Father's spirit children can enter their mortal estate. Adam and Eve received this injunction from a loving Father. "And God blessed them, and God said unto them, Be fruitful, and multiply, and replenish the earth" (Genesis 1:28). In the proclamation on the family, the importance of this commandment was reemphasized by the First Presidency and Council of the Twelve: "The first commandment that God gave to Adam and Eve pertained to their potential for parenthood as husband and wife. We declare that God's commandment for His children to multiply and replenish the earth remains in force. We further declare that God has commanded that the sacred powers of procreation are to be employed only between man and woman, lawfully wedded as husband and wife" (*Ensign*, November 1995:102).

Church leaders have emphasized that divinely given sexual urges help God fulfill His purposes, and hence are divinely approved. These feelings are intended to remind us of our responsibility to become parents for God's spirit children. They attract men and women to each other and give them a desire to marry and fulfill their divine natures, rather than remain single. What a sacred privilege! No wonder God holds individuals accountable for their procreative stewardship.

The power of procreation is a gift that enables men and women to act as co-creators with God in providing physical bodies for His spirit children. Because of its great importance in the eternal plan, President Kimball taught the importance of not delaying or inappropriately limiting the opportunity of parenthood (Kimball, *Teachings*, 324). Unless special circumstances exist (e.g., genetic problems, health considerations) every couple should anxiously desire to become parents. However, this responsibility requires considerable thought and planning, a consideration of the emotional and physical welfare of the mother, and the ability of the husband to function as a father and provider. Each couple must make this decision in a spirit of humility and prayer, seeking the Lord's blessing and guidance in fulfilling their responsibility (Benson, *Teachings*, 513).

The questions of how many children to have and how to space them require personal decisions each couple must make through the use of individual agency. . . .

With conception and pregnancy, couples join hands with God in the amazing and incomprehensible process of giving life. Who can fathom the biological and spiritual implications of procreation? Being partners with God as a co-creator is associated with spiritual dimensions which, for some, enhances the sexual experience. "When I was younger, on the occasion when we were trying to get pregnant, the sexual experience was accompanied by the most sublime joy," said one woman who is now beyond childbearing years. "It was wonderful to think that a new life might be conceived through that sacred act. I miss those days." Because of the effects of age, this woman has temporarily lost her ability to create life in partnership with God. However, she finds great joy in anticipating the possibility of childbirth and parenting throughout eternity.

When children are born, parents are created. Parenthood brings new opportunities for growth and happiness in what is perhaps the toughest undertaking in life. But parenthood is also associated with great blessings. It seems that as men and women learn to be good parents, they are blessed with growing experiences. They often develop traits that cannot be gained in any other way. Women learn what it means to have sorrow and conception multiplied. Men learn what it means to eat bread by the sweat of their face all the days of their lives (Genesis 3:16, 17, 19). In addition, they experience the joy that comes from interacting with their children throughout life.

Fortunately, we are given special gifts to help us fulfill our responsibilities as parents. Our premortal spiritual capacities, our genetic endowments, and our individual personalities suit us to our roles as mothers and fathers. Then, through righteous parenting, we begin to acquire some of the characteristics of our Heavenly Parents and become more like them.

TO EXPERIENCE PLEASURE AND JOY

Finally, sexual intimacy is intended to provide joy. Heavenly Father knew that marriage would require effort, but that it could not be all work and no play. Marital intimacy is a way in which couples find diversion together. It is a form of therapy. It is a nice distraction from paying the mortgage, earning a living, keeping the cars running, paying the bills, and dealing with the children.

Sexual relations are designed to lift a marriage relationship from the profane and mundane to a higher plane. The pleasure of physical intimacy should motivate a couple to treat each other with increasing kindness and consideration. Indeed, the feelings of love and caring generated through sexual union normally carry over into their nonsexual relationship as well (Robinson, 254). President John Taylor spoke of the power of marital intimacy to provide "life, happiness, and exaltation" to marriage. . . .

President Joseph F. Smith stated that sexual union blesses and sanctifies those who participate: "Sexual union is lawful in wedlock, and if participated in with right intent is honorable and sanctifying. But without the bonds of marriage, sexual indulgence is a debasing sin, abominable in the sight of Deity" (*Gospel Doctrine*, 309).

Church leaders have affirmed that sexual intimacy in marriage is intended to enrich marriage. "Husbands and wives do have physical and emotional needs that are fulfilled through sexual union. . . . Becoming as one flesh can be one of life's richest and most rewarding experiences" (*A Parent's Guide*, 49).

Lehi taught his son Jacob, "Men are that they might have joy" (2 Nephi 2:25). The pursuit and attainment of joy is one of the primary purposes of life. Joy is attained when our lives are in harmony with the will of God and his purposes, and when we are in harmony with each other. Sexual intimacy in marriage is one way in which joy is shared. . . .

The enjoyments of life rightfully include sensations and emotional feelings that are generated by being physically close to each other. It is relaxing and pleasurable for couples to massage, stimulate, and arouse each other. These passions, when kept in the bounds of propriety, become sanctifying and enriching to each spouse and to the marriage.

Men and women were anatomically created in such a way that feelings of acute pleasure are produced during sexual activity. . . .

SUMMARY

Sexual union in marriage is intended to be enriching and exciting, pleasurable and joyful. One young newlywed said, "I never dreamed before marriage that it could be the source of spiritual binding so strong that it has caused us both to cry with tears of great joy." This kind of joy comes when we understand why God has given us the gift of marital intimacy and when we use that gift wisely.

It comes when we are "one" in the highest sense of the word—one in purpose, desire, aspirations, and deeds. It occurs when we are faithful in our dedication to the marriage and place our spouse's sexual satisfaction ahead of our own. When this happens, we more fully understand why Elder Pratt called it "the very main-springs of life and happiness" (Robinson, 52).

From *Between Husband and Wife: Gospel Perspectives on Marital Intimacy* (2000)

8. Oliver Alden [pseudo.], " 'My God, My God, Why Hast Thou Forsaken Me?': Meditations of a Gay Mormon on the 22nd Psalm"

It might fairly be said that no ecclesiastical organization is more centered than the church in the idea of family as the focus of earthly life and of heavenly aspiration alike. "No other success can compensate for failure in the home," President David O. McKay was fond of quoting, and President Harold B. Lee proclaimed "the most important work you will ever do will be within the walls of your own home." And the home clearly held to be the ideal in this all-pervasive religious emphasis is one presided over by a righteous priesthood-holding husband and father, with a wife and mother at his side, and populated by children. In such a vision, no place has been found for the homosexual. In practice as well as theory, the church is a family-centered organization. A weekly meeting is designated "Family Home Evening," temple marriage is instilled in youth as the highest earthly goal they can aspire to, and sermons, structure, and socials generally revolve around the presumption of a congregation dominated by families. In addition, from its founding in 1830 and continuing to the present, the church has been marked by tenacious intragroup cohesion. Ward organization by geography, lay ministry, a rhetoric of chosenness and exclusivity differentiating Latter-day Saints from "gentiles," distinctive dietary practices, the general pervasiveness of LDS belief into all aspects of lived experience—these and myriad other factors create among Mormons powerful group identity. The consequence of both of these sets of circumstances is enormously devastating for those who have made the decision to self-identify as Latter-day Saints but, by virtue of homosexual orientation, find themselves alienated from the heart and soul of Mormon life. Many feel adrift from the world and outsiders to their religious community.

It took me three decades to bring myself to the point where I could admit that I am gay, even though the inclinations both emotional and, as I matured, sexual go back as far as I can recollect, to age six maybe, or eight. Even then, I recall sensing that something was terribly wrong, and I realized, with waxing horror at each stage of my growth, that my responses differed profoundly from what I was told they should be. The centerfolds my compatriots smuggled with them on junior high Boy Scout campouts (our troop's sponsor, an American Legion post, was untroubled by such things) merely repelled me. Even in high school, female anatomy never held for me any of the fascination that grew to be so all-consuming in the lives and conversations of my friends. I could never understand why it did not. On dates, I had to force myself to do the little that could, in view of my moral stance, be expected of me.

Even more difficult was realizing what it was that I felt instead; realizing that I was becoming something my society and my religion proclaimed to be wrong; realizing that my deepest emotions and inclinations were "defective"; realizing that I was turning into the sort of monster that I had been taught should horrify even me. As a young man, it is hard to comprehend these things and even harder to come to terms with them, with no guidance, with no answers, with no role models except laughingstocks, with no one who understands.

The mockery and derision cause great pain to those who grow up gay. Still, people give vent to their scorn, even in the Church. In recent years, I have sat in priesthood meeting and heard gays—and by extension myself—described as an "abomination in the sight of the Lord" (by a class member, not by the instructor) and have sat in stake conference and heard gays described as "vile" and "disgusting" (by the stranger next to me who volunteered that he hadn't darkened the Church door in thirty years, not by the apostle conducting the meeting). Of course, neither man guessed that he spoke of me. Nor did my former boss, who, unsuspecting, made it clear that he did not want a gay man working for him and would go to great lengths to ensure that this did not occur. For better or worse, I am one of the very great number of gays who do not fit society's stereotypes. I have stood, bemused, as people who assumed me to be straight explained to me, with great earnestness, how "you can always tell who they are." . . .

Why art thou so far from helping me, and from the words of my roaring? o my God, I cry in the daytime, but thou hearest not; and in the night season, and am not silent. PSALM 22:1–2

I never doubted God's ability to perform miracles, and the very manner of my conversion reaffirmed to me their reality and their availability in individual human lives. It is not surprising, then, that I had faith that God could perform a miracle here, too—a faith that was strengthened when I received my patriarchal blessing and heard, to my intense relief, its promise that I would marry and have children. I need not worry, I thought. The lepers in the New Testament were cured. God will cure this problem, too. Certainly, it was a righteous request. In fact, I wondered many times—and even asked priesthood leaders— why they couldn't just give me a blessing and make everything all right. After all, I certainly felt that I had experienced many other miracles.

My faith gave me strength enough to go for long periods believing that I really was (or at least soon would be) straight, and I identified myself as such to myself and others. True, every year and a half or so, something (usually something I could not restrain with mere effort or discipline, like a dream) would remind me of where my mind went if I did not keep it under absolute control. At such times, my faith that God would cure me would often waver. Once, when wondering why God had let me suffer this for so long, I received a peaceful spiritual assurance that I had voluntarily agreed in the pre-existence to take this on. I was not told why. Nonetheless, with great relief (and even greater hubris), I not only took this revelation to mean that I would be cured, but assumed that I could then go on to serve as an exemplar of how this was done, living proof of the rewards of faith. There would have been purpose to the suffering, I thought; it would benefit others as well. So I held on, and strove mightily to obey every commandment and to do all that was expected of me, to clutch the iron rod so tightly that even priesthood leaders suggested I was too hard on myself, and prayed fervently many times each day. And waited. For fourteen years.

Be not far from me; for trouble is near; for there is none to help. PSALM 22:11. . . .

Throughout this period, I also sought the help and advice of nearly all the men who served as my bishops. To their credit and to that of the Church, none ever reacted with unkindness or prejudice (the fact that I hadn't actually done anything may have played a part here), and each responded with care and concern and with his most sincere attempt to help. Unfortunately, the help was almost universally limited to offering comfort and encouragement and then referring me to more psychologists. True, one bishop did propose castration as an option, but I was not sure that he meant it entirely seriously, and I was sure (I knew him) that he was young, frightened, desperate to be able to offer any sort of solution, and generally in over his head on this one. Besides, his other idea—to bury myself in my career in the hopes of successfully suppressing all sexual impulses—was one I more or less adopted for the next decade. The result, naturally, is that I did not end up being straight, but did end up being fairly prosperous. This is not what I had in mind, of course, but it beats being gay and poor.

I also stumbled, at the end of the fourteen years, onto an informal group of Church members who met together to seek to overcome their homosexuality The group was diverse in every respect: age, occupation (construction workers, oddly, seem to have been disproportionately represented), degree of masculinity, degree of activity in the Church, marital status. Several even had children, which certainly suggested that they were able to be more physically responsive to women than I could imagine being. A few (all married) claimed that they had successfully overcome homosexuality. Of course, six months later, one of these was on the phone telling me that he felt torn between staying with his wife, his children, and the Church and chucking it all to go find the man of his dreams. Gradually, I began to figure out that what at least some of these men had meant when they said that they had overcome homosexuality was that they had managed to stop resorting to anonymous sexual encounters with other men. By that standard, certainly, I had never been gay at all. The problem was that I was still attracted exclusively to men. Worse yet, it was still men with whom I would find myself falling in love. . . .

All they that see me laugh me to scorn: they shoot out the lip, they shake the head, saying, He trusted on the Lord that he would deliver him: let him deliver him, seeing he delighted in him. PSALM 22:7–8

Things only got worse with time, as it became harder and harder to deny with any conviction that all those years of counseling, all those years of vigilance, all those years of prayer seemed to have availed me nothing. The homosexual drives, far from diminishing, took on ever more alarming strength from year to year, and then even from month to month, until they loomed nearly overwhelming. I had still not given in to them, but there began for the first time to be some close calls, and then others that slid closer still.

More terrified than I had ever been in my life, I discussed each of these with my bishop, who responded with an outpouring of patience and love and concern, but with no solutions, which manifestly pained him deeply. He strove to offer what encouragement he was able, and what balm he could for the self-loathing I so clearly evidenced, pointing out that I hadn't yet actually done anything serious, that temptation itself was no vice, that I ought, in view of the way I was actually still living my life, feel morally triumphant. "How could I?" I asked. He, if tempted by the sight of a woman, could curb his thoughts and walk away triumphant in his victory over acknowledged natural drives. For me, such victories were only another form of defeat, one more triumph in a battle no normal person should need to fight, one more shattering reminder that what lay at my very core was not something "righteous if kept within proper bounds," but something evil. "Even when I win," I recall telling him, "I lose." . . .

The decades of battling to a standstill my most basic drives had left me worn and exhausted. I felt like someone who had fallen over a cliff but caught onto a branch that he was grasping onto for dear life, wondering, as he felt his strength ebb and despairing of rescue, how much longer he could hold on. Still, I did not want to fall, did not want to become what I had been taught to despise. More than anything, I wanted to be able to face God with a clean record. If I lived, however, it seemed only a matter of time before this record would become tarnished. I decided that I would rather be dead. Unfortunately suicide, too, was said to be a serious sin. I regretted that there were no wars for which I could volunteer and in which I might be killed. So for countless evenings, as I said my prayers, I begged the Lord to take my life during the night.

My strength is dried up like a potsherd; and my tongue cleaveth to my jaws; and thou hast brought me into the dust of death. PSALM 22:15

. . . The main barrier to suicide, oddly, proved to be one of the Church's teachings. Not its teaching that suicide was a sin. I was already convinced that the choice lay between that and homosexuality, which was also a sin but somehow seemed much worse in the eyes of the Church. After all, I had never sat in meetings and heard someone call suicides an "abomination in the sight of the Lord." What I couldn't get around was the teaching that you took your mind intact into the next life. "What if I blow my brains out," I thought, "and then I wake up in the next world and I'm still gay?" What if suicide didn't actually work?

The other barrier was my bishop. He had watched me and listened to each stage of my struggles throughout the long and agonizing process. He may have lacked for grand solutions, my bishop, as my feelings jerked back and forth for weeks and months with the ebb and flow of my strength, as I struggled to endure one day only to plunge into utter despair the next, but he was always there, with love and compassion and caring greater than most human beings seem able to muster. He hurt for me. I doubt that as a straight man he will ever understand completely what it feels like to be gay, but he came closer in those days to understanding the pain that gay members of the Church endure than anyone I have ever seen, before or since. And for months he kept me alive, until one day, desperate, at wit's end, he finally blurted out that he would much rather that I went off to be gay than that I killed myself, thereby finally triggering in me the realization that the hatred of homosexuals that lay at the root of my suicidal drive did not ultimately come from my religion. It came from me.

From *Sunstone* (1995)

9. Dallin H. Oaks and Lance B. Wickman, "Same-Gender Attraction"

Historically, like most Bible-based denominations, the church depicted homosexuality as both a pathology and a grievous sin. Many Christian organizations have shifted to a more liberal acceptance of homosexuality as a legitimate alternative to heterosexuality. Two factors in particular compound the difficulty of a comparable shift in the church. First is the faith's understanding of sexuality in an eternal perspective. Because Latter-day Saints see marriage as an eternal institution and procreation as a power to be exercised by saved ("exalted") beings, heterosexuality becomes inscribed as a normative, eternal constituent of human identity. Second, Latter-day Saints have a tradition of quasi-biblical literalism. While liberal traditions have increasingly seen scripture as a product of inspired men writing under the influence of cultural forces, Mormons have resisted any trend that reinterprets scripture in the light of evolving mores. At the same time, LDS leadership has been emphatic in recent years in articulating limited but significant movement in their teachings on same-gender attraction. First, they acknowledge that a genetic predisposition to homosexuality may exist, for which homosexuals would not be morally responsible. Second, they have emphatically declared the need to treat homosexuals with respect and love, rather than condemnation and judgment. Church leaders thus distinguish between inclination or tendency, which is morally blameless, and action or behavior, which is not. Homosexuals who live a celibate life may hold church offices and serve honorable missions. Some gay Latter-day Saints rightly point out that celibacy is a tougher standard for homosexuals than for the unmarried, since the latter live with the hope of moving into an emotionally and sexually satisfying relationship. It is harder to say if many Mormon homosexuals are comforted by the that all homosexual feelings are an aberration that will be emended in the life to come.

———————————

PUBLIC AFFAIRS: *At the outset, can you explain why this whole issue of homosexuality and same-gender marriage is important to the Church?*

ELDER OAKS: This is much bigger than just a question of whether or not society should be more tolerant of the homosexual lifestyle. Over past years we have seen unrelenting pressure from advocates of that lifestyle to accept as normal what is not normal, and to characterize those who disagree as narrow-minded, bigoted and unreasonable. Such advocates are quick to demand freedom of speech and thought for themselves, but equally quick to criticize those with a different view and, if possible, to silence them by applying labels like "homophobic." In at least one country where homosexual activists have won major concessions, we have even seen a church pastor threatened with prison for preaching from the pulpit that homosexual behavior is sinful. Given these trends, The Church of Jesus Christ of Latter-day Saints must take a stand on doctrine and principle. This is more than a social issue—ultimately it may be a test of our most basic religious freedoms to teach what we know our Father in Heaven wants us to teach.

PUBLIC AFFAIRS: *Let's say my 17-year-old son comes to talk to me and, after a great deal of difficulty trying to get it out, tells me that he believes that he's attracted to men—that he has no interest and never has had any interest in girls. He believes he's probably gay. He says that he's tried to suppress these feelings. He's remained celibate, but he realizes that his feelings are going to be devastating to the family because we've always talked about his Church mission, about his temple marriage and all those kinds of things. He just feels he can't live what he thinks is a lie any longer, and so he comes in this very upset and depressed manner. What do I tell him as a parent?*

ELDER OAKS: You're my son. You will always be my son, and I'll always be there to help you. The distinction between feelings or inclinations on the one hand, and behavior on the other hand, is very clear. It's no sin to have inclinations that if yielded to would produce behavior that would be a transgression. The sin is in yielding to temptation. Temptation is not unique. Even the Savior was tempted.

The New Testament affirms that God has given us commandments that are difficult to keep. It is in 1 Corinthians chapter 10, verse 13: "There hath no temptation taken you but such as is common to man: but God is faithful, who will not suffer you to be tempted above that ye are able; but will with the temptation also make a way to escape, that ye may be able to bear it."

I think it's important for you to understand that homosexuality, which you've spoken of, is not a noun that describes a condition. It's an adjective that describes feelings or behavior. I encourage you, as you struggle with these challenges, not to think of yourself as a "something" or "another," except that you're a member of The Church of Jesus Christ of Latter-day Saints and you're my son, and that you're struggling with challenges.

Everyone has some challenges they have to struggle with. You've described a particular kind of challenge that is very vexing. It is common in our society and it has also become politicized. But it's only one of a host of challenges men and women have to struggle with, and I just encourage you to seek the help of the Savior to resist temptation and to refrain from behavior that would cause you to have to repent or to have your Church membership called into question.

PUBLIC AFFAIRS: *If somebody has a very powerful heterosexual drive, there is the opportunity for marriage. If a young man thinks he's gay, what we're really saying to him is that there is simply no other way to go but to be celibate for the rest of his life if he doesn't feel any attraction to women?*

ELDER OAKS: That is exactly the same thing we say to the many members who don't have the opportunity to marry. We expect celibacy of any person that is not married.

ELDER WICKMAN: We live in a society which is so saturated with sexuality that it perhaps is more troublesome now, because of that fact, for a person to look beyond their gender orientation to other aspects of who they are. I think I would say to your son or anyone that was so afflicted to strive to expand your horizons beyond simply gender orientation. Find fulfillment in the many other facets of your character and your personality and your nature that extend beyond that. There's no denial that one's gender orientation is certainly a core characteristic of any person, but it's not the only one.

What's more, merely having inclinations does not disqualify one for any aspect of Church participation or membership, except possibly marriage as has already been talked about. But even that, in the fullness of life as we understand it through the doctrines of the restored gospel, eventually can become possible.

In this life, such things as service in the Church, including missionary service, all of this is available to anyone who is true to covenants and commandments.

PUBLIC AFFAIRS: *So you are saying that homosexual feelings are controllable?*

ELDER OAKS: Yes, homosexual feelings are controllable. Perhaps there is an inclination or susceptibility to such feelings that is a reality for some and not a reality for others. But out of such susceptibilities come feelings, and feelings are controllable. If we cater to the feelings, they increase the power of the temptation. If we yield to the temptation, we have committed sinful behavior. That pattern is the same for a person that covets someone else's property and has a strong temptation to steal. It's the same for a person that develops a taste for alcohol. It's the same for a person that is born with a "short fuse," as we would say of a susceptibility to anger. If they let that susceptibility remain uncontrolled, it becomes a feeling of anger, and a feeling of anger can yield to behavior that is sinful and illegal.

We're not talking about a unique challenge here. We're talking about a common condition of mortality. We don't understand exactly the "why," or the extent to which there are inclinations or susceptibilities and so on. But what we do know is that feelings can be controlled and behavior can be controlled. The line of sin is between the feelings and the behavior. The line of prudence is between the susceptibility and the feelings. We need to lay hold on the feelings and try to control them to keep us from getting into a circumstance that leads to sinful behavior.

ELDER WICKMAN: One of the great sophistries of our age, I think, is that merely because one has an inclination to do something, that therefore acting in accordance with that inclination is inevitable. That's contrary to our very nature as the Lord has revealed to us. We do have the power to control our behavior.

PUBLIC AFFAIRS: *If we were to look back at someone who had a "short fuse," and we were to look at their parents who might have had a short fuse, some might identify a genetic influence in that.*

ELDER OAKS: No, we do not accept the fact that conditions that prevent people from attaining their eternal destiny were born into them without any ability to control. That is contrary to the Plan of Salvation, and it is contrary to the justice and mercy of God. It's contrary to the whole teaching of the Gospel of Jesus Christ, which expresses the truth that by or through the power and mercy of Jesus Christ we will have the strength to do all things. That includes resisting temptation. That includes dealing with things that we're born with, including disfigurements, or mental or physical incapacities. None of these stand in the way of our attaining our eternal destiny. The same may be said of a susceptibility or inclination to one behavior or another which if yielded to would prevent us from achieving our eternal destiny.

PUBLIC AFFAIRS: *You're saying the Church doesn't necessarily have a position on "nurture or nature"?*

ELDER OAKS: That's where our doctrine comes into play. The Church does not have a position on the causes of any of these susceptibilities or inclinations, including those related to same-gender attraction. Those are scientific questions—whether nature or nurture—those are things the Church doesn't have a position on.

ELDER WICKMAN: Whether it is nature or nurture really begs the important question, and a preoccupation with nature or nurture can, it seems to me, lead someone astray from the principles that Elder Oaks has been describing here. Why somebody has a same-gender attraction . . . who can say? But what matters is the fact that we know we can control how we behave, and it is behavior which is important.

PUBLIC AFFAIRS: *Is therapy of any kind a legitimate course of action if we're talking about controlling behavior? If a young man says, "Look, I really want these feelings to go away . . . I would do anything for these feelings to go away," is it legitimate to look at clinical therapy of some sort that would address those issues?*

ELDER WICKMAN: Well, it may be appropriate for that person to seek therapy. Certainly the Church doesn't counsel against that kind of therapy. But from the standpoint of a parent counseling a person, or a Church leader counseling a person, or a person looking at his or her same-gender attraction from the standpoint of "What can I do about it here that's in keeping with gospel teachings?" the clinical side of it is not what matters most. What matters most is recognition that "I have my own will. I have my own agency. I have the power within myself to control what I do."

Now, that's not to say it's not appropriate for somebody with that affliction to seek appropriate clinical help to examine whether in his or her case there's something that can be done about it. This is an issue that those in psychiatry, in the psychology professions have debated. Case studies I believe have shown that in some cases there has been progress made in helping someone to change that orientation; in other cases not. From the Church's standpoint, from our standpoint of concern for people, that's not where we place our principal focus. It's on these other matters.

ELDER OAKS: Amen to that. Let me just add one more thought. The Church rarely takes a position on which treatment techniques are appropriate, for medical doctors or for psychiatrists or psychologists and so on.

The second point is that there are abusive practices that have been used in connection with various mental attitudes or feelings.

Over-medication in respect to depression is an example that comes to mind. The aversive therapies that have been used in connection with same-sex attraction have contained some serious abuses that have been recognized over time within the professions. While we have no position about what the medical doctors do (except in very, very rare cases—abortion would be such an example), we are conscious that there are abuses and we don't accept responsibility for those abuses. Even though they are addressed at helping people we would like to see helped, we can't endorse every kind of technique that's been used.

PUBLIC AFFAIRS: *Is heterosexual marriage ever an option for those with homosexual feelings?*

ELDER OAKS: We are sometimes asked about whether marriage is a remedy for these feelings that we have been talking about. President Hinckley, faced with the fact that apparently some had believed it to be a remedy, and perhaps that some Church leaders had even counseled marriage as the remedy for these feelings, made this statement: "Marriage should not be viewed as a therapeutic step to solve problems such as homosexual inclinations or practices." To me that means that we are not going to stand still to put at risk daughters of God who would enter into such marriages under false pretenses or under a cloud unknown to them. Persons who have this kind of challenge that they cannot control could not enter marriage in good faith.

On the other hand, persons who have cleansed themselves of any transgression and who have shown their ability to deal with these feelings or inclinations and put them in the background, and feel a great attraction for a daughter of God and therefore desire to enter marriage and have children and enjoy the blessings of eternity—that's a situation when marriage would be appropriate.

President Hinckley said that marriage is not a therapeutic step to solve problems.

ELDER WICKMAN: One question that might be asked by somebody who is struggling with same-gender attraction is, "Is this something I'm stuck with forever? What bearing does this have on eternal life? If I can somehow make it through this life, when I appear on the other side, what will I be like?"

Gratefully, the answer is that same-gender attraction did not exist in the pre-earth life and neither will it exist in the next life. It is a circumstance that for whatever reason or reasons seems to apply right now in mortality, in this nano-second of our eternal existence.

The good news for somebody who is struggling with same-gender attraction is this: 1) It is that "I'm not stuck with it forever." It's just now. Admittedly, for each one of us, it's hard to look beyond the "now" sometimes. But nonetheless, if you see mortality as now, it's only during this season. 2) If I can keep myself worthy here, if I can be true to gospel commandments, if I can keep covenants that I have made, the blessings of exaltation and eternal life that Heavenly Father holds out to all of His children apply to me. Every blessing—including eternal marriage—is and will be mine in due course.

ELDER OAKS: Let me just add a thought to that. There is no fullness of joy in the next life without a family unit, including a husband, a wife, and posterity. Further, men are that they might have joy. In the eternal perspective, same-gender activity will only bring sorrow and grief and the loss of eternal opportunities.

From LDS Newsroom (2006)

10. Maxine Hanks, "Introduction"

Mormons rightly point out that the church has been progressive with regard to women in significant ways. A conception of deity that includes a female god, a theological view that makes salvation a joint enterprise, the elevation of Eve to status of heroine, early territorial suffrage for all women, and encouragement of and support for female education going back to the Nauvoo period—these and other features are all countercultural examples of liberal thinking about women's issues. But none of these considerations belie the fact that women are excluded from most substantive decision making in the church and from participation in most ordinances where the priesthood is required outside of temple rites. Maxine Hanks pointed out in her scholarly research that in the early LDS church years, women did participate in a variety of aspects of priesthood. There is also evidence that Joseph Smith originally intended a fuller role for women in the church and in the priesthood.

A vocal minority of women have encouraged the church leadership to reevaluate not only women's exclusion from the priesthood but also the fuller implications of the largely neglected doctrine of a Mother in Heaven. While many express hopes for continued development, no majority has emerged for more radical changes to women's roles. In part, this is a consequence of Mormons' deeply rooted belief that a living prophet is ordering and guiding the church according to the divine will. In part, it may indeed be a product of an authoritarian and conservative culture where dissent is generally frowned upon and seldom productive of meaningful change in any case. And in part, it may be a reflection of the fact that to the extent a feminist sensibility thrives in Mormondom, women consider the persisting ambiguity regarding the past history and eternal meaning of plural marriage a more vexing and relevant concern.

This anthology unites some of the feminist perspectives that have surfaced in Mormonism from the beginning of the Church of Jesus Christ of Latter-day Saints to the present. . . . I selected texts about priesthood authority and female deity that demonstrate an emerging feminist theology . . . its purpose is to illustrate women's religious equality . . .

This book also coincides with the 150th anniversary of the Relief Society (the women's organization of the LDS church), conceived by Sarah Kimball and founded in 1842 by Joseph and Emma Smith. The book's feminist voices remind us that the Relief Society once exercised authority and that "the Society should move according to the ancient priesthood." This feminist theology . . . works within the scope of Mormon theology and history . . .

Feminism has always existed in Mormonism. It makes sense that Mormon women would be feminists: within male-centered religion and discourse, feminism and feminist theology are necessary. . . . Not all feminists agree on theories or approaches; and most feminists do not belong in one category. The slogan "equality-versus-difference" has been used as a "shorthand to characterize conflicting feminist positions . . ." Feminists who believe that "sexual difference is an irrelevant consideration" stress equality. Feminists who advocate "needs, interests, and characteristics common to women as a group" stress difference" . . .

FIRST WAVE FEMINISM

The first wave of Mormon feminism coincided with its American counterpart. Nineteenth-century Mormon women demonstrated liberal and cultural feminism in their writing and activities . . .

Mormon feminism began with Emma Smith, wife of the prophet Joseph Smith. She "profoundly affected the development of [two] religious movements (Mormonism and the Re-organized church) . . . she became a force to be reckoned with, especially in financial and other practical matters affecting the Mormon church . . . she quietly but vigorously opposed the polygamous beliefs and practices which he [Joseph] sought to introduce into Mormon practice." As first president of the female Relief Society of Nauvoo, Illinois, Emma was "elected" and "ordained" to preside over women in the church; she received "a portion of the keys of the kingdom." Feminist assertions surfaced in the early Relief Society minutes. Emma Smith . . . exhorted sisters to pursue monogamy and denounce polygamy . . . claiming, "If there ever were any authority on this earth, she [Emma] had it—and had it yet."

Liberal feminism was expressed by Mormon women . . . through their labors to help build society. Mormon women mastered a range of employment skills and professions and gained prominent places in the public sphere. They became merchants, politicians, and scholars; the University of Deseret, founded in 1850, enrolled women. Mormon women managed wheat and silk industries. Utah had a higher percentage of women doctors and midwives than any other U.S. state . . . doctor Ellis Shipp alone trained 500 midwives and practitioners. Mormon women published an independent women's newspaper and young women's magazine for four decades. Women were granted suffrage in Utah in 1870 . . . nearly fifty years before the Nineteenth Amendment . . . and regained the vote in Utah after the Edmunds-Tucker law rescinded it in 1887. Between 1871 and 1920 Mormon women collaborated and travelled with eastern activists such as Elizabeth Cady Stanton and Susan B. Anthony to lobby for national women's suffrage.

Cultural feminism found outlets in the Mormon doctrine of a heavenly mother and female priesthood, implicit in Joseph Smith's discussions of God, the temple, and priesthood keys. Eliza R. Snow described the Mother in her 1845 poem, "Invocation: or the Eternal Father and Mother," now one of Mormonism's most loved hymns. Snow was widely regarded as a "priestess" and "prophetess" as well as "presidentess" of the Mormon women's organizations including the Relief Society. Founded in 1842, the women's Relief Society . . . was a benevolent society as well as a self-governing "kingdom of priests." Sarah Kimball, who first conceived the Relief Society, claimed upon its establishment that "the sure foundations of the suffrage cause were deeply and permanently laid." Later in 1850, she emulated male priesthood patterns by setting apart women "teachers" and "deaconesses." In 1882 the Society established the Deseret Hospital, staffed by women . . .

What was the result of all this Mormon liberal and cultural feminism? . . . Near the turn of the century one Church leader admitted . . . "While the auxiliary organizations have taken the right of way, the Priesthood quorums stand by looking on awe-struck." As a result, the Priesthood Correlation Program was conceived in 1908 to bolster male involvement in all aspects of the church, as well as to organize and streamline church structure in preparation for expansion. As correlation gained strength, women's authority diminished. Priesthood leaders began referring to the women's organizations as "auxiliaries." Female priesthood ordinance work was discouraged, and by the 1930s it was forbidden. Tension grew between male priesthood leadership and feminists who were experiencing loss of authority and position . . .

A potent symbol of Mormon women's loss of power . . . was the release of Emmeline Wells as president of the Relief Society. Citing her "frailty and age," President Heber J. Grant informed Wells he would release her. "Emmeline was stunned. None of her predecessors had been released, remaining in their office until their deaths." This was a lifetime appointment, like apostle or prophet. "The humiliation of a release was unbearable. Her spirit broken, Emmeline's health failed rapidly. Her daughter wrote a reproving letter to President Grant. He responded, "I had hoped that . . . I could reconcile [your mother to] . . . the judgement of all of the First Presidency and Twelve as the best and wisest thing to do . . ." Wells died the day Grant's letter was written. Her daughter believed she died of a broken heart.

SECOND WAVE FEMINISM

In the twentieth century, feminism evolved and diversified into a wide spectrum of approaches all grouped into the "second wave" of feminism in America. Mormon feminism again coincided with U.S. feminist movements, but emerged in at least three "Mormon waves" or "generations" [of its own]. Mormon feminism became an important counterbalance to the rise of Priesthood Correlation . . .

Mormon feminism . . . embraced American social movements (1910–1940s). During and after World War I church members interfaced with emerging national relief and social work organizations. Mormons such as Amy Brown Lyman developed large social projects. . . . Mormon social feminists gave birth to Relief Society Social Services, social programs and curriculum (linked to church welfare and social services), the Primary Children's Hospital, and other community projects. . . . Esther Peterson and Belle Spafford had great impact with social projects and reforms. During the 1940s social historians Juanita Brooks and Fawn M. Brodie reevaluated the past with an insight that helped give birth to revisionist history or "the New Mormon History" . . .

The LDS church Priesthood Correlation Program began its final push in 1960–1980, to place women under the male structure. The Relief Society magazine was discontinued by priesthood directive in 1970. With President Belle Spafford's release in 1974, all Relief Society funds, operations, and curriculum were brought under control of priesthood correlation and male leaders. The result of priesthood correlation was a stream-lined but all-male authority.

Mormonism's third feminist wave surfaced in the early 1970s, energized by a rediscovery of 1870s Mormon liberal feminism and . . . also responded to the decline of women's power in the church. Mormon feminism found expression in and outside of the church . . . in *Exponent II, Dialogue: A Journal of Mormon Thought,* and *Sunstone;* BYU's Women's committees, women's studies courses, and Women's Research Institute; and the Mormons for ERA; the Utah International Women's Year committee, the Alice Louise Reynolds forum; and increasing feminist and revisionist histories of Mormon women and Mormonism . . .

Male church leaders responded to Mormon feminism with unprecedented emphasis on the nuclear family and patriarchal authority during the 1970s. . . . The church opposed the Equal Rights Amendment, organized and funded efforts to defeat it. Tensions between male correlation and feminism reached a crescendo at the Utah International Women's Year conference in 1977, then peaked in the excommunication of Mormons for ERA president Sonia Johnson in December 1979. These events divided Mormon women as nothing in Mormon history ever had: they polarized feminists and non-feminists, fragmented feminists from each other, and left emotional scars still evident to the present . . .

Contemporary Mormon feminism (or its fourth wave) began in the mid-1980s . . . it includes the full spectrum of feminist approaches. Three prominent areas of focus are: theological discussion of a mother in heaven and female priesthood . . . social and historical research on Mormon women . . . and post-modern feminist critique. . . . These and related topics have prompted increasing discussions in non-church settings at Sunstone symposia, Mormon Women's Forum, women's studies programs in Utah (including BYU) and the women's retreats in Utah, the Midwest, New England, and California. Paradoxically, as feminism has been suppressed in the church, it has grown and evolved in the larger Mormon culture.

Each of Mormon feminism's four waves had different rally calls: for first wave liberal/cultural Mormon feminism it was woman's equality and suffrage; for second wave social feminism it was social reform; third wave Mormon feminists rallied to women's history and the ERA; fourth wave Mormon feminists seek women's authority and discourse.

Two conclusions emerge from a review of Mormon feminist texts: Mormon feminists say some of the same things over and over again, yet there is no unifying feminist consensus, we must validate our diversity . . . Mormon feminists repeat the rhetoric, texts, and causes of their liberal/cultural great-grandmothers . . . keep reinventing the wheel . . . unable to connect their work together in a continuous historical tradition; feminist work is born and then buried again with each new generation . . .

My sense is that current Mormon feminists are trying to overcome generational gaps and authoritative backlashes. Mormon feminism is building on the previous work of its feminist foremothers during the nineteenth and twentieth centuries . . . assuming feminism as a basic given and exploring new territories. In all their diversity Mormon feminists seem to know that one feminist view, one strategy, one struggle is not enough. They are refusing to reinvent the wheel . . .

EMERGING FEMINIST THEOLOGY

Theology, or simply the way we view God and our relationship to God, is the foundation of our religion. Mormon theology evolves: our concept of continuing revelation, absence of formal creeds, and inconsistency of doctrine through decades and diverse prophets allow Mormon theology speculative and dynamic freedom. Still, LDS scripture and authoritative male discourse are used as theological controls. Our authoritative discourse shows a lack of feminine theology; yet feminine deity is implicit in Mormon theology.

Mormon theology establishes the existence of a mother in heaven equal in glory and power to a father. Linda Wilcox notes that "little if any theology has been developed to elucidate her nature and characterize our relationship to her." For Mormon women, this gap between a dual-gender theological blueprint and an exclusively male theological construction communicates an authoritative omission of femaleness in our religion . . .

Feminist theology . . . reveals the feminine in our view of God and priesthood. Why undertake Mormon feminist theology? Because we cannot separate ourselves from the image of God . . . we cannot separate our social life from our beliefs . . . Mormon theology, history, and doctrine need to be reevaluated in light of women's participation, resistance, and perspectives. Historically, male perspectives have prevailed over women's concerns; thus men's efforts in history and theology are treated as if they are the complete story . . .

In recent years, many Mormons have come to agree that the female or feminine needs to fully emerge in Mormon theology, doctrine and church structure. What has been speculated but not decided on any official level is how that should be done. Should female theology come from the leading body of male apostles and prophets? . . . Should female theology emerge through women's consciousness? If so, how does this integrate with male leadership? Is it already happening? . . .

For church leaders, a female theology would require additional revelation, doctrine or scripture. For scholars, it means developing concepts of women's priesthood and Mother in Heaven within historic and theological frameworks. For many members, the divine feminine is an expression of personal experience with God. I would hope that all three approaches could converge in a collective or holistic expression of the feminine. . . . Ultimately, the development of feminist theology and restoration of women's authority in the church may depend on the Relief Society reclaiming its authority . . .

PRIESTHOOD

Mormon women receive priesthood power (or power of God) in several ways: through exercise of spiritual gifts such as blessings, healings, and prophecy (beginning 1830–1832); through Relief Society priesthood keys (in 1842); through the temple endowment (in 1843); through the call to preach the gospel (in 1850); and through temple marriage. Baptism and confirmation also convey God's power to exercise gifts of the spirit, such as testimony, visions, and blessings. Put simply, the church conveys priesthood power to women, yet . . . permission to use priesthood is granted only to men who are "ordained" to a priesthood office; women are not "ordained" but are "set-apart" to church positions as the means of conferral of priesthood to women.

Mormon women exercised the power of God in the church for 100 years. Nineteenth-century Mormon women administered some priesthood powers and ordinances. After the turn of the century women's exercise of priesthood power was discouraged and ultimately revoked, while men's priesthood exercise was expanded. If the momentum of women's nineteenth-century priesthood had been maintained, their priesthood may have been included in priesthood correlation and women might be exercising their priesthood power in the church today . . .

Formal church activation or ordination of women's priesthood power has been suggested by Mormon feminists for decades. If this were to happen women might not sense possession of something new but rather a loosening of bonds, a new freedom to use something they have always had, a spiritual liberation. Ultimately, the reactivation of women's priesthood powers may not be a matter of ordination but of women reclaiming their own authority.

The modern church has claimed that male Priesthood Correlation is the means of establishing Zion—a society of one heart with God. Perhaps creating Zion is a simple thing—the creation of equal partnership between men and women in the church. Just as Priesthood Correlation was necessary to prepare for the present growth of the church, the restoration of the female to Priesthood Correlation may be necessary for future growth. The church may not be able to grow into Zion without feminism. Neither patriarchy nor feminism are Zion; feminism modifies patriarchy to make Zion possible. Zion is a way of being, a way of living the kingdom of God within.

From *Women and Authority: Re-emerging Mormon Feminism* (1992)

11. Emily Milner, "Finding Myself on Google"

No one voice could possibly encapsulate the essence of what it means to be a woman in the contemporary church in America. But Emily Milner manages to capture the myriad tensions, transformations, and struggles that constitute this particular moment in the church's cultural evolution. Arguably, being male in the church is relatively easy, because the role entails a clear sense of priorities, and the man's spiritual, familial, and professional imperatives generally align: pursuing professional and personal growth is the best way to fulfill the provider role assigned by church teachings. In prior generations, church policy and cultural expectations alike assigned women the principal role of mother and nurturer, so conflict and uncertainty about their identity were at a minimum. But LDS couples are no longer admonished to have as many children as they can support; newly married women are no longer counseled to forgo education in favor of immediate childbearing; and women are encouraged from girlhood to pursue excellence, to attain the highest level of education they can, and to prepare for financial independence and self-sufficiency. This means they face the same challenges as women in larger society: trying to balance an impossible array of imperatives, with the difference that having children and raising a family is for Mormon women still the non-negotiable paramount priority of their mortal existence. The result for many is a life whose greatest joys are nonetheless tinged with the recognition of roads not taken, opportunities missed, and an appreciative audience of generally modest proportions. Milner's gift is in seeing in such a life glimpses of the holy without sentimentalism.

There are three actual references to me on Google. The first reference to Emily Milner, me, is on page six. Before that I wade through pages of references to not-me Emily Milners: genealogy charts, a talented high-school violinist, a devout Catholic from Georgia, a fourth-year physics major. The first two actual references to me are from a forum I haven't posted on in years; the last one comes from my husband, who e-mailed something to a political website last fall using my e-mail address. It's on page seven.

Most of the time I am grateful to be where I am, at home with my children. It is my season to be a mother: to watch my toddler's dandelion fluff hair spread out, halo-like, from static electricity; to see my son figure out how to blend one letter's sound into the next letter, and watch the delight on his face as he reads the words. These are my rewards for the daily diligence motherhood demands.

But sometimes, I wish I showed up on Google.

I have done nothing worthy of mention on Google for years, although it doesn't take much to be listed there: a page referencing employees at a business, a brief line in a newspaper article. In spite of the ease of appearing on Google, however, my presence there is almost nonexistent. I could set up a self-promoting website: Googling "Emily Milner" could yield results such as "brought dinner to her visiting-teaching sister on the same night she had Enrichment, even though she is on the planning committee and was swamped." If you clicked on the link, you would see a picture of me holding a bag full of hot breadsticks in one hand, and baked ziti casserole, my potluck special, in the other. The next result might say, "did not lose patience when her four-year-old wet the bed on the same morning that her two-year-old decided to strip off pajamas and diaper and pee all over everything." The link would be to a picture of me doing laundry with a resigned smile.

These are my accomplishments right now, and none of them is Google-worthy.

I don't remember much about the time right after I had my first child, Scott. Most of it runs together in a haze, except this conversation with my father. I had gone several days with very little sleep as I tried to nurse my baby, and I was frazzled when I answered the phone.

"How's my grandson?" he said. He sounded too cheerful. I could not handle cheer right then.

"I can't do this!" I sobbed. "I can't do this! I can't keep trying to nurse him! I can't go without sleep! I am a terrible mother! Why am I doing this?"

Dad stayed mostly quiet and let me cry it out.

"You'll make it through this," he told me. "You can do this."

But could I? All the books and magazines I had purchased during my pregnancy, *What to Expect When You're Expecting*, *Your Pregnancy Week by Week*, *Baby Talk*, and *American Baby*, had failed to prepare me for my complete inadequacy when presented with an actual baby. I couldn't feed him, couldn't get him to sleep, couldn't even experience that mythical mothering bond that was supposed to make all my sleepless nights worthwhile.

But Dad was right. I did it, because I had to, and every day I got a little better at diapering and feeding and entertaining.

Eventually I even got a good night's sleep. But I was right too: the person I was when I had Scott could not be a mother. I had to change. I gave up a part of myself to be a mother that I have never seen since. It's the part of me that wrote "A Translation and Commentary of Manuel Cañete's *Prologue to the Obras Completas del Duque de Rivas*" for my honors thesis. It's the part of me that checked my grades online every so often, just for fun, so I could see the rows of approving As. It's the part that loved school; every September I still get nostalgic for new pencils and crisp notebooks. And it is the part that, if I had played my cards differently, would have been right there on Google.

When Scott was seven months old I sang "Eensy Weensy Spider" to him for the first time. He sat up, still a bit wobbly in his balance, and laughed as I made the hand motions. He had never laughed like that before. I sang it for him over and over as he laughed and waved his arms. I wrote about it in my journal, as I wrote down other such mommying moments: little snippets of time that made me feel like a mother, instead of someone just filling in for the real mother, who would arrive any minute to take over and return me to my previous life. I have a list from Scott's first year: the time he held up his head and deliberately looked all around, very proud of himself; the time he stacked ten board books up in a row; the time he laughed at a bouncing Winnie-the-Pooh ball. I cataloged them for myself. I didn't have a report card anymore, no neat rows of letters announcing my performance level, but I had a few scrawled memories that meant I was trying to learn how to mother.

Scott was almost one when I first heard Sheri Dew's talk on motherhood, "Are We Not All Mothers?" The talk left me discouraged and uplifted at the same time. She said: "In the Lord's language, the word mother has layers of meaning. Of all the words they could have chosen to define her role and her essence, both God the Father and Adam called Eve 'the mother of all living'— and they did so *before* she ever bore a child. Like Eve, our motherhood began before we were born."

I wept as I listened to Sheri Dew speak, from a combination of the Spirit witnessing truth and my own feelings of inadequacy. If, as Sheri Dew said, my essential nature was that of a mother, and if I didn't like being a mother sometimes, what did that say about me? I felt like a terrible human being because Eve's mothering heritage was not my natural gift. I had to work at enjoying mothering, giving myself mommy pep talks. I missed the Googlable side of myself, and sometimes I resented my new job. I had no natural mothering in me! Every bit of mothering skills I had were ones I worked and prayed and sweated for. I was not Eve, not even close.

And yet—the uplifted side of me gained a better understanding of what it meant to be a mother. I read many books and magazine articles on mothering before I had Scott. I had listened for years to talks on the importance of mothers and their influence. But until I had him, I did not realize how much of motherhood was being in addition to doing.

There was a lot of doing involved in mothering: tidying, feeding hungry tummies, wiping noses and bottoms. There was so much doing, and so many voices telling me how to do things the right way, that doing obscured being. Sheri Dew was telling me that I needed a vision of my eternal nature, my eternal being, as a mother. She said: "Motherhood is more than bearing children, though it is certainly that. It is the essence of who we are as women. It defines our very identity, our divine stature and nature, and the unique traits our Father gave us." If, as Sheri Dew explained, I was in essence a mother, whether or not I felt like one, then I needed to humble myself and repent. I needed to discover the mothering side of me, and find joy in it.

I had Sheri Dew's words echoing in my heart when Scott turned one. That, to me, was a deadline: I'd had a year to get used to this baby, and now, as a righteous woman, as someone who wanted a row of celestial As, it was time for me to have another baby. This was because, I told myself, it was wrong to use birth control for too long. There were so many spirits waiting to come down, and it would be selfish of me to refuse them. This was my role now: I gave up being a student, and I was now a mother. I might not be naturally good at mothering, but perhaps what I lacked in quality I could make up for in quantity.

That's what I told myself when we started "trying" again.

A few weeks later, Matt was going to put Scott to bed. "Do you want to say good night?" he asked.

"I have a terrible headache," I told him. "It's just throbbing. I'm going to say good night from here." Scott gave me a hug and kiss and went off to say prayers with Matt. I lay on the couch flipping through channels. My head hurt. I had never gotten headaches like that before. I expected it to be gone the next day.

But it wasn't. After a few weeks I had seen my doctor, gotten a CAT scan, seen the doctor again, and ended up in front of a therapist so I could try biofeedback to control the pain, since other painkillers did not work.

"Before the biofeedback," he said, "I want to talk about what's going on in your life. Is there anything that could be causing the pain? Any stress?"

"Oh no," I said. "I have a one-year-old, but he's a good baby, and my husband's great, absolutely no complaints."

"So you're doing well then?"

"Yes, and we're even . . ." Here, baffling myself, I started to cry. "We're even trying to have another baby, our next one, because we're ready for that."

I did not realize how not ready for another baby I was until I untwisted all my convoluted logic in that therapist's chair. I had read various general authority quotes concerning birth control that made me feel like it would be sinful to prevent children from coming naturally any longer than a year or so. I don't know where I got the year limit from; it was just there somehow, maybe since babies are weaned at around a year. After a year's grace, it should be time to have a baby again.

Did I realize, my therapist asked, that the current general handbook is much less dictatorial than I'd assumed? That while members are encouraged to multiply and replenish the earth, the timing is left to the parents' prayers and discretion? Had I prayed about this? Had God told me it was time?

I had prayed about it, but had assumed that God's default answer would be yes. Of course it would be yes. Of course I would need to have another child, and soon. That is what I would need to do to be good, to be righteous, to be a celestial mother. To be Eve.

Is it possible, my therapist asked, that God is more merciful than that? Is it possible that it's okay for you to take some more time before your next baby, to continue getting used to this one, to figure out who you are as a mother? You've lost the student-self you were used to, and you haven't found your mother-self yet. Don't you think God is generous enough to give you more time?

The headache didn't go away for a long time. I wish I could define the moment when it left me. Eventually I felt comfortable enough with my mothering that I believed God would let me have some extra time between kids, because I could not pop them out every other year like some women could. And I even believed that it was all right for me to take that time. I did not need to be just like Eve all at once. I began to think of our next child not as "another baby" but as Norah, even before she was conceived.

Norah would be funny and passionate and strong-willed. She would be excited to play with Scott. Norah, my next child, was real.

The more I knew her spirit, the more I was able to think of welcoming her into our home. A few months after my headaches left, I became pregnant. I knew before the ultrasound that it would be Norah.

The night I went to have Norah, the nurse preparing me for my C-section was surprised to see me crying quietly. "Are you worried about the surgery?" she asked. "It's not that," I said. "I'm just scared to have another baby. I don't know if I can do this again. The pain is terrible, you never sleep, and it's really, really hard."

Poor nurse. She did not seem to know what to say. I was not excited like most other moms-to-be; I knew what was coming and I was frightened. She rubbed my hands and said, "You can do this. We'll get you through it."

They did.

Norah was perfect, and beautiful. I spent a day with her in the hospital, holding her and nursing her and feeling motherly. I held her little body and felt God's approval. She came when I was ready, and that was all right. In my mothering weakness, I was given sufficient grace.

As I write now, I'm thirty-six-weeks pregnant with my third child. His name is Dale. I was scared to have him too, until I began to think of him as my athletic, happy son Dale. God has blessed me with the gift of knowing who my kids are ahead of time, of knowing their names, so that I can prepare my difficult heart to receive them.

I have forgotten most of the doing tasks that come with a newborn. I have forgotten how much he is supposed to eat with every feeding, and the best way to hold his wobbly head. Used to the heft of my two-year-old, I do not remember newly born lightness. I can feel him bumping inside me, exploring his narrow world. Other women, when they get to thirty-six weeks, want the baby out. I like him inside, where I can feel him kick without hearing him cry. My body nurtures him automatically. When he emerges in a few days, I will become his mother, and the nurturing must be deliberate.

I will never show up on Google for my heroic two A.M. feedings or epic laundry battles. Some day the student side of me may resurface there. I still miss her. But my nurturing does not belong on Google. Nurturing, I am learning, is inherently private. To proclaim my mothering accomplishments is either to turn myself into a martyr-mother, or to trap the sublime with stumbling, sentimental words. If my nurturing lost its privacy, it would lose its identity. By embracing the inheritance of Eve's mothering birthright, I received a sacred anonymity: a private, holy grace.

From *Segullah: Writings by Latter-day Saint Women* (1996)

SEVEN

EDUCATION AND INTELLECTUALISM

A SIGNAL CHARACTERISTIC OF JOSEPH SMITH's ministry at the head of The Church of Jesus Christ of Latter-day Saints was his synthesis of the two poles of knowledge acquisition. He was at one and the same time a visionary, given to rapturous epiphanies, angelic visitations, and the gift of seership, and an enthusiastic and devoted student of languages, history, and culture. Joseph Smith's liberal eclecticism was marked by a confidence that worldly and spiritual learning were mutually reinforcing, and he initiated both a School of the Prophets and a university in Nauvoo to bring his vision of such a happy confluence to fruition. The revelation directing the establishment of the former unblinkingly mingled admonition to study "the law of the gospel" with a directive to gain knowledge of "things which are at home; things which are abroad." So in the School of the Prophets, "Lectures on Faith" mingled with the study of geography and languages. For several years after the Latter-day Saints settled in Utah, its members naturally dominated the educational system; diversification of the population led for a time to a division into secular and church schools. Amy Lyman gives below an account of a female Mormon's education in this era, from grammar school through training in Brigham Young Academy (located in a Provo, Utah, warehouse), and on to a career as an educator herself.

Having lost their isolated status in the Great Basin with the coming of the railroad in 1869, Latter-day Saints in Utah had to begin to contend with more than competing educational agendas. An array of cultural and intellectual influences permeated the territory (and after 1896 the state), threatening what the church saw as its spiritual purity and identity. Like Israel in the midst of foreign tribes and religions, Mormons in Utah experienced the tension between the idea of Zion and the offerings and allure of surrounding cultural riches. Late in the century, eminent LDS women as well as Apostle Orson F. Whitney called for the creation of an authentic "home literature" that would espouse Mormon values and ideals. Mormon women again led out in the 1920s, this time with a progressive appeal to education that was vocational and that qualified women as well as men to be "socially serviceable and financially independent." As the twentieth century progressed, and larger cultural influences continued to trickle into Utah, increasing numbers of Latter-day Saints began to cross borders in the opposite direction, especially to secure degrees at Midwestern and Eastern universities. In her reminiscence, historian Juanita Brooks illustrates one such pilgrimage to Columbia in New York City and the resultant discomfort of cultural collision.

Joseph Smith's hope of blending faith and intellect, which has a long history but was especially pronounced in nineteenth-century religious circles, met few serious challenges during the church's formative years. Even though his successor, Brigham Young, was more inclined to the pragmatic than the intellectual, he too could be fervent in praising the "spirit and power of research . . . planted within" us and in forecasting that the work of earthly renewal would be accomplished "by angels well instructed in chemistry." The harmonious union of faith and intellect was most powerfully challenged by the advent of Darwinism. Though individual leaders aligned themselves as partisans in the science wars, the official voice was generally a moderate one—as in the First Presidency statement on the Origin of Man, which is (undoubtedly deliberately) too ambiguous to serve as a clear statement of church teaching on human evolution. Chemist Henry Eyring, valued by the leadership for his measured rebuttals to anti-science voices among the church leadership, is represented here in his selection on "Science and Religion."

Like any Christian denomination striving to maintain unity and orthodoxy in the face of growth and secularizing influences, the church has struggled with the boundaries of dissent and repeatedly renegotiated the balance of authority and individualism that marks LDS membership. Eugene England was notable for his attempt to build bridges and find middle ground between those at the margins and at the center of the faith. The 1960s were particular fraught years for the church membership as opinions split over Vietnam, feminism, race—and historiography. Historian Juanita Brooks had alienated many of her co-religionists by publishing a critical account of the Mountain Meadow Massacre (where Mormon militiamen and Paiutes killed nearly all the members of a "gentile" wagon train in 1857) in 1950. In 1959, the newly launched academic journal *BYU Studies* got off to a rocky start with church leaders by publishing an article that shed unflattering light on nineteenth-century church observance (or non-observance) of the Word of Wisdom (the LDS health code).

The Mormon History Association formed in 1965 and soon pioneered a new model of history writing, "The New Mormon History," that endeavored to narrate the LDS past in a more naturalistic way, according to the canons of academic scholarship. Many of these developments caused concern among church leadership and growing alienation on the part of some academics and writers who resented what they saw as suspicion and anti-intellectualism. Eugene England tried to effect a compromise, or at least a détente, between the parties by launching an independent journal, *Dialogue*, which was followed by a similarly conceived magazine of independent thought, *Sunstone*. Observers have noted how the evolving accessibility to the church's own library and archival collections of historical materials has acted as a barometer of the goodwill between church leaders and scholars.

In a similar gesture of conciliation, historian Richard Poll described the competing attractions of faith and intellectualism in his influential essay, which he names the Iron Rod and the Liahona approach to the church. Here we find a broadly conceived, if somewhat reductive, way of thinking about two general reactions in Mormon culture to the irresolvable tension between authority and agency so interwoven in LDS theology.

The 1970s and 1980s introduced growing tensions in a church confronting challenges to biblical literalism, sexual mores, gender roles, and racial stereotypes. The church's lack of creedal statements is often celebrated as an invitation to doctrinal independence and speculation. "It feels so good not to be trammeled," said Joseph Smith on more than one occasion. One consequence of this anti-creedalism, however, is the difficulty of assessing the limits of orthodoxy. Compounding the problem is Mormonism's oft-commented-upon seeming evolution into an ethnic community. As a result, recent decades have witnessed the emergence of a relatively new phenomenon, the "cultural Mormon." In the concluding essays of this section, we find two women's voices who found different solutions to the matrix of obligations they feel toward profession and faith, gender and community(ies), and conscience and church. English professor

Marilyn Arnold finds the Book of Mormon, yet to be taken seriously by the vast majority of academics, to be a text that is supremely satisfying both at the level of affective response and spiritual resonance, and as a complex text that sustains sophisticated literary analysis. Laurel Thatcher Ulrich, a Pulitzer Prize–winning historian, situates herself amid the competing claims on her identity of intellect, Mormon culture, feminism, and Joseph Smith's teachings. Feminism in particular became for her a catalyst that empowered and shaped, rather than confounded or diminished, her religious faith.

1. Joseph Smith, "Revelation to the First Elders [Doctrine and Covenants 88:73–80, 117–41]"

Joseph Smith combined his role as prophet and revelator with consistent advocacy of education through more conventional means. In June 1831, Oliver Cowdery and William McLellin were commanded in a revelation to "do the work of printing, and of selecting and writing books for schools in this church, that little children may also receive instruction" (Doctrine and Covenants 55:4). Then, in the midst of his project to edit or "translate" the King James version of the Bible, Smith announced the inauguration of a "school of the prophets" to be held in a temple built for that (and other) purposes. The revelation directing such a project follows below. In the short term, Joseph Smith met with more than a dozen men in the chambers above Newel K. Whitney's Kirtland store. In a synthesis typical of Smith's tendency to collapse heaven into earth, the group studied scriptures and theology, but also government, geography, and languages. The school was thus one of antebellum America's early experiments in adult education, coming just years after Josiah Holbrook launched the Lyceum movement, which rapidly became a national phenomenon. The school held sessions during the winter months over the next few years, with another branch operating in Missouri under the leadership of Parley P. Pratt. In early 1836, Joseph Smith contracted with an Oberlin instructor, Joshua Seixas, to teach Hebrew to a large and enthusiastic group of Latter-day Saints. Once the Mormons were settled in Illinois, Smith's educational vision led to the founding of the University of Nauvoo. Mormon sponsorship of education would continue into the Utah period with the founding of the University of Deseret (now the University of Utah) only three years after settlement and the subsequent founding of what is now the largest church-affiliated university in America, Brigham Young University, in Provo, Utah.

20. Behold, I will hasten my work in its time; and I give unto you who are the first laborers in this last kingdom, a commandment, that you assemble yourselves together, and organize yourselves, and prepare yourselves; and sanctify yourselves; yea, purify your hearts, and cleanse your hands and your feet before me, that I may make you clean; that I may testify unto your Father, and your God, and my God, that you are clean from the blood of this wicked generation: that I may fulfil this promise, this great and last promise which I have made unto you, when I will.

21. Also, I give unto you a commandment, that ye shall continue in prayer and fasting from this time forth. And I give unto you a commandment, that you shall teach one another the doctrine of the kingdom; teach ye diligently and my grace shall attend you, that you may be instructed more perfectly in theory, in principle, in doctrine, in the law of the gospel, in all things that pertain unto the kingdom of God, that is expedient for you to understand; of things both in heaven, and in the earth, and under the earth; things which have been; things which are; things which must shortly come to pass; things which are at home; things which are abroad; the wars and the perplexities of the nations; and the judgments which are on the land; and a knowledge also of countries, and of kingdoms, that ye may be prepared in all things when I shall send you again, to magnify the calling whereunto I have called you, and the mission with which I have commissioned you. . . .

36. Therefore, verily I say unto you, my friends, call your solemn assembly, as I have commanded you; and as all have not faith, seek ye, diligently and teach one another words of wisdom; yea, seek ye out of the best books words of wisdom: seek learning even by study, and also by faith. Organize yourselves; prepare every needful thing, and establish a house, even a house of prayer, a house of fasting, a house of faith, a house of learning, a house of glory, a house of order, a house of God; that your incomings may be in the name of the Lord; that your outgoings may be in the name of the Lord; that all your salutations may be in the name of the Lord, with uplifted hands unto the Most High.

37. Therefore, cease from all your light speeches; from all laughter; from all lustful desires: from all your pride and lightmindedness, and from all your wicked doings. Appoint among yourselves a teacher, and let not all be spokesmen at once; but let one speak at a time, and let all listen unto his sayings, that when all have spoken, that all may be edified of all, and that every man may have an equal privilege.

38. See that ye love one another; cease to be covetous, learn to impart one to another as the gospel requires; cease to be idle, cease to be unclean; cease to find fault one with another; cease to sleep longer than is needful; retire to thy bed early, that ye may not be weary; arise early, that your bodies and your minds may be invigorated: and above all things, clothe yourselves with the bonds of charity, as with a mantle, which is the bond of perfectness and peace: pray always, that you may not faint until I come: behold, and lo, I come quickly, and receive you unto myself: Amen.

39. And again, the order of the house prepared for the presidency of the school of the prophets, established for their instruction in all things that are expedient for them, even for all the officers of the church, or in other words, those who are called to the ministry in the church, beginning at the high-priests, even down to the deacons: and this shall be the order of the house of the presidency of the school: He that is appointed to be president, or teacher, shall be found standing in his place, in the house, which shall be prepared for him. Therefore, he shall be the first in the house of God, in a place that the congregation in the house may hear his words carefully and distinctly, not with loud speech. And when he cometh into the house of God, (for he should be first in the house; behold this is beautiful, that he may be an example,)

40. Let him offer himself in prayer upon his knees before God, in token, or remembrance, of the everlasting covenant, and when any shall come in after him let the teacher arise, and with uplifted hands to heaven; yea, even directly, salute his brother or brethren with these words:

41. Art thou a brother or brethren, I salute you in the name of the Lord Jesus Christ, in token, or remembrance of the everlasting covenant, in which covenant I receive you to fellowship in a determination that is fixed, immovable and unchangable, to be your friend and brother through the grace of God, in the bonds of love, to walk in all the commandments of God blameless, in thanksgiving, forever and ever. Amen.

42. And he that is found unworthy of this salutation, shall not have place among you; for ye shall not suffer that mine house shall be polluted by them.

43. And he that cometh in and is faithful before me, and is a brother, or if they be brethren, they shall salute the president or teacher with uplifted hands to heaven with this same prayer and covenant, or by saying, Amen, in token of the same.

44. Behold, verily I say unto you, this is a sample unto you for a salutation to one another in the house of God, in the school of the prophets. And ye are

called to do this by prayer and thanksgiving as the Spirit shall give utterance, in all your doings in the house of the Lord, in the school of the prophets, that it may become a sanctuary, a tabernacle, of the Holy Spirit to your edification. 45. And ye shall not receive any among you, into this school save he is clean from the blood of this generation: and he shall be received by the ordinance of the washing of feet; for unto this end was the ordinance of the washing of feet instituted.

46. And again, the ordinance of washing feet is to be administered by the president, or presiding elder of the church. It is to be commenced with prayer: and after·partaking of bread and wine he is to gird himself, according to the pattern given in the thirteenth chapter of John's testimony concerning me. Amen.

From Doctrine and Covenants (1835)

2. Amy Brown Lyman, "Childhood"

Ironically, in a religious culture where plural marriage was practiced, Mormon women fared well educationally. Though not participants in either Kirtland's Hebrew school or the School of the Prophets, young women attended Kirtland High School and composed more than half the rolls of the Nauvoo schools. When the University of Deseret in Salt Lake City reopened in 1868 after a hiatus of some years, women composed almost 50 percent of the class.[1] (This occurred at a time when women were receiving less than 15 percent of bachelor's degrees awarded and fewer than 1 percent of women eighteen to twenty-one years of age were attending college.[2]) President Brigham Young said, "We believe that women . . . should . . . study law or physics or become good bookkeepers and be able to do the business in any counting house."[3] He also advised women to attend medical schools; consequently, the women's Relief Society supported a number of women who went east to obtain training. Romania B. Pratt Penrose, Ellis Shipp and Margaret Shipp Roberts (sister wives), together with Martha Hughes Cannon and many others, returned with degrees in hand to establish practices and teach classes in Utah. Eliza R. Snow even attempted to establish a Female Medical College in Utah. Soon, more female American medical students hailed from Utah than from any other state.[4] Utah education began as a nondenominational endeavor, but the situation grew complicated with the influx of non-Mormons after the Civil War. In the late nineteenth century, as today, control of educational systems could be hotly contested because of conflicting agendas informed by varying religious and secular commitments. Amy Lyman, who eventually served as General Relief Society president, alludes to a time of polarization, when "gentiles" controlled much of public education and Latter-day Saints retreated temporarily into church-sponsored academies.

I first attended school in the old United Order hall. The school was held in the large room which occupied all of the top floor and which was reached by an outside stairway. The ground floor and the cellar of this building were used as a tithing granary and storehouse, and it was in this building that for many years the Relief Society wheat of the ward was stored. I shall never forget my first day in school. The teacher was Mrs. Fanny Stewart, a tall, angular woman, intellectual and well-read, but very serious. Like the other beginners, I was afraid of her and of the older children as well.

It was a mixed school of several grades with seventy-five or eighty pupils. There were few textbooks, and equipment was very limited. At times the teacher was put to her wit's end to carry on a recitation with one group, keep other groups busy, and at the same time maintain order. This was indeed a very difficult task. The teacher was very conscientious, and she was determined to get good results in the matter of our intellectual development. She was more interested in seeing that we learned something than she was in finding out how we felt about what we learned. She succeeded in teaching us how to apply ourselves, and she made sure that our work was correct and well done. She certainly gave us a good start.

Mrs. Stewart was a widow, and she had the entire care of three young children. She used to bring her children, her mending, and her ironing to school, and at recess and noon she would mend or iron. She often allowed the older girls to iron during school hours. This they loved to do. The flatirons were heated on the large, oval stove which stood in the middle of the room.

We first learned the alphabet, and then we learned to read, spell, and write. Our books consisted of the old Wilson readers, which were exceptionally good, and the famous blue-backed spelling books. Our number work was taken from the blackboard. We used slates entirely for writing, with a slate pencil attached to the slate by a string tied through a hole in the slate frame. Lead pencils and paper for children were luxuries we had not dreamed of. Most of the older children had double slates which, of course, furnished more space. The girls usually had a little bottle of soapsuds and a wet rag or sponge for erasing or cleaning their slates. The boys, however, were not so particular. It was quite a task to keep slates clean and sweet smelling since saliva was often used when water was not handy or available. A large pail, with a dipper, placed in one end of the room, furnished us with drinking water—a far cry from our sanitary drinking fountains of today.

The next year the schools were better graded, and we were moved to the schoolhouse. Altogether, I had six teachers in the grades—three women and three men. They were all good and greatly loved teachers. I was especially fond of the three women, who made such fine impressions upon my mind that they have been an unceasing uplift to me all my life. In my third year, my older sister, Rose Brown (later Mrs. I. J. Hayes), was my teacher. She had just returned from the Brigham Young Academy, where she had graduated from the normal department under Karl G. Maeser. She was an efficient, up-to-date teacher, as gentle and kind and able in the schoolroom as she had always been in our home where, being ten years my senior, she was to me a second mother. For kindness and evenness of disposition, I have never known her to be surpassed.

My teacher in the eighth grade was Augusta Winters, later Mrs. Heber J. Grant. It was our good fortune that she came back to Pleasant Grove that particular year to be the principal of the school and the teacher of the seventh and eighth grades. She was an excellent and most interesting teacher. Having attended both the Brigham Young Academy and the University of Utah, she was especially well prepared. She had also taught school in a number of other places, including Salt Lake City. She had traveled a great deal—to California and even to faraway Maine. She used to tell us many interesting, new, and different things. She was not only well prepared as an instructor, but she was dramatic and humorous in her presentation of material; she constantly enlivened her teaching with interesting experiences, stories, and comments.

We admired and respected this excellent teacher for her fine traits of character, her intellectuality, her dignity and poise, and her splendid ability as a teacher. We loved her for her attractive personality, for her kindness and sympathy, as well as for her beauty and charm. She was our heroine, and we all longed to be like her.

In the fall of 1888, I entered the normal department of Brigham Young Academy. My sister Susan and I were driven to Provo by father in a farm wagon along with some furniture and supplies, and we were located in a large room near the school where we were to do light housekeeping. Each weekend provisions from home were sent to us across Provo Bench.

The school was then located in the old ZCMI warehouse near the railroad depot, where it had been housed since the fire had destroyed its original home, Lewis Hall, on Center Street. It occupied the whole second floor of the warehouse, with several offices and the laboratory on the ground floor.

To me the school was a surprise, a marvel, and a delight. It did not matter that the building was a plain, ordinary warehouse, nor that the desks were long, crude, table affairs, with chairs of the kitchen variety. It was the spirit and atmosphere of the institution which were so fascinating and satisfying. I had heard a great deal from my brothers and sisters and other former students about how Free the school was, how the spirit of the gospel permeated every quarter, and how the students regarded religion as the most important subject in the whole curriculum. I had anticipated much, but the reality exceeded my expectations, and I found that the wonders of the school had not half been told. That year seemed to me to be the happiest of my life, and the world such a fascinating place in which to live. It was during this period that I met and fell in love with my future husband, Richard R. Lyman—so why shouldn't it be the happiest time of my life?

As I think of it now, the school was really as remarkable as I then thought it was, for it featured those things which are most important in this life and in the life to come.

There were a number of excellent teachers, but the most important, best loved, and honored was, of course, Dr. Karl G. Maeser, who stood at the head and was really the soul of the institution. Tall and thin, dressed in a Prince Albert coat, he personified the idea of the old professor, and ruled the school like a general. Trained for his work in Old-World education centers, he was an educator of the first rank, a fine scholar, and a finished teacher. His enthusiasm and earnestness, his unwavering faith and spirituality, his fine character, and his daily life were a constant inspiration to his students and stimulated them to greater effort and accomplishment than they had thought possible. He loved the calling of a teacher and often said he hoped he would be able to teach in heaven. I was a member of his theology class, in connection with which we had a monthly testimony meeting, and I was also a member of his classes in history of education, theory and practice of teaching, and, occasionally elocution, when he substituted so ably for the teacher of that subject. Next to my own parents, Brother Maeser influenced my life. Our daily devotional exercises brought us all together each morning when there would be singing and prayer, a message from Brother Maeser or one of his associates, and special instructions, if there were any to give. . . .

The Domestic Department was established to look after students during out-of-school hours. In each boarding place, one student was appointed to act as monitor. It was his duty to look after the rest and report regularly in Domestic meeting, held monthly, as to how things were going, and whether school rules were being observed. Students were not expected to be out at night, even until seven o'clock, without special written permission from Brother Maeser himself. Nine o'clock was considered a late hour.

For recreation we had Polysophical Society which held forth every Friday night, when excellent literary and musical programs were given by the best talent available in the school. And once in five weeks there was a student dance in the school assembly hall which began at eight o'clock and closed promptly at twelve o'clock. We were so happy in those dances we did not notice the poor, splintered floor. We were not expected to frequent public dances. Nor did we. I never heard anyone complain, however, about school restrictions. Everybody seemed satisfied and happy.

I was graduated from the Normal School in June 1890, and was selected, with several others, to make a short speech at commencement exercises. It was customary then for a number of students to appear on the commencement program. . . .

A few weeks after my graduation I was engaged by Brother Maeser to go back to the "Y" and take charge of what was then known as the "Primary Department"; and under his supervision and direction, in the fall of 1890 I began my work as a teacher at a salary of $40 per month—one-third cash and two-thirds tithing scrip.

In 1891, the B.Y.A. was moved from its temporary home in the Z.C.M.I. warehouse to its new home on the new campus, in the northern part of the city, now known as the lower campus. The new building, College Hall, was considered a real palace by the students. Here we had central heat, a telephone, and other conveniences.

I taught in the Training School of the institution for four years and had the privilege during that time of working under President Benjamin Cluff, Jr., who was a constant inspiration to both his teachers and students, and Prof. George H. Brimhall, that dynamic and forceful teacher and builder of character, who was in direct charge of the Training School. In addition to my work in the

Training School, I taught, at different periods, needlework and physical education. During an emergency I served as matron of the school.

I used to feel at times that teaching in a Church school had its handicaps, especially for young women who loved fun, parties, and dancing as I did. The teachers were supposed to be very circumspect and to set a good example, which was rather hard on the younger faculty members. Party dresses with low necklines and short sleeves were not very common and were taboo for us.

One great disappointment that I remember distinctly was when I was advised not to take part in a grand masquerade ball given in the Provo Theater by the society folk of the town. It was really the ball of the season, and all of my girl friends dressed and masked for the occasion. I felt quite rebellious at being advised not to take part and argued that point with Brother Maeser. I told him I had been held down all my life, and that I was tired of being a bishop's daughter and a church school teacher. I think I even shed a few tears about it. But I finally gave in, and sat in the front row of the dress circle—we called it bald-headed row—with the older people, where I watched my friends enjoy all the fun that accompanied those old masquerade balls. . . .

Teaching children is always interesting whether in a private or public school. From the B.Y.A., I came to the schools of Salt Lake City, where under that able educator and gentleman, Dr. J. F. Millspaugh, who was then superintendent, I worked at a salary of $100 per month, which seemed a fortune to me. Professor William M. Stewart had offered me a position in the Training School at the University of Utah, but I felt that I had served my time in teacher-training work.

The Salt Lake City schools were then operating under a board of education which was anti-Mormon, and which a few years previously had reorganized the school system and eliminated practically all Latter-day Saint teachers, and had imported teachers from the outside to take their places. When I began teaching here in 1894, there were only a few Latter-day Saint teachers in the entire city. What a blessing that much of the prejudice against the Mormons has been overcome! I heard Anna Garlin Spencer, a brilliant American woman, say in an address that prejudice should be classed with other destructive forces such as war, poverty, and disease. It was always a mystery to me why some people who were so antagonistic to the Mormons chose to live among them.

From *In Retrospect: Autobiography of Amy Brown Lyman* (1945)

3. Orson F. Whitney, "Home Literature"

Mormon culture has long been torn between autonomy and assimilation, a sense of chosenness and exceptionalism on the one hand, and the pain of exile and a desire to participate in larger American culture on the other. But the leadership has recurrently sounded the alarm when the distance between Zion and Babylon grew worryingly small. "The people must be kept where the finger of scorn can be pointed at them," urged President Brigham Young.⁵ With the coming of the railroad in 1869, Mormon Utah's period of isolation was over, and before two decades had passed, voices were suggesting that LDS distinctness was being engulfed in the contaminated waters of the world. Mormon women's leaders such as Emmeline B. Wells and Susa Young Gates led the way, both urging and modeling a resistance to "gentile" values and the production of a literature by and for Latter-day Saints. In 1888, Apostle Orson F. Whitney took up the cause and issued an agenda-setting challenge to create a "home literature" that would combine artistic merit with an inspired moral vision. It was the Mormon equivalent of Ralph Emerson's Phi Beta Kappa address, a moment of abrupt rupture with cultural forbears and an invitation to a new birth. The timing was propitious because in the year of Whitney's summons to Mormon greatness, American best-seller lists were dominated not by past greats like Emerson, Henry Thoreau, Walt Whitman, and Edgar Allan Poe but by low-brow celebrities Hall Caine, Marie Corelli, A. C. Gunter, and Mrs. Humphrey Ward. Nevertheless, the response to Orson Whitney's appeal was an avalanche of didactic and utterly unremarkable literature. The church would have to wait until World War II for the emergence of its first authors of national stature.

Seek ye out of the best books words of wisdom; seek learning even by study, and also by faith.

The words I have quoted are the words of the Prophet Joseph Smith; or rather, they are the words of the Almighty through him to this people. A people who are popularly supposed to be enemies of education, despisers of learning, haters of books and schools, and of everything, in fact, that is pure, ennobling and refined. A greater mistake was never made, a crueler wrong was never committed, a more heinous moral crime was never perpetrated than when the

"Mormon" people, the Church of Jesus Christ of Latter-day Saints, were thus made odious in the eyes of mankind.

For, if it be a crime to filch from an individual his good name, that "immediate jewel of the soul," compared with which, as the poet tells us, to steal one's purse is to "steal trash," what must it be to rob a whole community of reputation? A community, too, with such a mission as ours; the spiritual enlightenment of a world, the salvation of the human race, the education, for this life and the life which is to come, of all who can be persuaded to enter the garden of God and partake, freely, of the precious fruits of the Tree of Knowledge, which, in the truest sense, is also the Tree of Life. To rob such a people of their good name, thus limiting their usefulness, and hindering them from fulfilling their great mission, which is to draw all men unto Christ by means of knowledge, wisdom and learning revealed from heaven and recorded in the best of books, is indeed a crime, not only against the immediate victims of the slander, but a crime against God and humanity.

But it is not my present purpose to pursue the subject to which this train of thought would naturally lead. It suffices me to know, and to testify, that this people are the friends, not the foes, of education; that they are seekers after wisdom, lovers of light and truth, universal Truth, which, like the waters of earth, or the sunbeams of heaven, has but one Source, let its earthly origin be what it may.

> Truth is truth, wher'er 'tis found,
> On Christian or on heathen ground.

And worthy of our love and admiration, whether far or near, high or low, whether blazing as a star in the blue vault of heaven, or springing like a floweret from the soil.

"Seek ye out of the best books words of wisdom; seek learning even by study, and also by faith."

Why did the Lord so instruct His Prophet? Why did the Prophet so teach his people? It was because God had designed, and His Prophet had foreseen a great and glorious future for that people. Chosen himself in weakness, so far as this world's wisdom was concerned, as a foundation stone of the mighty structure which is destined to tower heavenward, reflecting from its walls and glittering spires the splendors of eternity, he knew there must come a time, unless God, who cannot lie, had sworn falsely, when Zion, no longer the foot, but as the head, the glorious front of the world's civilization, would arise and shine "the joy of the whole earth"—the seat of learning, the source of wisdom, and the centre of political power, when side by side with pure Religion, would flourish Art and Science, her fair daughters; when music, poetry, painting, sculpture, oratory and the drama, rays of light from the same central sun, no longer refracted and discolored by the many-hued prisms of man's sensuality, would throw their white radiance full and direct upon the mirror-like glory of her towers; when the science of earth and the wisdom of heaven would walk hand in hand interpreting each other; when philosophy would drink from wells of living truth, no longer draining the deadly hemlock of error, to poison the pure air with the illusions of sophistry; when love and union would prevail; when war would sit at the feet of peace and learn wisdom for a thousand years; when Zion's sons and Zion's daughters, as famed for intelligence and culture as for purity, truth and beauty, "polished after the similitude of a palace," would entertain kings and nobles, yea, sit upon thrones themselves, or go forth, like shafts of light from the bow of the Almighty, as messengers and ambassadors to the nations.

Joseph saw all this; he knew it was inevitable; that such things were but the natural flowers and fruits of the work which God had planted. The roots of the tree might not show it so well—their mission is to lie hidden in the earth despised and trampled on of men—but the branches in a day to come would prove it. Joseph knew, as every philosopher must know, that purity is the natural parent of beauty; that truth is the well-spring of power, and righteousness the sun of supremacy. He knew that his people must progress, that their destiny demanded it; that culture is the duty of man, as intelligence is the glory of God. Rough and rugged himself, as the granite boulders of yonder hills, typical of the firm, unyielding basis of God's work, he knew, and his brethren around him knew, that on the rough, strong stones of which they were symbolical—the massive foundations of the past—the great Architect would rear the superstructure of the future; that the youth of Israel, their offspring, would be inspired to build upon the foundations of the fathers, and yet would differ from their fathers and mothers, as the foundations of a building must differ from the walls and spires.

What shall I say, my young brethren and sisters, what can I say to awaken in your hearts, if perchance it sleeps, the desire to realize this glorious anticipation? Alas! what can my poor pen indite, what can my feeble tongue utter to rouse within you this determination? I can only call upon God, in humility, to make my words as sparks of fire, to fall upon the tinder of your hearts and kindle them into flame. That from this hour your souls may be lit up with the light of your glorious destiny, that you may live and labor for God and His kingdom, not simply for yourselves and the perishable things of earth.

What else shall make us worthy of such a future? What are we here for? Why did we come? Was it to waste our time in folly and dissipation, to laugh away our lives, pursuing the phantom of pleasure as an idle boy might chase a butterfly from flower to flower? Was it to bow down to mammon, to worship a golden calf, or stain our souls, and blur the brightness of our minds, with the vices of the ungodly? Was this what our fathers and mothers foresaw? Was it for this they sacrificed and suffered, to bring us into existence, teach us the truths of heaven, and place us on the threshold of the mightiest mission ever given to men in the flesh?

The answer falls like a thunderbolt from heaven: "I give not unto you to live after the manner of the world." It echoes down the corridors of years: "If ye are Abraham's children, ye will do the works of Abraham." It speaks from earth, from air, from the roaring waters; it sounds from the depths of the oracular soul: "YE ARE AN EXAMPLE TO THE WORLD; FOLLOW NOT AFTER THEM!"

But what has all this to do with literature? you ask. More, perhaps, than is at first apparent. It is by means of literature that much of this great work will have to be accomplished; a literature of power and purity, worthy of such a work. And a pure and powerful literature can only proceed from a pure and powerful people. Grapes are not gathered of thorns, nor figs of thistles.

I am not here, my friends, to tickle your ears with tinkling phrases, to deliver a learned lecture on Greek and Roman mythology; to quote Hebrew and Latin, and stun you with sound, and bewilder you with a pedantic display of erudition. No! Experience has taught me that it is the heart, not simply the head, we must appeal to, if we wish to stir the soul. The intellect may shine, but it is the bosom that burns, and warms into life every movement that is born to bless humanity. I, therefore, speak to your hearts, and I would rather say three words by the power of the Holy Ghost than lecture here for three hours on the fables of Greece and Rome.

Wake up! ye sons and daughters of God! Trim your lamps and go forth to meet your destiny. A world awaits you; rich and poor, high and low, learned and unlearned. All must be preached to; all must be sought after; all must be left without excuse. And whither we cannot go, we must send; where we cannot speak we must write; and in order to win men with our writings we must know how and what to write. If the learned will only listen to the learned, God will send them learned men, to meet them on their own ground, and show them that "Mormonism," the Gospel of Christ, is not only the Gospel of truth, but the Gospel of intelligence and culture. The Lord is not above doing this. He is merciful to all men, not willing that any should perish, or have it to say they were unfairly dealt with. For over fifty years the Gospel has been preached to the poor and lowly. It will yet go to the high and mighty, even to kings and nobles, and penetrate and climb to places hitherto deemed inaccessible.

Our literature will help to take it there; for this, like all else with which we have to do, must be made subservient to the building up of Zion.

But remember this, ye writers and orators of the future! It is for God's glory, not man's. Let not vanity and pride possess you. Without humility there is no power. You must be in earnest. You must feel what you write, if you wish it to be felt by others. If the words you speak are not as red-hot embers from the flaming forge of a sincere and earnest soul, they will never set on fire the souls of your hearers. The days of buncombe and bombast are over. Over? They never had a beginning. Nothing really is that is not founded on fact.

"Seek ye out of the best books, words of wisdom; seek learning, even by study, and also by faith."

The advantages of learning over ignorance are so self-evident as to need no dissertation. Knowledge is power, in this world or in any other. The prophet Joseph is authority for the saying that "a man is saved no faster than he gets knowledge"; that "it is impossible for a man to be saved in ignorance"; "for," says he, "if he does not get knowledge, he will be brought into captivity by some evil power in the other world, as evil spirits will have more knowledge and consequently more power, than many men who are on the earth." The Prophet also says that whatever principles of intelligence we attain to in this life, they will rise with us in the resurrection; and if one soul by its diligence and faithfulness acquires more knowledge, than another, it will have just so much advantage in the world to come.

How little then they know of "Mormonism," who say and think it is opposed to education. "With all thy getting, get understanding" is no less a part of the "Mormon" creed than it is one of the pearls of the wisdom of Solomon.

"Seek learning, even by study, and also by faith."

The formation of a home literature is directly in the line and spirit of this injunction. Literature means learning, and it is from the "best books" we are told to seek it. This does not merely mean the Bible, the Book of Mormon, the book of Doctrine and Covenants, Church works and religious writings—though these indeed are "the best books," and will ever be included in and lie at the very basis of our literature. But it also means history, poetry, philosophy, art and science, languages, government—all truth in fact, wherever found, either local or general, and relating to times past, present or to come.

Yes, the Prophet even meant revelation, inspiration, immediate and direct; for does he not say, "seek learning by study, and also by faith?" Faith points to futurity, to things that will be; study pertains more to the past, to things that have been. History is temporal, prophecy is spiritual. The past is great, but the future will be greater. The dead letter may be precious, but the living oracle is beyond all price.

It is from the warp and woof of all learning, so far as we are able to master it and make it ours, that the fabric of our literature must be woven. We must read, and think, and feel, and pray, and then bring forth our thoughts, and polish and preserve them. This will make literature.

Above all things, we must be original. The Holy Ghost is the genius of "Mormon" literature. Not Jupiter, nor Mars, Minerva, nor Mercury. No fabled gods and goddesses; no Mount Olympus; no "sisters nine," no "blue-eyed maid of heaven"; no invoking of mythical muses that "did never yet one mortal song inspire." No pouring of new wine into old bottles. No patterning after the dead forms of antiquity. Our literature must live and breathe for itself. Our mission is diverse from all others; our literature must also be. The odes of Anacreon, the satires of Horace and Juvenal, the epics of Homer, Virgil, Dante and Milton; the sublime tragedies of Shakespeare; these are all excellent, all well enough in their way; but we must not attempt to copy them. They cannot be reproduced. We may read, we may gather sweets from all these flowers, but we must build our own hive and honeycomb after God's supreme design.

We will yet have Miltons and Shakespeares of our own. God's ammunition is not exhausted. His brightest spirits are held in reserve for the latter times. In God's name and by His help we will build up a literature whose top shall touch heaven, though its foundations may now be low in earth. Let the smile of derision wreathe the face of scorn; let the frown of hatred darken the brow of bigotry. Small things are the seeds of great things, and, like the acorn that brings forth the oak, or the snow-flake that forms the avalanche, God's kingdom will grow, and on wings of light and power soar to the summit of its destiny.

From *Contributor* (1888)

4. Editors, "Vocational Education"

In the early twentieth century, as industrialization galloped ahead, American education adapted by incorporating vocational tracks. Taking stock of an increasingly complex economy, this Mormon author is careful to applaud both manual and "non-productive" vocations, while raising subtle concerns and offering counsel that is strikingly progressive for a 1921 document. What are now called "white collar" professions are presented as a dangerous temptation for those attracted by a path to labor-free, easy money. Also striking is the author's awareness of the cost of national transformation from an agrarian to an industrial society: "In recent times our economic structure requires that the multitude live from the production of the few. It can result ultimately in nothing short of social disaster." The warning is reminiscent of the Romantic critique of technology first made by Rousseau, that is, that by relying upon specialized labor, we sacrifice self-sufficiency and court vulnerability. This concern has special resonance with a people commanded to be organized, according to Joseph Smith, so "that the brethren might eventually be independent of every encumbrance beneath the celestial kingdom."⁶ In the 1860s and 1870s, Brigham Young emphasized economic self-sufficiency as one means of establishing and safeguarding their overall religious and cultural autonomy in Utah, and self-reliance and self-sufficiency are watchwords of today's church welfare policy. Finally, this document reveals that even as Latter-day Saints have long emphasized traditional gender roles in family organization, women are encouraged to make their economic reliance on the husband a choice and not a necessity.

What is vocation? Whether it be making or mending shoes, setting broken bones, growing vegetables for the market, or preparing them for the dinner table; each type of work to be worth the name vocation, must serve a real need in our complex civilization. Society itself has determined that making alcoholic beverages is not a social need; it is, therefore, forbidden as a vocation. Because producing and preparing food and the mechanical trades do serve essential, basic needs, professional training of young people in these vocations is fostered by federal government appropriations and carried on by the states.

The tendency at this time is to over-crowd the non-productive vocations, especially in cities. The term non-productive is used here in reference to material production, such as agriculture, mining and manufacturing. There are, of course, many other forms of service equally honorable, and necessary to the life of a civilized community. Occupations having to do with transportation and distribution of goods require the services of a relatively large percentage of the population. In the more distinctly professional lines of work the percentage is smaller. The professions of nurse and teacher are not usually over-crowded. If either should become so the remedy lies in raising the standards of qualification in these vocations. The regular M.D. medical course is now too long, difficult and expensive to be readily over-crowded. This is not so true of law; this profession is especially liable to over-crowding now that so many young men have opportunities to complete a college course.

The greatest difficulty, however, is likely to be in non-productive vocations to which almost anybody of fair education and ability can be admitted. This group of vocations includes real estate, insurance, stock brokerage and others of like nature. To be of real service to the public persons who engage in these vocations should be professionally trained in the business. It happens now that many young men without vocational training of any sort, but with more affinity for easy money than for manual labor, just fall into one of these vocations and work it for all they can get out of it, with little or no regard for the public good. This is not said in condemnation of these vocations, but in their defense; they are an easy prey to the get-rich-quick and get-it-easy despoiler of his fellowmen.

The wise selection of a vocation and proper vocational training are among the most serious problems that confront the modern youth. They have generally received too little attention from parents, teachers, and community leaders. Wise decisions in these matters concerning not only the future usefulness and happiness of individuals, but also the stability and prosperity of the nation. In recent times our economic structure requires that the multitude live from the production of the few. It can result ultimately in nothing short of social disaster.

Sometime between the ages of fifteen and twenty years every youth, whether boy or girl, should give serious thought to qualifying for service in a vocation. The problem cannot be solved at one stroke. It may require several years of study and observation, wise counsel, and experimentation before a youth finds himself. He must discover his own abilities and interests and mould these to fit social needs. In any case he is likely to become more serious minded and more efficient through having a vocational purpose, even though he may later change his purpose.

A youth often fancies he wants to qualify in a profession of which he has but a surface knowledge. Better acquaintance with the work may reverse his opinion. He must learn, in part at least, by his own experiences, but he should be taught also to profit by the experiences of others, and his observation of the work others are doing.

Every girl should have ambition to qualify in two vocations—that of home making, and that of earning a living by other means whenever occasion requires. An unmarried woman is always happier when following a vocation in which she can be socially serviceable and financially independent. In no case should she be considered to accept an unworthy companion as a means of support. Any married woman may become a widow at any time; property may vanish as readily as husbands may die. Thus any woman may be under the necessity of earning her own living and helping to support dependents. Why should not she be trained for the duties and the emergencies of life?

From *Relief Society Magazine* (1921)

5. Juanita Brooks, "To Columbia"

Only in the early twentieth century did the church finally find a peaceful accommodation with America. Latter-day Saints began to end the practice of plural marriage in 1890, but three years later, at the 1893 World's Parliament of Religion, they were distinguished by being the only religious group banned from representation in a gathering that reached out to virtually all Christian denominations and nine other world religions. Even after statehood was at last accorded Utah in 1896, the U.S. Congress delayed three years before seating Utah's legally elected Senator Reed Smoot, a Mormon apostle, in 1907. Just over two decades later, Juanita Brooks was a thirty-year-old widow teaching English at the church-run Dixie Junior College in St. George, Utah. Previous to this decade, it was highly unusual for Latter-day Saints—especially those in the church's educational system—to venture east for further educational opportunities. Brigham Young University tried sending several professors to Chicago's Divinity School but halted the practice when they returned with critical perspectives church leaders found more harmful than helpful. When Brooks was offered a sabbatical opportunity in 1928, she immediately accepted and made plans to obtain a master's degree at Columbia University. Her experiences as a new arrival at the New York City campus capture moments of cultural contact and interaction that could be as disconcerting to the Utah Mormon as they were to her eastern hosts. The same adventuresome, independent streak that led Brooks to her Ivy League sojourn would later lead her to a momentous intellectual odyssey. She was one of the earliest Mormon historians to tell the difficult story of the infamous Mountain Meadows Massacre, when Mormon militiamen and Paiutes murdered more than a hundred immigrants in 1857. At a time when Latter-day Saints were still leery of fully opening their archives—and their past—to even faithful eyes, Brooks aroused antipathy from fellow church members and was unofficially blacklisted in her southern Utah LDS community. She thus went from marginalized Mormon in American culture to marginalized Mormon in her own.

I don't remember the date, but it was early in the spring of 1928 at a regular Monday morning faculty meeting. We met in a classroom adjoining the president's office, and I came in with a chew of squawbush gum in my mouth. For all my scorn of gum and my insistence that students should not chew gum in class, I had not been able to resist this, the result of an afternoon hour along the Santa Clara Creek. I knew that I would discard the gum before class, but had neglected to spit it out as I passed the wastepaper basket.

I had hardly taken my seat before Art Paxman began to sniff the air. "Squawbush gum!" he said. "Who's got squawbush gum?"

I glued my mouth shut, determined not to open it until I got out of there. I knew the odor was pleasant—pungent and different—and evidence that someone had spent some time gathering it. The gum was really not important except that I was embarrassed to have the attention focused on me.

Near the close of the hour President Nicholes announced that the board had consented to give one sabbatical leave each year. This would enable a teacher to take a year off for study on half pay, and come back with a raise in salary the following fall.

Brother Arthur K. Hafen had been longest in service here. Would he care to accept this offer?

"I couldn't possibly leave for a full year," Arthur K. said. "My family is large. I cannot take them and I cannot leave them. The older boys are at an age where it is hard for my wife to manage them, and her health is poor."

Next in seniority was H. L. Reid, who declined for the same reason. One or two others were named, but each only shook his head. President Nicholes turned to me.

"Don't look at me," I said. "I'll take it so quick it'll make your head swim."

"I move we give her a hand," Art Paxman said, "and have her explain how come she is here at this hour chewing squawbush gum. You know, of course, that young squaws gather and chew it as a mating bait. Big medicine for them—squawbush gum!"

Everybody laughed, the first bell rang for opening classes, and the meeting was dismissed. I very quickly disposed of the telltale gum and went about my regular classes.

I had given no thought to this possibility, but I knew exactly what I would do: I would go to Columbia University! Later I was often asked why I should choose to go all the way across the continent when I could as easily get a Master's at BYU or the University of Utah, or even at the University of California at Berkeley. I answered that I had always wanted to see the Statue of Liberty and to visit the New England area, and Boston. I wanted to see the homes and surroundings of the writers: Thoreau's Walden Pond, Emerson's, yes, and Louisa M. Alcott's home. Basically, though, it was because of Miss Mina Connell. If Columbia University had been good enough for my Normal Training Course instructor, it would do for me.

I didn't worry about the money, either. I knew that I had enough in savings to take me across the continent and to Columbia, and on $85 a month I could manage.

As I looked through the literature which came in answer to my written request, I was more certain than ever that I was doing the right thing. I would cross the continent on a Pullman Flyer, like the one that had given me such a fright in Moapa years before, and there would surely be adequate housing.

I traveled light: two medium-sized suitcases and a spacious purse held all my necessities. I boarded the train at Modena and arrived in the evening of the second day. We pulled into the underground station and unloaded. I went to the information desk and told a lady that I had come to go to Columbia University, and would like to secure living quarters within walking distance, if possible.

She made a telephone call, and directed me to the Morningside Residence Club, a home for women on the campus. In a very short time I had arrived, signed up and left my check, and was directed to a room on the seventh floor, facing north and east. It was very nice; I could tell even before I turned on the light.

Then I walked across the room, and opened my window to view the scene outside. Instantly a carillon in a nearby church began to play:

Lead, Kindly Light, amid the encircling Gloom,
Lead thou me on!
The night is dark, and I am far from home—
Lead thou me on!
Keep Thou my feet, I do not ask to see
The distant scene—one step enough for me.

This seemed directed at me, especially played for my benefit. At any rate it gave me a new feeling of security, of being right where I should be, and an assurance that things were really working out. From this time on, I tried to be at home every night in time for vespers. They became my private worship.

The next morning I was up and out early, eager to visit the campus. The bookstore was open, so I purchased a notebook, pencils, and a small guidebook covering not only the campus, but the whole area. The young man, seeing that I was from Utah, asked about my home town and background. He was Harold Bentley! Little could he guess how much I knew about him from his little girl friend, my former classmate at BYU.

Yes, Verna was here; she would get her Bachelor's degree in the spring, when he would get his Ph.D., and I hoped to get my Master's.

Verna later seemed happy to meet me, too. They had hoped to find someone to sit with their baby girl two or three hours a week, which I would be glad to do. I was more than happy to have met Hal, for he advised me to take my degree through the University instead of the Teachers' College. I was not interested in training teachers; my business was to teach college students. I learned the time and place for the initiation meeting for potential Master's degree candidates. Here we were told that there would be no record of our activities; we could attend such classes as we cared to; we would work at our own time and pace; we must just pass that final examination. One thing more: we must prepare a written study, a research paper under the direction of a graduate dean, who would work with a group not to exceed twenty students. His grade would be important, but not so important as that of the final test.

Soon after I arrived, the management announced that they were holding open house as a way of helping their people become acquainted, and urged us all to attend. I had not yet spoken to a soul in the building, nor had anyone spoken to me. So I dressed up as well as I could and went to the reception room, where chairs were set up in groups and rows, with a long table filled with plates of cookies and dainties, and at the end coffee, tea, postum, and several cold beverages. Not many had arrived when I served myself and sat in the second row near the center of the room.

Two well-dressed ladies followed soon after and filled in just in front of me. They seemed to be important; at least they were carrying on a lively conversation and greeted most of the others scattered about as if they were well-known.

"I heard the greatest joke the other day," one said to the other. "Doctor Blank told me that there was a Mormon in her department who was going out for his Ph.D. Can you imagine a Mormon getting a Ph.D.?" And they both laughed heartily.

What should I do? Should I sit and hear my people ridiculed and not say a word? And yet, I knew that I would have no influence here; I would be a reason for all the more ridicule. So I sweated it out and waited, as I was prompted to do.

"Oh, Dr. Somebody," one of them called out to another mature lady as she finished filling her plate. "Come over here and sit with us. Dr. Blank here has just told me the greatest joke. There is a Mormon in her department who is going out for his Ph.D.!"

"Where have you girls been? I know many Mormons who have Ph.D.'s. On our faculty some of our best teachers are Mormons. Dr. Lew Winsor and Dr. Keith Seegmiller are well-known in Cornell. And this man with the Bell Telephone laboratories, Harvey Fletcher, is a Mormon. They say he fills his ranks with University of Utah graduates, and they are getting too great a stronghold."

I returned my empty dishes to their place and left without having met a single person, but my heart was warm with the knowledge that someone else had spoken better for me than I could have spoken for myself. . . .

One of the girls who lived in the apartment house had come to be a speaking acquaintance, though we never said more than a good morning. Then she came to look me up. Would I like to go to the Alumni Banquet of the Naval Military Academy? No, I don't really know where it was held, and I had no reason to want to go. But it seemed very important to her. Her escort was bringing a friend along, and she must supply a date for him. I protested that I had no appropriate clothes. She would rent an outfit for me, and I could help select it. So she brought several dresses, and rigged me out with a wrap and shoes as well, so that I looked like any other girl going to a dance—any other plain girl, that is.

We went together in a cab, and found a place at a round table with an extra man and one other couple quite a distance from the speaker's stand. Everyone seemed in high spirits. When the band played "The Bells of St. Mary's," most of them kept the time with their spoon and glass, while many joined in singing the chorus.

Soon my escort drew a flask from his pocket and started pouring out the drinks. I had no idea what it was, but I knew that I must not drink it. Of course, I should have kept silent and pretended. But I didn't. When the glass was a little over half-full I held up my hand and said, "Whoa!"

A thunderbolt from heaven could not have created more of a sensation. His mouth dropped open; his hand froze in the air. After a pause, he set the bottle down.

"What did you say?" he asked, slowly and distinctly.

"I said 'Whoa,'" I answered. "That is a perfectly good word. It means *enough, cease, stop, desist, thank you.*"

"Smells like a barn to me," he said shortly. "What do you know about horses?"

"Well, I own a little bay mare of my own."

"Bay is not a color. It is a body of water almost surrounded by land."

"It is a color of a horse. There are sorrels and blacks, and dappled, but bays are most common."

His evening was ruined. He took his drink at a gulp and poured another. I don't remember what we ate. I remember only that the crowd became so noisy that the chairman rapped again and again for order, but no one paid any attention, and the speaker sat down. Some dance music was playing not far away as we got up from the table. The other two couples went over to dance, but my escort sprawled on a couch as though he had literally passed out. I walked to the ladies' room, and wandered about a little before I settled in a chair. My friends didn't dance long; they had also had more liquor than they could handle.

So we left my escort where he was, and got a taxi to take us home. We rode in silence most of the way—there seemed nothing to say to each other. I got out first and walked on toward the door; my friends followed after they had paid the driver. The girl missed her step as she reached the curb, and fell, in all her finery, into the gutter—or onto the pavement. Her escort seemed unable to give much assistance, but the cab driver came and got them onto their feet and headed toward the door. I paused a little before I went in, stopped a minute or two inside, and then opened the door a crack to look out. They were locked in a tight embrace in the corner.

The next morning I put my outfit back into its box, wrapped and tied it, and left it at the desk downstairs to be delivered to the girl who had ordered it. I did not see her again.

I remember the whole incident with a sense of embarrassment and shame. I wonder if, after the fatal "Whoa!" was out, I had smiled and said "Forgive me, please. That's plenty, thank you," perhaps we could have passed it off and found a subject for discussion which was more fitting to the occasion.

From *Quicksand and Cactus: A Memoir of the Southern Mormon Frontier* (1982)

6. Eugene England, "The Possibility of Dialogue: A Personal View"

Like all faith organizations, the church works to effect a fruitful synthesis of faith and reason and of community-mindedness and independent thought. Tensions can be especially acute in these areas, given a hierarchy every bit as stratified as the Catholic Church, and conditions for self-direction (lay priesthood, personal revelation, scripture fluency) as pronounced as in any Protestant tradition. But the church prophet has more sway with Latter-day Saints than the pope has with Catholics; combined with a pervasive rhetoric of certainty peculiar to Mormon expressions of faith, doubt and dissent become especially marginalized in almost any form. Eugene England was a leading LDS mediator of these centrifugal forces during the late twentieth century. He worked for a more expansive conception of the church, one that would accommodate the faithful, the faithless, and the searching within the tent of a Mormon culture that he saw as larger than any set of orthodox creedal statements. Passionate in his faith, England was also relentless in his questioning and in his life and essays modeled possibilities to unite the spirit and intellect. The word dialogue, *which unifies the piece below, reflected his ideal of the faithful life as an ongoing conversation and became the name of the journal he co-founded in 1966.* Dialogue: A Journal of Mormon Thought *continues to serve as a forum for Latter-day Saints seeking freely to question Mormon orthodoxy in the theology, historiography, and culture. When another journal for Mormon intellectuals launched in 1975, intending the "free and frank exploration of gospel truths as they relate to the complexities of today's society" (Sunstone description), Eugene England wrote the editors expressing mild disappointment in his own journal's failure to succor "those who face special problems in developing their faith" and cautioning the new periodical's board to "put your loyalty to this work of saving souls above everything, above your own prestige and ambitions, your academic standards."⁷*

Prove all things; hold fast that which is good.

—Paul the Apostle

The paradoxical words of Paul quoted above are an obvious place to begin to consider the possibilities of dialogue about a Christian religion and its cultural heritage. The words are familiar to our time. "Examine. Test. Prove." The demand for reevaluation and for proof and the pressure toward thoroughgoing skepticism continue in our universities and mount in our society generally. The voices against dogmatism (especially religious dogmatism) grow in the land. And here is Paul, who brought Christianity to the Western world, speaking the same words. "Prove all things": consider all things; look at all possibilities; examine your inherited prejudices and evaluate again even your cherished beliefs; be open to what might be a new understanding—a new faith.

But, of course, Paul was no mere skeptic. The Christian apostle would have us give our searching a meaning, not allow it to serve as an easy posture. He also said, "Hold fast that which is good": respect certitude as well as doubt; commit yourself to the good you find; give yourself to the possibilities that begin to prove out; live the faith that is given you in your seeking—however deeply you continue to test that faith and examine others.

A Book of Mormon prophet named Alma understood this paradox. He knew that "faith is not to have a perfect knowledge" but is a willingness to "experiment" in new realms, to give place in our hearts for new words and not cast them out prematurely with our unbelief. He knew what it is to prove and also hold—to be open to seeds of potential meaning and being, continually both to test and to nourish them (because they can only be properly tested if nourished) until the good seeds produce fruit that is "most precious" (see Alma 32:27–42).

Paul's challenge and Alma's experiment have been deeply significant to my own experience of the possibilities of life and to my faith in the process of dialogue as a way to discover life's possibilities. I have tasted the precious fruit of faith in specific things; I have been able, in all my proving, to discover and to continue to hold some things fast as certainties—faith in the divinity of Christ and in the saving power of his teachings and Atonement, faith in the divine mission of his Church and his modern prophets—and the deep hunger of my soul has been fed as I have given myself to this faith. At the same time, I have sensed the risk of choice, the limitation of commitment to a defined context in this world that is full of richly complex possibilities and allows us only finite vision into their worth. Yet I have found that my very specific faith does not cut me off from this rich complexity; it actually intensifies and informs with meaning my involvement in it.

I am motivated, in my relationship to Christ and my desire to build his Kingdom, by both the questing openness and the loving authority exhibited in his life and in his revelations to his prophets. I think and act within a specific context of Mormon faith that defines my life and shapes my soul. I relate to my wife and children and friends and use my time in terms of the counsel of the Church and the heritage of Mormon experience. But my very grasp on this specific direction, this "iron rod," turns me out to all people and their experience in desire for dialogue with them. The very principles I accept as definitive of my life warn me to be continually open to the revelation of new possibilities for my life from both God and man.

My faith encourages my curiosity and awe; it thrusts me out into relationship with all the creation. The Christ I have come to know through my Mormon faith affirms the world as good and each of its people as eternally precious; he insists that my words and actions be integrated with each other and relevant to that world—that they not just speak to it but really make the connection. My faith in him encourages me to enter into dialogue.

Such a dialogue seems to me to depend on some initial commitment to values, to some beliefs that give a person a place from which to speak and a purpose for speaking. It can be engaged in best by those who hold fast that which is good. But such a dialogue depends also on willingness to prove all things. We must be willing to consider that anything we believe or base our lives upon may be a partial truth—at best something seen (as Saint Paul also said) "through a glass darkly"—or even may be dead wrong. We must take seriously the jovial words of the distinguished Mormon chemist, Henry Eyring, "In this Church we don't have to believe anything that isn't true."

A dialogue is possible if we can avoid looking upon doubt as a sin—or as a virtue—but can see it as a condition, a condition that can be productive if it leads one to seek and knock and ask and if the doubter is approached with sympathetic listening and thoughtful response or that can be destructive if it is used as an escape from responsibility or the doubter is approached with condemnation.

A dialogue is possible if, in trying to describe our findings and convictions, we can be honest with ourselves and each other, if we can use traditional forms and conventions without letting them become lies or idols. We must be witnesses for all that is real to us and no more, recognizing the eternal dignity of truth which gives it claim finally over expediency and even perhaps charity.

But a dialogue can realize its full possibilities only if there is charity, if we can speak with sensitivity to each other's framework or ability to hear and speak in order to communicate for each other's welfare, not to justify or exalt ourselves at each other's expense. We must truly listen to each other, respecting our essential brotherhood and the courage of those who try to speak, however they may differ from us in professional standing or religious belief or moral vision. We must speak and listen patiently, with good humor, with real expectation, and then our dialogue can serve both truth and charity.

Joseph Smith, one of the prophets to whom I give my faith, has recorded the voice of the Lord urging men to be "anxiously engaged in a good cause . . . and bring to pass much righteousness; for the power is in them, wherein they are agents unto themselves" (Doctrine and Covenants 58:27–28). I am motivated by my belief in that power and agency to test the possibilities that the journal we here begin can be successful in fostering many kinds of valuable dialogue. I am also motivated by partial agreement with Episcopal Bishop James A. Pike that "The church should be a launching pad and not a comfort station." (It should be both.) And I am motivated by the challenges to intelligent and creative discipleship made again and again by the leaders of the Church.

The faith I hold fast impels me to speak and to listen; it impels me to express honestly and fully and as gracefully as possible the convictions that shape my life, to try to demonstrate the things I find as I think and do research and experience the holy. It impels me to listen carefully and always. My faith as a Mormon encourages by specific doctrines my feeling that each man is eternally unique and god-like in potential, that each man deserves a hearing and that we have something important to learn from each man if we can hear him—if he can speak and we can listen well. Dialogue is possible to those who can. Such a dialogue will not solve all of our intellectual and spiritual problems—and it will not save us; but it can bring us joy and new vision and help us toward that dialogue with our deepest selves and with our God which can save us.

From *Dialogue: A Journal of Mormon Thought* (1966)

7. Richard D. Poll, "What the Church Means to People Like Me"

In Fyodor Dostoevsky's famous Grand Inquisitor episode, the aged cardinal lectures a returned Jesus Christ that churchmen "have vanquished freedom and have done so to make men happy . . . we are ready to endure the freedom which they have found so dreadful." Authoritarian religion always runs the risks of making its adherents into passive beings. "When our leaders speak, the thinking has been done," wrote an LDS editor in an official publication.[8] President George Albert Smith subsequently repudiated the message as "an embarrassment" inconsistent with church teachings.[9] But its publication reflects one extreme of the authority/ individual seesaw in Mormon culture. Latter-day Saints are enjoined by scripture to accept the prophet's words "as if from mine own mouth" (Doctrine and Covenants 21). Yet even the autocratic President Brigham Young was "afraid that this people have so much confidence in their leaders that they will not inquire for themselves of God whether they are led by him. I am fearful that they settle down in a state of blind self-security, trusting their eternal destiny in the hands of their leaders with a reckless confidence that in itself would thwart the purposes of God."[10] "I know not save the Lord commanded me," says an obedient Adam when queried on the reasons for his sacrifice (Moses 5:6); "I want the liberty of thinking and believing as I please. It feels so good not to be trammeled," said the freethinking Joseph Smith.[11] Mormon culture embraces both polarities, often in opposition rather than synthesis. Historian Richard Poll finds in the Book of Mormon apt symbols of the twin faces of the LDS attitude toward spiritual commitment: the iron rod, to which the faithful cling, and the brass compass, which requires personal initiative for its working. The symbols have become part of Mormon cultural vocabulary.

My thesis is that there are two distinct types of active and dedicated Latter-day Saints. I am not talking about "good Mormons" and "Jack Mormons," or about

Saints in white hats and pseudo-Saints in black. No, I am talking about two types of involved Church members who are here tonight, each deeply committed to the Gospel but also prone toward misgivings about the legitimacy, adequacy, or serviceability of the commitment of the other.

The purpose of my inquiry is not to support either set of misgivings, but to describe each type as dispassionately as I can, to identify myself with one of the types, and then to bear witness concerning some of the blessings which the Church offers to the type I identify with. My prayer is that this effort will help us all to look beyond the things which obviously differentiate us toward that "unity of the faith" which Christ set as our common goal.

For convenience of reference, let me propose symbols for my two types of Mormons. They have necessarily to be affirmative images, because I am talking only about "good" members. I found them in the Book of Mormon, a natural place for a Latter-day Saint to find good symbols as well as good counsel.

The figure for the first type comes from Lehi's dream—the Iron Rod. The figure for the second comes also from Lehi's experience—the Liahona. So similar they are as manifestations of God's concern for his children, yet just different enough to suit my purposes tonight.

The Iron Rod, as the hymn reminds us, was the Word of God. To the person with his hand on the rod, each step of the journey to the tree of life was plainly defined; he had only to hold on as he moved forward. In Lehi's dream the way was not easy, but it was clear.

The Liahona, in contrast, was a compass. It pointed to the destination but did not fully mark the path; indeed, the clarity of its directions varied with the circumstances of the user. For Lehi's family the sacred instrument was a reminder of their temporal and eternal goals, but it was no infallible delineator of their course.

Even as the Iron Rod and the Liahona were both approaches to the word of God and to the kingdom of God, so our two types of members seek the word and the kingdom. The fundamental difference between them lies in their concept of the relation of man to the "word of God." Put another way, it is a difference in the meaning assigned to the concept "the fulness of the Gospel." Do the revelations of our Heavenly Father give us a handrail to the kingdom, or a compass only?

The Iron Rod Saint does not look for questions, but for answers, and in the Gospel—as he understands it—he finds or is confident that he can find the answer to every important question. The Liahona Saint, on the other hand, is preoccupied with questions and skeptical of answers; he finds in the Gospel—as he understands it—answers to enough important questions so that he can function purposefully without answers to the rest. This last sentence holds the key to the question posed by my title, but before pursuing its implications let us explore our scheme of classification more fully.

As I suggested at the outset, I find Iron Rods and Liahonas in almost every L.D.S. congregation, discernible by the kinds of comments they make in Gospel Doctrine classes and the very language in which they phrase their testimonies. What gives them their original bent is difficult to identify. The Iron Rods may be somewhat more common among converts, but many nowadays are attracted to the Church by those reasons more appropriate to Liahonas which I will mention later on. Liahona testimonies may be more prevalent among born members who have not had an emotional conversion experience, but many such have developed Iron Rod commitments in the home, the Sunday School, the mission field, or some other conditioning environment. Social and economic status appear to have nothing to do with type, and the rather widely-held notion that education tends to produce Liahonas has so many exceptions that one may plausibly argue that education only makes Liahonas more articulate.

Parenthetically, some of the most prominent Iron Rods in the Church are on the B.Y.U. faculty.

Pre-existence may, I suppose, have something to do with placement in this classification, even as it may account for other life circumstances, but heredity obviously does not. The irritation of the Iron Rod father confronted by an iconoclastic son is about as commonplace as the embarrassment of the Liahona parent who discovers that his teen-age daughter has found comfortable answers in seminary to some of the questions that have perplexed him all his life.

The picture is complicated by the fact that changes of type do occur, often in response to profoundly unsettling personal experiences. The Liahona member who, in a context of despair or repentance, makes the "leap of faith" to Iron Rod commitment is rather rare, I think, but the investigator of Liahona temperament who becomes an Iron Rod convert is almost typical. The Iron Rod member who responds to personal tragedy or intellectual shock by becoming a Liahona is known to us all: this transition may be but is not necessarily a stage in a migration toward inactivity or even apostasy.

My present opinion is that one's identification with the Iron Rods or the Liahonas is more a function of basic temperament and of accidents than of pre-mortal accomplishments or mortal choices, but that opinion—like many other views expressed in this sermon—has neither scriptural nor scientific validation.

A point to underscore in terms of our objective of "unity of the faith" is that Iron Rods and Liahonas have great difficulty understanding each other—not at the level of intellectual acceptance of the right to peaceful co-existence, but at the level of personal communion, of empathy. To the Iron Rod a questioning attitude suggests an imperfect faith; to the Liahona an unquestioning spirit betokens a closed mind. Neither frequent association nor even prior personal involvement with the other group guarantees empathy. Indeed, the person who has crossed the line is likely to be least sympathetic and tolerant toward his erstwhile kindred spirits.

I have suggested that the essential difference between the Liahonas and the Iron Rods is in their approach to the concept "the word of God." Let us investigate that now a little.

The Iron Rod is confident that, on any question, the mind and will of the Lord may be obtained. His sources are threefold: Scripture, Prophetic Authority, and the Holy Spirit.

In the Standard Works of the Church the Iron Rod member finds far more answers than does his Liahona brother, because he accepts them as God's word in a far more literal sense. In them he finds answers to questions as diverse as the age and origin of the earth, the justification for capital punishment, the proper diet, the proper role of government, the nature and functions of sex, and the nature of man. To the Liahona, he sometimes seems to be reading things into the printed words, but to himself the meaning is clear.

In the pronouncements of the General Authorities, living and dead, the Iron Rod finds many answers, because he accepts and gives comprehensive application to that language of the Doctrine and Covenants which declares: "And whatsoever they shall speak when moved upon by the Holy Ghost shall be scripture, shall be the will of the Lord, shall be the mind of the Lord, shall be the word of the Lord, shall be the voice of the Lord, and the power of God unto salvation" (68:4). This reliance extends to every facet of life. On birth control and family planning, labor relations and race relations, the meaning of the Constitution and prospects for the United Nations, the laws of health and the signs of the times, the counsel of the "living oracles" suffices. Where answers are not found in the published record, they are sought in correspondence and interviews, and once received, they are accepted as definitive.

Third among the sources for the Iron Rod member is the Holy Spirit. As Joseph Smith found answers in the counsel of James, "If any of you lack wisdom, let him ask of God . . . ," so any Latter-day Saint may do so. Whether it be the choice of a vocation or the choice of a mate, help on a college examination or in finding "Golden Prospects" in the mission field, healing the sick or averting a divorce—in prayer is the answer. The response may not be what was expected, but it will come, and it will be a manifestation of the Holy Spirit.

Implicit in all this is the confidence of the Iron Rod Latter-day Saint that our Heavenly Father is intimately involved in the day-to-day business of His children. As no sparrow falls without the Father, so nothing befalls man without His will. God knows the answers to all questions and has the solutions to all problems, and the only thing which denies man access to this reservoir is his own stubbornness. Truly, then, the person who opens his mind and heart to the channels of revelation, past and present, has the iron rod which leads unerringly to the Kingdom.

The Liahona Latter-day Saint lacks this certain confidence. Not that he rejects the concepts upon which it rests—that God lives, that He loves His children, that His knowledge and power are efficacious for salvation, and that He does reveal His will as the Ninth Article of Faith affirms. Nor does he reserve the right of selective obedience to the will of God as he understands it. No, the problem for the Liahona involves the adequacy of the sources on which the Iron Rod testimony depends.

The problem is in perceiving the will of God when it is mediated—as it is for almost all mortals—by "the arm of flesh." The Liahona is convinced by logic and experience that no human instrument, even a prophet, is capable of transmitting the word of God so clearly and comprehensively that it can be universally understood and easily appropriated by man.

Because the Liahona finds it impossible to accept the literal verbal inspiration of the Standard Works, the sufficiency of scriptural answers to questions automatically comes into question. If Eve was not made from Adam's rib, how much of the Bible is historic truth? If geology and anthropology have undermined Bishop Ussher's chronology, which places creation at 4000 B.C., how much of the Bible is scientific truth? And if our latter-day scriptures have been significantly revised since their original publication, can it be assumed that they are now infallibly authoritative? To the Liahona these volumes are sources of inspiration and moral truth, but they leave many specific questions unanswered, or uncertainly answered.

As for the authority of the Latter-day prophets, the Liahona Saint finds consensus among them on Gospel fundamentals but far-ranging diversity on many important issues. The record shows error, as in Brigham Young's statements about the continuation of slavery, and it shows change of counsel, as in the matter of gathering to Zion. It shows differences of opinion—Heber J. Grant and Reed Smoot on the League of Nations, and David O. McKay and Joseph Fielding Smith on the process of creation. To the Liahonas, the "living oracles" are God's special witnesses of the Gospel of Christ and His agents in directing the affairs of the Church, but like the scriptures, they leave many important questions unanswered, or uncertainly answered.

The Iron Rod proposition that the Spirit will supply what the prophets have not gives difficulty on both philosophical and experimental grounds. Claims that prayer is an infallible, almost contractual, link between God and man through the Holy Spirit find Liahona Mormons perplexed by the nature of the evidence. As a method of confirming truth, the witness of the Spirit demonstrably has not produced uniformity of Gospel interpretation even among Iron Rod Saints, and it is allegedly by the witness of that same Spirit—by the burning within—that many apostates pronounce the whole Church in error. As a method of influencing the course of events, it seems unpredictable and some of the miracles claimed for it seem almost whimsical. By the prayer of faith one man recovers his lost eyeglasses; in spite of such prayer, another man goes blind.

All of which leaves the Liahona Mormon with a somewhat tenuous connection with the Holy Spirit. He may take comfort in his imperfect knowledge from that portion of the Article of Faith which says that "God will yet reveal many great and important things. . . ." And he may reconcile his conviction of God's love and his observation of the uncertain earthly outcomes of faith by emphasizing the divine commitment to the principle of free agency, as I shall presently do. In any case, it seems to the Liahona Mormon that God's involvement in day-to-day affairs must be less active and intimate than the Iron Rod Mormon believes, because there are so many unsolved problems and unanswered prayers.

Is the Iron Rod member unaware of these considerations which loom so large in the Liahona member's definition of his relationship to the word of God? In some instances, I believe, the answer is yes. For in our activity-centered Church it is quite possible to be deeply and satisfyingly involved without looking seriously at the philosophical implications of some Gospel propositions which are professed.

In many instances, however, the Iron Rod Saint has found sufficient answers to the Liahona questions. He sees so much basic consistency in the scriptures and the teachings of the latter-day prophets that the apparent errors and incongruities can be handled by interpretation. He finds so much evidence of the immanence of God in human affairs that the apparently pointless evil and injustice in the world can be handled by the valid assertion that God's ways are not man's ways. He is likely to credit his Liahona contemporaries with becoming so preoccupied with certain problems that they cannot see the Gospel forest for the trees, and he may even attribute that preoccupation to an insufficiency of faith.

As a Liahona, I must resist the attribution, though I cannot deny the preoccupation.

Both kinds of Mormons have problems. Not just the ordinary personal problems to which all flesh is heir, but problems growing out of the nature of their Church commitment.

The Iron Rod has a natural tendency to develop answers where none may, in fact, have been revealed. He may find arguments against social security in the Book of Mormon; he may discover in esoteric prophetic utterances a timetable for that Second Coming of which "that day and hour knoweth no man . . ." His dogmatism may become offensive to his peers in the Church and a barrier to communication with his own family; his confidence in his own insights may make him impatient with those whom he publicly sustains. He may also cling to cherished answers in the face of new revelation, or be so shaken by innovation that he forms new "fundamentalist" sects. The Iron Rod concept holds many firm in the Church, but it leads some out.

The Liahona, on the other hand, has the temptation to broaden the scope of his questioning until even the most clearly defined Church doctrines and policies are included. His resistance to statistics on principle may deteriorate into a carping criticism of programs and leaders. His ties to the Church may become so nebulous that he cannot communicate them to his children. His testimony may become so selective as to exclude him from some forms of Church activity or to make him a hypocrite in his own eyes as he participates in them. His persistence in doubting may alienate his brethren and eventually destroy the substance of his Gospel commitment. Then he, too, is out—without fireworks, but not without pain.

Both kinds of Latter-day Saints serve the Church. They talk differently and apparently think and feel differently about the Gospel, but as long as they avoid the extremes just mentioned, they share a love for and commitment to the Church. They cannot therefore be distinguished on the basis of attendance at meetings, or participation on welfare projects, or contributions, or faithfulness in the performance of callings. They may or may not be hundred percenters, but the degree of their activity is not a function of type, insofar as I have been able to observe. (It may be that Iron Rods are a little more faithful in genealogical work, but even this is not certain.)

Both kinds of members are found at every level of Church responsibility—in bishoprics and Relief Society presidencies, in stake presidencies and high councils, and even among the General Authorities. But whatever their private orientation, the public deportment of the General Authorities seems to me to represent a compromise, which would be natural in the circumstances. They satisfy the Iron Rods by emphasizing the solid core of revealed truth and discouraging speculative inquiry into matters of faith and morals, and they comfort the Liahonas by resisting the pressure to make pronouncements on all subjects and by reminding the Saints that God has not revealed the answer to every question or defined the response to every prayer.

As I have suggested, the Iron Rods and the Liahonas have some difficulty understanding each other. Lacking the patience, wisdom, breadth of experience, or depth of institutional commitment of the General Authorities, we sometimes criticize and judge each other. But usually we live and let live—each finding in the Church what meets his needs and all sharing the Gospel blessings which do not depend on identity of testimony.

From *Dialogue: A Journal of Mormon Thought* (1967)

8. Henry Eyring, "Science and Religion"

The church emerged at a historical moment when Baconianism was ascendant, that is, an Age of Jackson enthusiasm for the scientific method so rampant that even religion, if it was not to be discarded as a regressive affair of the heart, had to exhibit the scientist's regard for evidence, esteem for progress, and the same cool, rational embrace of sound reasoning. Early Mormon theologians such as Apostles Parley P. Pratt and Orson Pratt expounded and defended the church accordingly. Well into the twentieth century, the church found science, rationalism, even archaeology, to be allies in its quest for converts and validation. This changed abruptly in the 1950s, when Joseph Fielding Smith, Mormon apostle (and future church president) and prolific writer, characterized science and true religion as mutually hostile. The Church Educational System also retrenched in these years, emphasizing faith-affirming instruction over inquiry and intellectual curiosity. Highly respected Mormon scientists James E. Talmage and John A. Widtsoe were both apostles, but with their passing Joseph Fielding Smith had no counterweight in the apostolic quorum. Defense of the sciences, and of their compatibility with religious truth, fell largely upon the shoulders of one of the church's most prominent scientists. The theoretical chemist Henry Eyring was a Princeton professor, Wolf Prize and National Medal of Science winner, and president of the American Association for the Advancement of Science. He engaged Joseph Fielding Smith in civil debate on the subject of evolution and was influential in championing the church's official position of scientific openness and tolerance during a contentious era.

Once when I was speaking at the University of Utah as part of a panel on man in the cosmos, I built my talk around the famous question of Pontius Pilate, "What is truth?" After my talk, a young man in the audience stood up and said, "Well, Dr. Eyring, they tell me that what you do is put religion in one compartment and your science in another. Isn't that inconvenient? For instance, I want to propound a question to you. In the *Young Women's Journal,* Joseph Smith is reported to have said that people are living on the moon." He continued, "Now, Dr. Eyring, we know there is no oxygen on the moon, so that couldn't possibly be true. What do you say to this question?"

I answered about as follows: "I especially appreciate being asked that question, because it is easy to answer, and I like easy questions better than hard ones. As a Latter-day Saint, like any other honest man, I am obliged to accept only the truth. I simply have to investigate whether men live on the moon. I am reasonably certain they don't, but we'll soon know by direct exploration. If we don't find them there, they don't live there. As a Latter-day Saint, my problem is as simple as that.

"Many times men of importance have statements attributed to them they never made. I think that if J. Golden Kimball said all the things he is credited with saying, he would have had to talk even more than he did, and he did very well.

"Now what about the Prophet Joseph Smith? I don't know whether or not he said men live on the moon. But whether he did or not troubles me not in the least. A prophet is wonderful because he sometimes speaks for the Lord. This occurs on certain occasions when the Lord wills it. On other occasions, he speaks for himself, and one of the wonderful doctrines of this Church is that we don't believe in the infallibility of any mortal. If in his speculations the Prophet thought there were people on the moon, this has no effect on my belief that on other occasions, when the Lord willed it, he spoke the ideas that the Lord inspired him to say. It is for these moments of penetrating insight that I honor and follow him."

There is a further point that needs emphasis. The gospel is not the people in the Church. The gospel is not even the people who direct it. *The gospel is the truth.* One will have difficulty finding better men than we have presiding over the Church at present and than we have had in times past. Still, they are human beings, as we are.

Some people have pointed to some member of the Church and said, "Now, Dr. Eyring, that's one of your brethren, and he's not what he ought to be." My answer is this: "Well, you ought to see what he'd be like if it weren't for the Church." We have to keep firmly in mind at all times the two aspects of the Church: its divinely inspired perfect side, and its human side.

Perhaps I can say it another way. This Church would have been perfect if the Lord had not let people into it. That is where the mistake seems to have been made, but we understand this, too. The Church is part of the Lord's wonderful plan to work with you and me. Mankind is thus singled out because of man's divine origin and transcendent destiny.

I could leave the Church and abandon its teachings if I could figure out some way to do so honorably and consistent with my desire to know the truth, no matter what the source. I find myself unable to build out of my experience an acceptable case for disbelief. In fact, the case favors belief. It goes something like this:

1. The physical universe exhibits striking characteristics: the complexity of the nucleus, the exactness of the atom, the unity of life, the predictability of the everyday world, and the enormity and longevity of space.
2. Not only is the universe complex, exact, orderly, and predictable, but it is also running down. The second law of thermodynamics indicates that since a closed system can only run down and can never get wound up in the first place, either there are some exceptions to these natural laws we don't know about or the physical universe is not a closed system. That is, there is something or

someplace outside the physical world from which energy was obtained to fire the "big bang."

3. The combination of intelligence and power that assembled the materials and energy, set off the "big bang," and provided order, complexity, exactness, and precision in the physical universe is called the Creator, the Supreme Being, God, and so on.

4. As scientists believe that nature is not capricious, and therefore we can expect things we can't measure to behave in ways similar to things we can, it is reasonable to assume that the Creator's world is also a place of order, complexity, exactness, and precision. This is an example of the importance of postulates in science and religion. In order to seek to learn truths about the physical world we must *assume* some things we can't prove. (An example is uniformitarianism— the proposition that the rules as we now observe them were the same in the past and will be in the future and that therefore we can understand the past and predict the future based on what we observe now.) Similarly, in order to seek for truth in spiritual things, we must adopt some basic assumptions or postulates that also can't be proved.

5. Basic spiritual assumptions or postulates might include: (a) God exists; (b) God has curiosity and interest in what he has created; (c) God knows me; (d) God is at least as compassionate and just as the good people I know.

6. The truth of these postulates is determined by seeing if the results of "experiments" can be best predicted by their adoption. That is, as we experience life, study history, and seek communion with God, is what we find best explained by the acceptance of our postulates?

7. God is tolerant of our efforts. He's willing to have truth discovered "line upon line, precept upon precept." That is, he doesn't mind that we don't yet know everything about science, or religion.

8. The gospel is the truth. All truth is part of the gospel regardless of how the truth has been learned.

9. The safest course is to work like the dickens and do even more than is required to be done. That's the way I get the most freedom to maneuver.

10. Most important, the foregoing nine points don't answer *all* the questions. If I take everything I know from the scriptures and the prophets, and everything I know from science, and reconcile them, I still have as many unanswered questions as I have ones with answers. No intellectual approach nails down everything. In this life, there will always be unanswered questions. In fact, each answer seems to raise more questions. That's the way it is in science, too, and

I don't apostatize from science for that reason. Actually, that's what makes science, and religion, fun. Faith is feeling good about myself, feeling good about God, and muddling along after truth as best I can.

11. Finally, perhaps a believer never does more disservice to religion than to support the truth with bad arguments. The listener spots the obvious errors, becomes impatient, often "throws out the baby with the bath," and turns away, even from true religion.

As parents and teachers, we pass on to our children and pupils our world picture. Part of this picture is religious and part of it deals with the world around us. If we teach our pupils some outmoded and nonessential notions that fail to hold water when the students get into their science classes at the university, we run grave risks. When our protégés shed the bad science, they may also throw out some true religion. The solution is to avoid telling them the world is flat too long after it has been proved round. Don't defend a good cause with bad arguments.

So, I am certain that the gospel, as taught in The Church of Jesus Christ of Latter-day Saints, is true. It's a better explanation of what I observe in science than any other I know about. There are still lots of things I don't know, but that doesn't bother me. I'm a happy muddler. The gospel simply asks me to find out what's true as best I can and in the meantime to live a good life. That strikes me as the best formula for living there could be.

———————————

From *Reflections of a Scientist* (1983)

9. Marilyn Arnold, "Unlocking the Sacred Text"

With well over 150 million copies in print, the Book of Mormon is by far the most widely distributed book ever produced by an American. Yet its omission from surveys of American culture or religious history is indirectly explained by Catholic sociologist Thomas O'Dea's jest that "The Book of Mormon has not been universally considered by its critics as one of those books that must be read in order to have an opinion of it." The Book of Mormon is so shrouded in supernaturalism—angels, gold plates, and "holy interpreters"—that disputes over its purported origins and transmission have historically co-opted any interest in the text as a text. Latter-day Saints have perhaps unwittingly been complicit in this miscarriage, as they have long emphasized the record's importance as a manifestation of

Joseph Smith's prophetic calling. In other words, they have made its objective reality, rather than its theology, stories, or other textual content, the focus of attention. In recent years, an array of scholars from Jacob Neusner to Jan Shipps to Nathan Hatch to Daniel Walker Howe have chided theologians and historians for disregarding the book as a key to religious, cultural, or historical understanding of an era and a people. In the late twentieth and early twenty-first centuries, The University of Illinois, Penguin, Doubleday, and Yale have all published editions, facilitating its entry into college curricula. In this selection, novelist and Willa Cather specialist Marilyn Arnold makes a pitch for the Book of Mormon as a work of significant literary value and complexity.

Unlike the scientist of faith, who studies the work of the Creator every time he or she enters the laboratory or the field, the English teacher studies the product of the human mind, relentlessly pursuing meaning and delight in the written word. To the onlooker there may seem to be little connection between literary studies and religious faith; but to me there is an almost inseparable bond. In fact, it was not until I began to read sacred texts with the skills I had acquired in studying nonsacred texts that the eyes of my understanding truly began to open. Most assuredly, my training in literary analysis has enhanced my reading of scripture and my testimony of its divine origin.

Of the many hundreds of texts I have read, none has touched me more profoundly than the Book of Mormon. Without question, it is the greatest book I have ever encountered. The near-perfect blend of poetry and truth is, in my view, simply unequaled. I confess, however, that I have not always appreciated its greatness, and for too many years my reading was sporadic and merely dutiful. I knew that the Book of Mormon contained some splendid passages, but as a whole it had not grabbed me and shaken me into a realization of its unparalleled magnificence. Three things transformed the book for me, though it was not I that changed the book, but the book that changed me. The first transforming event was my decision to read the Book of Mormon in earnest, from cover to cover, investing the same concentrated energy that I would accord a complex and masterful literary text. The second transforming event grew out of the first: it was the decisive entrance of the Spirit into my study of the book, and hence into my life, with unprecedented intensity and constancy. The third transforming event also grew out of the first: it was the prayerful desire to experience the great change of heart described by King Benjamin and Alma, to be more than an "active Mormon," to be spiritually born as a child of Christ.

These three events, in concert, permanently transformed my inner life. They implanted in my soul an indescribable love of the Book of Mormon, of the gospel of Jesus Christ, and of his church. At the time this change was occurring, my friends may have recognized the same lengthy frame and the same silly grin they had always known, but I knew I was not the person they had charitably tolerated all those years. It was as if I harbored a sweet secret that I was too shy to talk about. I now wanted desperately to live more purely, to correct my innumerable character flaws, to abandon my sins. What happened to me during that period of intense study, prayer, and self-assessment remains with me still.

Since that time, I have undertaken a yet more concentrated study of the Book of Mormon, and with each reading it almost magically expands to meet my increased ability to comprehend it. Truly, this is no ordinary book, and I am grateful that the practice of literary analysis, though anything but an exact science, has given me useful tools in the study of sacred texts. Then, too, the Book of Mormon has its parallels with good fiction, for both contain narratives that offer insight into human experience. And while fiction is not true in a literal sense, it can most surely be true in an absolute sense. But the Book of Mormon is much more than fiction, for it is factually true as well as philosophically and morally true. The Book of Mormon is more than history, too.

All readers, specialists or not, have much in common, and like most, I am drawn to great texts out of love. Consequently, emotion, positive or negative, to some extent shapes my reading and accompanies my objective responses to the written word. We should not be embarrassed by an emotional response to genuine greatness. The emotion that overwhelms me when I read an exceptional text like the Book of Mormon bears no resemblance to the cheap tears that are the stock in trade of tasteless popular literature. Such tears are induced by shallow notions, stereotypical characters, and shopworn images rather than by truth and artistry. Countless years of studying written texts have, I hope, fixed in me some small ability to distinguish between the good and the bad, the true and the false, the genuine and the spurious, the original and the imitative. When I read a book, I no longer have to ask with Hamlet, "Is this an honest ghost?"

In my experience, the first few pages of a book are critical; if a book is deceitful, its opening pages will betray it. I challenge anyone to apply that test to the Book of Mormon. Can an honest reader of the following lines doubt that Nephi is who he says he is and that he writes what he knows to be absolute truth?

> I, Nephi, having been born of goodly parents, . . . and having seen many afflictions in the course of my days, nevertheless, having been highly favored of the Lord in all my days; yea, having had a great knowledge of the goodness and the mysteries of God, therefore I make a record of my proceedings in my days. . . .
>
> And I know that the record which I make is true; and I make it with mine own hand; and I make it according to my knowledge. (1 Nephi 1:1, 3)

Nephi's forthrightness is apparent in every line. He opens by naming himself, paying homage to his parents and his God, and bearing testimony about his record. Thus, we learn immediately that the narrative voice belongs to someone who is candid, respectful, dutiful, and grateful, someone who is likely to cut a very straight course. No hedging, no circumventing, no embroidering the truth. In fact, the very structure of verse three projects Nephi's sincerity through the use of three sturdy parallel clauses, all beginning with the words "And I" followed by a single syllable verb: "And I know," "and I make," "and I make." That same sincerity is also conveyed through word repetition. The first sentence contains a subordinate clause that introduces the words "I make," words that Nephi deliberately repeats in the two independent clauses that follow. Nephi's prompt self-introduction takes on added significance, too, as we come to realize that throughout the Book of Mormon the Lord and his servants almost invariably announce who they are, while Satan and his servants rarely do. The honest have nothing to hide; the devious have everything to hide. By immediately announcing his identity and fealty, therefore, Nephi serves reliable notice that he is who he says he is and that he intends to prepare a true record.

Although I consider other factors, my preference in approaching a text is to appraise its value by examining the internal evidence the text itself presents. History, biography, critical theory, and literary fashion are all legitimate and interesting doors through which to enter and interpret a piece of literature. But to limit analysis to one or more of those approaches is, I think, to remain in the foyer rather than to enter the living quarters of the work. It is to assess, merely, and never possess. Whatever frustrations the Book of Mormon presents to the historian or the anthropologist, it lends itself particularly well to my brand of close textual reading. In fact, external information about the record's creation and its cultural setting is so sparse that the words on the page are very nearly the reader's only tangible resource. Except for concurrent biblical history and archaeological findings in Mesoamerica, we are largely ignorant of the world that engendered the Book of Mormon.

Coincidentally, because the Book of Mormon arrives with so few cultural trappings, the diligent, spiritually attuned seeker can study and appreciate it with no specialized academic preparation for the task, no extensive historical background, and no external biographical data. Even so, I regard it as a great personal blessing that my formal training is of the sort that adds significantly to my study of the Book of Mormon. Possibly I "see more" because I am trained to see more. Most certainly, the Spirit finds me a readier pupil than I might otherwise have been. . . .

My point is simply this: The Book of Mormon is an inspired text whose possibilities could not be exhausted in a lifetime of study, much less a lifetime of pulling isolated passages for Sunday lessons and talks. I am particularly blessed to be a student of literary texts, for my academic pursuits have enriched, even prompted, my study of scripture. More than that, the Spirit that sometimes illuminates sacred texts for me also seems to lend insight and discernment to my reading of nonsacred texts. In all, the felicitous merging of these two important strands of my study and my life has immeasurably increased my understanding and appreciation, not only of books, but of the very essence of study and life.

From *Expressions of Faith: Testimonies of Latter-day Saint Scholars* (1999)

10. Laurel Thatcher Ulrich, "A Pail of Cream"

Mormon women who pursue an academic vocation are caught in several crosshairs. If they choose to be mothers, then like all professional women they experience the conflicts of career and child-bearing and rearing. And in addition to the familiar faith and intellect conflicts often aggravated by academic training, they may feel more acutely than most the competing appeals of a modern, feminist sensibility and a religion rooted in traditional gender roles and values. Historian Laurel Thatcher Ulrich adds to this mix the contrast of "small western town" (she was born in Sugar City, Idaho), with an adult life spent in northeastern cities and Ivy league settings. Ulrich has negotiated the paradoxes and potential mine fields of her life exceptionally well: she is a MacArthur Fellow, tenured professor at Harvard, winner of both the Pulitzer and the Bancroft prizes—and a committed

Latter-day Saint. This mini memoir chronicles how the disparate influences and ingredients of her life became a source of inspiration and fruitful productivity. Rather than seeing her own feminist orientation as incompatible with the church, Ulrich finds it a coherent extension of the vibrant feminist strain she discovered in early Utah Mormonism. And her integration of the public and the private, the exceptional and the very ordinary, became a hallmark of her own celebrated brand of history-writing.

Sometime in fifth grade, I decided I wanted to be a writer. When I was in high school I began submitting my best poems to *Seventeen*, cherishing the occasional words of encouragement I received with rejection slips. In my senior year, the editors invited me to write a short piece for a feature on how teens in various parts of the United States celebrated Christmas. I suppose they picked me because I lived in a town that evoked the smell of cookies baking, even though it was named for a sugar beet factory that had long since closed. "Sugar City Magic" was published in December 1957 during the first quarter of my sophomore year at the University of Utah.

For the most part *Seventeen*'s editors were satisfied with my effort to turn the mundane facts of life in a small western town into local color. They kept my description of my dad buying Christmas nuts at the Sugar City Mercantile, "a combination grocery store, butcher shop, shoe store, dry goods store, dress shop and summer fishing headquarters," and my reference to an elderly neighbor who came to our house on the day before Christmas "with her traditional present: sugared doughnuts." But they balked at the sentence that described "the youngest sheep farmer" in town bringing us a gift of lamb chops for Christmas morning breakfast. In the published version that became "The youngest dairyman in our neighborhood arrived with a pail of thick cream for our Christmas morning breakfast." I hooted at that pail of cream, telling everybody I knew that it was a New York fantasy, that the dairy farmers in Sugar City used milking machines, sold most of their milk in bulk to the farmers' co-op, and refrigerated the rest in narrow-necked glass bottles with paper caps. The cream rose to the top, leaving a band of yellow above the thin blue milk. It did not come in pails. . . .

I did not publish another personal essay for almost fifteen years. Although I majored in English and minored in journalism in college, the more I learned about writing, the less confident I was that I had anything to say. I continued to write humorous pieces, usually in verse, for family and friends. After moving to Boston with my husband in 1960, I managed to publish a few short pieces on New England writers for the *Relief Society Magazine*, a Mormon periodical for women, but I was unsure of my ability to write for a broader audience until some friends and I produced *A Beginner's Boston*, a guidebook for newcomers, in 1966. Originally created as a fund-raising project for the Mormon congregation in Cambridge, Massachusetts, it was widely distributed after a favorable review in the *Boston Globe*. . . .

After that, my writing moved in two directions, one activist and personal, the other academic. Having succeeded in our first publishing venture, several of the women who worked on *A Beginner's Boston* volunteered to edit a special women's issue of *Dialogue: A Journal of Mormon Thought*, a scholarly and literary journal published in California. As the introduction explained, "The Women's Liberation movement was then in full flower, making converts and causing all women to search their souls before reaffirming their traditional commitments." Within a few years we were producing an independent newspaper called *Exponent II* in honor of a feminist-suffragist periodical published in Utah from 1872 to 1912. Meanwhile, I completed a part-time M.A. program in English at Simmons College, and after my husband took a teaching position at the University of New Hampshire, I began a Ph. D. in early American history. As I am fond of telling my graduate students, I did not choose my field or my graduate school. I simply took advantage of what was available in a small state university. Seminars with Charles E. Clark and Darrett Rutman, both former journalists, emphasized good writing as well as rigorous scholarship, and I was hooked. As I delved into what to my Rocky Mountain eyes seemed remote and exotic material, I discovered new intellectual interests and another way of being a writer.

In 1976, I published both my first scholarly article and an essay for *Dialogue* in which I discussed an encounter between my oldest son, then fifteen, and a new neighbor who, on hearing about the birth of our fifth child, exclaimed, "Your poor mother! She's got them spread all over the place." I was a puzzle to more than one person in Durham. About the same time, the wife of one of my professors rushed over to me at a community gathering and said, "Congratulations!" When I looked puzzled, not being sure that she had even noticed my pregnancy, she completed the thought: "For getting your article accepted. Babies don't count." Well, I thought, babies may not count, but they certainly

demand attention. Writing personal essays helped me work out the contra-
dictions in my life as a wife, mother, teacher, scholar, active churchgoer, and
emerging feminist. My personal essays were directed not at those who found
my life incomprehensible, but at Latter-day Saint women who were struggling
with the same dilemmas I faced. They (and I) needed reassurance that motherhood and religious faith were compatible with intellectual ambitions. We found
our answer in history.

Many of us had grown up knowing about the heroism of pioneer ancestors who had participated in the epic trek across the United States, but few of
us knew anything about the Mormon feminism. We did not know that Utah
women voted and held office fifty years before women in the eastern United
States, nor that polygamist wives and mothers had attended medical school,
published newspapers, and organized cooperative enterprises. When we read
the original *Woman's Exponent*, we were astonished at how confident these
pioneer women were and how earnestly they insisted on their right to participate in public life and work. In enthusiasm, we no doubt missed many of the
ironies in their stories (nobody wanted to think of polygamy as a liberating
force). Still, we found in this forgotten aspect of Mormon history models for
religious commitment, social activism, and personal achievement that seemed
far more powerful than the complacent domesticity portrayed in popular magazines or in our own congregations.

I doubt that I would have had the courage to begin graduate school without
the support of Latter-day Saint women—living and dead. Yet, when it came
to choosing a graduate specialization, I did not choose Mormon history. In
part that was a practical decision. Given the resources available to me at the
University of New Hampshire, it would have been next to impossible to write a
dissertation in western history. But there were even more compelling reasons,
I think, for my decision to write about early America. In researching that first
scholarly article, a study of seventeenth-century funeral sermons, I discovered
the attractions of strangeness and the liberation in working with material that
seemed opaque and alien. In personal essays I was all-present, accountable to
the world and people I loved. Moving backward in time, I was able to establish
a critical distance in my own life and culture. There was no point in advocacy.
I had to sit back and try to understand.

My experience growing up in a rural community, reading scriptures, learning to bottle fruit, knit, and embroider dishtowels, listening to my grandfather's
stories about the old West, and hearing my grandmother talk about giving

birth to twelve children on a homestead in Idaho surely had something to do with my ability to write about religion, frontier life, childbirth, housework, and community. My own experiences as a wife, mother, and Sunday school teacher also contributed to my work. But my success as a scholar probably had more to do with my need to transcend those time-honored roles. I celebrate ordinary, anonymous, forgotten women, but even as a teenager I sought and achieved visibility by publishing. Although I have received mail addressed to Martha Ballard and have been identified on at least one college campus as a midwife, I am only a little bit like my eighteenth-century heroine. Like her, I was raised to be an industrious housewife and a self-sacrificing and charitable neighbor, but sometime in my thirties I discovered that writing about women's work was a lot more fun than doing it. . . .

In one of the last lectures in "Women, Feminism, and History," a Harvard core class that explores the relationship between feminist consciousness and history, I explain how the discovery of the nineteenth-century Mormon periodical *Woman's Exponent* changed my life. I illustrate the point with overhead transparencies of the cover of the first issue of *Exponent II*, founded in 1972 as the "spiritual descendant" of that pioneer newspaper. Because the course functions both as a survey of central themes in women's history and as an introduction to the personal uses of history, it seems appropriate to include my own story. By acknowledging my religious affiliation, I not only complicate students' understanding of twentieth-century feminism, I empower them to talk about their own connections to the past. But my moment of self-revelation comes at the end of a course that asked them to master a great deal of unfamiliar material, beginning with Christine de Pisan's *City of Ladies* (1405) and ending with Maxine Hong Kingston's *The Woman Warrior* (1976). I want them to see the many uses of history as well as the many ways of being a woman in times past.

At a critical point in my own life, history empowered me. It sent me to school, taught me a new way of being a writer, and gave me a critical perspective on my own dilemmas. But it was the women's movement that brought me to history. Together, feminism and history helped me to find a different sort of "magic" in my rural upbringing.

From *Journal of American History* (2002)

EIGHT

CONTEMPORARY RELIGIOUS LIFE

"WHAT THE MORMONS DO," British author Charles Dickens wrote in 1851, "seems to be excellent; what they say, is mostly nonsense."[1] Filtering out the satirist's bite, an important insight remains true: The norms of worship and praxis of The Church of Jesus Christ of Latter-day Saints are unexceptional and often admired. Mormon theology—especially in its early, more speculative dimensions—is more prominent in the public imagination than in LDS consciousness. Media coverage of Latter-day Saints and popular understanding tend to focus on unorthodox conceptions of the godhead, additional scriptures, peculiar notions of the soul's pre-mortal existence, or the possibility of "becoming like God." Yet to be a Latter-day Saint, as to be a member of any faith community, is arguably much more about how one lives one's religion on a daily basis than about creedal commitments or doctrinal understanding. To be an "active" Mormon, in other words, is much more a function of home visiting, testimony (or witness) bearing, and temple attending than of believing a set of doctrines about the origin of God, the kinship of Jesus and Satan, or the eternal status of plural marriage.

The following documents, while reflective of LDS theological underpinnings, sample the core dimensions of Mormonism as a lived experience. They do so by charting seminal moments in the religious journey of believing Latter-day Saints interspersed with glimpses of representative participation in the rhythms of Mormon religious life. Latter-day Saint participation in the life of the community formally begins when a newborn child is publicly given a name and a blessing. The process of acculturation and indoctrination begins when at the age of three, Mormon children begin gospel instruction and baptismal preparation in the "Primary." Once they reach the age of eight, LDS children are baptized and continue in the Primary organization until they reach age twelve. At that time, the young men are generally ordained deacons in the Aaronic Priesthood and join the Young Men's program, while the girls join the Young Women's program. At that point, in addition to Sunday meetings, they convene one night a week for youth meetings. A few years later, as LDS youth enter high school, they begin attendance at "seminary." In areas of heavy Mormon concentration (in the American Intermountain West), these classes are often held during school hours. In the rest of the country, however, LDS teens converge at the local chapel or a private home at 6 or 7 A.M. every school day for an hour of study that progresses from Old Testament, to New Testament, to Book of Mormon, to church history. During these years, frequent service projects, summer camps known as youth conference, Sunday meetings, and Standards Night are also attended by committed youth members.

After high school, young Mormon men who have remained committed to the church sometimes attend university for a year before "turning in their papers," that is, passing a series of worthiness interviews along with physical and dental exams and submitting paperwork indicating their preparedness and willingness to serve full-time missions. If young women make the same choice, their eligibility comes at age nineteen rather than eighteen. Because a mission call comes subject to the inspiration of the church leadership, independent of any candidate's preference, the designated field of service can literally be any of the church's more than four hundred missions. The day when the mission call arrives is therefore one of the most anxiously anticipated in the life of a Latter-day Saint. Even after a two-year commitment (eighteen months in the case of "sister" missionaries or senior couples), Mormons can look forward to a lifetime of church service, as the lack of a professional clergy means every member will bear a portion of the burden of leadership. Upon their release from service, returned missionaries are encouraged to pursue two immediate goals: education and marriage. When marriage does occur, it signals both a terminus and a beginning in a Latter-day Saint's life narrative. It is an end, insofar as a temple marriage is held out as the supreme religious goal and spiritual achievement throughout their young lives. All youth programs and church teachings make temple marriage the most important aspiration a young Latter-day Saint can nourish, and its obtainment is in that sense the most significant outward measurement of the success of parental teaching and church training. At the same time, given the Mormon theology of the family—wherein a couple sealed in the temple by priesthood authority, who are faithful to their temple covenants, found a new family dynasty of everlasting duration—the marriage represents an epochal beginning in both time and eternity.

While the temple orientation of Latter-day Saints and their view of the family's eternal nature are unique among Christians, visitors from other denominations would find much in Mormon lived religion entirely familiar. Latter-day Saints sing hymns of crossing the plains and weathering Missouri persecution, but their hymn books are also replete with Protestant standards. Their "sacrament" or Lord's Supper is administered by young men, but it commemorates the same supreme sacrifice of God's son that a billion other Christians observe. Many Latter-day Saints hold a semi-informal family service on Monday nights, with song, a lesson, and games, but they also engage in the rituals of family prayer and scripture reading found among the devout everywhere. And when they come together to bury their dead, they usually retell a narrative that is both strange and familiar. They tell of the soul's journey that began aeons ago, as spiritual progeny of a Heavenly Father and Heavenly Mother, and that passes through this life on the way to endless learning, progress, and life among the gods. They express sorrow and tears at the parting but find hope and comfort in the familiar New Testament promise of a resurrection and a day when all tears will be done away.

1. Dennis Clark, "A Name and a Blessing"

Unlike other Christians who baptize or christen infants, male LDS Melchizedek Priesthood holders formally bless and name babies during the first few weeks or months of their lives. This practice is rooted in both New Testament precedent and modern Mormon scripture. Jesus Christ blessed little children during his New Testament ministry and continued the practice during his post-resurrection appearance in the New World according to the Book of Mormon. In the early days of the church, Joseph Smith received a revelation instructing priesthood holders to continue the practice of blessing children and officially recording their names on the membership roles of the church (Doctrine and Covenants 20:70). Today, priesthood holders form a circle and take the baby in their arms to perform this ritual. As voice of the blessing, the infant's father or another male close to the family invokes God the Father (usually as "Heavenly Father"), then bestows upon the child its name. He then blesses the infant, pronouncing hopes of health, counsel, and general guidance. These blessings generally take place on fast Sundays (first Sunday of the month) in front of the entire congregation, but they can also be performed in homes or other appropriate places. The poem below describes this ritual from the perspective of an onlooker but radiates the feelings of a fasting LDS father groping for inspiration and pleading for the care and future spiritual growth of his child. Following the prayer, the father usually holds up the infant for the congregation to see.

---

the father and his friends, holding
the holy high priesthood and the infant,
stand in a circle, facing each other,
right hands supporting the baby—
rising, falling to gentle it—
left hands on the next near neighbor shoulder,
on the stand before the meeting of saints
this fast and testimony sunday;
having forsaken food for thought,
having sought for the companionship of
the holy ghost (a spirit of promise),
considering the creation
of bodies (his, his wife's and god's)
he is to name and bless, the father now
closes his eyes to shut the world out,
bows his head to see the child,
begins talking with god into
the microphone so the congregation
may share revelation of fatherhead;
like making an application
he labels the frightened child,
then plunges into blessing if the ghost
lures him down, under forms and records to
that silence of mind where spirit
speaks freely in the depths of life,
of deaths; and hears, searching experience

for knowledge of this child that he may learn
to bless it, then asks father god
to signify thru spirit he
has found resources to impart by mind
to help his child grow into resonance
with the child jesus, the man christ.

From *Dialogue: A Journal of Mormon Thought* (1970)

2. "Questions and Answers About Baptism"

*Sacrament service, the weekly worship service in the church, is attended by the
entire family. Given the number of infants and small children in a typical Mormon ward, speakers must sometimes exert themselves to be heard. After sacrament meeting, the congregation breaks up by age groups for the next two hours of
meetings. Beginning at age three, children begin to attend the ward "Primary." For
the next five years, they receive gospel instruction with a central focus on preparing for their baptism. Mormons reject the doctrine of original sin and believe that
personal guilt (and therefore punishment) only follows upon the deliberate choice
to sin. Age eight is designated by Mormon scriptures as "the age of accountability."
That is why Latter-day Saints do not practice infant baptism and are referring to
personal sin when they characterize baptism as being for "the remission of sins."
Preparation entails learning the essentials of the faith, particularly belief in Jesus
Christ, and in his atonement through which personal forgiveness and salvation
are possible. Ideally, children by the age of eight have the stirrings of their own
"testimony," or spiritual conviction of such standard principles as Heavenly Father
loves them, Jesus is their Savior, the Church of Jesus Christ of Latter-day Saints is
His church, and that the current church president is God's prophet on the earth.
Before their baptism, children are interviewed by the bishop, intended to ensure
their preparation has made them as prepared and self-aware about their pending
baptism as an eight year old can be. A church publication directed at the children
is intended both to answer basic questions and allay worries that might occur to
young minds contemplating the daunting specter of a ritual where they are in the
public spotlight.*

DO I MAKE A PROMISE WHEN I AM BAPTIZED?

Yes. You promise to keep Heavenly Father's commandments. He promises that you can live with Him in His kingdom. These promises are called covenants.

WHERE WILL I BE BAPTIZED?

Where possible, you will be baptized in a font in a stake center. If you cannot be baptized in a font, you may be baptized anywhere approved by your bishop or branch president, such as a pond or ocean. There has to be enough water to cover you completely. That's what baptism by immersion means.

WHY IS BAPTISM IMPORTANT?

It's more than important—it is necessary. Jesus Christ said that people must be baptized to belong to His Church and enter the kingdom of God (see John 3:5).

IS BAPTISM SCARY?

No. The person baptizing you holds onto you the whole time. You are under the water for only a moment.

WHAT DO I NEED TO DO TO PREPARE TO BE BAPTIZED?

Want to be baptized.
Keep the commandments.
Be willing to live the teachings of Jesus Christ and follow His example.
Be interviewed by your bishop or branch president.

WHY AREN'T BABIES BAPTIZED IN OUR CHURCH?

Children are born innocent. Heavenly Father and Jesus Christ give parents eight years to teach their children the gospel so their children can learn right from wrong before they become accountable for their sins. (See D&C 68:25.)

WHO CAN BAPTIZE ME?

A priest in the Aaronic Priesthood or a man who holds the Melchizedek Priesthood.

WHEN CAN I BE BAPTIZED?

You need to be at least eight years old (see D&C 68:27).

WHAT WILL THE PERSON BAPTIZING ME SAY?

"Having been commissioned of Jesus Christ, I baptize you in the name of the Father, and of the Son, and of the Holy Ghost. Amen" (D&C 20:73).

WHAT HAPPENS AFTER BAPTISM?

After you are baptized, you are confirmed a member of The Church of Jesus Christ of Latter-day Saints and you receive the gift of the Holy Ghost. You are then accountable for your sins, and you need to repent when you do something wrong. Before you take the sacrament each week, you should repent of whatever you did wrong that week and ask for forgiveness. Then when you take the sacrament, you covenant to take upon yourself the name of Jesus Christ, which means you will always try to remember Him, follow His example, and obey Him. When you do this, you are promised that His Spirit will be with you.

WHAT WILL I WEAR WHEN I AM BAPTIZED?

White clothing usually borrowed from your stake, district, or mission.

DO THE SCRIPTURES TELL ABOUT PEOPLE WHO WERE BAPTIZED?

Yes! Here are some you can read about:

Adam: Moses 6:64–65

Alma: Mosiah 18:8–16

Jesus Christ: Matthew 3:13–17

3,000 in one day: Acts 2:38–41

Paul: Acts 9:17–18

Limhi and his people: Mosiah 25:17–18

Zeezrom: Alma 15:12

Joseph Smith: Joseph Smith–History 1:68–71

———————

From *Friend* (2008)

3. Antonia Purina Honrado, "They Gave Me a Copy with All of the Pages"

Since the earliest days of Christianity in America, conversion narratives have celebrated the actions of God in bringing salvation to his elect. While most evangelical Christians point to a moment in their lives when they experienced the redeeming grace of Jesus Christ in such accounts, Latter-day Saints are more likely to reflect on when they came to "know" that the Book of Mormon, and by extension the church teachings, were true. In the logic of LDS testimony, the truthfulness of that scriptural record gives implicit assurance that Joseph Smith, its translator, was acting as God's prophet. Therefore, the truthfulness of the complete version of the gospel he restored follows as a matter of course. (The Book of Mormon is, in this sense, the "keystone" of the religion.) The convert's resulting testimony or personal conviction of the correctness of their religion is often shared in public settings as a mark of their spiritual maturity and commitment to the church and its tenets. The following account is taken from a collection of such Mormon conversion narratives, titled Converted to Christ Through the Book of Mormon. *Its author, Antonia Purina Honrado, relates a familiar LDS pattern of encountering the Book of Mormon, reading and praying over its message, and becoming convinced of the truthfulness of the church. She describes the meaningful milestones in her own conversion over a period of six years from the time she first came in contact with the Mormon scripture. Using language patterns that are commonplace within such "testimonies" she explains how the Book of Mormon brought her closer to Jesus Christ and changed her life. The Book of Mormon continues to serve as the chief sign of Latter-day Saints' demarcation from other Christian groups who believe in the principle of sola scriptura, or the Bible's sufficiency as a record of God's word.*

One Sunday morning, almost six years ago, I met a young man in my building on his way to church. He was neatly groomed and greeted me with a smile. I noticed a certain book in his hand. He wasn't reading it, just carrying it with a cluster of other books. Nevertheless, for some reason that book caught my attention, so I asked him what it was. He replied it was a Book of Mormon, showing me the blue cover. I proceeded by asking him if I could have it, and without hesitation, he gave it to me. Looking at his watch, he said he was going to be late for the meetings and scurried off, leaving me with no explanation of this book that caught my eye.

I began at once my investigation of this book, reading it and pondering over its contents. It offered me something more than I had previously felt by my studies of other books of religion. I had been looking for something all my life. You see, I was baptized and raised in the Catholic Church. My parents were faithful members and taught me the ways of God, but I felt there was something missing. Therefore, at the young age of sixteen, I began my search for that something.

Attending churches and listening to their different doctrines only left me more discouraged. Nothing seemed to satisfy me. I even began to doubt my own beliefs about God and His existence. However, this new book in my possession offered me insights to such things as the heavens, God the Father, our Savior Jesus Christ, and the Resurrection. I felt the power of this book, which later on helped me to understand more about life. My studies increased, and I began to read it every night, comparing its teachings with those in the Bible, reading parts here and there.

One night, after meditating over what I had previously read in the book, I decided to apply the scripture in Mormon 9:21, which reads, "Behold, I say unto you that whoso believeth in Christ, doubting nothing, whatsoever he shall ask the Father in the name of Christ it shall be granted him, and this promise is unto all, even unto the ends of the earth." I believed in Jesus Christ, so I asked the Father if this book was true and if He could tell me. Then, I crawled into bed feeling good, anxiously awaiting the answer to my supplication.

The following morning, I woke up after a dream in which I knew that God heard my simple prayer. He really does live, and this book that caught my eye contains His word. Never before had I felt something so strong. This, also, helped me understand the death of my son that would occur months later. I knew that God lived and cared about me.

After this experience, which I call a revelation, after my prayer over the Book of Mormon, I desired to learn more about this true book. Some time had passed since the boy had given me it, and I hadn't seen him since.

I began knocking on doors in the building, asking if they knew of this boy and the Mormon church. Most of the people replied negatively, while others had never even heard of the Mormon religion. My search went on for six years to find somebody who knew something about the Mormons. Now that I look back, if I had known the complete name, The Church of Jesus Christ of Latter-day Saints, I could have looked it up in the phone book and saved me years of searching.

Not being able to find the boy or his religion, I continued on with my reading and enjoying all the wonderful truths within its pages. I never was able to read the entire book, though.

One afternoon when I arrived at home, I found out that my grandchildren had needed a coloring book. The Book of Mormon must have caught their eye, too, as they decided to mark their favorite passages. By the time they were finished, the book was colored up and ripped into pieces. The only part remaining intact was from the picture of Samuel the Lamanite to the end of the book.

For the next few years, I read and reread the books of 3 Nephi to Moroni, while continuing my search for the church of the book.

In August 1988, six years from the time I first received the book, my prayers were answered again. I met a Mormon lady who wrote down my address and said she'd send missionaries to visit me. When those two young men knocked on my door, I knew they would help me come to the end of my search.

One of the first teachings Elder Claypool and Elder Jorgensen shared with me was about the importance of prophets, then Joseph Smith, then the wonderful Book of Mormon. I anxiously took out my battered copy, showing them I had a part. Then they gave me a copy with all the pages.

My joy was only beginning in the gospel of Jesus Christ. I felt so much closer to Him because of the book. Thanks to the Book of Mormon, and the clear teachings of the elders, the commandment and privilege of baptism was easy to accept. I knew it was what God wanted me to do. I knew it was what I wanted to do.

From *Converted to Christ Through the Book of Mormon* (1989)

4. Boyd K. Packer, "Counsel to Young Men"

One peculiarity of the church is how ecclesiastical authority is hierarchical and widely diffused at the same time. Earthly priesthood authority is centered in the church president, then the First Presidency as a governing quorum. The Mormon prophet is sometimes likened to the Catholic pope, although the LDS leader has much greater sway over the actual praxis of faithful members than his counterpart.[2] Next in line is the Quorum of the Twelve Apostles, then the Quorums of the Seventy, then area seventies, stake presidents, and bishops. Every male member of the church, from young boys to senior apostles, has a file leader who supervises him in his priesthood stewardship. At the same time, every male member of the church is eligible to hold the priesthood by formal ordination. The following document implicitly encompasses two salient experiences in the life of LDS males. First is the conferral of that priesthood, which generally happens at the age of twelve

*when a boy is ordained a deacon. The offices of teacher and priest follow at ages
fourteen and sixteen. These three offices (in addition to bishop) constitute the
Aaronic Priesthood, also called the lesser or preparatory priesthood. Once boys
become deacons, they are initiated into a second ritual, which is attendance at
the semiannual priesthood session of the General Conference, which is beamed
by satellite television or radio from the Conference Center in Salt Lake City to
thousands of priesthood groups worldwide. The following talk was delivered at
such a convocation (the other four sessions of a General Conference are open to
all, member and nonmember, who choose to attend or listen). Boyd K. Packer, a
senior apostle in the Quorum of the Twelve, in the context of a retrospective of his
own life, counsels young holders of the Aaronic Priesthood, conveying both general Christian themes and particular Mormon perspectives on priesthood, sexual
morality, and the LDS health code known as the Word of Wisdom.*

Young men speak of the future because they have no past, and old men speak
of the past because they have no future. I am an old man, but I will speak to
the young men of the Aaronic Priesthood about your future.

The Aaronic Priesthood you hold was restored by an angelic messenger.
"The ordination was done by the hands of an angel, who announced himself as
John, the same that is called John the Baptist in the New Testament. The angel
explained that he was acting under the direction of Peter, James, and John, the
ancient apostles, who held the keys of the higher priesthood, which was called
the Priesthood of Melchizedek."

"The power and authority of the lesser, or Aaronic Priesthood, is to hold the
keys of the ministering of angels, and to administer in outward ordinances, the
letter of the gospel, the baptism of repentance for the remission of sins, agreeable to the covenants and commandments."

You have been ordained to an office in the priesthood of God and given
divine authority that is not and cannot be held by the kings and magistrates
and great men of this earth unless they humble themselves and enter through
the gate that leads to life eternal.

There are many accounts in the scriptures of young men serving. Samuel
served in the tabernacle with Eli. David was a young man when he faced Goli-
ath. Mormon's service began when he was 10. Joseph Smith was 14 when he

received the First Vision. And Christ was 12 when He was found in the temple teaching the wise men.

Paul told young Timothy, "Let no man despise thy youth."

When I began my teaching career, President J. Reuben Clark Jr., the First Counselor in the First Presidency, had spoken to teachers. His words went into my heart and influenced me ever since.

President Clark described youth as "hungry for things of the Spirit [and] eager to learn the gospel." He said: "They want it straight, undiluted. They want to know . . . about our beliefs; they want to gain testimonies of their truth. They are not now doubters but inquirers, seekers after truth."

President Clark continued: "You do not have to sneak up behind this spiritually experienced youth and whisper religion in [their] ears; you can come right out, face to face, and talk with [them]. . . . You can bring these truths to [them] openly. . . . There is no need for gradual approaches."

Since then I have taught young people in the same way that I teach adults.

There are some things you need to understand.

The priesthood is something you cannot see nor hear nor touch, but it is a real authority and a real power. . . .

You are a son of God. You lived in a premortal existence as an individual spirit child of heavenly parents. At the time of your birth, you received a mortal body of flesh and blood and bone in which to experience earth life. You will be tested as you prepare yourself to return to our Heavenly Father.

I ask you the same question that Paul asked the Corinthians: "What? know ye not that your body is the temple of the Holy Ghost which is in you, which ye have of God, and ye are not your own?"

Your gender was determined in the premortal existence. You were born a male. You must treasure and protect the masculine part of your nature. You must have respectful, protective regard for all women and girls.

Do not abuse yourself. Never allow others to touch your body in a way that would be unworthy, and do not touch anyone else in any unworthy way.

Avoid the deadly poisons of pornography and narcotics. If these are in your life, beware! If allowed to continue, they can destroy you. Talk to your parents; talk to your bishop. They will know how to help you.

Do not decorate your body with tattoos or by piercing it to add jewels. Stay away from that.

Do not run with friends that worry your parents.

Everywhere present is the influence of Lucifer and his legion of angels. They tempt you to do those things and say those things and think those things that would destroy. Resist every impulse that will trouble your spirit.

You are not to be fearful. The Prophet Joseph Smith taught that "all beings who have bodies have power over those who have not." And Lehi taught that all "men are instructed sufficiently that they know good from evil." Remember, the prayerful power of your spirit will protect you. . . .

If you have been guilty of sin or mischief, you must learn about the power of the Atonement, how it works. And with deeply sincere repentance, you can unleash that power. It can rinse out all the small things, and with deep soaking and scrubbing, it will wash away serious transgression. There is nothing from which you cannot be made clean.

With you always is the Holy Ghost, which was conferred upon you at the time of your baptism and confirmation. . . .

You young men should not complain about schooling. Do not immerse yourself so much in the technical that you fail to learn things that are practical. Everything you can learn that is practical—in the house, in the kitchen cooking, in the yard—will be of benefit to you. Never complain about schooling. Study well, and attend always.

"The glory of God is intelligence, or, in other words, light and truth."

"Whatever principle of intelligence we attain unto in this life, it will rise with us in the resurrection."

We are to learn about "things that are above, and things that are beneath, things that are in the earth, and upon the earth, and in heaven."

You can learn about fixing things and painting things and even sewing things and whatever else is practical. That is worth doing. If it is not of particular benefit to you, it will help you when you are serving other people. . . .

The reality of life is now part of your priesthood responsibilities. It will not hurt you to want something and not have it. There is a maturing and disciplining that will be good for you. It will ensure that you can have a happy life and raise a happy family. These trials come with responsibility in the priesthood.

Some of you live in countries where most of what you eat and some of what you wear will depend on what can be produced by the family. It may be that what you can contribute will make the difference so that the rent is paid or the family is fed and housed. Learn to work and to support.

The very foundation of human life, of all society, is the family, established by the first commandment to Adam and Eve, our first parents: "Multiply, and replenish the earth."

Thereafter came the commandment, "Honour thy father and thy mother: that thy days may be long upon the land which the Lord thy God giveth thee."

Be a responsible member of your family. Take care of your possessions— your clothing, your property. Do not be wasteful. Learn to be content.

It may seem that the world is in commotion; and it is! It may seem that there are wars and rumors of wars; and there are! It may seem that the future will hold trials and difficulties for you; and it will! However, fear is the opposite of faith. Do not be afraid! I do not fear.

———————————

From *Ensign* (2009)

5. Lee Tom Perry and Daniel Lyman Carter, "As Now We Take the Sacrament"; Mabel Jones Gabbott and Rowland H. Prichard, "In Humility, Our Savior"; and Karen Lynn Davidson and Hans Leo Hassler, "O Savior, Thou Who Wearest a Crown"

Latter-day Saints center their Sabbath worship service on the sacrament, or their version of the Catholic Eucharist or Protestant Communion. Like their Christian brothers and sisters, they eat and drink (bread and wine in the early years, bread and water today in keeping with the LDS health code known as the Word of Wisdom, which eschews alcoholic drinks) in remembrance of the suffering of Jesus Christ, as described in Matthew 26. Mormons also do so as a reaffirmation of their baptismal covenants, which include the taking upon oneself of Christ's name and the promise to keep his commandments and always remember him. In addition to New Testament accounts of the sacrament, Latter-day Saints have recourse as well to a Book of Mormon account, wherein the resurrected Lord instituted the practice among a righteous group of New World disciples (3 Nephi 18:7; 20:3; 26:13). The sacrament prayers are given in Mormon scripture (D&C 20:75–79; Moroni 4 and 5) and must be recited with exactness before the emblems of Christ's body and blood are passed to worthy congregants. The sacrament portion of the Sunday meetings is a time of heightened reverence and community participation, as male members of the local congregation, usually Aaronic Priesthood holders, prepare, bless, and pass the sacrament. While priests, generally young

men between the ages of sixteen and eighteen, break the bread, the congrega-
tion sings a sacrament hymn, like the ones presented in this section. Then
deacons (twelve to fourteen years of age) and teachers (fourteen to sixteen
years of age) distribute the bread and water to the congregation in silence.
Those who deem themselves out of harmony with the Holy Spirit, because of
personal transgression or for other reasons, are expected to decline the sacra-
ment. After all have partaken who wish to, the meeting resumes with sermons
("talks") and music.

AS NOW WE TAKE THE SACRAMENT

As now we take the sacrament,
Our thoughts are turned to thee,
Thou Son of God, who lived for us,
Then died on Calvary.
We contemplate thy lasting grace,
Thy boundless charity;
To us the gift of life was giv'n
For all eternity.

As now our minds review the past,
We know we must repent;
The way to thee is righteousness—
The way thy life was spent.
Forgiveness is a gift from thee
We seek with pure intent.
With hands now pledged to do thy work,
We take the sacrament.

As now we praise thy name with song,
The blessings of this day

Will linger in our thankful hearts,
And silently we pray
For courage to accept thy will,
To listen and obey.
We love thee, Lord; our hearts are full.
We'll walk thy chosen way.

IN HUMILITY, OUR SAVIOR

In humility, our Savior,
Grant thy Spirit here, we pray,
As we bless the bread and water
In thy name this holy day.
Let me not forget, O Savior,
Thou didst bleed and die for me
When thy heart was stilled and broken
On the cross at Calvary.

Fill our hearts with sweet forgiving;
Teach us tolerance and love.
Let our prayers find access to thee
In thy holy courts above.
Then, when we have proven worthy
Of thy sacrifice divine,
Lord, let us regain thy presence;
Let thy glory round us shine.

O SAVIOR, THOU WHO WEAREST A CROWN

O Savior, thou who wearest
A crown of piercing thorn,
The pain thou meekly bearest,

Weigh'd down by grief and scorn.
The soldiers mock and flail thee;
For drink they give thee gall;
Upon the cross they nail thee
To die, O King of all.

———————————

No creature is so lowly,
No sinner so depraved,
But feels thy presence holy
And thru thy love is saved.
Tho craven friends betray thee,
They feel thy love's embrace;
The very foes who slay thee
Have access to thy grace.

———————————

Thy sacrifice transcended
The mortal law's demand;
Thy mercy is extended
To ev'ry time and land.
No more can Satan harm us,
Tho long the fight may be,
Nor fear of death alarm us;
We live, O Lord, thru thee.

———————————

What praises can we offer
To thank thee, Lord most high?
In our place thou didst suffer;
In our place thou didst die,
By heaven's plan appointed,
To ransom us, our King.

O Jesus, the anointed,

To thee our love we bring!

From *Hymns of The Church of Jesus Christ of Latter-day Saints* (1985)

6. Margaret Rampton Munk, "Service Under Stress: Two Years as a Relief Society President"

The bishop of a ward expends tremendous time and energy in his calling. He is responsible for all finances, care of the poor, pastoral counseling, oversight of the youth, coordination of all activities, and conduct of worship services. Equally taxing, however, can be the work of the ward's Relief Society president. Her work includes not just presiding over the women's program (counterpart to the male Mormon priesthood organization), but also directing much of the welfare assistance that takes place in her ward. She assesses the needs of those on church support, supervises home visits, oversees child care where mothers are sick or incapacitated, and coordinates meal preparation and delivery to those same homes. These functions, and over a hundred other roles in local congregations, are staffed by lay members, as no leaders at the ward or stake levels are paid for their services. Given the absence of a local professional clergy, members are acculturated from their youth to accept requests to give generously of their time and talents when called upon. Contributing to the spirit of volunteerism is the Mormon belief that bishops and other leaders are endowed with a mantle of authority that gives them access to inspiration. The "callings" that they issue are accordingly seen as coming from the Lord. In addition, those so called are "set apart" by priesthood authority and given the spiritual gifts and inspiration requisite to their responsibilities. Because all callings are temporary (most last from one or two to five or six years in the case of a bishop), members rotate in and out of many in their lifetime, often fulfilling two or more simultaneously in small wards and smaller "branches." Service commitments can require an hour or two a week for minor callings or as much as twenty hours a week for those in bishoprics, stake presidencies, and Relief Society presidencies.

I spent two years as Relief Society president in our ward in the Washington, D.C. Stake, from June 1976 to July 1978. I had never contemplated having this experience, certainly not while in my thirties with such small children. We had lived in the ward only nine months, and I had never served in a Relief Society presidency. I had never been president of anything except a group of college girls who wore purple dresses on Wednesdays. As an adult, I had never really lived in a typical ward, having gone from student wards to seven years in the mission fields of Asia. I did not fit my own image of a Relief Society president at all. My first thought was, "But I don't even bake bread!"

I was taken by surprise. I didn't know what to expect. Two years later, I was still surprised.

Every ward is unique; consequently the challenges of one Relief Society president are different from those of another. Several factors made our ward different; each has challenged me and other ward leaders, including my husband, who now serves as bishop of the same ward.

Any large city attracts people from their original homes and extended families—many for professional or educational reasons, some because they are trying to "find themselves" in a new and more varied environment, and still others because they want simply to escape. Church members are scattered over a large area. Washington also attracts many visitors—tourists, people dealing with the federal government, patients in the city's three large government and military hospitals, all located within our ward boundaries.

Such a location causes a great deal of coming and going and constantly shifting ward membership. Reorganization is endless, and it is often difficult just to know who is here, not to mention making ward members feel welcome and meeting their personal needs. Loneliness is a problem for some, especially those who are living alone or who have recently left home. In spite of our efforts to provide activities and opportunities for Church members to meet socially, some still feel isolated and alone. Members in large cities are more likely to turn to the Church for help in times of illness or trouble than to distant families and neighbors. Transportation needs to be provided for women who do not drive and are either incapacitated or lack confidence to use public transportation. Hospital patients, even though not members of our ward, need visitors and concerned friends, and their families often need transportation, housing, and encouragement. Other visitors sometimes call upon local Church members for housing, transportation, sight-seeing guidance, babysitting, and other services.

Young, single people entering the city without definite goals or attempting to escape from problems often find themselves emotionally lost and discover that their problems have somehow moved with them. They change apartments often, have frequent crises in their personal relationships, get into financial straits, and sometimes become physically and mentally ill. They tend to seek out father and mother substitutes among the older members of the ward and request frequent counseling and practical help. . . .

Aside from these special problems, my two years were full of things familiar to any Relief Society president anywhere, though unexpected or only dimly foreseen when I began.

I shopped for and delivered groceries to needy families, itemized each purchase, and submitted the bills to the ward clerk. I became the object of good-natured ribbing for coming in for my monthly paycheck. I learned that Relief Society nurseries are notorious sources of potential friction, and I studied diplomacy helping my education counselor pacify mothers who wanted their babies' diapers changed and mothers who did not, mothers whose children were allergic to the morning's snack, mothers who wanted their children to have milk or juice during the morning and nursery volunteers who had to clean up the milk or juice, volunteers who were angry with the Primary for getting into the Relief Society toy box, mothers and volunteers who disagreed about how to handle a child who hit, bit, or cried continually, women who did not want to help in the nursery, and mothers who were willing to take their turn but were not happy about the way things were done.

I solicited contributions to the Nauvoo Women's Monument fund but avoided telling my sisters how they should feel about the Equal Rights Amendment. (Subsequent use of Mormon women for political purposes in neighboring Virginia made me extremely grateful that the ERA had won early approval from the Maryland legislature.) I called and interviewed visiting teachers, which was time-consuming but the very best means of getting to know the women. I worked with the bishop to keep Relief Society staff positions filled, oriented new board members, and tried to encourage these women when I was fully sharing their insecurities.

I reported our doings to the editor of the ward newspaper and arranged for displays in the trophy case. I attended meetings, organized meetings, presided over meetings, and held meetings to plan meetings. I dealt with last-minute crises before meetings, crises which often began with a phone call at 8:00 on a Tuesday morning. Our Relief Society produced four major ward socials during the two years and three others for women only; we catered food for six wedding receptions.

I visited sick women, new mothers, newcomers, families with financial and personal problems, and people whose help I needed. I visited homes, hospitals, and a nursing home where one of our members lived. I rented and delivered three wheelchairs and one commode. I stood helplessly by as a rescue squad arrived at the apartment of a woman who had suffered a stroke, and my husband made what was for him the ultimate sacrifice by allowing the children and me to care for her little white dog for three days. I received calls for advice on husbands who had not come home when expected and babies with severe diaper rash.

I recruited volunteers for a great variety of activities—temple assignments, compassionate service, food and help for socials, dinners for visiting Church dignitaries, and ward fund-raising projects, including experimental studies at the National Institutes of Health for which Church members often volunteered as subjects. I became an exchange and referral center for housing, used furniture and clothing, employment, telephone information, transportation, babysitting, house sitting, and care of the elderly. I wrote well-deserved thank-you notes to the many people who helped me, and ordered and distributed Relief Society manuals in Spanish and English. One cold December night, I delivered six large turkeys to the six women who would be roasting them for the ward Christmas dinner.

Several times our home became headquarters for newcomers, the temporarily homeless, and passers-through. These ranged from a woman whose husband had been seriously injured in an automobile accident in Germany and sent to Walter Reed hospital to a poor little soul who claimed to have been left stranded at a Washington airport by a boyfriend who had promised to marry her. (The first woman rented an apartment and stayed to become an active member of our ward during her husband's long recuperation. The second, after regaling me with more and more fantastic stories of her life and making many long-distance telephone calls from our kitchen, finally boarded a bus for California. Her story turned out to be a fabrication, and our last news of her was a postcard from somewhere in Oklahoma.)

I met and talked with counselors at LDS Social Services about our mutual efforts to help women with serious emotional problems. I kept an ear open to the needs of some twenty new mothers during one year and helped when two ward members died. I sang in the stake Relief Society chorus and organized

Christmas carolers and small singing groups for socials. I attended baptisms of new converts and tried to ease them into a new way of life and a new circle of friends. I coordinated schedules with the Relief Society of the ward which shared our building.

I made announcements concerning coming events, bulk food orders, craft fairs, classes, tickets, lost and found items. I helped two new Relief Society secretaries struggling to take attendance discreetly in sacrament meeting, where there were always new and unfamiliar faces, and in four separate weekly sessions of Relief Society—Tuesday morning, Sunday morning, Young Adults, and Spanish speakers.

This catalogue is extremely full of "I's," and that is not as it should be. I have tried to show the great variety of things with which a Relief Society president may become involved, but I do not mean to suggest that I did all these things single-handedly. I used to sit in the chapel during sacrament meeting, looking from one woman to the next, realizing that I felt a great gratitude to almost every one for help willingly given. I am not an administrator by inclination; I would rather do twice as much work myself than ask someone else for help. This calling was good for me because I could not possibly do everything myself. I found that most people were very willing to help; but it was still painful to ask, and the most beautiful words in the world became, "I'd be glad to." It is a tribute to the women of our ward that I heard those words far more often than "I'm afraid I can't."

I had devoted counselors whom I came to love, even though we did not start out as a naturally compatible group. Their interests and abilities lay in areas such as homemaking activities where my own were weak. We had excellent teachers, an experienced and beloved secretary, a dedicated visiting teacher supervisor, and many women who gave time, talent, and service.

I offer this long list only to understand better why this calling so dominated my life for two years. At times when I felt overwhelmed, I was advised to delegate responsibility. I tried, but I learned that delegation both reduced my load and added something back to it. Each time I asked someone to help, it also became my duty to follow through—to explain responsibilities, show interest, and lend necessary support.

If anyone asked me, "What were the hardest things about your job?", I would answer without hesitation, "The telephone and Sundays." Perhaps this is because these two aspects most affected my family, and I worried and felt guilty over having to divide my time and attention among so many people in addition to them.

When I was called to my position, the bishop assured me that I was to put my family first. I tried hard to do this, but I found it more easily said than done. My husband was very supportive and soon realized, if he had not before, that I had a full-time job. Busy with a demanding profession of his own, he helped me in many ways, washing more dishes in those two years than in all the thirty-six that preceded them. I felt the children could not be expected to be so under-standing or flexible. Perhaps at first I overcompensated by involving them too often in my activities. I was deeply hurt by one or two remarks indicating that women in our ward were not accustomed to a Relief Society president with small children in tow. (My predecessor had had grown and teenaged children and had served for six years.) I was bewildered by this seeming intolerance from other women; after all, motherhood was supposed to be our most impor-tant calling. But this problem soon faded, perhaps because I had been overly sensitive and the problem had been more perceived than real. . . .

I had never spent much time on the telephone, and we had lived quite hap-pily for five years in the Philippines without one. Now, although I seldom got a bishop's middle-of-the-night calls, I found that the box on the kitchen wall could be a tyrant. Calls often began before 8:00 in the morning and contin-ued until 11:00 at night, many the inevitable fruit of delegated responsibility. I remember only one day in the two years when there were no Relief Society-related phone calls. Perhaps something was wrong with our phone that day. . . .

And Sundays! I have heard many busy Church members concede that Sun-day is a day of rest for them only in the sense that they exchange their weekday labors for ecclesiastical ones. For me, Sundays of those two years were char-acterized by an intensification of the same kind of labor which dominated the other six days of the week. . . .

At times the job was manageable, although I had to learn, with my bishop's good advice, that I could not possibly do all that I might like. The second year, in general, was easier than the first, as I gained confidence, experience, and knowledge of whom to call upon for help. But there was never a let-up for long, and several times I felt that something in me would give under the strain. My husband, who is used to seeing me take on too much, let me cry and rage, and then encouraged me to buck up and finish the job. I did, but in looking back through my little notebooks, I can easily understand why the pressure some-times exceeded my tolerance point. . . .

Several impressions and concerns stand out from my experience of those two years.

I am a reasonably social person, and I enjoy and appreciate my friends; but I also need and enjoy a considerable amount of solitude. One of the greatest values of my Relief Society job was that I developed relationships with many fine people whom I would otherwise have known only slightly. But I often thought of a story about Senator Edward Kennedy who, surrounded by a crush of people at a political rally, would sometimes mutter to an aide, "T.M.B.S. !"— too many blue suits. It was his signal that he needed to escape and be alone for a while. I knew that feeling very well. I was determined to do all I could for the women in the ward and not to let my family suffer. Most of the time I think I succeeded, but I paid a price. Being overly organized and self-controlled put a real strain on me, and I had to sacrifice almost all of my time to write, read, or pursue other solitary interests. . . .

I discovered reserves and sources of strength upon which I could call. Our family was healthy throughout two winters of record cold. The children were ill only once, with chicken pox, and I did not expect the Lord to spare us that after we had just housed a family of infected little cousins. In looking back, a sort of "loaves and fishes" miracle must have occurred in my behalf, giving me more time than there was in a day and more capacity than normal to do things.

But my weaknesses also became more obvious. I was disappointed when I was not able to speak with necessary frankness for fear of being thought unkind or unhelpful, when I overreacted to criticism, when I showed my weariness and impatience at the end of a busy day to the children or to someone who had innocently made the phone ring once too often, when I let myself get too busy to exercise and pray thoughtfully, and when I reacted to a new problem in the ward with tension and dread as well as sympathy. I was relieved to hear our bishop, released just after I was following seven years of service, say that he now found it good to hear of problems with concern but without feeling direct, personal responsibility.

Working closely with priesthood leaders and learning about the operation of a ward was an education by itself. To see a group of men who are also fathers and full-time breadwinners willingly assume responsibility for the temporal, social, and spiritual welfare of some 500 people is remarkable, and not to be found, so far as I know, outside the LDS Church. I began to understand the responsibilities which a bishop and his counselors carry and gained an enduring respect for the men who take them on. Working with the leaders of our ward was almost entirely a positive experience. I had known our bishop for many years as a former Congressman from Utah, a friend, and erstwhile political opponent (successful) of my father. He took a fatherly interest in me and was extremely kind and encouraging. Several times the thought of the large load he had been carrying for six years prevented me from adding to it by telling him I wasn't sure I could continue.

Only occasionally did I feel disadvantaged operating in the priesthood-dominated councils of the ward or sense a bit of kindly condescension, but I did become more keenly aware of the limited role women play in Church policy making. Except for the hour-long monthly ward correlation meetings, which all auxiliary presidents attended, I was the only woman present at the ward executive meetings, and I was invited to those only to discuss welfare matters. At the time, this was an interesting new experience, but in retrospect I wonder why over 50 percent of the Church membership should be so under-represented. I saw situations where needs could have been better met if more women had been actively involved in planning and decision-making. I also felt sometimes that a woman's (and a man's) own desires and interests should be considered before ward callings were made, and that the secrecy surrounding those callings and releases was probably unnecessary. I did not become a crusader for the priesthood for women. I had more than enough to do already. But I came to feel that women could and should participate more directly and in greater numbers in making plans and decisions which have such a great effect upon their lives and their families.

I regret I was not able to find time for closer involvement with inactive ward members. I understand now, as I did then, that my own ambivalence toward inactivity as well as lack of time contributed to this situation. Several members of my immediate family are estranged from the Church. Some of them receive home teachers, attend church occasionally, and have a cordial relationship with Church leaders. Others want to be left entirely alone. These are people I love and, I think, understand. I do not share their feelings, but I respect them and know that preaching and prodding would be the very least helpful and effective thing I could do. On the other hand, I have heard many inspiring stories and expressions of gratitude for the home or visiting teacher whose persistent interest and friendliness has led an inactive member back to a way of life which he or she is grateful to have found again. I did have, and maintain, a good relationship with one inactive member as her visiting teacher. I made some cautious contacts with some of the women in our ward who had declined in the past to have visiting teachers or any involvement with the Church, but to say that I was not aggressive would be an understatement.

It was also difficult to make time for neighbors, friends outside the Church, and even friends in other wards, though we had many house guests and managed some social life of our own. I'm sure I was not the first to notice a certain incompatibility between the Church's growing emphasis on "friendshipping" and missionary work and the burgeoning number of meetings and activities which consume our time.

It was easy to explain to other Mormons what I was doing with my time. The words "Relief Society president" communicated immediately and quite accurately. But to most non-Mormon friends and acquaintances, the job meant nothing at all. Many of my neighbors are working mothers whose children are in school. My husband works in an office of professional people, most of whom also have professional spouses. As I met these people and was asked inevitably, "Do you work?", there was always a deep breath and a pause on my part. I could not bear to say "no," as I had never worked harder in my life. I could say, "I stay at home with my children," but that would hardly have given an accurate picture. . . .

From *Dialogue: A Journal of Mormon Thought* (1986)

7. Laury Livsey, "A Day in the Life of a Missionary"

On June 25, 2007, church leaders gathered at the Missionary Training Center in Provo, Utah, to celebrate an evangelistic milestone: 177 years after Joseph Smith's brother, Samuel, first set out to proselytize with a knapsack filled with copies of the Book of Mormon, the one millionth LDS missionary was beginning his two-year service. He joined the other 53,000 full-time young men and young women who were then evangelizing in the church's four hundred plus missions around the world. These missionaries receive intensive evangelistic and linguistic training (more than fifty languages taught) at one of the church's seventeen Missionary Training Centers. Though most Christians accept the implicit responsibility bestowed upon them by "the Great Commission," the directive the resurrected Jesus Christ gave to his apostles to preach his gospel in all the world, LDS youth have proved especially responsive to the call. Several factors probably contribute: Mormon youth attend a four-year course of gospel instruction every school day (before or during class hours) that acquaints them with church teachings and sets up the expectation of missionary service. Youth serve at their own (or their family's) expense so many prospective missionaries begin saving money at an early age. As sociologists of religion generally recognize, a high standard of sacrifice and personal investment tends to enhance rather than hinder religious commitment. And given the emphasis from the leadership on mission service (recent leaders have called it a "duty" for young men but "welcome" young women), the mission serves as a conspicuous marker of church commitment and temple worthiness.

———————————————————

Come along as we follow two sets of missionaries through two typical days of hard work, personal growth, and blessings.

Your assignment is to follow missionaries on a typical day to find out what it is missionaries do. So you check the address once more and find you're on the right street. You pass a pile of tree branches and a discarded computer printer. Next to that is a stone pedestal, with a bowling ball sitting majestically on top. Interesting, you think.

As you continue walking, you see what must be the elders' apartment. It's not easy to find as it is tucked behind a wall and beneath several large citrus trees.

When you step inside, the first thing you notice is how clean the apartment is. However, luxury isn't the first word that leaps to mind. The living room is a little light on furniture, and since Elder Brown and Elder Paventy have already claimed the small couch, Elder Burton and Elder Smith get the floor. The hard floor.

It's seven in the morning, and the four missionaries in the California Anaheim Mission are reading from a study guide and doing some role-playing while preparing for a day of proselyting.

Meanwhile, 40 miles to the north, in the California San Bernardino Mission, Elder Graham is sitting at his desk studying, while his companion, Elder Majeran, is at the kitchen table reading. Their apartment used to be a garage but has been converted to an apartment. At least any oil spills from the structure's previous tenant are now covered by carpeting.

Ah, the life of a missionary.

Even though it's safe to say both apartments won't be included in a home and garden magazine, it really doesn't matter. The missionaries are trying to keep costs down, and they mainly need a place to sleep and study anyway. For the rest of the day, they're doing what they were called to do.

Two days, two missions, two companionships. This is what happened.

TUESDAY IN ANAHEIM

Elder Tim Paventy and Elder Brian Burton have been missionaries for 17 months. Their missions are winding down, but they're not. After going over their schedule, they're out the door by 9:30.

Like many of the missionaries in this mission, they drive cars. So Elder Burton loads up the trunk with copies of the Book of Mormon and *Lamb of God* videos. Elder Paventy hops in the passenger side, and off they go. The first visit is to a less-active member and his nonmember wife.

9:42 A.M.

As the two missionaries walk through an apartment complex, they see a repairman. His name is Gene, and he has a sewed-on badge on his shirt to prove it. Elder Paventy stops him and asks him if they can talk for a minute. Gene waves them off, saying he's too busy.

"We tried," Elder Paventy says.

A few minutes later the missionaries are visiting the part-member family from Colombia. The husband was baptized there before moving to the United States. He explains his Sunday job has kept him from becoming active again, and he's pleased his wife has agreed to talk to the elders. She is very interested in what they have to say and has lots of questions. Elder Burton, who speaks Spanish, explains things and reads scriptures with her. "When I read the Book of Mormon, I feel the same way I do when I read the Bible," she says. Elder Burton smiles.

It's a very productive meeting, and another appointment is scheduled.

"She is really good," Elder Burton says as he walks toward the car. He understands as a missionary you live for moments like that.

11:05 A.M.

The elders are both enthusiastic because they know their next appointment is with an investigator who is committed to baptism. As they walk to their meeting, a woman approaches the missionaries. She tells them she attended church a few times when she lived in Arizona and would like to know where the nearest chapel is. They write down her address and phone number and tell her they'll make sure the missionaries assigned to her area stop by for a visit.

As the elders approach the home of their scheduled appointment, Elder Burton says, "I think we should sing here. It will be a good time to do it, and I know she'll feel the Spirit."

On a recent tour of this mission, Elder Richard H. Winkel of the Seventy challenged the missionaries to sometimes sing to their investigators. "Elder Winkel promised us our investigators will feel the Spirit. We don't sound great when we sing, but the Lord blesses the people listening and allows the Spirit to come through. We really like doing it, and it has caught on in our mission," Elder Burton says.

Elders Burton and Paventy are greeted warmly by the investigator, a middle-aged woman whose daughter joined the Church in Hawaii. The mother saw how her daughter changed and wanted to know why. The daughter called the mission home and requested the missionaries visit her mother. A few weeks earlier they did, and here they are for another discussion.

Before they leave, the missionaries do ask if they can finish with a song. They sing "Love Is Spoken Here." No, they're not the world's best singers. But they're right. You can feel the Spirit.

12:18 P.M.

The elders need to back the car out of a driveway, so Elder Paventy jumps out and directs Elder Burton. "Mission rule," Elder Paventy explains. "Whenever we're backing out, one of us has to check for traffic." Safely on the road, they're now on their way to the Anaheim Shores condominiums for some tracting. "Let's go knocking," Elder Burton says enthusiastically.

Nobody lets them in, but it's not for lack of trying. "Sometimes that's just how it is," Elder Paventy says.

1:40 P.M.

After a quick lunch, the missionaries stop at a nearby park to look at their schedule. As they check their planners, they decide how to spend the rest of the afternoon. "We have the two member visits to do, and we could tract a little more while we're out," Elder Burton says. They're in agreement, and that becomes the plan.

2:32 P.M.

The member visits are short, and more tracting follows. In one apartment complex, the missionaries stop a woman and her daughter and talk to them. The woman explains that she's familiar with the missionaries and the Church, but tells them she isn't interested. Elder Paventy tries one more time for an appointment, but she politely refuses.

"Anything you do as a missionary is stepping out of your comfort zone," Elder Paventy says. "In high school you were looking for your comfort zone. But I've found that on my mission I'm looking to get out of my comfort zone.

I'm always searching for ways to do something more." Maybe at one time it would have seemed odd to go up to complete strangers and talk to them about the Church. But not now. "The Lord has really blessed me that way," he says.

4:13 P.M.

Elder Paventy and Elder Burton are at it again. This time it's with a man in his 20s. As they walk through a neighborhood they stop to talk to him. They engage him in a conversation for several minutes, but he doesn't give them his address or phone number.

4:29 P.M.

It's getting close to dinner. That night they have two more appointments scheduled. But it's time for you to part ways with these missionaries. You're off to the California San Bernardino Mission, and there is Los Angeles rush-hour traffic to battle.

WEDNESDAY IN MONTCLAIR

9:28 A.M.

Elder Darren Majeran and Elder Josh Graham say a prayer, grab their bike helmets, and head out the door. No car for them. They need to get to Bonnie Brae Street for an appointment with an investigator, but they have a little time before that so they go on two callbacks to people they'd met last week. They pedal down the driveway and onto the street.

9:55 A.M.

There is no answer at either home, so back on the bikes they go. Their investigator on Bonnie Brae likes what he has heard about the Church, but he is having a problem understanding the concept of the priesthood and authority. They're prepared to try to answer his questions.

10:07 A.M.

The investigator seems happy to see the missionaries. He has read two of the pamphlets the elders left with him on their last visit, and he's prepared to discuss them. He seems very earnest in his desire to learn. He's just not sure he can accept what they are teaching.

11:20 A.M.

"I thought it went okay," Elder Majeran says after the meeting. "It's just going to take some time."

Next stop: the corner of Harvard Street and Ramona Avenue. The missionaries lock their bikes to a stop sign and begin going door to door. Elder

Majeran and Elder Graham go to 19 houses, but very few people are home, and nobody invites them in.

12:15 P.M.

The missionaries break for lunch and talk about what just happened and what's ahead. Elder Graham has been a missionary for about seven months, and he's settled into a daily routine. "I guess the work has been the way I expected it to be. I haven't done quite as much teaching as I thought we would," he says. "But when you do, and you see people make changes in their lives and know you've been a part of that, it's great."

He continues: "If we tracted for a whole day and did nothing else, we'd probably get in maybe two or three doors."

"We do a lot of talking through screens," Elder Majeran adds. "But we usually have pretty good success once we get in."

Today won't be one of those days, however.

1:22 P.M.

It's more of the same in the afternoon, although there is something to look forward to tonight. A family committed to receive baptism is scheduled for a sixth discussion, and another family in the ward has invited the missionaries to dinner.

7:03 P.M.

With dinner concluded ("The chicken was really good. Sister Wilson is a great cook," Elder Graham says), the missionaries end up teaching a discussion to a person referred to them by a member. That is followed by the discussion to the family scheduled to be baptized.

9:35 P.M.

Another day is complete. Elder Majeran is tired but happy. "Not bad. We got a lot done today," he says. As they change from their proselyting clothes and get ready for bed, they make phone calls to the zone leaders and the ward mission leader.

Your job is done too. You realized after two days that missionary work is still challenging. It takes a lot of hard work and effort, and there are highs and lows. But both companionships remained optimistic and excited about missionary work. All four told you that being missionaries is what they need to be doing.

You shake hands and say good-bye. Your work is done. But theirs isn't.

After all, tomorrow awaits.

From *New Era* (2000)

8. Truman G. Madsen, "House of Glory"

Joseph Smith taught that "in any age of the world" the object of gathering the people of God was the same—"to build unto the Lord an house whereby he could reveal unto his people the ordinances" of his temple.[3] Within months of organizing the church in 1830, Smith began to gather converts to the Kirtland, Ohio, and Independence, Missouri, areas. Within a few years, a magnificent temple (45 feet at the eaves) would be reared in Kirtland at great financial sacrifice. The Latter-day Saints were expelled from Missouri before they could complete a similar structure there, but they dedicated a temple in Nauvoo, Illinois, in 1846. Arrival in Utah was followed by a series of temples, the most famous, in Salt Lake City, being finished in 1893. As of 2014, more than 170 Mormon temples were in operation or planned. Unlike a chapel or ward meetinghouse (of which there are many thousands), temples are not used for normal church services and are not open to the public. In the temple, Latter-day Saints participate in rituals, make specific covenants, and receive the promise of powerful blessings. A principal feature of Mormon temple worship is the belief that rituals performed therein are of eternal, rather than merely temporal, duration. Couples married in the temple, for instance, are "sealed" together for time and for eternity. Individuals who receive their "endowments" are promised spiritual blessings insofar as they keep covenants to observe specified gospel laws, including obedience, sacrifice, chastity, and consecration. In 1840, Joseph Smith taught for the first time that certain gospel rituals, like baptism, could be performed on behalf of those who had died without hearing and accepting the gospel. "Baptisms for the dead," along with endowment and sealings, are likewise vicariously performed in the temples by members standing in for deceased ancestors or other persons. In the remarks that follow, Truman Madsen, a popular teacher and writer, addressed a range of less formalized aspects of temple worship and the meaning of temples for Latter-day Saints.

The Salt Lake Temple was dedicated with a sense of sacrifice and gratitude that maybe we moderns have not reached. Forty years! Forty thousand people gathered just to see the laying of the capstone! And Lorenzo Snow, then one of the Twelve, led them in the Hosanna Shout. And then Wilford Woodruff, who had had a dream years before that he would somehow be involved in the dedication of that temple (and he was by now the President of the Church), promised that a strict reading of the requirements of worthiness would not be imposed on the members attending the dedicatory services provided they come feasting and repenting. . . .

Well, during a twenty-three-day period of dedicatory services averaging two thousand each session, some eighty thousand people were regenerated. President Woodruff's entry in his journal at the end of that year was: "The greatest event of the year [1893] is the dedication of the Salt Lake Temple. Great power was manifest on that occasion."

The scriptural phrase that brings all that into a theme is that we are to receive in temples, through temples, from temples, "power from on high" (D&C 95:8). Christ is the source of that power. The temple is His. Every symbol in and out of that sacred structure points toward Him and, as a cup carries water, transmits the Holy Spirit.

Now to be specific in terms of needs that all of us feel strongly about in our time. It is a characteristic fact that the Lord has commanded the sacrifice of temple building at the times when apparently our people were least able to build them; and the sacrifice has been immense. But sacrifice "brings forth blessings."

In the 1830s the Brethren kept inquiring. They didn't have our heritage, and they didn't understand even what the word *temple* meant. They kept asking, What is it we are doing? Well, we build a temple. What for? And Joseph Smith told them on one occasion, "nor could Gabriel explain it to [your] understanding." But prepare, he told them, for great blessings will come.

Yet in a preparatory revelation (see D&C 88) the purposes of the temple are outlined. It's called "a house of prayer, a house of fasting, a house of faith, a house of learning, a house of glory, . . . a house of God." Prepare yourselves, it says, "sanctify yourselves . . . and [God] . . . will unveil his face unto you." (D&C 88:68, 119.)

Let's discuss each of those purposes.

A house of prayer. "Make yourselves acquainted," said the Prophet, "with those men who like Daniel pray three times a day toward the House of the Lord." There is a true principle involved in literally facing the house of God as one prays and as one praises the Lord. The Prophet, as he led a group of faithful Saints through the Nauvoo Temple not yet finished (he did not live to see that day), said to them, "You do not know how to pray to have your prayers answered." But, as the sister who recorded that brief statement testifies, she and her husband received their temple blessings, and then came to understand what he meant.

A modern Apostle, Elder Melvin J. Ballard, said once to a group of young people about solving their problems: "Study it out in your own minds, reach a conclusion, and then go to the Lord with it and he will give you an answer by that inward burning, and if you don't get your answer I will tell you where to go; go to the House of the Lord. Go with your hearts full of desire to do your duty. When in the sacred walls of these buildings, where you are entitled to the Spirit of the Lord, and in the silent moments, the answer will come." . . .

"A house of prayer, a house of fasting, a house of faith, a house of learning." One of the men who touched my life was Elder John A. Widtsoe of the Council of the Twelve, a man who graduated summa cum laude from Harvard after three instead of the usual four years, who was given in that last year an award for the greatest depth of specializing in his field (which was chemistry); but they also gave an award that year for the student who had shown the greatest breadth of interests, which he also received. Elder Widtsoe wrote perceptively about the temple and temple worship. I heard him say in sacred circumstances that the promise was given him by a patriarch when he was a mere boy in Norway, "Thou shalt have great faith in the ordinances of the Lord's House." And so he did. I heard him say that the temple is so freighted with depth of understanding, so loaded with symbolic grasp of life and its eternal significance, that only a fool would attempt in mere prosaic restatement to give it in a comprehensive way.

I heard him say that the temple is a place of revelation. And he did not divorce that concept from the recognition that the problems we have are very practical, very realistic, down-to-earth problems. He often said, "I would rather take my practical problems to the house of the Lord than anywhere else." In his book *In a Sunlit Land* he describes a day when, having been frustrated for months in trying to pull together a mass of data he had compiled to come up with a formula, he took his companion, his wife, to the Logan Temple to forget his failure. And in one of the rooms of that structure there came, in light, the very answer he had previously failed to find. Two books on agrarian chemistry grew out of that single insight—a revelation in the temple of God.

The temple is not just a union of heaven and earth. It is the key to our mastery of the earth. It is the Lord's graduate course in subduing the earth, which, as only Latter-day Saints understand, ultimately will be heaven—this earth glorified.

A house of learning? Yes, and we learn more than about the earth. We learn *ourselves*. We come to comprehend more deeply, in an environment that surrounds one like a cloak, our own identity, something of the roots that we can't quite reach through memory but which nevertheless are built cumulatively into our deepest selves—an infinite memory of conditions that predate memory. The temple is the catalyst whereby the self is revealed to the self. . . .

The temple is a house of learning. And it is intended that therein we not simply learn *of* or *about* Christ, but that we come to *know Him*. It has always impressed me that in the Joseph Smith Translation the classic passage about the hereafter when many will say, "Lord, Lord, did we not do this and that?" is rendered more fittingly. The King James Version says that Christ will respond, "I never knew you." The Joseph Smith Translation renders it, "You never knew me." (Matt. 7:23; JST Matt. 7:33.)

This is the gospel of Jesus Christ. This is the restored Church of Jesus Christ. This is the church that teaches us that we can have a direct and immediate living relationship with the living Christ. And we inscribe on temples, "Holiness to the Lord," "The House of the Lord." He told us, and He didn't qualify it, that as regards our preparation, "all the pure in heart that come into it shall see God" (D&C 97:16). Elder Orson Pratt points out that this promise specifically relates to a temple not yet built, a temple to be erected in the center city, the New Jerusalem, wherein someday Christ actually will dwell; and wherein, therefore, any who enter will meet Him. But again, Elders John A. Widtsoe, George F. Richards, Joseph Fielding Smith, and others have borne witness that the promise is more extensive than that; that it applies now. It is a promise that we may have a wonderfully rich *communion with* Him. *Communion!* That is to say that we are not simply learning propositions *about,* but that we are in a participative awareness *with*.

Occasionally we struggle in amateur research in Church history to understand what kind of a portrait, in terms of sheer physical appearance, one could draw of Christ if we simply utilized what modern witnesses have said about their glimpses of Him. It's an impressive portrait. But one thing perhaps we sometimes neglect in that curiosity is an awareness or a seeking for an awareness of His personality, of those subtler realities that we already recognize in other persons in all variations but which have been perfected in Him. What would it be like to be in His presence, not simply in terms of what you would see but what you would feel? To give us one clue, He says, "Listen to him, who is pleading your cause before [the Father], saying, Father, behold the sufferings and death of him who did no sin [that is to say, committed none, but he knows sins, for he experienced temptation to do them all], in whom thou wast well pleased; behold the blood of thy Son which was shed, . . . wherefore, Father, spare these my brethren." (D&C 45:3–5.) That's a glimpse of the compassion that one comes to feel in communion—the feeling with, the feeling for, that He has. He is the one personality of whom it cannot truthfully be said: "You don't know me. You don't understand me. You don't care about me." Because of what He went through, He does know, He does understand, He does care. And He has had us sacrifice to build sacred houses where the linkage of His heart, His "bowels of compassion," can merge with ours.

The temple is a place of learning to know Him.

And now the phrase "a house of glory, a house of God." One of the most tender moments of my spiritual life was the day that Rose Wallace Bennett, an author I knew, told me that as a little girl she was present in the dedicatory services of the Salt Lake Temple. She described also the day Wilford Woodruff had a birthday, his ninetieth, when it was a little girl's privilege to take forward to him in the Tabernacle ninety roses in a setting of some eight thousand children between the ages of eight and twelve, all dressed in white. They had gathered to honor him; and then as he had come into the building (under some pretense that there was need of an organ repair), they arose and sang, "We Thank Thee, O God, for a Prophet." She could not talk about what it felt like to see his tears, or again, what it was like to be in the temple, without herself weeping. But what she said to me was: "Young man, my father brought me to the edge of City Creek Canyon where we could look down on the temple. I testify to you that there was a light around the temple, and it was not due to electricity."

There are such phrases in all the authentic literature that has to do with temple dedications: "light," "glory," "power." Even some who were not members of the Church at Kirtland came running, wondering what had happened. They wondered if the building was on fire. It was; but with what the Prophet called "celestial burnings," the downflow of the power of the living God, like encircling flame as on the day of Pentecost. A prayer for that had been offered by the Prophet and by his father, and it was fulfilled. (See D&C 109:36–37.)

What is glory? Well, it is many things in the scriptures. One strand of meaning is often neglected. If we can trust one Hebrew student, the Hebrew word equivalent to glory, *kabod,* refers in some of its strands to physical presence. Just as a person says in common parlance today, "he was there in all his glory," so the Old Testament often uses this word for God. In the Psalm that refers to the glory (Ps. 8) there are two changes that are crucial. The King James Version reads, "Thou hast made [man] a little lower than the angels, and hast crowned him with glory and honour." Probably what that verse said originally was, "Thou hast made [man] a little lower than the Gods, and hath crowned him with a *physical body* and with honor." This is the truth. The body is a step *up* in the scales of progression, not a step down. God is God because He is gloriously embodied; and were He not so embodied, He would be less than God.

The privilege of attending the house of God is in effect to have our physical beings brought into harmony with our spirit personalities. And I have read, but cannot quote perfectly, can only paraphrase, the testimony of President Lorenzo Snow to the effect that participating in the temple ceremonies is the only way that the knowledge locked in one's spirit can become part of this flesh; thus occurs that inseparable union, that blending, which makes possible a celestial resurrection. It is as if, if I may mix the figure, we are given in the house of God a patriarchal blessing to every organ and attribute and power of our being, a blessing that is to be fulfilled in this world and the next, keys and insights that can enable us to live a godly life in a very worldly world, protected—yes, even insulated—from the poisons and distortions that are everywhere.

That is the temple. And the glory of God, His ultimate perfection, is in His house duplicated in us, provided we go there with a susceptible attitude.

From *Five Classics by Truman G. Madsen* (1994)

9. Clark T. Thorstenson, "Discovering My Icelanders"

No one would doubt that sex, sports, and money are the three most popular topics on the Internet. But a 1999 Time cover article named genealogy, or family history, as number four.[4] Mormon interest in family history was generated when Joseph Smith taught that through the performance of temple ordinances, family relationships could be made eternal. Lending theological impetus to the genealogical research was his added teaching that ordinances necessary for salvation, such as baptism, could be performed by proxy for those who died without such an opportunity in this life. Together, these beliefs provide a powerful motivation for Latter-day Saints to "seek out their dead." Smith in fact taught that salvation for the dead was the most important work members could engage in, and the last decades of the twentieth century and the first of the new millennium saw an explosion in the construction of Mormon temples, dedicated to that purpose.

Nationally, interest in family history research began at about the same time as the early Latter-day Saints. The New England Historical and Genealogical Society was organized in 1845. Utah's version followed in 1894, and Salt Lake City is now the hub of an astoundingly massive and efficient family history project. Over seven hundred professionals and volunteers assist some fifteen hundred daily visitors at the church's Family History Library to trace their "kindred dead," relying upon millions of rolls and fiche of microfilm and hundreds of thousands of published sources. Thousands of rolls of additional microfilm pour in monthly, produced by hundreds of volunteers photographing records in dozens of countries at any one time. The church's searchable databases now comprise more than a billion names, and their FamilySearch.org Web site receives billions of hits annually. But most inspiring to members are the myriad stories of what they consider to be divine guidance along their paths to seeking out their own ancestors.

The term *Icelander* has a special meaning in the immediate area of Spanish Fork, Utah. The "Icelanders," as they are affectionately known, came to Utah as converts in the late 1800s from the Westman Islands just off the coast of Iceland. They settled in the southeast corner of Spanish Fork, which was known as the "bench," and they had such an impact upon the other settlers that the area rapidly became known as "Little Iceland."

Both of my father's parents were born in Iceland, and my father taught me that being an "Icelander" was akin to being one of noble birth and heritage. I have always believed that and have held a special place in my heart for anyone with a heritage common to mine.

My father died when I was just a child, and my grandparents died shortly after; so when it came time for me to search out the information for my four-generation sheets, I had to turn to records that were either incorrect or incomplete. Family records were almost nonexistent, and church and community archives contained so many inaccuracies that I became frustrated. After hundreds of exasperating hours at the Brigham Young University branch library as well as the Church genealogical library in Salt Lake City, and even with assistance from skilled genealogists, I still had not been able to complete the four-generation sheets as asked by the Church. But I never gave up, and I regularly enrolled in genealogy classes in hopes that someday there would be a breakthrough.

About two years ago, as I sat in a ward genealogy class, I raised my hand and gave vent to my consternation, explaining that I had done all I could but was unable to complete the task required. I still remember the teacher's reply: "Brother Thorstenson, if you have done everything possible that you know how to do and still can't complete the worksheets, the Lord will open the way for you."

Her words were stated so firmly and in such a positive way that I felt she was right and I would be helped.

Some two weeks later I received a telephone call telling me that a man from Iceland who was visiting in Spanish Fork thought he might possibly be a relative of mine. In just a moment of conversation with Marino Gudmundsson, I learned that his grandfather and my grandfather were first cousins and that Dr. Thorstein Jonsson (former mayor of the Westman Islands) was a common great-grandfather! Marino was a nonmember, but missionaries who had just opened Iceland for missionary work, after our having no missionaries there for almost one hundred years, had contacted him. During their conversation he remembered that he had heard of Mormon relatives who had gone to Utah. His curiosity about Utah and the possibility of relatives being there led him to make a special trip just to get acquainted with them.

The words, "The Lord will open the way" were literally ringing in my ears as I conversed with this intelligent and intriguing relative who seemed to have all the missing genealogical information I needed. I felt I had known him all my life, and soon we became close personal friends.

About three weeks after he and his wife, Gudrun, returned to Iceland, I received a package in the mail containing five generations of names on my father's side, a photograph of my great-grandfather, and clippings from books and articles about my family. He also said I had a large number of living relatives in Iceland and that a visit by me would open all the records I needed for genealogy.

I had always dreamed of going to Iceland, but in three trips to Europe I had never been able to arrange to go that far north. This past spring, however, an assignment to the Nordic countries opened the way, and almost before my wife and I realized it, our airplane was landing at Keflavik Airport in Iceland.

To our dismay, no one met us at the airport, even though we had written to Marino more than a month prior to our departure informing him of our flight plan and requesting that he meet our plane if possible, since we knew no one else in the country. After a short wait, we boarded a bus for a forty-five-minute ride into Reykjavik, the capital city of Iceland, and were delighted to see two missionaries in the crowd looking for us. They informed us that Marino was in The Netherlands and would be unable to return during our short stay. Imagine my disappointment! I could feel my opportunity for genealogy work slipping away.

The elders took us to our hotel and then told us of the church meeting schedule and the opportunities they had arranged for us to speak. After they left, I looked out the window at the gray clouds, the dark seas, and the recently fallen snow and felt despair. In spite of the opportunity to be of service to the Saints, I felt I was about to lose my one great chance to serve my kindred dead.

About that time the phone rang and a pleasant female voice asked for me by my first name. She said her name was Valborg, that she was a cousin of mine, and that Marino had told her I would be in Iceland. She wondered if I could arrange my schedule to meet with her and other family members the following day. "The Lord will open the way" rang again in my ears.

My spirits soared. On Sunday we spoke to the missionaries, in Sunday School, in sacrament meeting, and at a fireside to the forty or so members and investigators who were eager to hear someone from Church headquarters.

Between church meetings, Valborg came to our hotel and took us to a fine, large home where we found a dozen elderly and middle-aged relatives who were just as anxious to meet us as we were to meet them. As soon as we were introduced, I pulled family group sheets from my briefcase and asked them to help me fill in information I was missing, which they were pleased to do. Most of them were children of my grandfather's brothers, and they related many stories about my family that spiritually buoyed me up. They were warm and friendly and seemed delighted that we could be with them. They were even more expressive when I told them they were the only direct relatives I had ever met on my Icelandic side of the family. Afterwards, I could have floated back to the hotel, I was so happy.

The next day they arranged for us to fly to the birthplace of my grandparents, the Westman Islands. Mechanical problems delayed the flight two hours, but when we landed, another cousin was there to greet us. He showed us the home where my grandfather was born and then took us to the cemetery, where we were able to obtain vital information from family headstones. He even took us to a nursing home to see his mother, who could remember my grandfather when she was a small child.

Again, miracles seemed to be continuously forthcoming. The Westman Islands were almost destroyed by a small volcano several years ago. The lava destroyed over four hundred homes and came within half a block of where my grandfather was born. Volcanic ash buried the cemetery, but international student volunteers joined natives and hauled away the ten feet of ash that covered the headstones. Despite the natural disasters, the genealogical data I needed was there waiting for me. Even my cousin, Bogi Sigurdsson, turned out to be a miracle. He could verify all the data I received because as a youth he had memorized his ancestral line for six generations.

Because the flight to the Westman Islands was so late arriving, we only had three hours on the island before we had to return to Reykjavik. With much emotion and love, we departed. My ancestors were now real, personal, and, I felt, nearby.

On our third and final day in Iceland, my cousin Valborg came to the hotel and took us shopping. And then, as a last-minute gesture, she invited us to her home for light refreshments before we departed for the airport. Her husband, Sighvatur, and their child were there to greet us, and we enjoyed being together.

Then another miracle occurred. Just before we were to leave, Sighvatur said he wanted to show us his den and collection of Icelandic books. Time was short, but to be courteous we went upstairs to see them. To my amazement, he pulled a book from the shelf which contained the biography of my great-grandfather, Thorstein Jonsson. A cursory glance told me immediately that it contained further family records and information of considerable value. I had started copying feverishly when he, almost casually, pulled out an ancient handwritten document and said, "You might be interested in this. It's the genealogy of Thorstein Jonsson."

I literally trembled as he handed it to me and I leafed through the pages—thirty-two in all—handwritten. It provided a complete record of Thorstein Jonsson's family back to A.D. 1124! It even included a paragraph in Thorstein Jonsson's own handwriting saying he had read it, reviewed it, and could unequivocally state that it was accurate! Again I could have floated away. Then Sighvatur told me that he was going to give the original document to a museum for preservation, but that he had photocopied it and would like to present a copy to me.

As we left for the airport, I thought to myself, "If Marino had been here, I probably would never have gone to the home where the only copy of this document was to be found, and consequently I wouldn't have received it."

I don't remember much more. The flight home was smooth, the food was good, the people were pleasant. All I remember is the words, "The Lord will open the way for you."

———————

From Ensign (1981)

10. Ruth M. Gardner and Vanja Y. Watkins, "Families Can Be Together Forever"; and Janice Kapp Perry, "I Love to See the Temple"

Church leaders teach that "all roads lead to the temple." A Book of Mormon scripture asks of the recently baptized, "after ye have gotten into this strait and narrow path, I would ask if all is done? Behold, I say unto you, Nay" (2 Nephi 31:19). Spiritual progress after baptism is largely marked by temple milestones. At age twelve, church youth participate in temple trips where they are baptized for deceased persons. Before departing on their missions, generally at eighteen, young men receive their "endowment," which is a series of promised blessings predicated on obedience to covenants they make in a sacred ritual. Young women generally receive their endowments preparatory to marriage, unless they too serve as missionaries at age nineteen or older and go to the temple at that time. For returned missionaries and converts, the capstone temple experience is the temple marriage (or "sealing" for those already wedded). In this ceremony, bride and groom are united in a priesthood ritual that gives the conditional promise of a union beyond the grave and the right to posterity in perpetuity. At this moment a new eternal unit is forged, at the same time it is incorporated into an eternal family tree. Children born to such a union are considered "born in the covenant" and automatically form part of that eternal family unit. (Married converts may be sealed to their children who were not born under the covenant.) As the children grow up in an observant LDS home, they will repeat the cycle. While the theological details may escape them, children are responsive to the safety and security of family ties, and the ubiquitous Mormon mantra, "families are forever," establishes early on the indissoluble connection in LDS minds between temples and enduring family bonds. The following two popular children's songs provide additional reinforcement.

FAMILIES CAN BE TOGETHER FOREVER

I have a family here on earth.
They are so good to me.
I want to share my life with them through all eternity.

[Chorus]

Families can be together forever
Through Heavenly Father's plan.
I always want to be with my own family,
And the Lord has shown me how I can.
The Lord has shown me how I can.

———————————————————————

While I am in my early years,
I'll prepare most carefully,
So I can marry in God's temple for eternity.

[Chorus]

I LOVE TO SEE THE TEMPLE

I love to see the temple.
I'm going there someday
To feel the Holy Spirit,
To listen and to pray.
For the temple is a house of God,
A place of love and beauty.
I'll prepare myself while I am young;
This is my sacred duty.

———————————————————————

I love to see the temple.
I'll go inside someday.
I'll cov'nant with my Father;

I'll promise to obey.
For the temple is a holy place
Where we are sealed together.
As a child of God,
I've learned this truth;
A fam'ly is forever.

From *Hymns of The Church of Jesus Christ of Latter-day Saints* (1985) and *Children's Songbook of The Church of Jesus Christ of Latter-day Saints* (1989)

11. Brenda Williams, "My Terrible, Horrible Day"

Most LDS priesthood rituals follow a tightly prescribed format and occur in formal settings (like baptisms, sacrament prayers, and grave dedications) or moments of conspicuous need (such as blessing of the sick). The most striking exception to this rule is the father's blessing. The benediction pronounced by a patriarch upon his children is a common scriptural motif. Isaac blessed Jacob, Jacob in turn blessed his twelve sons, while the Book of Mormon patriarch Lehi gave a final blessing to his sons and even a servant before his own death (women were apparently either ignored or unmentioned). In the LDS faith, fathers similarly bless their children (including daughters), but at times of transition, crisis, or special need, rather than as the final act of a departing father. In many Mormon homes, it is customary for a father to bless his children on the first day of a new school year, when they depart for college or military service, or at other times that represent moments of anxiety and upheaval. But children are also encouraged to request such blessings at any time when the pressures of their lives, a personal problem, or a pending decision looms especially large. Done in the intimacy of a home, without official supervision or in conjunction with a life milestone, a father's blessing becomes the occasion for the father to express his love and concern and respond in a sensitive way to the particular, and often unvocalized, needs of a child. The practice is thus a prompt to the father to maintain worthiness so he will have the requisite inspiration and a catalyst to family unity. The blessing is performed by the authority of the Melchizedek Priesthood. Similar blessings of counsel or comfort may be administered to wives and to non-family church members as well.

I sat alone at the edge of my bed, balancing my thick biology book as I attempted to study for the next day's test. I slowly turned through the complicated chapter on cellular respiration, my jaw tight as I tried to concentrate. But it was useless.

I looked up at the glow-in-the-dark stars clustered above my bed, dull in the light of my lamp, the sharp edges blurring as my eyes filled with tears. I had done a horrible job that evening trying out for the play. It had been my first attempt at high school theater. Although untrained in the arts of dancing, acting, and singing, I had undertaken the challenging musical tryouts at the urging of my friends. I hadn't done well. My dancing on the first night and my singing audition seemed about average. But tonight had been the final test, the portion I had counted on for success—a memorized humorous monologue, performed in under a minute, before the critical eyes of the director and audition board. I had prepared for my monologue days in advance, writing and memorizing the script carefully until I was certain I could perform it even in my sleep. But when I had reached the school, I couldn't think clearly. I was not only nervous but also tired and worried about my two difficult tests scheduled for the next day. I tried to remember my lines, those words that I knew so well, but they slipped from me in fragments and spilled out shaky and uncertain.

A hot tear brushed my lips, and I tried to muffle a sob. Nothing seemed to be going right the past few weeks. Between the recent cold distance of one of my closest friends, the stress of my difficult schedule, and the nagging doubts of applying to college, I was finding my senior year to be nearly impossible. And now, after the embarrassment of tonight's audition, I didn't know how I could study or even sleep. I shut my biology book and placed it on the floor, emotions roiling as I buried my head in my pillow.

Then I heard my door open and the concerned voice of my mother. "Do you need a blessing?" she asked softly. I looked up, tempted to send her away. My puffy red face, streaked by wetness, held the imprint of my pillow's seams. But I knew, even as I pulled myself into a sitting position so that I could see both my parents in my doorway, that tonight a blessing was what I needed most of all. I nodded wordlessly, sniffing a bit as I stood and followed my parents across the hall into their room.

I've heard of blessings given by pioneers. And even in modern times I've heard of blessings for fire victims, children in comas, and people who are not expected to survive. I had a testimony of the priesthood before that night. I had been given my patriarchal blessing two years prior and knew of the unique truthfulness and love it contained. But as my father placed his hands on my head that evening, I could feel divine power in his phrases, in the gentle pressure of his hands. His blessing swept past my superficial wants into what I needed to hear most. And as he concluded, my heart sang at the power in those words, those simple, healing words that I knew were not his. My father couldn't remember what he had said, but I could, and my dark tangle of stress and fears had loosened into a soft and gentle peace.

I smiled at my mother, grateful for her inspired suggestion. As I turned around and hugged my father, I could feel in the warmth of his arms an echo of the love of my Heavenly Father and His Son, both watching and caring for me more than anyone else ever could. I felt so grateful for that single modest blessing, those quietly powerful, comforting words. That night I slept deeply for the first time in weeks, unworried and sure of my future as a beloved daughter of God.

From *New Era* (2001)

12. Kathleen Flake, "How to Bury a Prophet"

Church leaders have counseled Latter-day Saints to make funerals appropriately solemn occasions, but they are also to be celebrations of lives well lived and opportunities to teach the LDS plan of salvation. Although Mormons believe that the departed return to the presence of God and loved ones, they still—in conformity with scriptural admonition—"weep for the loss of them that die." As with Christian funerals generally, Mormon services include prayers, sermons, sentimental tributes, hymns, and special music. Speakers are encouraged to focus on the atonement of Jesus Christ and his redemptive mission. After the funeral services, typically held in local meetinghouses where the deceased attended church, family members and close friends assemble for a graveside service where a Melchizedek Priesthood holder dedicates the grave to remain undisturbed and hallowed until the resurrection. Latter-day Saints are generally buried, out of respect for the body, rather than being cremated, although local customs or personal preference may dictate otherwise. President Gordon B. Hinckley was the fifteenth prophet of the church and one of the most beloved. Though little ceremony is accorded a Mormon prophet, the membership feels immense respect. Often, for instance, audiences will rise and spontaneously sing the anthem "We Thank Thee O God for a Prophet" when the church president enters an assembly hall or auditorium before an address. In the case of a prophet's funeral, however, little distinguishes the service from that which attends the passing of any other member. So how do you bury a Mormon prophet? The same way you bury a normal Latter-day Saint.

The Latter-day Saints buried their prophet on Saturday. Thousands attended the service in person and millions more faithful watched in chapels around the globe, as well as on the internet. What they saw was an unusually personal ceremony for a very public man who led and to large degree defined the contemporary Church of Jesus Christ of Latter-day Saints. Notwithstanding the numbers and titles of participants, Gordon Hinckley's funeral was a family affair both in word and sacrament. It was an extraordinary display of what makes Mormonism tick.

Gordon Hinckley died at the age of ninety-seven, having been in the church's leading councils since 1958 and serving as its fifteenth president since 1995. He shaped the church through a half century of growth in one hundred and seventy countries. A third of its present membership joined during his tenure as president. Displaying remarkable vigor late in life, he met with church members on every continent, responding to their needs with curricular, welfare, and building programs whose costs are impossible to imagine and no one will admit. He met the press to a degree unequaled and with an openness heretofore unknown among Mormonism's leadership. This effort too was largely successful. No less a cynic than CBS's Mike Wallace admitted that Hinckley "fully deserves the almost universal admiration that he gets." He was, as *Newsweek*'s Jon Meacham said, "a charming and engaging man, an unlikely prelate—and all the more impressive for that." The same could be said of his funeral.

Hinckley's funeral was an unlikely but impressive mix of the sacramental and the mundane, in large part because it observed Mormonism's custom that families bury their dead. The family designs the memorial program, participates actively in it, and performs the ordinances that send their loved ones off to the next life. Yes, the chapel in this case was the LDS Conference Center that held 21,000 mourners; the lay pastor who conducted the meeting was Thomas Monson, Hinckley's presumptive successor as "prophet, seer, and revelator;" and the music was provided by the three-hundred-plus member Mormon Tabernacle Choir. But, in all other essentials, the service was performed by the family. A son gave the invocation. Monson conducted at the request of the family, he said, not by ecclesiastical right. The eulogy was given by a daughter who described her father's life as half-way point in a now seven-generation story of sacrifice, death, and survival that is the Mormon saga. Explicitly gathering the millions watching into that story, she declared "we are one family sharing an inheritance of faith." Friends with high titles spoke next.

Though the requisite list of Hinckley's ecclesiastical accomplishments was given, it was subordinated to his success as a courageous and amusing friend and a successful husband and father. Another daughter gave the benediction: "We are buoyed by the knowledge that we will see him again as family, as friends."

Hinckley's sons and daughters with their spouses led the casket out of the hall and between an honor guard of church authorities. Cameras followed the mourners, focusing on his five children, twenty-five grandchildren and sixty-two great-grandchildren who formed the cortege to the cemetery. There, possibly most surprisingly, the eldest son dedicated the grave without fanfare. Notwithstanding the presence of the entire church hierarchy, the son stepped forward to pronounce: "By the authority of the Melchizedek priesthood, I dedicate this grave for the remains of Gordon B. Hinckley, until such time as thou shall call him forth." Then, church leaders were "dismissed," as Monson put it. As the church teaches is the case in the afterlife, only the family remained.

Families are, as Latter-day Saints like to say, forever. What they don't say is that the church is not forever. It is only the instrument for endowing families with the right and duty to mediate the gifts of the gospel to their members, thereby sealing the willing among them as families in the life to come. This was Hinckley's message as a prophet. As he would have it and as the best Mormon funerals do, his message was embodied and enacted by his family who blessed him in death, no less than in life. This is how the Latter-day Saints, at least, bury a prophet.

From *Sightings* (2008)

$$\text{N O T E S}$$

Preface

1. "Style Guide—The Name of the Church," Newsroom, The Church of Jesus Christ of Latter-day Saints. Available at: http://newsroom.lds.org/style-guide. Accessed February 21, 2011. See also Diane Connolly, "Church of Jesus Christ of Latter-day Saints," in *Reporting on Religion: A Primer on Journalism's Best Beat*, ed. Debra L. Mason (Westerville, Ohio: Religion Newswriters Association, 2006), 74–75.
2. *Associated Press Stylebook*, "The Church of Jesus Christ of Latter-day Saints" (New York: Associated Press, 2004), 48, 215.
3. "Community of Christ: General Denominational Information," Community of Christ. Available at: www.cofchrist.org/news/GeneralInfo.asp. Accessed February 21, 2011; "Growth of the Church," Newsroom, The Church of Jesus Christ of Latter-day Saints. Available at: http://newsroom.lds.org/topic/church-growth. Accessed February 21, 2011.
4. Richard F. Burton, *The City of the Saints and Across the Rocky Mountains to California*, ed. Fawn M. Brodie (New York: Knopf, 1963), 224.

1. Theology and Doctrine

1. Bob Mims, "Mormons: High Conservativism, Low Divorce, Big Growth," *Salt Lake Tribune*, March 6, 1999. Available at: http://archives.his.com/smartmarriages/; Census Bureau, *Statistical Abstract of the United States 1997: National Data Book* (Washington, D.C.: U.S. Department of Commerce, 1997); Christian Smith, *Soul Searching: The Religious and Spiritual Lives of American Teenagers* (New York: Oxford University Press, 2005), 38–40.

2. Scattering of the Saints

1. Newell G. Bringhurst and John C. Hamer, eds., *Scattering of the Saints: Schism within Mormonism* (Independence, Mo.: John Whitmer, 2007). This text helps explain the core differences between the various theological and social factions of Mormonism.

2. Parley P. Pratt, "A Dialogue Between Joe Smith and the Devil," *New York Herald*, August 25, 1844.

3. E. Watson, ed., *Manuscript History of Brigham Young, 1801–1844* (Salt Lake City, Utah: Smith Secretarial Service, 1968), 170–71.

4. Wilford Woodruff to Heber J. Grant, March 26, 1887, Church History Library, The Church of Jesus Christ of Latter-day Saints, Salt Lake City, Utah.

5. "Letter of Appointment," available at: www.strangite.org/Reveal.htm#SECTION-1. Those outside the Strangite church consider the letter a forgery.

6. Hard numbers are impossible to come by. A range of statistics is discussed in Vickie Cleverley Speek, "From Strangites to Reorganized Latter Day Saints: Transformations in Midwestern Mormonism, 1856–79," in *Scattering of the Saints: Schism within Mormonism*, ed. Newell G. Bringhurst and John C. Hamer (Independence, Mo.: John Whitmer Books, 2007), 142–44.

7. Joseph Wood, *Epistle of the Twelve* (Milwaukee, Wisc.: The Church of Jesus Christ of Latter Day Saints [Williamite], 1851).

8. Wood, *Epistle*, 9–10, 18–20.

9. Larry Watson, "The Church of Jesus Christ (Headquartered in Monongahela, Pennsylvania), Its History and Doctrine," in *Scattering of the Saints*, 194.

10. As two historians note, "The current location of the original document is unknown, making it virtually impossible to answer questions about dating and authorship. Various copies are in circulation, but no one has come forward claiming any of these as the original." See Richard Neitzel Holzapfel and Christopher C. Jones, "'John the Revelator': The Written Revelations of John Taylor," in *Champion of Liberty: John Taylor*, ed. Mary Jane Woodger (Provo, Utah: Religious Studies Center, Brigham Young University, 2009), 273–308.

11. Joseph W. Musser, *The Journal of Joseph W. Musser, 1872–1954* (n.p.: Pioneer Press, 1948), 9.

12. Brian C. Hales, "I Have Been Fanatically Religious: Joseph White Musser, Father of the Fundamentalist Movement." Available at: www.mormonfundamentalism.com/JWM-Bio.html.

3. Gathering to Zion

1. "To All the Saints Abroad," *Elders Journal* 1, no. 4 (August 1838): 54.

2. "To the Elders of the Church of Latter-day Saints," in Joseph Smith, *History*, 2: 254–55.

3. Sarah M. Kimball, "Auto-Biography," *Woman's Exponent* 12 (September 1, 1883): 51.

4. Minutes, Nauvoo Female Relief Society, April 28, 1842. Church History Library, The Church of Jesus Christ of Latter-day Saints, Salt Lake City, Utah.

5. Paul E. Dahl, " 'All Is Well . . .': The Story of 'the Hymn That Went around the World,' " *BYU Studies* 21, no. 4 (Fall 1981): 523.

6. John Langeland, "Scandinavia, the Church in," in *Encyclopedia of Mormonism*, ed. Daniel H. Ludlow. (New York: Macmillan Publishing Company, 1992), 3: 1264.

7. James E. Talmage, "The Story of Mormonism," *Improvement Era* 4, no. 9 (July 1901), 692–698.

8. Editors Table, *Improvement Era* 6, no. 2 (December 1902), 150.

9. "An Address. The Church of Jesus Christ of Latter-day Saints to the World," *Improvement Era* 10, no. 7 (May 1907): 483.

4. Government and Politics

1. Joseph F. Smith, "The Truth About Mormonism," *Out West* 23 (1905): 242.

2. Garth L. Mangum, "Welfare Projects," in *Historical Atlas of Mormonism*, ed. S. Kent Brown, Donald Q. Cannon, and Richard H. Jackson (New York: Simon and Schuster, 1994), 140.

5. Race and Ethnicity

1. *The Evening and Morning Star* 2, no. 14 (July 1833): 109–111.

2. Matthias Cowley, *Wilford Woodruff* (Salt Lake City, Utah: Deseret News Press, 1909), 351.

3. Bruce R. McConkie, "All Are Alike unto God," in *I Believe: A Retrospective of Twelve Firesides and Devotionals, Brigham Young University, 1973–1985* (Provo, Utah: Brigham Young University, 2006), 75–84.

6. Sexuality and Gender

1. "How the Public Perceives Romney, Mormons," Pew Forum on Religion and Public Life, December 4, 2007. Available at: www.pewforum.org/Politics-and-Elections/How-the-Public-Perceives-Romney-Mormons.aspx.

2. Daniel H. Ludlow, ed., *Encyclopedia of Mormonism* (New York: Macmillan, 1992), 3: 1095.

3. Joseph Lee Robinson, *Journal and Autobiography of Joseph Lee Robinson*, 50, Church History Library, The Church of Jesus Christ of Latter-day Saints, Salt Lake City, Utah.

4. Editor's Table, *Improvement Era* 15, no. 11 (September 1912): 1042–43.

5. James R. Clark, comp., *Messages of the First Presidency*, 6 vols. (Salt Lake City, Utah: Bookcraft, 1965–1975), 4: 199–206.

6. L. John Nuttall, "Helps in Teacher-Training," *Improvement Era* 27, no. 5 (March 1924): 429–30.

7. Tim B. Heaton, Kristen L. Goodman, and Thomas B. Holman, "In Search of a Peculiar People: Are Mormon Families Really Different," in *Contemporary Mormonism: Social Science Perspectives*, ed. Marie Cornwall, Tim B. Heaton, and Lawrence A. Young (Urbana: University of Illinois Press, 1994), 100.

7. Education and Intellectualism

1. Leonard J. Arrington and Davis Bitton, *The Mormon Experience* (New York: Random House, 1979), 337.
2. "Projecting Bachelor Degree Recipients by Gender," *Postsecondary Opportunity* 102 (December 2000), 8–11; Mabel Newcomer, *A Century of Higher Education for American Women* (New York: Harper and Brothers, 1959), 46.
3. Brigham Young, "Obeying the Gospel—Recreation—Individual Development," *Journal of Discourses* 13 (July 18, 1869): 61.
4. Claudia L. Bushman, *Mormon Sisters: Women in Early Utah* (Logan: Utah State University Press, 1997), 58–59.
5. Brigham Young, "The Value of Attending Meetings—Gentile or Gentilism—Isolation—Preaching—Zion," *Journal of Discourses* 12 (August 16, 1868): 272.
6. Joseph Smith, *History of the Church*, 1: 269.
7. Eugene England, "Letter to the Editor," *Sunstone* 1, no. 1 (Winter 1975): 5.
8. "Sustaining the General Authorities of the Church," *Improvement Era* 48, no. 6 (June 1945): 354.
9. Letter from George Albert Smith to J. Raymond Cope, December 7, 1945, cited in "A 1945 Perspective," *Dialogue: A Journal of Mormon Thought* 19, no. 1 (Spring 1986): 38.
10. Brigham Young, "Eternal Punishment—Mormonism," *Journal of Discourses* 9 (January 12, 1862): 150.
11. "History of Joseph Smith," *Millennial Star* 20 (1858): 774.

8. Contemporary Religious Life

1. Charles Dickens, "In the Name of the Prophet—Smith!" *Household Words* (July 19, 1851): 385.
2. To cite one of many examples, the Catholic Church maintains an official opposition to abortion at least as emphatic as Mormonism's. Yet statistics reveal that Catholics obtain them at a rate even higher than that of their Protestant counterparts. Mormons, in contrast, undergo abortions at a rate dramatically lower than the national average. See "Abortion and Pregnancy Rates by State," Guttmacher Institute, www.agi-usa.org/pubs/state_facts99.html.
3. Andrew F. Ehat and Lyndon W. Cook, eds., *The Words of Joseph Smith* (Orem, Utah: Grandin Book, 1991), 212.
4. Margot Hornblower, "Genealogy: Roots Mania," *Time*, April 19, 1999, 54–55.

REFERENCES

Chapter One

1. Joseph Smith, "Latter Day Saints," in *He Pasa Ekklesia: An Original History of the Religious Denominations at Present Existing in the United States*, comp. I. Daniel Rupp (Philadelphia: J. Y. Humphreys, 1844), 404–10. Public domain.

2. Joseph Smith, *The Book of Mormon: An Account Written by the Hand of Mormon, Upon Plates Taken from the Plates of Nephi* [3 Nephi 9–11] (Palmyra, N.Y.: E. B. Grandin, 1830), 472–80. Public domain.

3. Oliver Cowdery, "Letter to W. W. Phelps on Aaronic Priesthood Restoration," *Messenger and Advocate* (Kirtland, Ohio) 1, no. 1 (October 1834): 13–16. Public domain.

4. Joseph Smith, "Extract from the Prophecy of Enoch [Moses 7]," *The Evening and the Morning Star* (Independence, Mo.) 1, no. 3 (August 1832): 18–19. Public domain.

5. Joseph Smith, "A Vision [Doctrine and Covenants 76]," *The Evening and the Morning Star* (Independence, Mo.) 1, no. 2 (July 1832): 10–11. Public domain.

6. Joseph Smith, Journal, Journal Account of Kirtland Temple Visitations [Doctrine and Covenants 110] (1836), Church History Library, The Church of Jesus Christ of Latter-day Saints, Salt Lake City, Utah. Public domain.

7. Joseph Smith, "Letter from Joseph Smith [on Baptisms for the Dead]" [Doctrine and Covenants 128], *Times and Seasons* 3, no. 23 (October 1, 1842): 934–36. Public domain.

8. Stan Larson, "The King Follett Discourse: A Newly Amalgamated Text," *BYU Studies* 18, no. 2 (Winter 1978): 193–208. Used by permission of Brigham Young University Studies.

9. Joseph F. Smith, "Vision of the Redemption of the Dead [Doctrine and Covenants 138]," *Improvement Era* 22, no. 2 (December 1918): 165–70. Public domain.

10. First Presidency (Heber J. Grant, Anthony W. Ivins, and Charles W. Nibley), " 'Mormon' View of Evolution," *Improvement Era* 28, no. 11 (September 1925): 1090–91. Used by permission of The Church of Jesus Christ of Latter-day Saints. © By Intellectual Reserve, Inc.

11. First Presidency and Quorum of the Twelve Apostles (Gordon B. Hinckley, Thomas S. Monson, James E. Faust, et al.), "The Family: A Proclamation to the World," *Ensign* 25, no. 11 (November 1995): 102. Used by permission of The Church of Jesus Christ of Latter-day Saints. © By Intellectual Reserve, Inc.

12. First Presidency and Quorum of the Twelve Apostles (Gordon B. Hinckley, Thomas S. Monson, James E. Faust, et al.), "The Living Christ: The Testimony of the Apostles," *Ensign* 30, no. 4 (April 2000): 2–3. Used by permission of The Church of Jesus Christ of Latter-day Saints. © By Intellectual Reserve, Inc.

Chapter Two

1. Isaac Russell, "Isaac Russell's Letter to the Saints in England," *History of the Church*, 3:343–44. Used by permission of the Church History Library, The Church of Jesus Christ of Latter-day Saints. © By Intellectual Reserve, Inc.

2. Brigham Young, "An Epistle of the Twelve," *Times and Seasons* 5, no. 15 (August 15, 1844): 618–20. Public domain.

3. Lyman Wight and George Miller, "Lyman Wight to the First Presidency—Preaching the Gospel to the Indians and Proposing to Migrate to Texas," *History of the Church*, 6:255–57. Used by permission of the Church History Library, The Church of Jesus Christ of Latter-day Saints. © By Intellectual Reserve, Inc.

4. James J. Strang, "Pastoral Letter" (1845). Public domain.

5. Jason W. Briggs, "Revelation," *The Messenger* 2 (1851): 1. Public domain.

6. William Smith, *Epistle of the Twelve* (Milwaukee, Wisc.: Sentinel and Gazette Steam Press Print, 1851): 1–18. Public domain.

7. Sidney Rigdon, Joseph H. Newton, William Richards, and William Stanley, *An Appeal to the Latter-day Saints* (Philadelphia: Printed for the authors, 1863), 60–71. Public domain.

8. John Taylor, Revelation, September 27, 1886. Original text not extant. Public domain.

9. David Whitmer, *An Address to All Believers in Christ: By a Witness to the Divine Authenticity of The Book of Mormon* (Richmond, Mo.: n.p., 1887), 30–45. Public domain.

10. Joseph Musser, "Announcement," *Truth* 1, no. 1 (June 1, 1935): 1–2. Public domain.

11. Wallace B. Smith, Revelation on Priesthood [RLDS D&C 156]; *Book of Doctrine and Covenants* (Independence, Mo.: Herald Publishing House, 2007): 206–8. Used by permission of the Community of Christ.

12. Stephen M. Veazey, "A Defining Moment," *Community of Christ Herald* 156, no. 5 (May 2009): 12–19. Used by permission of the Community of Christ.

Chapter Three

1. Joseph Smith, "Plat for the City of Zion," Church History Library, The Church of Jesus Christ of Latter-day Saints, Salt Lake City, Utah. Public domain.

2. Sarah Studevant Leavitt, "Autobiography," in *Women's Voices: An Untold History of the Latter-day Saints, 1830–1900*, ed. Kenneth W. Godfrey, Audrey M. Godfrey, and Jill

Mulvay Derr (Salt Lake City, Utah: Deseret Book, 1982), 26–33. Used by permission of the Deseret Book Company.

3. Artemisia Sidnie Meyers, "Haun's Mill Massacre Account," in *Bones in the Well: The Haun's Mill Massacre, 1838: A Documentary History*, ed. Beth Shumway Moore (Norman, Okla.: Arthur H. Clark Company, 2006), 103–107. Used by permission of the Arthur H. Company at the University of Oklahoma Press.

4. James B. Allen, Ronald K. Esplin, and David J. Whittaker, "Vilate Kimball to Heber C. Kimball, September 21, 1839," in *Men with a Mission, 1837–1841: The Quorum of the Twelve Apostles in the British Isles* (Salt Lake City, Utah: Deseret Book, 1992), 356–57. Used by permission of the Deseret Book Company.

5. Elizabeth Ann Smith Whitney, "Reminiscence," in *In Their Own Words: Women and the Story of Nauvoo*, ed. Carol Cornwall Madsen (Salt Lake City, Utah: Deseret Book, 1994), 198–205. Used by permission of the Deseret Book Company.

6. First Presidency (Joseph Smith, Sidney Rigdon, and Hyrum Smith), "A Proclamation, to the Saints Scattered Abroad," *Times and Seasons* 2, no. 6 (January 15, 1841): 273–77. Public domain.

7. Eliza R. Snow, "The Female Relief Society," *Woman's Exponent* 1, no. 1 (June 1, 1872): 2; and *Woman's Exponent* 1, no. 2 (June 15, 1872): 10. Public domain.

8. William Clayton, "Come, Come, Ye Saints" ["All Is Well"], in *Hymns of The Church of Jesus Christ of Latter-day Saints* (Salt Lake City, Utah: The Church of Jesus Christ of Latter-day Saints, 1985), no. 30. Public domain.

9. Wilford Woodruff, *Wilford Woodruff's Journal, 1833–1898, Typescript*, ed. Scott G. Kenney, 9 vols. (Midvale, Utah: Signature Books, 1983–84), 3:120–23, January 21, 1847. Original in Church History Library. Used by permission of Signature Books.

10. William Atkin, "Handcart Experience," *Union* (St. George, Utah), May–June 1896. Public domain.

11. Valborg Henrietta Louise Rasmussen, *Valborg: An Autobiography of Valborg Rasmussen Wheelwright* (Salt Lake City, Utah: Pioneer Music Press, 1978), 20–33. Used by permission of Mona Wheelwright Lowe.

12. First Presidency (Joseph F. Smith, John R. Winder, and Anthon H. Lund), "Christmas Greeting to Saints in the Netherlands," *Der Stern* 13, no. 1 (January 1908): 3–6. Public domain.

13. Bruce R. McConkie, "Come: Let Israel Build Zion," *Ensign* 7, no. 5 (May 1977): 115–18. Used by permission of The Church of Jesus Christ of Latter-day Saints. © By Intellectual Reserve, Inc.

Chapter Four

1. Oliver Cowdery, "Governments and Laws in General," *Messenger and Advocate* (Kirtland, Ohio) 1, no. 11 (August 1835): 163–64. Public domain.

2. Joseph Smith, *General Smith's Views of the Powers and Policy of the Government of the United States* (Nauvoo, Ill.: Printed by John Taylor, 1844). Public domain.

3. Margaret L. Scott, "Margaret L. Scott: Beloved Brother," in *Army of Israel: Mormon Battalion Narratives*, ed. David L. Bigler and Will Bagley (Spokane, Wash.: Arthur H. Clark

Company, 2000), 66–68. Used by permission of the Arthur H. Clark Company at the University of Oklahoma Press.

4. Brigham Young, "Proclamation by the Governor," Special Collections—Manuscripts, Marriott Library, University of Utah, Salt Lake City. Public domain.

5. Martha Hughes Cannon, *Letters From Exile: The Correspondence of Martha Hughes Cannon and Angus M. Cannon, 1886–1888*, ed. Constance L. Lieber and John Sillito (Salt Lake City, Utah: Signature Books, 1989), 253–56. Used by permission of Signature Books.

6. First Presidency and Quorum of the Twelve Apostles (Wilford Woodruff, George Q. Cannon, Joseph F. Smith, et al.), "To the Saints," *Deseret Weekly News*, April 11, 1896, 532–34. Public domain.

7. Reed Smoot, U.S. Congressional Record, 59th Congress, 2nd Session, 1906, vol. 41, part IV (Washington, D.C.: Government Printing Office, 1907), 3, 268–81. Public domain.

8. Susa Young Gates, "The History of Woman Suffrage in Utah, 1900–1920," in *The History of Woman Suffrage*, 6 vols., ed. Ida Husted Harper (New York: National American Woman Suffrage Association, 1922), 6:644–50. Public domain.

9. J. Reuben Clark, General Conference Address, in *Conference Report*, October 1936, 111–15. Used by permission of The Church of Jesus Christ of Latter-day Saints. © By Intellectual Reserve, Inc.

10. Sonia Johnson and Karen S. Langlois, "All on Fire: An Interview with Sonia Johnson," *Dialogue: A Journal of Mormon Thought* 14, no. 2 (Summer 1981): 27–47. Used by permission of the Dialogue Foundation.

11. Judith Rasmussen Dushku, "A Time of Decision," *Dialogue: A Journal of Mormon Thought* 14, no. 4 (Winter 1981): 110–16. Used by permission of the Dialogue Foundation.

12. Harry Reid, "Faith, Family, and Public Service," Brigham Young University Forum Address, October 9, 2007. Used by permission of Harry Reid.

13. Mitt Romney, "Faith in America," address at The George Bush Presidential Library, College Station, Texas, December 6, 2007. Used by permission of the Associated Press.

14. First Presidency (Thomas S. Monson, Henry B. Eyring, and Dieter F. Uchtdorf), "Preserving Traditional Marriage and Strengthening Families," letter to church leaders in California, June 29, 2008. Used by permission of The Church of Jesus Christ of Latter-day Saints. © By Intellectual Reserve, Inc.

Chapter Five

1. Parley P. Pratt, *The Autobiography of Parley Parker Pratt, One of the Twelve Apostles of the Church of Jesus Christ of Latter-day Saints, Embracing His Life, Ministry and Travels, with Extracts, in Prose and Verse, from His Miscellaneous Writings*, ed. Parley P. Pratt Jr. (New York: Russell Brothers, 1874), 49–62. Public domain.

2. Jane Elizabeth Manning James, "Autobiography" [n.d.], Church History Library, The Church of Jesus Christ of Latter-day Saints, Salt Lake City, Utah. Public domain.

3. Parley P. Pratt, "The Standard and Ensign for the People," in *Journal of Discourses* (Liverpool: F. D. Richards, 1855), 1:172–185. Public domain.

4. Brigham Young, "Spiritual Gifts—Hell—The Spirit World—The Elders and the Nations—The Lamanites—The Temple," in *Journal of Discourses* (Liverpool: F. D. Richards, 1855), 2:136–45. Public domain.

5. Joseph Fielding Smith, "Appointment of Lineage," in *The Way to Perfection: Short Discourses on Gospel Themes* (Salt Lake City, Utah: Genealogical Society of Utah, 1931), 42–48. Used by permission of The Church of Jesus Christ of Latter-day Saints. © By Intellectual Reserve, Inc.

6. Helen Sekaquaptewa, "My Church," in *Me and Mine: The Life Story of Helen Sekaquaptewa* (Tucson: University of Arizona Press, 1969), 234–44. Used by permission of the University of Arizona Press.

7. Lacee A. Harris, "To Be Native American—and Mormon," *Dialogue: A Journal of Mormon Thought* 18, no. 4 (Winter 1985): 143–52. Used by permission of the Dialogue Foundation.

8. First Presidency (Spencer W. Kimball, N. Eldon Tanner, and Marion G. Romney), "Revelation Extends Blessings of Gospel," *Church News*, June 17, 1978: 3. Used by permission of The Church of Jesus Christ of Latter-day Saints. © By Intellectual Reserve, Inc.

9. Joseph Freeman, "A Momentous Weekend," in *In the Lord's Due Time* (Salt Lake City, Utah: Bookcraft, 1979), 1–6. Used by permission of the Deseret Book Company.

10. Chieko N. Okazaki, "Baskets and Bottles," *Ensign* 26, no. 5 (May 1996): 12–13. Used by permission of The Church of Jesus Christ of Latter-day Saints. © By Intellectual Reserve, Inc.

11. Esmeralda Meraz Amos, "El Evangelio," in *All God's Children: Racial and Ethnic Voices in the LDS Church*, ed. Cardell K. Jacobson (Springville, Utah: Bonneville Books, 2004), 139–47. Used by permission of Cedar Fort.

Chapter Six

1. "Revelation," *Deseret News* (Extra), September 14, 1852: 26–28. Public domain.

2. Eliza R. Snow, "My Father in Heaven," *Times and Seasons* (Nauvoo, Ill.) 6, no. 17 (November 15, 1845): 1039. Public domain.

3. Annie Clark Tanner, "Marriage in Polygamy," in *A Mormon Mother: An Autobiography of Annie Clark Tanner*, 3rd ed. (Salt Lake City, Utah: University of Utah Library Tanner Trust Fund, [1983] 1991), 57–69. Used by permission of the University of Utah Library.

4. Wilford Woodruff, "Official Declaration," *Deseret Weekly News*, October 4, 1890: 476. Public domain.

5. James E. Talmage, "The Eternity of Sex," *Young Woman's Journal* 25, no. 10 (October 1914): 600–604. Public domain.

6. Virginia Budd Jacobsen, "Book Review of *New Patterns in Sex Teaching*," *Relief Society Magazine* 23, no. 10 (October 1936): 631–32. Used by permission of The Church of Jesus Christ of Latter-day Saints. © By Intellectual Reserve, Inc.

7. Stephen E. Lamb and Douglas E. Brinley, "Sexual Intimacy in Marriage," in *Between Husband and Wife: Gospel Perspectives on Marital Intimacy* (Salt Lake City, Utah: Deseret Book, 2000), 17–26. Used by permission of the Deseret Book Company.

8. Oliver Alden [pseudo], " 'My God, My God, Why Hast Thou Forsaken Me?': Meditations of a Gay Mormon on the 22nd Psalm," *Sunstone* (August 1995): 44–55. Used by permission of the Sunstone Foundation.

9. Dallin H. Oaks and Lance B. Wickman, "Same-Gender Attraction," LDS Church Public Affairs interview, 2006. Available at: http://newsroom.lds.org/ldsnewsroom/eng/public-issues/same-gender-attraction. Used by permission of The Church of Jesus Christ of Latter-day Saints. © By Intellectual Reserve, Inc.

10. Maxine Hanks, "Introduction," in *Women and Authority: Re-emerging Mormon Feminism*, ed. Maxine Hanks (Salt Lake City, Utah: Signature Books, 1992): xi–xxix. Used by permission of Maxine Hanks.

11. Emily Milner, "Finding Myself on Google," *Segullah: Writings by Latter-day Saint Women* 3, no. 2 (Summer 2007): 2–4. Used by permission of Emily Milner.

Chapter Seven

1. Joseph Smith, Oliver Cowdery, Sidney Rigdon, and Frederick G. Williams, comps., *Doctrine and Covenants of the Church of the Latter-day Saints: Carefully Selected from the Revelations of God* (Kirtland, Ohio: F. G. Williams, 1835), 100–108. Public domain.

2. Amy Brown Lyman, "Childhood" in *In Retrospect: Autobiography of Amy Brown Lyman* (Salt Lake City, Utah: General Board of Relief Society, 1945), 15–23. Used by permission of The Church of Jesus Christ of Latter-day Saints. © By Intellectual Reserve, Inc.

3. Orson F. Whitney, "Home Literature," *Contributor* 9, no. 8 (June 1888): 297–302. Public domain.

4. Editors, "Vocational Education," *Relief Society Magazine* 8, no. 4 (April 1921): 247–49. Public domain.

5. "Juanita Brooks, "To Columbia," in *Quicksand and Cactus: A Memoir of the Southern Mormon Frontier* (Salt Lake City, Utah: Howe Brothers, 1982), 300–309. Used by permission of Utah State University Press.

6. Eugene England, "The Possibility of Dialogue: A Personal View," *Dialogue: A Journal of Mormon Thought* 1, no. 1 (Spring 1966): 8–11. Used by permission of the Dialogue Foundation.

7. Richard D. Poll, "What the Church Means to People Like Me," *Dialogue: A Journal of Mormon Thought* 2, no. 4 (Winter 1967): 107–17. Used by permission of the Dialogue Foundation.

8. Henry Eyring, "Science and Religion," in *Reflections of a Scientist* (Salt Lake City, Utah: Deseret Book, 1983), 98–103. Used by permission of the Deseret Book Company.

9. Marilyn Arnold, "Unlocking the Sacred Text," in *Expressions of Faith: Testimonies of Latter-day Saint Scholars*, ed. Susan Easton Black (Salt Lake City, Utah: Deseret Book, 1996), 193–200. Used by permission of the Deseret Book Company.

10. Laurel Thatcher Ulrich, "A Pail of Cream," *Journal of American History* 89, no. 1 (June 2002): 43–47. Used by permission of the Organization of American Historians.

Chapter Eight

1. Dennis Clark, "A Name and a Blessing," *Dialogue: A Journal of Mormon Thought* 5, no. 3 (Autumn 1970): 93. Used by permission of the Dialogue Foundation.

2. "Questions and Answers About Baptism," *Friend* 38, no. 8 (August 2008): 24–25. Used by permission of The Church of Jesus Christ of Latter-day Saints. © By Intellectual Reserve, Inc.

3. Antonia Purina Honrado, "They Gave Me a Copy with All of the Pages," in *Converted to Christ Through the Book of Mormon*, ed. Eugene England (Salt Lake City, Utah: Deseret Book, 1989), 98–100. Used by permission of the Deseret Book Company.

4. Boyd K. Packer, "Counsel to Young Men," *Ensign* 39, no. 5 (May 2009): 49–52. Used by permission of The Church of Jesus Christ of Latter-day Saints. © By Intellectual Reserve, Inc.

5. Lee Tom Perry and Daniel Lyman Carter, "As Now We Take the Sacrament," in *Hymns of The Church of Jesus Christ of Latter-day Saints* (Salt Lake City, Utah: The Church of Jesus Christ of Latter-day Saints, 1985), no. 169; Karen Lynn Davidson and Hans Leo Hassler, "O Savior, Thou Who Wearest a Crown," in *Hymns*, no. 197. Used by permission of The Church of Jesus Christ of Latter-day Saints. © By Intellectual Reserve, Inc.; and Mabel Jones Gabbott and Rowland H. Prichard, "In Humility, Our Savior," in *Hymns*, no. 172. Used by permission of Cheryl L. Gabbott.

6. Margaret Rampton Munk, "Service Under Stress: Two Years as a Relief Society President," *Dialogue: A Journal of Mormon Thought* 19, no. 2 (Summer 1986): 127–45. Used by permission of the Dialogue Foundation.

7. Laury Livsey, "A Day in the Life of a Missionary," *New Era* 30, no. 6 (June 2000): 60–65. Used by permission of The Church of Jesus Christ of Latter-day Saints. © By Intellectual Reserve, Inc.

8. Truman G. Madsen, "House of Glory," in *Five Classics by Truman G. Madsen* (Salt Lake City, Utah: Deseret Book, 2001), 273–85. Used by permission of the Deseret Book Company.

9. Clark T. Thorstenson, "Discovering My Icelanders," *Ensign* 11, no. 8 (August 1981): 25–27. Used by permission of Clark T. Thorstenson.

10. Ruth M. Gardner and Vanja Y. Watkins, "Families Can Be Together Forever," in *Hymns of The Church of Jesus Christ of Latter-day Saints* (Salt Lake City, Utah: The Church of Jesus Christ of Latter-day Saints, 1985), no. 300. Used by permission of Barbara Townsend; and Janice Kapp Perry, "I Love to See the Temple," in *Children's Songbook of The Church of Jesus Christ of Latter-day Saints* (Salt Lake City, Utah: The Church of Jesus Christ of Latter-day Saints, 1989), 95. Used by permission of Janice Kapp Perry.

11. Brenda Williams, "My Terrible, Horrible Day," *New Era* 31, no. 9 (September 2001): 34–36. Used by permission of The Church of Jesus Christ of Latter-day Saints. © By Intellectual Reserve, Inc.

12. Kathleen Flake, "How to Bury a Prophet," *Sightings*, February 7, 2008. Used by permission of Kathleen Flake.

INDEX

Book of Mormon: as aid in conversion, 393–95; attempted sale of copyright of, 83–84; as inspired text, 377–81; plates of, 6–7; as record of Indian ancestors, 223, 224, 227–29, 249–51; selection from, of Christ's visit to Nephites, 10–12; summary of, 7; translation of, 3, 7, 14; witnesses of, 85

Briggs, Jason W., 72–74

Brigham Young Academy, 344–47

Brigham Young University, Indian Education program at, 257

Brinley, Douglas E., on sexual intimacy, 305–11

Bushman, Virgil and Ruth, 252–53

Cain, 240, 243

California, 167; Proposition 8 ballot initiative in, 219–21

Campbell, Beverly, 199, 200, 202

Cannon, George Q., 174

Cannon, Martha Hughes: letter of, to her husband, 171–74; as member of state legislature, 189

canon, 16–17

Carlin, Thomas, 132

Carter, Daniel Lyman, composed hymn music, 401

Catholic Church: Eucharist of, 399; hierarchy of, 296, 362; opposed California Proposition 8, 220; pope of, likened to LDS prophet, 362, 395; priesthood in, 279, 296; sex education and, 301, 302; Trinitarian deity of, 49; as vehicle for human salvation, 2, 302

Catt, Carrie Chapman, 187, 191–92

celestial kingdom, 22–23

children: creation of, 308–9; as part of family, 48; salvation of, 39; teaching, about sex, 301–4

choice. See agency

Christ, light of, 240–43

Christianity: Judaism and, 234, 235–36; primitive, 1

Church of Christ (McLellin), 82

Church of Christ (Rigdonites), 77

Church of Christ (Temple Lot), 82

Church of Christ (Whitmerites), 82

Church of Jesus Christ (Bickertonites), 78

Church of Jesus Christ of Latter Day Saints (Strangites), 65–72

Clark, J. Reuben, on welfare plan, 193–96

Clayton, William, hymn written by, 133–35

Community of Christ. See Reorganized Church of Jesus Christ of Latter Day Saints

Conference on Families, 204–7

conferences, 60–61

conversion narratives, 107–11, 142–49, 231, 249–54, 392–95

Council of Seven Friends, 89

Cowdery, Oliver: on government, 155, 158–60; helped select Twelve Apostles, 82; received vision with Joseph Smith, 25–26; on restoration of priesthood, 12–16; went to Canada to sell Book of Mormon copyright, 83–84

creation, 35, 36–38, 45–46, 297–98, 300

crime, 159

Darwinism, 45

Davidson, Karen Lynn, hymn written by, 401–3

dead, salvation of, 27–32, 40–44, 422–23; of children, 39

death, 133–35

Declaration of Independence, 161

Delaware Indians, 226–29

Democratic Party, 175, 191, 210–14

Denmark, 142

Dialogue: A Journal of Mormon Thought, 362–66, 383

Dushku, Judith Rasmussen, on choosing to have a child, 157, 203–10